THE CIVIL WAR BATHROOM READER

☞ THE ☜
CIVIL WAR
BATHROOM READER

HISTORIC READING FOR
YOUR PRIVATE MOMENTS

SWEETWATER
PRESS

SWEETWATER
PRESS

ISBN-13: 978-1-58173-737-0

Cover and book design by Miles G. Parsons
Contributor: Rita Doughty

Printed in the U.S.

THE PECULIAR INSTITUTION

From the time America was founded, slavery wrenched the nation. Tobacco farmers in Virginia employed indentured servants from Europe—travelers who were promised a fixed labor term in exchange for the voyage to the New World. A little over a decade later, plantation owners began buying African slaves. Slaves soon became the essential component of the economy in the agrarian South. Their excruciating labor, guaranteed for a lifetime and beyond since slaves' children became the lifelong property of the slaveholders, fueled the life of the plantations, from planting to harvest and back again.

Slavery never took hold in the Northern states to any appreciable degree. New England was populated with small farms—not the large-scale plantations found in Virginia, the Carolinas, and beyond. Few groups in the South opposed slavery with much conviction during the colonial years.

Still, the problem of slavery in a land founded on democratic ideals emerged early, at the nation's birth. Founding Father Thomas Jefferson sought to deal with slavery in the Declaration of Independence and foretold the heavy toll it would exact on the fledgling nation, writing to a friend, "We have the wolf by the ears, and we can neither hold him, nor safely let him go. Justice is in one scale, and self-preservation in the other." Jefferson infamously owned slaves on his Virginia farm and almost certainly fathered illegitimate children with Sally Hemings, a slave he owned.

The Constitution prevented slaves from becoming free—even if they escaped to a free state. When framers of the Constitution enacted the Three-Fifths Compromise, evidence of society's growing fissures over slavery's existence could not be ignored. The Compromise stated that slaves were to be counted as three-fifths of a person when using population figures to determine how many Congressional seats were awarded to states. Southerners, hoping to gain political clout, wanted slaves considered full citizens.

VOICES OF DISSENT

Calls for an end to slavery grew during the late eighteenth century. Rhode Island, for example, outlawed slavery in 1774—two years before America declared its independence with Thomas Jefferson's eloquent, if unobserved, phrase, "All men are created equal."

In 1787, the Northwest Ordinance created an outline for gradually ending slavery. It designated a defined area in the present-day Midwest as an area to be made up of between three and five states, with each being a free, non-slave, state. It put limits on slavery for the first time.

Then came cotton. Even as other slave-dependent Southern crops, such as tobacco and rice, neared saturation, demand for cotton crops soared simultaneously with Eli Whitney's invention of the cotton gin in 1794. This created the need for yet more slaves. Cotton production across America, principally in the South, grew from 100,000 bales at the turn of the nineteenth century to 4.5 million at the dawn of the Civil War.

Cotton was in demand in Europe, Whitney's machine created a need for slaves to harvest the crops, and production roared in the wake of the Louisiana Purchase in 1803. The South's dependence on exporting cotton explains, in part, why Northern politicians were eager to pass protective tariffs, trade taxes that threatened the Southern economy. Politicians battled endlessly over tariffs during the decades leading up to the Civil War. As president, Jefferson expanded the nation's cotton-friendly terrain when he bought the Louisiana territory from Napoleon. John C. Calhoun, a two-time vice president, railed against tariffs and endorsed "nullification," the idea that states can ignore federal laws considered unconstitutional. Andrew Jackson avoided war only by passing a revised tariff.

COMPROMISE AND BORDER WARS

As slavery grew in importance across the South and declined in the North, attitudes hardened in both regions. Economic and political clout hung in the balance, shifting much of the debate from moral grounds to ones predicated on maintaining, as well as expanding, power and influence.

Beginning in 1820, several key events set the country on an inescapable path toward war. Many historians believe war became inevitable the moment Dutch traders brought African slaves to Virginia in the seventeenth century. If so, prior to Fort Sumter's first shots in 1861, four decades provided the final dash to destruction.

It began with the Missouri Compromise in 1820. Part of the territory acquired in the Louisiana Purchase, Missouri created a furor when it was identified as a slave state. To satisfy concerns over an imbalance between free and slave states, Missouri was admitted to the Union only after it was decided that Maine would come in simultaneously as a free state. The compromise negotiated in Congress also called for any future states in the American West to be free if located north of Missouri's lower state line.

The latter provision became a boiling point three decades later, leading to the cleverly named Compromise of 1850. For a conflict predicated on uncompromising sides, the Civil War's preamble is filled with nothing but compromises, it seems.

Vast property gained through America's participation in the Mexican War, which ended in 1848, led to the creation of all or parts of seven modern states: Utah, New Mexico, Arizona, Nevada, California, Colorado, and Texas. When California proposed to enter the Union as a free state, Southerners fought back, concerned that the balance between free and slave states—then deadlocked at fifteen apiece—would be upset. Congressional negotiation led to California's admission as a free state, but only after it ushered in tightened fugitive slave laws and allowed for other western territories to make their own call on whether to be free or slave states.

That brief sigh of relief disappeared within a few short years.

By 1853, slavery once again morphed into the hottest of political hot potatoes. The culprit was the building of a national railroad. Land issues tied to ensuring a rail line all the way across the country led to yet another compromise, this one known as the Kansas-Nebraska Act (apparently, even the politicians got tired of naming everything a compromise after a while). So, what did the Kansas-Nebraska Act do? It decided who played in the Orange Bowl, of course.

Okay, not really.

Instead, the Kansas-Nebraska Act gave those territories the power to decide if, in fact, they would become slave or free states. Just one problem—that all but negated the Missouri Compromise. This is where the uncompromising part of the drama begins to take shape. For the next seven years, furious, bloody battles raged in Kansas.

Election fraud, land squabbles, brawling, murder, and political intimidation marked the daily reality in Kansas and Missouri during the years leading up to the Civil War, leading to an ignominious nickname: "Bleeding Kansas."

The Kansas-Nebraska Act allowed for public to vote which way the future states would decide their status on slavery, prompting a rush of abolitionists (those who wanted slavery to end for moral reasons), free-staters (those against slavery for moral and economic reasons), and pro-slavery newcomers to descend upon the fledgling Midwestern territories. They shared a common tactic: violence. Barbarism exploded across the region, embodied by zealous abolitionist John Brown's 1856 massacre at Pottawatomie Creek, where Brown and his sons killed five unarmed people. A free-stater named James Montgomery became a notorious campaigner, engaging in raids, attacks, and other violent actions during 1858.

Free-state supporters prevailed when Kansas entered the Union as a free state in January 1861, just months before the Civil War began.

BEECHER'S BIBLES

Background: In Kansas

The 1854 Kansas-Nebraska Act let settlers in those territories vote on allowing slavery. A fiasco followed. Adamant supporters from each side flooded into Kansas with plans to stuff ballot boxes with votes favoring their position. Their tactics were so violent that the territory became known as "Bleeding Kansas."

Meanwhile: Back in New York

Preeminent preacher Henry Ward Beecher condemned slavery from the pulpit. He thought if more abolitionists moved to Kansas, their collected votes would ensure it became a free state.

Beecher knew his plan required financial backing and used his position to raise money for the Emigrant Aid Society. At a church meeting of "emigrants" planning to relocate to Kansas, Beecher pledged to buy Sharps rifles, costing $25 each, if the church would ante up a matching amount. The group raised $625 to buy rifles and a box of twenty-five Bibles.

On to Kansas

Wagonloads of crates were shipped to Kansas, all marked "Beecher's Bibles" (labeling them "Weapons" would surely be suspicious). More than nine hundred Sharp's rifles were sent to arm the antislavery settlers. Henry Ward Beecher considered the rifles to be even greater moral weapons than the Bible.

Little Bits of Trivia

- Beecher's sister, Harriet Beecher Stowe, wrote the powerful novel Uncle Tom's Cabin.
- John Brown, who plotted the Harper's Ferry massacre to create a nation of former slaves, was originally from the Bleeding Kansas territory.

- "Beecher's Bibles" was applied to all breech–loading weapons. With an effective range of only five hundred yards, the Sharps rifles were least preferred by Federal commanders, who thought the guns wasted ammunition.
- After the war, Robert E. Lee accepted the presidency at Washington College (now Washington and Lee University) in Lexington, Virginia. Beecher helped raise funds for the school.

Mary Tepee

Many Zouave regiments had *vivandières*, females dressed in a uniform similar to the men. Mary Tepee, or "French Mary," was the vivandière of the 114th Pennsylvania Infantry, or "Collis's Zouaves."

Mary was on almost every battlefield where the regiment fought, including Gettysburg, carrying water and bandages into battle and even sustaining her own war wound. Her regiment was known for its precision on the drill field.

Zouave Troops

Their Origins: Tough, brave French Army soldiers in Africa in the 1830s

How They Came to America: Elmer Ellsworth, a family friend of Abraham Lincoln, patterned a Chicago troop after the dashing, heroic French-African mercenaries.

What They Did: Ellsworth's Chicago "US Zouave Cadets" were known for their elaborate drills performed at double-quick pace with clockwork precision. They toured the North in parades and drill competitions, giving impressive, award-winning exhibitions.

How to Pronounce the Word: zoo-ahh-vah

Who They Fought For: Zouave regiments were organized in both the North and South, modeled after Ellsworth's Cadets.

What They Wore: Zouave uniforms of the Civil War resembled the brightly-colored clothes worn by the French-African troops. The exact uniform varied by regiment.

- Most regiments wore red turbans with white bands intertwined with orange tinsel (a fez with a tassel), short waist-length blue jackets with gold trim, baggy red trousers, gaiters or leggings, and a sash.
- The "Richmond Zouaves" of the 44th Virginia Infantry wore a blue jacket, orange trousers, and white gaiters.

Pros of the Uniforms: The brightly colored uniforms made the regiments stand out on the drill field, where they looked smart in their precision performances.

Cons of the Uniforms: The brightly colored uniforms made the regiments stand out on the battlefield, where they became easy targets.

How the Uniforms Fared Throughout the War: For the most part, as the war dragged on, regiments found it more and more difficult to replace tattered and worn parts of their unique uniforms. Many of the Zouave soldiers eventually turned to the regular army-issue uniforms. Some troops, such as the 95th Pennsylvania Volunteer Infantry ("Gosline's Zouaves"), were able to secure private funding (i.e., Philadelphia citizen John M. Gosline) for replacement clothing and kept wearing the special uniforms until the war's end.

What Became of Elmer Ellsworth: In 1861, Ellsworth organized the 11th New York Infantry, called the "Fire Zouaves," because they were recruited from New York City's different fire departments.

The 11th New York marched into Washington to defend the Union's capital. On May 24, 1861, while the unit was following orders to seize Alexandria, Virginia, Colonel Ellsworth took down a Confederate flag hanging on the Marshall House Inn. The innkeeper, James T. Jackson, was not pleased by this, and he retaliated by shooting Ellsworth dead. In turn, Private Francis E. Brownell shot and killed Jackson.

President Lincoln was grief stricken at the loss of his friend, and he had Ellsworth's body lie in state at the White House before being returned to New York for burial. Ellsworth became known as a "war hero," even though he had never been in combat. His regiment changed their nickname to "Ellsworth's Avengers."

An American Legion drill team in Zouave uniforms appeared on *The Ed Sullivan Show* in the 1950s.

MARTYRDOM AND JOHN BROWN

Zealot seems too mild a word for John Brown. Lunatic fits the bill better.

Abolitionist nonpareil Brown roused a band of like-minded, fire-breathing souls to stamp out slavery. They brooked no opposition and no divergent viewpoints, and they paid no heed to the slightest hint of nuance.

Brown first made a name for himself when he led his sons on a bloodthirsty quest for vengeance in Kansas. In 1856, he led an attack that left five settlers dead. The unarmed victims, Brown pronounced, were killed in retaliation for the plundering of Lawrence, which was a fiercely anti-slavery town that had been recently attacked by so-called pro-slavery "border ruffians" from Missouri.

Brown's Biblical fury burned even more hotly after spilling the blood of innocent citizens. Short of complete emancipation for all of the nation's slaves, Brown would not be appeased. Or, as Brown's acquaintance and eloquent freed slave Frederick Douglass later put it, "I could live for the slave; John Brown could die for him."

Brown's rigid sensibility captivated prominent slavery opponents, particularly in the abolitionist hub of Boston.

Brown spent his childhood in rural Ohio, growing up as part of an intensely religious family. He hated slavery as a boy, a feeling that deepened in adulthood.

Twice married, Brown fathered twenty children and led his family on a threadbare existence.

His first claim to fame came in Kansas during the 1850s, when he rampaged with his sons. Brown moved to Boston in 1857, and with the backing of noted abolitionists, he began plotting a slave uprising he believed would roar across the South. With twenty-one men, Brown headed for the federal armory in Harpers Ferry, then Virginia, now in present-day West Virginia. Douglass, sensing the inevitable, declined an offer from Brown to participate.

Brown and his men captured the armory and several other

buildings upon their arrival in October 1859. He sent two freed slaves to announce their arrival and stir an uprising. None came. Matters unraveled from there. Brown and his men took local citizens as prisoners and barricaded themselves in a building beside the armory.

Federal troops arrived, under the command of future Confederates Robert E. Lee and Jeb Stuart. Lee sent Stuart under a truce flag to demand surrender; Brown refused. A quick surge by Lee's men led to Brown's capture. The two-day raid led to the deaths of five men by Brown's gang, including a freed black. A ten-day trial led to a guilty verdict, and, on December 2, Brown was executed by hanging.

The raid on Harpers Ferry failed in every way imaginable, but still became a significant event. Brown's calm demeanor at trial and at his hanging—he left a note prophetically proclaiming "that the crimes of this land will never be purged away but with blood"—made him an instant martyr in the North. Noted pacifist Henry David Thoreau offered rapturous praise. What later became known as "The Battle Hymn of the Republic" even came from a song titled "John Brown's Body."

Southerners viewed Brown's raid and plan to use freed slaves to attack slaveholders as proof of Northern determination to destroy them. Harpers Ferry served as a major flashpoint and moved the nation inexorably closer to war.

Look Who's Watching

As with so many episodes surrounding the Civil War and its key players, Harpers Ferry offered a number of ironies and coincidences.

Starting, of course, with the U.S. military men called in to quell Brown and his men. Robert E. Lee and Jeb Stuart would soon become two of the most important members of the Confederate Army.

Brown's hostages in the raid included George Washington's great-grandnephew. This notable hostage even supplied Brown with a Washington heirloom—a sword—that Brown sported during the siege.

Later, at Brown's public hanging, witnesses included the famous stage actor and future Lincoln assassin John Wilkes Booth. A Virginia military professor who would later gain fame as "Stonewall" Jackson was also present, as was Edmund Ruffin, who fired the first shot of the war at Fort Sumter, South Carolina, in 1861.

Blacks in the Confederate Army

Yes, the Confederate Army used blacks—not usually as troops, but laborers. They were sometimes forced at gunpoint, and under Union fire, to dig trenches, build fortifications, and establish or strike camp.

As the war dragged on, some Confederate troops favored blacks serving as soldiers, too. An equal number of Southerners argued against the idea. Jefferson Davis did take the opportunity to make a declaration, but it was not implemented before the war ended.

CLAY THE COMPROMISER

Much like modern politicians, such as Kansas Republican Senator Bob Dole or Massachusetts Democrat and Speaker of the House Tip O'Neill, Kentuckian Henry Clay was known during the mid-nineteenth century for his acumen as a political dealmaker.

Clay shaped the last compromise of the years leading to the Civil War in 1850. In the wake of vast territories won in the Mexican War—and the controversy over whether those lands would be free or slave when accepted into the Union—Clay, then in his seventies, forged yet another deal. He had earlier put together the Missouri Compromise and a compromise on tariffs.

Clay pushed a series of five acts that rewarded both slaveholders and opponents of slavery. The package included the Fugitive Slave Act, a measure that bolstered slave owners by mandating the return of escaped slaves while promising severe penalties for runaways.

Clay urged the opposing factions in the slavery debate "to pause at the edge of the precipice" of national strife and inevitable suffering for both sides. Massachusetts Senator Daniel Webster, who rarely shared any common political ground with Clay, realized the urgency of the moment and made an equally impassioned plea for compromise.

It wouldn't be enough. War broke out a decade later.

Raising Cane in the Senate

During an era filled with notorious acts, few could be compared with the infamous feud between Republican Senator Charles Sumner of Massachusetts and South Carolina's Democratic Congressman, Preston Brooks.

In May 1856, as the border wars raged in Kansas, Brooks assaulted Sumner at his desk on the Senate floor and beat him bloody and unconscious using a metal-topped cane.

Brooks calmly walked out of the near-empty Senate chamber as a handful of witnesses looked on in horror and shock.

Sumner returned to the Senate after several years of rehabilitation and coping with the after-effects of the attack. When he resumed his political career, Sumner remained a fierce abolitionist. He also became a key adviser to President Lincoln during the war. Sumner fought any manner of compromise with the South in the run-up to the war and considered the Reconstruction policies endorsed by Lincoln and his successor, Andrew Johnson, to be too forgiving toward the South.

Brooks' attack was provoked by a speech about Kansas and the Border Wars that had been delivered by Sumner a few days earlier. In a lengthy oratory, Sumner assailed the authors of the Kansas-Nebraska Act, Democratic Senators Andrew Butler of South Carolina and Stephen Douglas of Illinois. The Act had put the decision of whether states allowed slavery in the hands of voters.

Sumner hammered Butler for his affair with "the harlot, Slavery" and then added personal slurs. Brooks, who also happened to be Butler's nephew, raged over Sumner's insults.

He found Sumner at his Senate desk just after adjournment. Brooks told Sumner that his speech was "a libel on South Carolina." Then, Brooks beat the senator and left him unconscious. The episode ignited fury in the North and South, with both men becoming heroes and villains simultaneously, depending upon regional perspective.

Brooks soon resigned his seat in the wake of a Congressional censure, though he was quickly reelected. He died seven months later, at the age of thirty-seven.

Sojourner Truth

Best known for her scorching "Ain't I a Woman" speech, Sojourner Truth's remarkable life included a lengthy role as a beacon of dignity and freedom.

Born Isabella Baumfree in 1797, the future Sojourner Truth, who took the name in a fit of inspired Christianity at age forty-six, was a New York slave. She left her master in 1826, a year before state-enforced emancipation took effect. By the mid-1840s, she had moved to Massachusetts and met leading abolitionists William Lloyd Garrison, Frederick Douglass, and others. Garrison published Truth's memoirs in 1850. A year later, she delivered her most famous speech at a women's convention in Ohio, bluntly outlining the injustices and cruelties suffered by blacks and women.

During the Civil War, Truth pushed for blacks to join the Union forces. Her grandson fought with the famed 54th Massachusetts Regiment, the all-black fighters depicted in the movie *Glory*. Truth died in 1883. By the time of her death, she had long since gained widespread reverence across America.

WHEN A PERSON IS NOT A PERSON: DRED SCOTT

Another influential step in the march toward war occurred in 1857 with a Supreme Court ruling in the case of Dred Scott, a slave who engaged in a decade-long series of legal battles aimed at winning his freedom.

The court, under Chief Justice Roger B. Taney, decreed that no one who was black, whether slave or free, could be considered an American citizen. In turn, blacks had no right to sue in federal court. Taney's decision went beyond that, and it held that blacks lacked rights at all. This freed whites to enact (or not) justice however they saw fit.

As Civil War historian David Blight told PBS, "In the wake of the Dred Scott decision, spring of 1857, to be black in America was to live in the land of the Dred Scott decision, which, in effect, said, 'You have no future in America.'"

Scott's journey from itinerant slave to iconic symbol of injustice stretched across many years, states, and owners. His first owner took Scott from Virginia to Alabama, then, to Missouri. An army surgeon, John Emerson, bought Scott in the wake of his original owner's death. They moved to Illinois, a free state, shortly after. In 1836, Emerson and Scott moved to what was then known as the Wisconsin Territory. Although Scott could have sued for his freedom during his twelve-year long stint living in Illinois and Wisconsin, he did not. Scott married a slave, who had two children with him. Emerson also owned the rest of the family.

Emerson died in 1843. Scott, now back in St. Louis, sued Emerson's widow after she offered him to an army captain. After first trying to buy his freedom from her and being refused, Scott went to court.

He lost the first court case in 1847. Three years later, Scott and his family won their freedom in a decision handed down by a circuit court. Missouri's Supreme Court reversed that decision in 1852. After another round of appeals, Scott's case reached the U.S. Supreme Court, setting the stage for the historic, decisive ruling in 1857. Five of the nine Supreme Court justices at the time came from slave-owning families.

Scott's original master's sons bought Scott after the Supreme Court decision and gave him his freedom. It was short-lived; Scott died a year and a half later.

Uncle Tom's Cabin

Harriet Beecher Stowe and her explosive, anti-slavery novel added fuel to an already raging fire upon its publication in 1852. The daughter of a prominent Connecticut minister, Harriet Beecher married a theologian, Calvin Stowe, in 1836. At the time, she was teaching in Cincinnati, where the specter of slavery first entered Harriet's consciousness because of the city's proximity to slave state Kentucky across the river.

After the Stowes moved back to the Northeast a decade or so later, she began work on a fictional account of slavery's cruelty and injustices. It sold ten thousand copies during its first week and went on to become a best-seller across the North and winning plaudits in international circles and brickbats in the South, where it was banned.

Plenty of contemporary critics and lay readers alike have questioned the book's literary merits, but its influence on the already strained relationship between the North and the South remains indisputable. Stowe, one of nine children, came by her forthright views honestly. Her brothers included noted abolitionist orator Henry Ward Beecher.

When Abraham Lincoln met Stowe at the White House in 1862, he said by way of introduction, "So you're the little woman who wrote the book that started this great war."

THE UNDERGROUND RAILROAD

If you're thinking Amtrak, think again. The Underground Railroad was, instead, a loose coalition of abolitionist blacks and a smaller number of whites who were bent on helping fugitive slaves find freedom by escaping the South for the Northern states and Canada.

Rather than trains, they used established safe locations and all manner of paths, roadways, passes, and other designated routes to help ferry slaves to freedom. Historians and other experts credit the Underground Railroad with inspiring the modern Civil Rights movement.

The Underground Railroad began in the late-eighteenth century and expanded into a series of stops and safe houses where fugitives could find shelter on their harrowing journeys. Quakers and others participated in the network, which took its name and jargon—the safe hiding spots were known as "depots" and "stations" while "stockholders" contributed supplies—from the new rail system being laid across America.

For slaves, merely escaping their plantations required acts of daring. If they made it past that first barrier—that had a minimum threat of whippings that would take them to the brink of death— fugitive slaves could then begin a dash to freedom across swamps, creeks, mountains, and many other obstacles, all in an environment where no one could be trusted. In most cases, the runaway slaves traveled at night.

Between its launch in the 1780s and the end of the Civil War in 1865, about 100,000 slaves made their way to freedom with the help of the Underground Railroad, according to various estimates. Successful escapees included Frederick Douglass, who broke free in 1838 from Baltimore. His situation was typical in that almost all successful escapes involved slaves on the run from the Upper South rather than the Deep South, which posed obvious additional barriers owing to its increased distance from Northern refuge.

Escaping slavery became even more complicated in the 1850s. As part of the Compromise of 1850, a Fugitive Slave Act was enacted that allowed for the arrest of runaway slaves in Northern territory.

Harriet Tubman

The Underground Railroad helped slaves to freedom because of innumerable acts of courage from its "conductors" and other volunteers, but none shined like Harriet Tubman. Dubbed "Moses" by grateful blacks, Tubman overcame slavery and oppression to become an iconic hero.

Born Araminta Ross around 1820—she later changed her first name to Harriet in honor of her mother—Tubman was a slave in Maryland. She worked as a servant, and as she grew, worked in the fields. Some time in the mid-1840s, she married a free black named John Tubman. She escaped to freedom in 1849 with a few other slaves after hearing rumors that they would all be sold. Her husband stayed behind.

Tubman made her way to Pennsylvania, eventually settling in Philadelphia. Working with Underground Railroad hero William Still and others, Tubman became a "conductor" and led daring missions into the South. In all, she helped more than three hundred slaves escape, though when she went back for her husband, she found that he had remarried in her absence. Frustrated authorities offered a whopping $40,000 bounty for Tubman's capture, but she evaded arrest thanks to unerring pluck, luck, and intelligence.

Tubman later worked as a nurse and a cook for the Union Army. She died in 1913.

ELECTION OF 1860

Slavery divided the Democratic Party, and, in one of the many ironies of the Civil War, led to the election of the man who would abolish the practice once and for all—Abraham Lincoln.

Today the South tilts reliably toward the Republican Party, but in the nineteenth century and through the first half of the twentieth, the region was known for its allegiance to the Democrats as the then-called "Solid South." The nickname emerged to describe Dixie's Democratic preference from Reconstruction through the 1940s, when Harry Truman's military integration led many Southerners to begin voting for Republican candidates.

With the election of 1860 approaching, Democrats of different sensibilities, including those who wanted slavery maintained in its present form and those who wanted to see it expand to other states and territories, fought among themselves and wound up with three diluted candidacies. The party's northern base chose Lincoln's old Illinois rival, Stephen Douglas, as the Democratic nominee. Southern Democrats nominated Kentuckian John C. Breckinridge, while a third faction opted for a Tennessean, John Bell.

The Republican Party arrived in 1854 and was built on a loose coalition of smaller political parties and the Whig Party. The Whigs fell out of favor among abolitionists in the wake of the border wars and the compromise of popular sovereignty. Though John C. Frémont lost the Republicans' first presidential election in 1856 (his slogan: "Free soil, free labor, free speech, free men, Frémont"), the party made a solid showing in Congressional races during its early years.

Republicans proved far more unyielding in their views on slavery than the Whigs, prompting many Democrats across the South to threaten secession if a Republican candidate won the presidency in 1860.

That, of course, is exactly what happened. Lincoln, a one-term Congressman who had built his reputation on a failed Senate campaign against Douglas in 1858, was the surprise Republican nominee in 1860. Considered more moderate than some of his rivals and benefiting from his "western" base of Illinois, Lincoln became president at fifty-one.

Lincoln won, in large part, because the Democrats split their votes among Douglas, Breckinridge, and Bell. He won all the free states, but none of the slave states, a telling sign of the nation's bitter division.

He succeeded James Buchanan, who might be best described as America's answer to Neville Chamberlain when it came to the issue of slavery.

After Lincoln's election in November 1860, seven Southern states seceded during a six-week span that began on December 20, 1860. In order, they were South Carolina, Mississippi, Florida, Alabama, Georgia, Louisiana, and Texas. Lincoln's advisers, including Secretary of State William H. Seward, told the president to let the states go without comment or threat of retribution. They told Lincoln to rely, instead, on the departed states' inevitable failure to prosper outside the Union.

He took office in March 1861. Several weeks before his inauguration, Lincoln stood on a platform in his home state while awaiting his train for Washington. Looking at the familiar faces before him, Lincoln left no doubt that he recognized the perilous journey ahead, describing the looming duties of the presidency as "a task before me greater than that which rested upon Washington."

He was right.

THE PRESIDENTS:
ABRAHAM LINCOLN

"… The better angels of our nature."
"Four score and seven years ago …"
"A house divided against itself cannot stand."

Other than Shakespeare and Yogi Berra, few people in the English-speaking world have delivered more memorable words than Abraham Lincoln, who, before becoming the slogan for a state (Illinois is "The Land of Lincoln") and a political party (Republicans still refer to theirs as "The Party of Lincoln"), carved a place for himself on Mount Rushmore with the greatest presidential acumen and grace under pressure in American history.

Summing up Lincoln's legend in a few paragraphs is impossible. After all, Lincoln biographies still arrive by the dozens each year, nearly 150 years after his death in 1865 at the hands of infamous assassin John Wilkes Booth. In recent years, histories and biographies have considered everything from Lincoln's mental health (at minimum, he was a man of severe melancholy) to physical attributes (which may or may not be related to a lifelong degenerative disease, according to one recent posited medical theory) to his sexual preferences (yes, really).

There isn't a shred of Lincoln mania that hasn't been, or won't soon be, explored.

America's sixteenth president towers over the nation long after his death because he managed to bind a severed Union while presiding over the single most destructive and divisive time in the nation's history. While there are plenty of issues to debate, such as the notion that Lincoln once thought it a sound notion to free all slaves and send them to Liberia or the fact that he suspended habeas corpus during the war, all but a handful of historians and experts acknowledge his overwhelming political skill in the face of excruciating demands.

Born in Kentucky in 1809, Lincoln's boyhood of hard work (rail-splitting, farming) and relentless ambition resonate as real-life examples of the American Dream. He came from humble means and longed to escape the rigors of backbreaking labor. Lincoln's mother died when he was nine, but his stepmother nurtured young Abe and instilled a love of learning and reading in him.

Lincoln disdained slavery. At the same time, he endorsed racist notions of blacks being intellectually inferior and opposed mixed marriages. His father moved the family to Indiana and Illinois, where Lincoln built his legal and political career. His analytical, cerebral approach and dry humor emerged from his years of arguments before small-town juries in the Midwest. He dabbled in mythmaking, as well: Lincoln painted himself as a man of modest means long after he had established a highly successful legal practice working on behalf of the railroad companies.

Although he was not an especially religious man, Lincoln drew upon the Bible heavily in his speeches and writings, conjuring vivid images and metaphors to hammer a point home. When that tactic failed, the lanky lawyer loved nothing more than a ribald joke—or three.

He married the former Mary Todd of Kentucky during his days as a lawyer in Springfield, Illinois. Todd came from an aristocratic, slaveholding family and was first courted by Lincoln's future political rival, Stephen Douglas. The Lincolns had four sons, though only one survived into adulthood.

Lincoln knew failure and sorrow, humbling qualities that enhanced his stature as he persevered through personal and political crises. These included the premature deaths of his children (two sons died during childhood while Lincoln was alive and a third died as a teenager after the president had been killed), his wife's shaky stability, and an array of military leaders who lacked a killer instinct. When he found one who possessed the skills needed, Lincoln never wavered in his support of General Ulysses S. Grant. "I can not spare this man," Lincoln said of Grant. "He fights."

Booth snuck into Lincoln's private box at Ford's Theatre on April 14, 1865 and shot Lincoln in the head. Only five days after the surrender at Appomattox, Lincoln was taken to a room across the street and died the following morning, at the age of fifty-six. Secretary of War Edwin M. Stanton looked at the slain president and said, "Now he belongs to the ages," though some believe he said "angels."

Inaugural Intrigue

Before Abraham Lincoln made it to the White House, the threat of assassination loomed. His two-week tour through the Midwest and Northeast in February 1861 was marred by an assassination plot to kill him at the Baltimore train station as he switched trains for the final leg to Washington. Famed detective Allen Pinkerton learned of the plot, and he worked with Lincoln and his advisers to orchestrate a change in itinerary and logistics to help the president reach Washington safely. Along the way, Lincoln donned a shawl and posed as an invalid, a detail that was extrapolated into Lincoln dressing in drag out of fear. The image persisted among Lincoln's rivals and critics in the North and South.

THIS MEANS WAR

Neither side was ready for war when it arrived in 1861. For starters, the bedraggled capital of Washington only had roughly five hundred troops guarding it and, once Virginia officially seceded after the attack on Fort Sumter, only the Potomac River stood between it and the enemy. Military men, government workers, and others in Washington routinely defected to the Southern cause or passed along information they considered helpful to the enemy. Hysteria and rumor swept through Washington. Its citizens were convinced the city would soon be overrun by Southerners and Southern sympathizers.

Both sides had little modern, effective weaponry to speak of, relying instead on leftovers from the Mexican War and other relics. Amazingly, with bedraggled, threadbare forces and few supplies, neither the North nor the South began building their armies through the draft until the conflict was more than a year old.

The war began, fittingly, in Charleston Harbor, in South Carolina, the first state to secede. The harbor included a man-made granite island known as Fort Sumter, where Major Robert Anderson presided over sixty-eight soldiers beginning in December 1860, the same month that South Carolina seceded. Anderson was surrounded by artillery batteries on nearby islands and towns, so Lincoln's Cabinet believed it best to evacuate and avoid an unwinnable standoff.

Instead, the president, who made an unsuccessful attempt at reconciliation during his March inaugural speech, decided to send basic necessities to Anderson while promising not to send weapons. He would not bolster Anderson and his men unless the fort came under attack.

Less than a week after Lincoln made his decision, Jefferson Davis approved an ultimatum to be delivered by Confederate Commander P. G. T. Beauregard, a former artillery student of Anderson at West Point. Anderson refused Beauregard's demand for evacuation, and on

April 12, a sixty-seven-year-old Virginia newspaper editor named
Edmund Ruffin fired the first shot of the Civil War. Miraculously,
none of the Union men died during a thirty-four-hour barrage of
four thousand rounds. Anderson surrendered, with Beauregard
granting gracious terms, including a gun salute to the American flag.
That salute led to the war's first death—that of Union Private Daniel
Hough, killed by a cannon misfire on April 14.

Four for Fighting

The events at Fort Sumter cemented the Confederacy
in the minds of like-minded observers. It quickly grew from
seven states to eleven after the first battle of the Civil
War. North Carolina, Tennessee, Arkansas, and Virginia
joined the Confederacy in the wake of Beauregard's attack
on the federal fort, putting the full Confederate States of
America in place for the duration of the war. All rejoined
the United States soon after the Union claimed military
victory in April 1865.

Uniforms and Variables

Union and Confederate soldiers alike wore uniforms of shirts, jackets, and trousers. Style, color, and accessories varied widely not just between the North and South, but from regiment to regiment.

At the beginning of the war, when the first troops to take up the cause were from state militia, soldiers showed up wearing their different militia uniforms. Later, both federal governments tried to issue uniform regulations, which were met in the clothes distributed to the soldiers. The men themselves, however, put their own personal stamp on everything they wore out of pride, sentiment, or sheer necessity.

On both sides, many shirts they wore under their uniform jackets were acquired by each soldier instead of by governmental issue. Almost all shirts were pullover style, with a wide neck and short collar, to which a stiff formal collar could be buttoned when necessary. You can bet that soldiers didn't often think it was, though.

Soldiers either bought shirts, or more often, for sentimental reasons, wore shirts that had been homemade by loved ones out of gingham or calico. Most shirts did not have pockets. The vests they wore had pockets, though.

Underwear, called "bishops," took the form of two-piece long johns. Covering arms and legs, these undergarments were made out of cotton or wool, usually in red or white.

Notes on Confederate Colors

Gray: Color varied greatly
- Cadet gray – Light gray
- Confederate gray – Clear, medium tint
- Steel gray – Light-bluish color
- Tuscaloosa gray – Brownish hue
- Richmond gray – Dark gray

Butternut: Civilian clothing was dyed with shells from butternuts, with resulting colors ranging from light beige to dark brown.

A Union Soldier's Uniform

In the North, factories worked under contract with the Federal government to manufacture uniforms.

- Shirts: flannel or wool; colored dark blue, light blue, gray, or white
- Trousers: wool or jersey; light blue (some regiments wore dark blue)
- Jacket: dark blue; four-button loose-flannel fatigue jacket (or sack coat); frock coat (single-breasted, long to the knees, with light blue trim or piping) for dress uniforms
- Overcoat: many styles, typically a greatcoat for winter (long over the knees with a cape over the shoulders)

A Confederate Soldier's Clothes

Notice, we don't say "uniforms" for the Confederate soldiers. As in all other aspects of supplying this war, Confederate troop dress started out uniform, but as time wore on and funds depleted, became more of a "make-do" mix-and-match system. From the beginning, because of a lack of factories, all the Confederate uniforms were hand-sewn and homemade.

- Jackets: Gray jackets or frock coats
- Trousers: heavy wool or a wool/cotton blend; light blue or gray; high-waists worn loose enough not to pop suspenders when bending over or sitting while leaving enough room for long underwear beneath
- After spring of 1862: Butternut colors, civilian clothes, and captured Union clothing supplies were all common sights

Union Underwear

When uniforms were issued by the government, some poor midwestern Union recruits were unfamiliar with cotton underwear and its function. They gamely followed the advice of more seasoned vets who told them it was the dress uniform to be worn on the outside of their pants during parades.

WEAPONS

Firearms

During the early war years, many Confederate soldiers used their own shotguns and hunting rifles. As warfare matured, two main rifle types emerged for both armies: the Enfield and the Springfield. Soldiers rolled and packed their own cartridges for each.

Springfield Musket
Manufactured in: Springfield, Massachusetts
Description: Muzzle-loading percussion cap
Caliber (muzzle opening): .58
Weight: 9 pounds, 12 ounces
Effective range: 500 yards
Number manufactured during Civil War: 670,000

Enfield Musket
Manufactured in: England
Description: Muzzle-loading
Caliber (muzzle opening): .577
Weight: 9 pounds, 3 ounces
Effective Range: 900 yards
Number manufactured during Civil War: 920,000

Could Have Been Weapons, But Weren't
Swords

Most foot soldiers did not carry swords; only officers and cavalry did.

Bayonets

Bayonets were not a main source of inflicting war wounds, since most opposing soldiers feared the bayonet and would rather retreat than risk being penetrated by one. Bayonets were, however, handy around camp for cooking over open fires and scratching itchy backs.

Socket bayonets fit over the end of the musket barrel and were triangularly shaped, with dull edges and a sharp point. When bayonets were actually used, they usually resulted in wounds fatal from infection.

Knives
While Confederate soldiers carried knives and displayed them prominently, they were most often used for chopping wood at camp. Union soldiers kept small jackknives in their pockets for utility purposes.

We see a lot of pistols in Civil War photographs, but soldiers were discouraged from carrying them. Pistols were heavy and required a different set of tools for loading ammunition. They would be a heavy burden on soldiers, in addition to everything else they were already loaded down with.

"Why then," you ask, "are they in the pictures?"

Many times, war photographers staged photo opportunities. These "journalists" supplied the small weapons to the soldiers just long enough to snap the photos.

MORE SOLDIERS' EQUIPMENT

Items They Carried
Soldiers carried on their back forty to fifty pounds of uniform pieces, musket equipment, and other gear.

- Canvas haversack: contained a mess kit and some personal items. Soldiers soon learned to tar them for weatherproofing.

- Canteen: covered in wool for insulation and sealed with a cork

- Cartridge box with shoulder straps

- Belt

- Cap box

- Bayonet scabbard and frog

- Personal items: pocketknife, watch and chain, small Bible, tobacco (pipes, cigars, snuff, chewing tobacco)

- Wool blanket for warmth

- Gum blanket to serve as a poncho or as a tent floor

Footwear
- Socks: wool, cotton, or linen; hand-knitted (women back home knitted pairs upon pairs of socks to send to the front); Soldiers quickly learned to tuck their pant legs inside their sock tops to keep chiggers from crawling up their legs.

- Shoes: either boots or brogans; Hands-down the most common was the Jefferson bootee, which Jefferson Davis popularized as U.S. Secretary of War. Quite simply, they were thick leather, black boots with a square loose toe, tight around the instep. They required some effort to put on or take off.

FYI: A mess kit included a tin cup, tin plate, knife, fork, and spoon.

Hats

- Kepi: The forerunner of today's baseball caps, kepis, also known as "forage caps" or "bummer caps," were cheap and easy to replace. They had a crown that stuck straight up with a cardboard brace.

- Havelock: Because the kepi did not offer any protection from sun or rain, a piece of cloth called a Havelock buttoned onto or fit over the kepi and hung down over the neck and ears.

- Slouch hat: The broad-brimmed slouch hat, name notwithstanding, was part of the Union dress uniform. One popular version, called the Hardee hat after Confederate General William Hardee, was black with a wide brim turned up on one side and pinned with a brass eagle pin.

- Other hats: Soldiers wore a wide variety of other kinds of hats, including the wheel hat with its stiff leather brim and a round top; straw hats; skimmers for summer weather; panama or plantation hats; wool stocking caps in colder weather; stovepipe hats, and derbies.

When soldiers in camp needed additional supplies, they could visit the sutler, a sort of traveling salesman. Sutlers followed encampments and served to provide soldiers with goods they did not receive from the army, such as tobacco, candy, tinned meats, shoelaces, medicines, fried pies, and newspapers. In a true example of supply and demand economics, sutlers charged outrageous prices for their wares, but the soldiers would pay any price if they were desperate enough.

Unrelated Notes on Shoes

1. Fortunately, by 1861, shoes were finally being made in pairs: one for the left foot, one for the right. At the war's start, only very poor people still wore shoes made to fit either foot.

2. Having enough shoes was a continual problem for the Confederate armies. In fact, their raid to get military supplies and boots is said to be one contributing factor to the Battle of Gettysburg.

OUTMODED WEAPONS

When the war started, most weapons in federal arsenals—both those still in the Union and those in the South captured by the Confederacy—were smoothbore muskets. Close cousins to the muskets used almost a hundred years earlier in the American Revolution, they were known as "Brown Bess." Notoriously inaccurate, smoothbores had a time-consuming loading procedure and relatively short range, less than a hundred yards.

Of the more than 570,000 arsenal weapons on hand, only forty-six thousand were modern rifles. The rest were outdated flintlock and smoothbore muskets. In the North, the modern Springfield rifle was in production by mid-1861. In the South, gun repair shops updated the donated rifles and flintlocks into precision shooting instruments.

Before they matured to the realities of weaponry, some regiments came up with what we recognize now as completely ineffective arms:

- Lances: a nine-foot wooden staff tipped by a foot-long blade (used by Union troops from Philadelphia).
- Pikes: six-foot wooden shaft with a steel point to throw or jab (used by Confederate forces★).

★Georgia governor Joseph E. Brown favored pikes for state troops. The soldiers named one version after him: The "Joe Brown pike" was made from two pieces of timber banded together with iron and had a spring-activated fifteen-inch blade.

THE PRESIDENTS: JEFFERSON DAVIS

Jefferson Davis and Abraham Lincoln shared several similarities in their backgrounds, a fact that no biographer can resist mentioning. Both were born in log cabins, and both were born in the state of Kentucky. In addition, both Lincoln and Davis served in the Black Hawk War, a dispute over territorial rights between the Black Hawk tribe and the government.

Of course, both served as president during the Civil War.

Davis, unlike Lincoln, moved to the Deep South as a child, while the Lincolns went on to Indiana and Illinois. His father named Jefferson, the youngest of ten children, for his favorite president, Thomas Jefferson.

The Davises moved briefly to Louisiana and then to Mississippi, where the patriarch found success in the cotton business. By the end of his schooling, Jefferson Davis gained acceptance at West Point. He graduated in 1828, ranking last in his twenty-three-member class, which included Davis' future Confederate general, Robert E. Lee.

Early military assignments included a stint under the command of future president Zachary Taylor. Despite Taylor's objection, Davis married Taylor's daughter, Sarah, in 1835. She died of malaria several months later, sending Davis into seclusion in Mississippi for most of the next decade.

He reemerged in 1844 in a successful bid for a Mississippi Congressional seat. A year later, he married again, this time to Varina Powell of Natchez, Mississippi.

Davis left Congress in 1846, opting to lead a volunteer regiment in the Mexican War. He won kudos for courage under fire in several battles and suffered a shot to the foot in 1847. A series of political adventures followed, including a brief tenure as a U.S. Senator from Mississippi, a failed gubernatorial bid in his home state, and a Cabinet position under President Franklin Pierce, for whom he served as secretary of war.

Though he favored the expansion of slavery, Davis did not favor secession at first, owing to his awareness of Southern inferiority in military preparation and capabilities. Still, when secession came, Davis went along. In February 1861 at the Confederate constitutional convention, he was named acting president. A subsequent election in November awarded him a six-year term.

Davis presided over the Confederate government until its dissolution in 1865.

The Minie Ball

Named after Claude Minié, it was actually a small, hollow-based bullet. Advantages over previously used bullets:

- easily loaded
- traveled farther
- better accuracy

Minie balls were the ammunition of choice for both sides and were the reason many Civil War soldiers lost limbs. Instead of a clean shot, minie balls exploded on contact, fragmenting and shattering bones, but leaving the limbs still attached. The army surgeon's quick response was invariably to amputate.

CIVIL WAR BATTLE TIMELINE: 1861

Only a small percentage of the military action during the Civil War occurred in big battles like Gettysburg or Antietam. Although most were comparatively small skirmishes, more than ten thousand military actions took place. Virginia, by far, saw the most fighting, where more than two thousand military actions were waged. In comparison, Tennessee, which saw the second-most hostility, hosted almost 1,500 actions, while all of the acts of war combined in Mississippi, Louisiana, Alabama, and South Carolina did not even match Virginia's number.

March 4: Abraham Lincoln inaugurated sixteenth U.S. president
April 12–13: Bombardment and surrender of Fort Sumter, South Carolina
June 10: Engagement at Big Bethel, Virginia
July 5: Engagement at Carthage, Missouri
July 11: Engagement at Rich Mountain, Virginia (later West Virginia)
July 21: First battle of Manassas (Bull Run), Virginia
July 26: George McClellan replaces General Irvin McDowell in commanding the Union Army of the Potomac
August 10: Battle of Wilson's Creek, Missouri
August 28–29: Battle of Hatteras Inlet, North Carolina
September 12–20: Siege and capture of Lexington, Missouri
October 21: Battle of Ball's Bluff, Virginia
November 7: Battle of Belmont, Missouri
November 7: Battle of Port Royal Sound, South Carolina
November 8: The Trent Affair in Havana
December 9 & 26: Engagements at Chusto-Talasah, Indian Territory
December 26: Battle of Hominy Creek

Union Officers

Edward Baker
William F. Bartlett
Egbert B. Brown
Don Carlos Buell
John Buford
Ambrose Burnside
Benjamin "Beast" Butler
Joshua Lawrence Chamberlain
George Custer
Ulrich Dahlgren
Francis M. Drake
David Farragut
Edward Ferrero
Francis Fessenden
Andrew Foote
John Charles Frémont
Ulysses S. Grant
Henry W. Halleck
Winfield Scott Hancock
Martin D. Hardin
Joseph A. Haskin
William Hazen
Joseph Hooker
O. O. Howard
Philip Kearny
James Ledlie
James McCleary
George Meade
David Moore
Halbert E. Paine
Ely Parker
Alfred Pleasanton

Henry Pleasants
John Pope
Theodore Read
John Reynolds
William S. Rosecrans
Winfield Scott
Philip Sheridan
William T. Sherman
Dan Sickles
Charles Stone
Thomas W. Sweeney
George H. Thomas
Davis Tillson

THE ANACONDA PLAN

This plan sprang from the mind of Winfield Scott, a seventy-five-year-old war hero who presided over the Union troops when the Civil War began. Scott suffered from gout, and at this point in life was a little larger than most military men. Scott had put on so many pounds in his later years that he was unable to mount a horse.

The crusty general, who gained fame for his heroics in the War of 1812, was known as "Old Fuss and Feathers" in wry tribute to his resolute dedication to military protocol.

Still, Scott could hatch a plan. The Union commander recognized the North's inherent advantages in population, financial muscle, and manufacturing. To capitalize on these imbalances, he proposed to cut off the Southern ports while sending between sixty thousand and eighty thousand men into Confederate territory to divide the South. It was aimed at strangling the economic life out of the South.

Scott's plan made sense, but was a long shot initially, because the Navy lacked sufficient equipment, since it consisted of only forty-two ships at the time. In addition, the vast Southern coast encompassed more than three thousand miles. Lincoln approved Scott's plan in April, whereupon Scott pronounced the strategy as, yes, "The Anaconda Plan."

DIXIE DREGS

At the dawn of the Civil War, the differences between the Union and the soon-to-be-born Confederacy went beyond slavery. The North had twice as many people, with 22 million to the South's 9 million, including a 4 million population of slaves who could not help in the military effort. It had five times as many factories (100,000 to twenty thousand), and ten times as many workers in those factories (1.1 million to 100,000). In addition, the South controlled only 20 percent of the nation's bank deposits when the war began, another indication of comparative economic weakness.

All of these economic elements symbolized the North's headlong pursuit of the twentieth century future that would boast an industrialized, urban society while eschewing its agrarian past. In contrast, the South found itself mired in the plantation society of tobacco, cotton, and slave labor.

The First Aircraft Carriers

We're not talking about the U.S.S. *Nimitz* here. Think smaller scale. In 1861, the Union army added a "flight deck" to a coal barge and renamed the craft, *George Washington Parke Custis*. This carrier once pulled a Union balloon for thirteen miles at an altitude of one thousand feet.

That same year, John LaMountain used the boat Fanny to tow his balloon at an altitude of two thousand feet above the James River.

Both Union and Confederate engineers also employed tugboats to pull their reconnaissance balloons along.

WHOSE SIDE ARE YOU ON ANYWAY?

On April 19, 1861, less than a week after the surrender of Fort
Sumter, another ominous sign jolted the Union. It occurred in
Baltimore, a city boasting a sizable population of Southern
sympathizers. As a border state, Maryland's loyalties were conflicted
despite its decision to remain part of the Union. A Massachusetts
regiment on its way to Washington came under attack by a mob of
pro-Confederate citizens and secessionists who singled out the Union
troops as they made their way through the city while transferring
between train stations. The attackers threw rocks, stones, and anything
else they could find as the regiment struggled to make its way to
Camden Station. Soldiers eventually fired on the attackers, leading to
the deaths of four members of the regiment and twelve civilians
involved in the assault on the federal troops. The episode spooked
President Lincoln, who was already dealing with a nervous capital
city engulfed in rumor as it looked across the Potomac to the South.
Now, it became clear that Maryland, to the capital's north, could also
prove harrowing for the Union capital.

The Medal of Honor

Sergeant William H. Carney of the 54th Massachusetts
was awarded the Congressional Medal of Honor for
bravery during the July 18, 1863, attack on Fort Wagner.
Carney retrieved the regiment's flag, taking bullets in the
head, chest, right arm, and leg. He was the first of twenty-
three blacks to win the Medal of Honor for service during
the Civil War, although it was not awarded until thirty-
seven years later.

Lincoln Branded as "Tyrant"

One of President Lincoln's most controversial decisions came in the wake of the Baltimore riots. Against the opinion of Supreme Court Chief Justice Roger Taney—the man behind the Dred Scott decision that proclaimed blacks had no rights because they weren't citizens—the president suspended habeas corpus, the legal tenet that prevents American citizens from being arrested and held without lawful basis.

Lincoln made the decision because of fears that Maryland would secede. He also hoped to quell riots and trouble stirred up by various militias. Taney declared the president's action unconstitutional, but Lincoln ignored Taney's censure.

In September 1862, Lincoln suspended the writ of habeas corpus again, this time throughout the nation. On the Confederate side, President Jefferson Davis also suspended habeas corpus in a bid to hold the fragile new nation together.

Lincoln wisely noted that the suspension of one Constitutional guarantee—habeas corpus—was worth it in light of the fact that there would cease to be a government to honor the federal constitution if the Union collapsed.

Nonetheless, he suffered criticism for his decision. Critics dubbed him a tyrant, a common refrain today among Southern sympathizers (yes, they still exist), libertarians, and some conservatives.

BATTLE OF MANASSAS (BULL RUN)

The first true battle of the Civil War occurred in the Virginia town of Manassas, about thirty miles southwest of Washington. A stream called Bull Run courses through that part of the state, providing the more common name of the battle. Confederate General P. G. T. Beauregard, the man responsible for launching the attack on federal forces at Fort Sumter in Charleston Harbor, led the Confederate Army of the Potomac, opposed by Union troops under the command of Irvin McDowell. Beauregard and McDowell had been classmates at West Point.

Attitudes and ambience surrounding the battle at Manassas are best summed up in one word: delusional. McDowell's men, like most soldiers in the early years of the Civil War, had little or no experience in battle. Beyond that, they expected to cruise to victory. During marches on the way to confront the Confederate soldiers, McDowell's soldiers often dropped out of formation to pick blackberries and engage in other less-than-disciplined endeavors. A retinue of politicians, reporters, and various other attendant hangers-on made for a genial atmosphere often described by eyewitnesses and historians as a picnic-like affair.

Neither side fought with much distinction as they went to battle on July 21. Confederate soldiers began to retreat, but were spurred to fight on by freshly arrived reinforcements from the Shenandoah Valley. The battle also created at least one legend, that of Thomas "Stonewall" Jackson.

As newspaper accounts described it, Confederate General Barnard Bee, a South Carolinian, informed Jackson, leader of a Virginia brigade, that Bee's men were being forced to give ground. Jackson vowed to fight the federal troops at the point of bayonets, prompting Bee to remark, "Oh men, there are Jackson and his Virginians, standing behind you like a stone wall." Whether it was intended as compliment or insult remains uncertain. Bee died the following day, preventing him from providing a point of clarity on the matter, but it cemented a reputation, and a nickname, as Jackson became "Stonewall" and his men were ever after known as "Stonewall's Brigade."

In any event, the Confederates carried the day, sending McDowell and the Union troops into panicked retreat. Chaos reigned as the hordes of onlookers were stampeded by terrified Union soldiers scampering for safety. As the tide turned, Jackson urged his men to charge and "yell like the furies," inspiring the first airing of the famed, high-pitched "Rebel Yell."

The two sides sustained 4,700 casualties in the engagement— 2,950 on the Union side, and 1,750 Confederates.

Name Game

Manassas or Bull Run? Sharpsburg or Antietam? Yes, before Americans debated tastes-great-less-filling, arguments arose over the names of Civil War battles, and still do, to some extent. The disagreements stemmed from proclivities in the North, which tended to name battles for the nearest river or stream, and the South, which favored the nearest town or railroad junction. So Southerners prefer Manassas or Manassas Junction, while Northerners opt for Bull Run, the name of an adjacent stream.

NOT READY TO RUMBLE

Armies in the North and South shared the common trait of not being ready for war in 1861. The United States had sixteen thousand officers and soldiers at the time of the Civil War; the Confederacy, obviously, had to build its forces from scratch. More than three hundred U.S. officers defected to the Southern side at the conflict's outbreak.

Though the men became more seasoned as the war dragged on, their officers often failed to make similar progress. That's because the Civil War offers a vivid example of technology outstripping tactics and conventional battlefield wisdom. Over and over again, commanders on both sides sent their men to slaughter by attacking fortified troops who had dug in with repeating rifles and advanced artillery. Improved weaponry—faster and more accurate than anything seen before in combat—overwhelmed the preferred Napoleonic-style tactics of attacking the enemy. In the Civil War and beyond, those in a fortified defensive position held a decided advantage, especially before the advent of aerial attacks.

Both armies suffered from a dearth of innovative tacticians, though most historians generally agree that the South fared better in this regard with Robert E. Lee, Stonewall Jackson, and James Longstreet. As the war went on, the North benefited from some stellar strategists, as well, such as Ulysses S. Grant, and of course William T. Sherman, who turned the war in favor of the Union and finished off the weakened Confederates with unflagging aggression.

Soldiers in the war tended to be WASPs—White Anglo-Saxon Protestants—between eighteen and thirty-nine years old. Most came from rural areas. One might think the proliferation of farm boys meant the soldiers were handy with guns and practiced at shooting, but inaccurate firing and poor handling of guns plagued both armies through most of the war.

During the war's first year or so, both armies relied on volunteers. (Drafts were instituted later, leading to riots in New York and elsewhere). As with most wars, the wealthy ruling class served in disproportionately lower numbers, benefiting from the ability to hire surrogates or exploit other means of avoiding military service.

Nothing Uniform About It

Everyone thinks of the Union in blue and the Confederacy in gray, but in the war's early months, telling the two sides apart confused the soldiers and commanders as much as anyone else. The problem stemmed from a lack of uniformity in uniforms: Both sides were ragtag bunches, with some streamlined uniforms of blue and gray on appropriate sides—and plenty of militias and volunteer soldiers from various towns wearing whatever material (and color) was handy.

CONFEDERATE COMMANDERS: THOMAS "STONEWALL" JACKSON

Other than Robert E. Lee, no one stands taller among military leaders of the Confederacy than Thomas "Stonewall" Jackson. He established his reputation at the First Battle of Bull Run, where a colleague gave him his nickname. Jackson's later campaigns and efforts would make "Stonewall" a household name, one that, to most observers, connoted immovable determination and military grit.

Jackson's men dubbed him "Old Blue Light," a reference to the piercing quality of his bright blue eyes.

Born in Virginia, Jackson came from humble means and had an itinerant, off-and-on education. Despite that, he proved to be a tireless worker and made it to West Point. There he doggedly made his way from the depths of his class, graduating seventeenth in 1846. He immediately left for the Mexican War upon graduation and served with distinction, earning a couple of promotions and making his first acquaintance with Lee, his future Confederate boss.

Jackson took a job as a teacher at the Virginia Military Institute before later siding with the South in the Civil War. He built his legend with daring, bold military maneuvers at the Battle of Chancellorsville and during the Valley Campaign of 1862. Other major battles Jackson served in include Antietam and Fredericksburg.

A stern teetotaler and rigid man of faith, Jackson possessed a variety of quirks and eccentricities. He sucked on lemons incessantly and had a hypochondria streak of stunning proportions.

It was a gaggle of Confederates on watch duty, and not pepper, that did Jackson in. At dusk on May 2, 1863, at Chancellorsville, a Southern soldier mistakenly shot Jackson. His left arm was amputated and he later contracted pneumonia as a result of the wound. Jackson died eight days later, a dreadful blow to Lee and the Southern army.

MAN OF INACTION

Less than a week after the Confederates dealt the Union a defeat at Bull Run, President Lincoln dumped Irvin McDowell as commander and installed George McClellan in his place.

The rise of McClellan led to almost comical hesitation on the part of the Northern army, much to the frustrated president's dismay. McClellan was a dashing, charismatic, and beloved figure among his men. At the same time, he was vainglorious, paranoid, and painfully cautious.

McClellan built his reputation on a couple of early, minor victories in the war and by fostering a disciplined, orderly regimen on the green Civil War troops. Once his troops were ready, McClellan had no idea how they should be employed. He invariably underestimated his forces and their potential while overestimating the size and skill of enemy troops. McClellan repeatedly shrank from battle when pressing his advantage would have led to victory, most famously at Antietam, despite one of McClellan's men having found a lost copy of Lee's battle plans before fighting began, and during the Peninsula Campaign, both in 1862.

McClellan was just thirty-four when he replaced McDowell. His dithering led Lincoln to demote the man revered as "Young Napoleon." Of his reluctance to engage in battle, Lincoln famously remarked, "If General McClellan does not want to use the Army, I would like to borrow it."

MEDICINE ON THE HOME FRONT

Advances in medicine made baby-steps since the Declaration of Independence. Epidemic diseases such as smallpox, typhoid, and malaria continued to decimate entire town populations.

Doctors staying home from war were no better prepared than the surgeons in the field. At that time, even the few legitimate medical schools offered only one year of training. Many doctors simply obtained their certifications from diploma mills.

Physicians of the 1860s employed herbal and botanical remedies, some of which we now know to do more harm than good. Drugs typically found in the doctor's bag included cathartics (or "purgatives"), emetics (to induce vomiting), and smelling salts (to revive faint feelings).

- Quinine was given in large doses to treat malaria. It was also a smallpox treatment, a painkiller, and an inflammation treatment.
- Paregoric, or camphorated, tincture of opium, was a pain reliever, a sedative, a cough suppressant, and an anti-diarrhea treatment. It was often used as a pediatric drug to settle restless babies.
- Calomel, or mercurous chloride (i.e., mercury), both a laxative and a disinfectant, it was applied in a variety of ways: given to slave children to expel worms, to adult slaves to treat swollen eyes, to infants to correct dysentery, and even to treat ague and fever.
- Laudanum, or extract of opium, was used as a sedative and pain reliever. It was widely prescribed for everything from colds and meningitis, to heart problems in adults and children.
- Camphor was a stronger sleep aid or fever reducer when opium didn't do the trick. Today, it is used in embalming fluid and moth repellent, as well as an ingredient in anti-itch cream and cough suppressant.
- Digitalis was used for dropsy, a condition of swelling due to fluid in the organs. It is still used today for atrial fibrillation.

SLAVE HEALTH

While conditions varied from one plantation to another, slaves often lived in unhealthy environments. Their lack of defense against disease and its spread was directly related to immune systems compromised by overwork, poor nutrition, and unsanitary living conditions.

Flies and mosquitoes found plenty of reason to live around the slave housing, where decaying food scraps and human waste made fertile breeding grounds. Beyond being ever-present pests, many of those same mosquitoes carried yellow fever or malaria. And the people of that time did not yet know the connection between mosquitoes and malaria.

Drinking water contaminated by all manner of waste, including human, quickly led to epidemics of cholera, dysentery, typhoid, and hepatitis, as well as parasitic worms in the lungs, liver, blood vessels, gall bladder, and intestines.

Doctors were only called in to treat slaves when a condition threatened their ability to perform their work. For example, a slaveholder would consult the local doctor for help when a male slave suffered frostbitten fingers.

But, for the most part, slave medical care was accomplished at home. The mistress of the house took her responsibility of caring for the ill slaves seriously. She kept a medicine chest stocked with popular remedies of bleeding, vomiting, and purging: cathartics, teas, oils, salts, and calomel. She didn't hesitate to dispense her medicines.

Some Home Remedies Administered by Plantation Wives

Symptoms: fever, headache, slight delirium, constant pain, sore throat (quite possibly, this was malaria)

Treatment: bleeding and blistering, doses of calomel and castor oil

Symptom: lockjaw

Treatment: bleeding and blistering, doses of salts

CONFEDERATE CAPITAL LOCATIONS

Just as the United States' national capital bounced around from Philadelphia to New York City, to Baltimore, before settling in D.C., so did the capital of the Confederacy.

Montgomery, Alabama

When the first seven states seceded from December 1860 to February 1861, it made sense to hold governmental meetings in the geographic center of South Carolina, Georgia, Alabama, Florida, Mississippi, Louisiana, and Texas. This center was Montgomery, Alabama.

Jefferson Davis was sworn in as President of the Confederate States of America at the Alabama capitol building on February 9, 1861.

Today, elementary classes across Alabama take field trips to the capitol, where they can stand on a gold star marking the exact spot on the capitol steps where Davis stood to take the oath of office. Then they cross the street to tour the First White House of the Confederacy, where Davis lived with his family for about three months.

Richmond, Virginia

When Virginia seceded in April, the capital was moved to the larger and more cosmopolitan city of Richmond. Like in Alabama, the Virginia capitol building doubled as the Capitol of the Confederacy for almost four years.

The Executive Mansion in Richmond, built in 1811 for the Brockenbrough family, housed Davis's family from 1861 to 1865. Shortly after the war's end, it served as a schoolhouse. Today, a National Historic Landmark, it is the site of the Museum of the Confederacy.

Danville, Virginia

With Union forces marching on Richmond, the Confederate government evacuated on April 2, 1865, to Danville, Virginia, on the North Carolina border. The temporary capital relocated to Major W. T. Sutherlin's home, until news of Lee's surrender a week later forced Davis to flee again.

The Sutherlin house is now the home of the Danville Museum of Fine Arts and History. It is listed on the National Register of Historic Places.

Bumbling and Stumbling Redux

The Union suffered embarrassment at the First Battle of Bull Run in July 1861—and then provided an encore performance of dubious distinction two months later at Ball's Bluff.

Located thirty miles from Washington across the Potomac River, Ball's Bluff was the site of a Union plan that centered on crossing the river and capturing Leesburg. Instead, it led to the capture of seven hundred Union soldiers and a congressional inquiry. Matters unraveled almost before they began. A group led by Colonel Edward Baker, a U.S. Senator from Oregon and friend of President Lincoln, reached the summit of Ball's Bluff, where, with nowhere to hide, they were easily picked off by Confederate forces under the command of Brigadier General Nathan Evans.

Baker and his men, serving under Union Brigadier General Charles Stone, were routed. Baker died in the battle. Stone took the fall, accused of treason and sent to jail for six months. He was later released, but never again given any significant military responsibilities.

THE TRENT AFFAIR

As war took shape, governments in the North and South worried what the response would be from Europe, particularly France and England. Southern cotton was a popular and necessary trading item for cloth makers in Europe, while grain from the North also was shipped overseas.

The Confederate government began a bid for alliance with Britain and France. At minimum, the Southerners wanted official recognition of their newly formed government.

In October 1861, Confederate President Jefferson Davis named John Slidell of Louisiana and James M. Mason of Virginia as ministers to France and England, respectively. Mason and Slidell secured a successful passage out of Charleston by boat and eventually made their way to Cuba, where they boarded the Trent, a British mail ship and merchant vessel.

Captain Charles Wilkes, commander of the U.S.S. *San Jacinto*, got wind of the mission while scouring for intelligence during a stop in Havana just after the Trent's departure with Mason and Slidell aboard. Wilkes sailed and soon caught up with the Trent, firing shots across the British ship's bow. A boarding party sent by Wilkes to the Trent seized Mason and Slidell and brought them back to the San Jacinto. They were brought north as prisoners and, as Wilkes celebrated, the British government fumed.

Britain demanded that Slidell and Mason be freed—and that the Union apologize for its actions. The president recognized the grievous mistake, even if he rued the release of Mason and Slidell, hardly innocent bystanders.

"One war at a time," Lincoln said before freeing the Confederate emissaries. Though the Brits were mildly mollified, and provided informal but unofficial recognition to the Confederacy for a time, the South never managed to secure the official recognition it so desperately sought from European nations.

EVERY THORN HAS ITS ROSE

Confederate spy Rose O'Neal Greenhow became a bit of a tabloid sensation during the Civil War. A Washington doyenne, Greenhow counted the high and mighty as friends and confidantes, from presidents and senators to military men and socialites. Among her closest friends: South Carolina's John C. Calhoun, the man behind nullification and a former vice president. Known as "Wild Rose" in reference to her complexion, and perhaps temperament, Greenhow was married to Dr. Robert Greenhow, who worked at the State Department and provided his wife with an informal education in politics. He died in 1854.

As a widow, Greenhow retained her social standing and caught the eye of a Confederate colonel. Already convinced of the South's cause through her earlier friendship with Calhoun, Greenhow needed little prompting to take up spying for the Confederacy. Her seductive charms played on male vanity—and procured valuable information, including the Union's strategic plans for the First Battle of Bull Run. Those details helped Beauregard and the Confederates whip the Union at the first significant battle of the war. Jefferson Davis, the Confederate president, credited her with providing the decisive blow at Bull Run with her secret messages about Union strategy.

Eminent detective Allan Pinkerton took the bloom off the Confederacy's rose, nabbing Greenhow in August 1861. Ten months later, she was paroled to the South. Davis sent her to Europe to promote the Confederate cause soon after she was released. During her time abroad, Greenhow published a well-received memoir and met with dignitaries, including Queen Victoria. She died in 1864 near the North Carolina coast aboard a lifeboat while trying to outrun a Union blockade. Greenhow's death stemmed, in part, from the ballast of clutching $2,000 in gold on her person—the royalties from her memoir's sales.

CONFEDERATE COMMANDERS: ROBERT E. LEE

Like Lincoln, the legend of Robert E. Lee supercedes any and all biographical fact. The legend, beginning with his death in 1870, alludes that the Confederate general never made a military mistake, never spoke an unkind word, and never erred in judgment.

The truth, of course, is far messier than that, but Lee, by almost any historical measure, remains one of the most admired and capable military leaders in American history. His father, "Light Horse Harry" Lee, served with distinction during the Revolutionary War but later endured financial hardship. He died when Robert was eleven.

Robert E. Lee graduated with honors from West Point and gained attention, as many Civil War officers did, during the Mexican War. President Lincoln made several overtures to Lee to assume command of federal forces in the run-up to the Civil War; Lee declined the offers. He opposed secession, but when his native Virginia seceded in April 1861, Lee followed.

Jefferson Davis tapped Lee as a military advisor in the Confederacy. In the summer of 1862, he sent Lee into the field, where he remained for the rest of the war. Bold and daring tactics distinguished Lee on the battlefield. Signature victories include Second Bull Run, Fredericksburg, and Chancellorsville. Loyal to his men and beloved in return, Lee and his horse, Traveller, became Southern icons.

Later historians have questioned Lee's disastrous forays into the North during the war. At Sharpsburg (or Antietam) in 1862, he avoided collapse by the narrowest of margins. He absorbed his most infamous and devastating loss in July 1863 at Gettysburg. Lee's ordered assault on Union troops, known as Pickett's Charge, led to instant carnage and doomed the Confederate forces to defeat. If Union commander George Meade had been more aggressive and pursued Lee and his retreating, battered troops, the South may have been finished then and there. Instead, Meade let Lee escape back to Virginia—and thereby extended the war by two years.

The emergence of Ulysses S. Grant as the Union's top military leader spelled the end for Lee and the Confederacy. Finally, after a string of ineffectual generals, the Union found a commander who was Lee's equal—and who was willing to take the battle to his enemy. Lee and Grant had both played successful roles in the Mexican War, and in 1865 they met in a mournful, respectful manner at Appomattox Court House to end the Civil War.

The Marble Man

Lee's iconic status has led him to become known as The Marble Man. After the war, Lee, unlike Jefferson Davis and other prominent Confederates, urged reconciliation and supported the Reconstruction efforts of President Andrew Johnson. He privately frowned upon public criticisms of the North by noted members of the former rebel government and military. He favored educating freed slaves, but he opposed giving blacks the right to vote. Shortly after the war ended, Lee accepted an offer to become the president of Washington College, now known as Washington and Lee University. He and his family are buried on the campus.

Lee and Arlington National

Robert E. Lee remains one of the most admired men in American military history, but his grave is not to be found at Arlington National Cemetery. Instead, it's at Washington and Lee University.

Despite the absence of a revered military hero in the nation's most honored military burial ground, Lee and Arlington National Cemetery are forever linked. That's because Lee and his wife, the great-great granddaughter of Martha Washington, lived in her parents' home, Arlington House, for thirty years. During the Civil War, the federal government seized it and, eventually, made the property into a military cemetery.

As for Lee's abandoned house, it can be toured today on the grounds of Arlington National Cemetery.

THE FIRST THANKSGIVING

Okay, we know you're too smart for us to tell you that Thanksgiving began during the Civil War. We know you've heard the story of Thanksgiving since you were in kindergarten, maybe earlier. We know that the Pilgrims of Plymouth colony celebrated the very first Thanksgiving with the native Indians in 1621, after surviving their first year in the New World.

But let us convince you that the First Official Thanksgiving National Holiday was observed during the Civil War.

Yes, it's true that several presidents observed one-time Thanksgiving holidays, starting with George Washington. In fact, Washington declared November 26, 1789, as a national day of thanksgiving and prayer. (NOTE: He limited it to that one day in that one year.)

By 1817, New York State had begun celebrating Thanksgiving Day as an annual festivity. And, within the next thirty years or so, it was getting to be a tradition in many states. (NOTE: It still was not a national holiday.)

Finally, in 1864, President Lincoln declared Thanksgiving a national holiday in his aptly-named 1863 Thanksgiving Proclamation. Lincoln stated that the holiday would be observed on the last Thursday of November. We believe he chose this day to commemorate the Mayflower landing at Cape Cod.

The story doesn't end here, though. In 1939, President Franklin Roosevelt declared Thanksgiving Day would be on the fourth Thursday of every November. This is because, sometimes, the last Thursday of the month can also be the last day of the month.

Roosevelt thought it would help stores prepare for the Christmas holiday to have a little more time between the two celebrations. (Not that stores care too much these days—what with Christmas decorations going up right after the back-to-school sales.)

OBSERVATION BALLOONS IN THE UNION ARMY

Both the North and the South used observation balloons for reconnaissance missions. With Lincoln always ready to try new technology, and with the backing of better resources, the North did it first and accomplished more.

Engineer John Wise built the first balloon for the Union army. Before it could be used, though, it came loose from its lines. Union soldiers shot it down to avoid capture by Confederates.

John LaMountain did his best to provide his balloon services to the Union Army. He was first to make aerial reconnaissance and first to do so during an untethered flight. But he did not know the right people, and so he did not get the backing needed to stay employed. In early 1862, General McClellan dismissed LaMountain, and his career as a military aeronaut ended.

Thaddeus Lowe, on the other hand, did know the right people. In turn, he was favored by the Union Army and given the resources necessary to get his plans "off the ground." It was Lowe who suggested sending telegrams from the floating balloons to commanders on the ground.

When Lincoln established the Balloon Corps in the summer of 1861, Lowe was in charge. Powered by gas from the capital city's gas lines, the balloon Union made the first official military balloon flight near Washington, D.C.

By fall, portable gas generators had been added to the arsenal, and balloons were moved out into the field. On September 24, 1861, Lowe telegraphed intelligence about Falls Church, Virginia, to troops in Arlington, Virginia, more than three miles away. Union troops made warfare history, aiming and firing accurately at their Confederate targets without actually seeing them.

Before the Balloon Corps disbanded in August 1863, its fleet consisted of the Union, plus Intrepid, Constitution, United States, Washington, Eagle, and Excelsior. Ranging in size from fifteen thousand to thirty-two thousand cubic feet, and able to climb to five thousand feet, they were crucial in such battles at Fredericksburg and Fair Oaks.

In response to the Union Army's recon balloons, Confederate commanders learned to enforce nightfall blackouts in camp, as well as create dummy camps and gun placements.

"Silk Dress" Balloons

The Confederate Army formed a small balloon corps in 1862 when Captain John Randolph Bryan built a hot-air balloon out of a varnish-coated cotton envelope. Without equipment to fill the craft with hydrogen, Bryan launched the tethered balloon with hot air. While aloft over Yorktown, Virginia, Bryan sketched a map of Union positions.

Another Confederate balloon was made of different colored silk panels. Rumors abound that it was made from silk dresses donated by patriotic Southern women. Though it was, actually, made from silk, it wasn't fashioned from recycled dresses. This balloon was filled with gas in Richmond, Virginia, and towed into location first by train, then by a tugboat (which then ran aground in the James River and was captured by Union troops).

The third Confederate balloon, also made of silk, suffered a similar fate when it was blown from its tethers and captured by Union soldiers.

DESERTION OF SOLDIERS

Why Did Men Desert?

Officers noticed a correlation between mail call and desertions. After soldiers received letters from home, detailing their families' living conditions—cold, hunger, eviction, destitution—many men decided it was time to take care of business at home.

Poor Southerners did not really identify with the Southern cause. When they read in letters from home how wealthy merchants profited from their loved ones' hard work, raising prices again and again, the soldiers quit trying to understand what they were fighting for.

Especially in the South, soldiers were sensitive to ill-use by their superiors, and they would not stand for being treated like slaves. Harsh commanders had a higher desertion rate than their more compassionate colleagues.

In the North, Democrats were not entirely on board with going to war. Frequently, articles in Northern newspapers openly encouraged desertion.

Did Any Specific Event Affect the Desertion Rate?

In April 1862, the Confederate Congress passed the "Twenty Slave Law" excusing any man owning twenty or more slaves from service in the Confederate Army. This didn't go over well with soldiers who didn't own slaves. It wasn't long after the law passed that many poor Southern soldiers decided they were through with fighting the rich man's war.

What Methods Did Soldiers Use to Desert?

For a while, soldiers surrendered as prisoners of war, to be paroled after their capture. But, then both sides stopped paroling prisoners, so that didn't work anymore.

Wealthy soldiers, who could easily get a pass home, took furlough or sick leave and never came back. Poor soldiers were kept at the

front. For them, the choice was simply to go home without the
excuse of leave.

How Did Men Get Away With It?

Especially in the South, deserters would band together and hide
in the woods and in caves. They used their collective firepower to
discourage any military search parties sent to round them up. Local
sympathizers would help smuggle food and clothing to them.

Both in the North and South, the stigma of desertion among
civilians quickly fell away, and AWOL soldiers found accomplices in
their families and neighbors. Whole communities were known to
back up their men—either by hiding them and protesting ignorance,
or by force, if necessary—when military search parties came through
reclaiming deserters.

How Many Men Deserted?

In the Union Army, the desertion rate grew to two hundred a
day by 1863. By the war's end, more than 500,000 men were listed as
deserters. The desertion rate among black soldiers was slightly higher
than average; their complaint was almost always that they had been
treated not as soldiers, but as slaves.

In the Confederacy, more than 40 percent of Southern soldiers
had left without leave by the end of 1863. By 1865, hundreds of men
were deserting every day.

What Were the Consequences of Desertion?

When caught, deserters were sentenced to court-martial (two-
thirds of wartime court-martials were for desertion charges). That is,
if they were given the formality of a trial. Deserters were likely to be
shot, either on sight, or killed by firing squad or hanging. Those
deserters fortunate enough to escape execution could expect to be
branded with the letter *D*.

THE MAN WITHOUT A COUNTRY: CLEMENT L. VALLANDIGHAM, PART I

Who was Clement Vallandigham?

Vallandigham was an Ohio preacher's son married to a Maryland planter's daughter. A loud, vocal Democrat, Vallandigham believed in states' rights and was against the Civil War, Unionism, and Abraham Lincoln.

Vallandigham served in the United States House of Representatives from 1858 to 1863. He had been heard to say that he wanted to restore "the Federal Union as it was forty years ago," and he did his best, opposing every act or measure that Republicans introduced regarding the war effort.

How does Ambrose Burnside fit into this story?

In 1863, General Burnside was commanding the U.S. military district composed of Ohio, Indiana, Illinois, Michigan, and eastern Kentucky. In the spring of that year, Burnside issued General Order No. 38, mainly to target Vallandigham, who was campaigning for the Democratic nomination for Ohio governor.

Burnside's order said that anyone who made statements against the federal government would be tried for treason. So, what did Vallandigham do? He made a strong speech that urged soldiers to desert from the Army. He also warned the Union that if the war continued, the western states (specifically Ohio) just might secede themselves and join the Confederacy. To be fair, he also stressed the value of his peace platform, criticizing violent resistance to the law and emphasizing using the power of the ballot box to cause change.

Burnside gave orders to have Vallandigham arrested on charges of treason.

What Happened at the Military Trial in Cincinnati?

First of all, there really wasn't much of a case. Without substantial evidence, and with prosecution witnesses supporting Vallandigham's claim of running on a peace platform, it didn't look like the trial would last long. He was found guilty anyway and sentenced to two years in military prison.

The Peace Society

One of the largest antiwar organizations in the South, the Peace Society, focused on spreading discord among soldiers and civilians and encouraging desertion. Its thousands of Unionist members from Mississippi, Tennessee, Alabama, Georgia, and Florida, were so powerful that, in the 1863 election, they sent six delegates to the Confederate Congress to advocate ending the war and rejoining the Union.

THE MAN WITHOUT A COUNTRY: CLEMENT L. VALLANDIGHAM, PART II

What happened after Vallandigham was convicted of treason?

Democrats, and even some Republicans, protested the verdict and prison sentence. They were appalled that a civilian could be sentenced by a military court for simply making speeches. The findings were escalated all the way to President Lincoln.

What did President Lincoln do?

President Lincoln didn't like Vallandigham, and he didn't like the thought of pardoning someone who urged desertion when the deserters themselves were dealt with by swift execution. But he saw how this could be a potential political fiasco for his upcoming run for reelection, should the Ohio Congressman be made a martyr. So, Lincoln, "split it down the middle," and reduced the sentence to banishment to the South.

What happened when Vallandigham was banished to the South?

From Cincinnati, Vallandigham was shipped via the gunboat Exchange to the Union Army's headquarters at Murfreesboro, Tennessee.

Even though he had been banished from the Union, Vallandigham still was a Union loyalist. The Secessionists in Tennessee didn't want him there, either. He was ordered off Confederate soil.

Vallandigham was the only man banished from both the United States and the Confederate States.

What happened after Vallandigham left the South?

He traveled to Canada, and continued his bid for Ohio Governor from his hotel room there. He won the Democratic nomination by a vote of 411 to eleven. However, he lost the election by 100,000 votes.

Did Vallandigham ever get to come back home?
In 1864, Vallandigham put on a beard disguise and stuffed a pillow under his clothes. Then he traveled back to Ohio. And, wouldn't you know it: when Lincoln heard about it, he got a big laugh at the mental image.

Copperheads

Clement Vallandigham was known to be one of the most outspoken Copperheads.

Copperheads were Northern Democrats who wanted to work out some kind of compromise with the Confederate states. They were probably named for the poisonous snake.

Or, they could have been named for the penny—they wore lapel buttons that they had cut from copper coins depicting the goddess of liberty.

THE MAN WITHOUT A COUNTRY: CLEMENT L. VALLANDIGHAM, PART III

What happened to Vallandigham after the Civil War ended?

After the Civil War, Vallandigham went back to practicing law. During an 1871 case, he was showing the court how a murder victim might have actually killed himself. He proved his point quite well when he accidentally—and fatally—shot himself. He died from the wound at the age of fifty-one.

Is there anything else we should know about Vallandigham?

His friends called him "Valiant Val."

What's the deal with "The Man without a Country?"

In 1863, Edward Everett Hale published a fictional short story in *The Atlantic Monthly* about the lifetime of Philip Nolan. Hale's main character had been sentenced to live out his days on U.S. Naval ships, never to see his home country again, after cursing America during a court-martial trial. Hale modeled the character Philip Nolan after Clement L. Vallandigham.

Today, Hale's writing is more quickly recognizable than Vallandigham's name. In fact, in 1973, a television movie adaptation of Hale's story featured actor Cliff Robertson (who later played Spider-Man's Uncle Ben Parker—the one who said, "With great power comes great responsibility") as Philip Nolan and Beau Bridges as the story's narrator.

TRAGEDY AND JEFFERSON DAVIS

Jefferson Davis and the Taylor family: Jefferson Davis's life was marked by heartbreak that enveloped his first marriage and even his first in-laws. Serving under Commander Zachary Taylor (the future president) Davis fell in love with Taylor's daughter, Sarah. Taylor was against the match, and Davis even considered challenging him to a duel to win Sarah's hand.

In 1835, against his commander's objections, Davis married Sarah anyway. Their happiness lasted only three months, when she died of malaria. Davis was a young widower, one who had not had time to gain much favor with his father-in-law.

The Taylor tragedies continued. Zachary's son, Richard, married the daughter of a French Creole planter in 1851. They quickly had two sons and three daughters. Both sons, Richard Jr. and Zachary, died of scarlet fever during the Civil War. At the time, General Richard Taylor was serving the Confederate Army as a brilliant and well-respected commander.

Tragedy in Jefferson Davis's Own Family: It took Jefferson Davis almost ten years to get over the loss of his first wife, but he remarried, to Varina Howell. They had six children. Only two daughters—Varina "Winnie" Anne and Margaret "Maggie" Howell—outlived their father. Only Maggie married and had children of her own.

- In 1854, Davis's first child, son Samuel Emory, died of measles at two years old.
- In 1864, five-year-old Joseph Evan, who Davis once called "his hope and greatest joy in life," died from an accident in the Confederate White House. Little Joe fell from a porch banister and died almost instantly.
- In 1872, William "Billy" Howell died of diphtheria when he was eleven years old.
- In 1878, Jefferson Jr. died of yellow fever at age twenty-one.
- In 1898, Winnie died at age thirty-four of malarial gastritis.

BLACK TROOPS IN THE UNION ARMY

The abolitionists were ready to send black troops into battle from the beginning of the war, and Congress authorized recruiting black soldiers in 1862. After Lincoln's Emancipation Proclamation, black men finally began to really serve their country. It is generally agreed that their enlistment ultimately made the difference between whether the North would win or lose the war.

Remember, the Emancipation Proclamation only freed slaves in rebelling states. Those slaves still held in Union states were not freed at that time. So, enlisting in the U.S. Army was a fast-forward to freedom for thousands of slave men. Most of the black men who joined the Army were slaves from border states, or they were escaped slaves from the Confederacy who had risked pursuit by dogs and pistol shot to reach Union lines.

More than 185,000 black Americans fought in the Civil War; thirty-seven thousand of them died. By the end of the war, black soldiers in 166 regiments made up almost 10 percent of the U.S. Army. In comparison, black civilians made up less than 1 percent of the North's population.

As in civilian life, black soldiers met with discrimination and skepticism. While President Lincoln and General Grant supported the idea of including black soldiers in the nation's defense, many other commanders, including Sherman, were not so sure. In many regiments, black soldiers were assigned the most menial labor tasks, but in others, their officers made sure they received lessons in reading and writing along with studies in tactics and drill practice.

Black privates received a $10 monthly payday, compared to the white private's $13 each month. In protest of the inequality, several black regiments actually refused to accept the $10 each month, working without any pay at all. They were also given a smaller clothing allowance than whites, and they received even worse medical care than white soldiers. And if you'll remember, nobody got good medical care.

Finally, for the most part, the black regiments were under the charge of white commanders. No black soldier was ever promoted to a rank above captain, and there were barely one hundred black officers in the entire Union Army.

Timeline Milestones

April 1862: The war's first black regiment, the 1st South Carolina, is formed when General David Hunter frees all the slaves on the South Carolina coast. Lincoln reverses the order and fires Hunter.

September 27, 1862: The first officially recognized black regiment is formed, the 1st Regiment Louisiana Native Guards, composed of free blacks from New Orleans.

January 25, 1863: The first black regiment from the North is formed by the governor of Massachusetts. Abolitionist and wealthy Bostonian Colonel Robert Gould Shaw is assigned command of the 54th Massachusetts Volunteers.

May 27, 1863: The first time African-American troops are used in combat, during the siege of Port Hudson, the Corps D'Afrique, raised and supplied on orders from General Banks.

June 7, 1863: The first important engagement in which black troops took part. At Milliken's Bend, Louisiana, 1,500 Texans attack a smaller force of black and white Union troops. Union commanders are duly impressed by the show of bravery.

July 16, 1863: The six hundred men of all-black 54th Massachusetts fend off a Southern charge on James Island in South Carolina.

July 18, 1863: The 54th Massachusetts assaults a Confederate position at Fort Wagner, South Carolina, part of the attempt to take Charleston. Frederick Douglass's two sons are among those who charged the battery and survived; 272 men did not return.

Governments During the Civil War (1861 to 1865): The United States of America

Administration and Cabinet

Office	Name	Term
President	Abraham Lincoln	1861–1865
	Andrew Johnson	1865–1869
Vice President	Hannibal Hamlin	1861–1865
	Andrew Johnson	1865
Secretary of State	William H. Seward	1861–1869
Secretary of the Treasury	Salmon P. Chase	1861–1864
	William P. Fessenden	1864–1865
	Hugh McCulloch	1865–1869
Secretary of War	Simon Cameron	1861–1862
	Edwin M. Stanton	1862–1868
Secretary of the Interior	Caleb Blood Smith	1861–1863
	John Palmer Usher	1863–1865
	James Harlan	1865–1866
Secretary of the Navy	Gideon Welles	1861–1869
Postmaster General	Montgomery Blair	1861–1864
	William Dennison	1864–1866
Attorney General	Edward Bates	1861–1864
	James Speed	1864–1866

- Simon Cameron was forced to resign as secretary of the war amid allegations of corruption and financial mismanagement.

- In ill health and bored with his position, Caleb Smith resigned as secretary of the interior in December 1862. He died eleven months later.

- President Lincoln asked Montgomery Blair to resign from the postmaster general position for political considerations.

- Salmon P. Chase was appointed Supreme Court chief justice after Roger Taney died in October 1864.

- Edward Bates, who wanted to be named chief justice of the Supreme Court for status reasons, resigned when he was overlooked for the position.

- William P. Fessenden replaced Chase as secretary of the treasury in 1864. The following year, he resigned to return to his Senate seat.

- John Usher, who had served as the assistant secretary of the interior under Caleb Smith, was the first cabinet member Andrew Johnson replaced upon taking office.

- Andrew Johnson did not have a vice president.

Governments During the Civil War (1861 to 1865): Confederate States of America

Administration and Cabinet

Office	Name	Term
President	Jefferson Davis	1861–1865
Vice President	Alexander H. Stephens	1861–1865
Secretary of State	Robert A. Toombs	1861
	Robert M. T. Hunter	1861–1862
	Judah P. Benjamin	1862–1865
Secretary of the Treasury	Christopher G. Memminger	1861–1864
	George A. Trenholm	1864–1865
	John H. Reagan	1865
Secretary of War	Leroy P. Walker	1861
	Judah P. Benjamin	1861–1862
	George W. Randolph	1862
	James A. Seddon	1862–1865
	John C. Breckinridge	1865
Secretary of the Navy	Stephen R. Mallory	1861–1865
Postmaster General	John H. Reagan	1861–1865
Attorney General	Judah P. Benjamin	1861
	Thomas Bragg	1861–1862
	Thomas H. Watts	1862–1863
	George Davis	1864–1865

- Frustrated and bored as secretary of state, Robert A. Toombs resigned within months to command a Georgia regiment in Virginia.
- Robert Mercer Taliaferro Hunter resigned to serve in the Confederate Senate from Virginia through the rest of the war.

- Because of Judah P. Benjamin's brilliance as attorney general, Jefferson Davis appointed him secretary of war when Leroy Walker left. Without any military experience, Benjamin acted as Davis's mouthpiece and was roundly criticized for all military blunders. When Benjamin resigned, Davis rewarded his loyal friend by appointing him secretary of state.

- Amid accusations of responsibility for the government credit's collapse, Christopher G. Memminger resigned.

- In the last days of the Confederacy, George Trenholm resigned due to illness (though some say he made off with all the Treasury's gold).

- Leroy Pope Walker left to serve as a brigadier general in the Army.

- A Confederate Army General, George Randolph served less than eight months as secretary of war.

- James A. Seddon retired, and Thomas Bragg returned to practicing law.

- Thomas Hill Watts was elected governor of Alabama in 1863.

THE REST OF THE STORY:
JUDAH P. BENJAMIN (1811-1884)

By now, you've gathered that Judah Benjamin was a pretty sharp guy. He served as U.S. Senator and held three Confederate cabinet positions: Attorney General, Secretary of War, and Secretary of State.

We're sure you're curious about the man who Varina Howell Davis described in her memoirs as Jefferson Davis's "right hand."

Early Background: Benjamin was born in the British West Indies to Jewish parents. We don't usually bring up religion, and Benjamin didn't either. However, his critics were quick to reference his religious affiliation. It is important to note that in 1852 Benjamin was the first acknowledged Jew elected to the U.S. Senate.

Yale Law School: Benjamin attended Yale Law School from age fourteen to seventeen. According to some sources, he was expelled for stealing. Others say that was an after-the-fact accusation made shortly before Southern secession to dirty Benjamin's name, and that Benjamin left because his father could not afford tuition. We know for sure that Benjamin left Yale before graduating.

The Married Life: Benjamin fell in love with his tutoring pupil Natalie St. Martin, from an old New Orleans Creole family. They married in 1833, but their happiness did not last.

Natalie was known for extravagant spending and promiscuity, not intelligence. She was wholly disinterested in Benjamin's politics. In 1845, Natalie took their young daughter Ninnette and moved to Paris, supposedly for the child's education. There have been suggestions that she left amid scandalous rumors.

Benjamin remained devoted to his family, visiting them in France each summer. He never divorced Natalie, but he didn't spend much time with her again, either.

Public Distinction: While a U.S. senator, Benjamin built a reputation as an eloquent speaker. Some historians list him alongside Daniel Webster and John C. Calhoun as one of the great Senate orators.

Bonding in Washington: During this time, Benjamin met Jefferson Davis in Washington. Davis insulted Benjamin on the Senate floor, and Benjamin challenged him to a duel. Davis apologized publicly, and they developed a mutual respect and friendship.

A Lincoln Assassination Conspiracy Theory? No Way! Yes, Benjamin cooked up a plan using a Confederate spy ring in Canada to attack Northern states on the Canadian border. Yes, some raids occurred, although unsuccessful. Yes, John Wilkes Booth was connected to those Confederate agents. But no, Benjamin and Davis were not responsible for Lincoln's assassination.

Get Out of Town! When the Confederate government fell, Benjamin disguised himself as a French journalist named Monsieur Bonfals (French for "Mr. Good Disguise") and fled to England. There, Benjamin rebuilt his law career.

Legacies of a Lifetime: In 1868, Benjamin wrote a classic British commercial law text, *Treatise on the Law of Sale of Personal Property*, still known today by law students as "Benjamin on Sales."

Benjamin died in 1884 and was buried in Paris. He never wrote a memoir, never returned to the United States, hardly mentioned his role in the Confederacy, and burned his papers shortly before his death. In 1938, the Paris Daughters of the Confederacy donated a memorial headstone for his simple grave.

THE VICE PRESIDENTS: HANNIBAL HAMLIN (1809-1891)

Maine native Hannibal Hamlin served as Lincoln's vice president during his first term. We don't hear much about Hamlin's tenure, and he himself realized that the office of vice president didn't offer much power or respect. In fact, while he was second in line behind Lincoln, Hamlin told others he was the most unimportant man in Washington, calling his job "a fifth wheel on a coach" and the vice president "a contingent somebody."

Read the Hannibal Hamlin facts listed below. Give yourself one point for each item you already knew. Then tally your points.

1. Hamlin was named after Hannibal of Carthage, who crossed the Alps on elephants.
2. Hamlin was physically fit, athletic, and had a dark complexion.
3. In Maine, Hamlin served in the state legislature and as a state representative to the U.S. Senate.
4. Hamlin was a devout abolitionist and a temperance supporter.
5. Hamlin's contemporaries remarked on the luck he enjoyed in his lifetime. For instance, in 1844, he was one U.S. Senator invited to attend the U.S. Navy frigate Princeton's new gun demonstration. However, he missed the sailing. One of the guns exploded, killing several statesmen on board.
6. Hamlin was disgusted by the many senators who attended session while intoxicated. He told friends that at least one-third of the congressmen left the daily sessions drunk, and as many as two-thirds left a long executive meeting inebriated.
7. Hamlin enjoyed playing cards, dancing, and attending the theater.
8. Hamlin's wife, Sarah Jane, died from tuberculosis in 1856. Less than six months later, he married Sarah Jane's half-sister, plain but sweet Ellen, who was the same age as one of his sons.
9. Hamlin switched from the Democratic Party to the Republican Party in 1856 over the issue of slavery.

10. Hamlin was elected governor of Maine and inaugurated on January 8, 1857. He resigned seven weeks later to begin a third term as senator.
11. The nomination for vice president was a shock. When he was notified while playing cards, Hamlin expressed dismay that the delivery of the news upset a particularly good hand he held.
12. During the campaign, opponents played dirty politics, suggesting that Hamlin was a mulatto trying to pass as white.
13. One campaign sign combined the ticket into a single name: "Abra/Hamlin/coln."
14. Hamlin did not meet Lincoln until after the elections. Why? After Lincoln got the surprise Republican nomination for president, he was advised not to rock the boat: no speeches or interviews, or even traveling from Illinois. So, Lincoln stayed put and did not meet Hamlin until after they had both won.
15. Hamlin was disappointed that Lincoln didn't quickly move for emancipation and enlisting black soldiers. Two of Hamlin's sons later commanded Negro units.
16. Lincoln showed Hamlin an early draft of the Emancipation Proclamation. Hamlin suggested some wording changes that Lincoln incorporated.
17. While still vice president, Hamlin enlisted in the Maine Coast Guard.
18. After the Union's loss at Fredericksburg, rumors circulated that Lincoln would resign to Hamlin.
19. In the 1864 election, Lincoln chose Democrat Andrew Johnson for his running mate.
20. Hamlin returned to the U.S. Senate (1869–1881) and was appointed U.S. minister to Spain (1881–1882).
21. Hamlin retired to Bangor, Maine. At age eighty-one, Hamlin collapsed and died while playing cards.

How'd You Do?

15-21 Points = A Real Hamlin Historian
8-14 Points = You Probably Know More About the Pied Piper
0-7 Points = That's About What We Scored, Too

THE VICE PRESIDENTS: ANDREW JOHNSON (1808-1875)

Andrew Johnson wasn't vice president long enough for us to say much about any policy he affected during that time. But we can talk about his life before the campaign, the election, the inauguration, and of course, his presidency.

Life Before the Campaign: Andrew Johnson was a poor Tennessee native who began his career as an illiterate tailor's apprentice. In 1827, at the tender age of eighteen, Johnson married sixteen-year-old Eliza McCardle. This, as it turns out, makes him the president who married at the earliest age. Eliza taught him how to read and write.

By marriage, Johnson bettered his life station, began a lifetime political career, and even purchased a few slaves, but he never shook his hatred for the planter aristocracy. By 1857, he had been elected one of Tennessee's U.S. senators.

When Tennessee seceded from the Union, naturally, all of the state's congressmen resigned from the federal government—except Johnson. Known for being stubborn, he simply refused to leave the Senate floor.

In 1861, Johnson was named a member of the Joint Committee on the Conduct of War. Then in 1862, he was appointed military governor of Tennessee after the Union occupied most of the state. He ruled the territory with an iron fist. One of his more successful tactics in subduing secessionists was to take civilians hostage and demand local compliance to his rules as their ransom. He even took seventy secessionists prisoner in retaliation for Confederates imprisoning seventy East Tennessee Unionists in Mobile.

The Election: When the Southern senators had left for home after secession, Johnson had remained on the Senate floor. He had been the only delegate still standing from the South, and he wasn't hard to miss. It didn't take long for Lincoln to hear about Johnson and his persistence. When it came time to pick a running mate for his second bid at presidency, Lincoln chose Johnson, hoping that the Tennessee Democrat would widen the ticket's appeal in border states.

The Inauguration: All accounts agree that, on inauguration day, Andrew Johnson's speech on the Senate floor was a mess. With slurred speech, Johnson gave "a rambling, incoherent" address which shocked and confused many in attendance. It was not a good first impression.

One story offers that he was drunk during the inauguration. Some say he was nervous, and had one sip of whiskey to calm his nerves, then one more, then one more. Here's another story: He was recovering from typhoid and a little weak on his feet. Perhaps it was a combination of both. By the way, Johnson was also a target in the Lincoln assassination plot. While John Wilkes Booth took out the president, George Atzerodt was assigned to Johnson. But Atzerodt chickened out.

Johnson's Presidency

- Johnson offered a $100,000 reward for Jefferson Davis's capture. The amount was divided among Union Brigadier General James Wilson's men.
- Johnson offered $25,000 for Jacob Thompson's capture. Johnson believed Thompson was in on the Lincoln murder plot. A former U.S. secretary of the interior, Thompson sided with the Confederacy, serving as a Confederate agent in Canada toward the end of the war.
- Everyone knew Johnson hated the Confederacy, so all were surprised at his leniency during Reconstruction (because of it, the Republican Congress vetoed most of his bills).
- In May 1865, Johnson pardoned all former Confederates who took an oath of loyalty to the Union and accepted emancipation.
- To defy the Republicans, one of Johnson's last acts as president was to pardon all unpardoned former Confederates on Christmas Day 1868.

THE VICE PRESIDENTS: ALEXANDER HAMILTON STEPHENS (1812-1883)

Of course, here, we're talking about the vice president of the Confederate States of America.

Prevalent Physical Descriptions
- "Wispy" (he only weighed about ninety pounds)
- "Tubercular"
- "A little, slim, pale-faced consumptive man" (this one was from Abraham Lincoln)

Aliases
- Nicknamed "Little Ellick"
- Known as "The Great Commoner" by his fellow congressmen

Background
- Born in Georgia to poor parents
- Orphaned at age twelve and raised by an uncle
- Graduated first in his class at the University of Georgia
- Became a planter and slave owner, with a reputation as a "humanitarian master" because he opposed whipping slaves and separating their families

Early Politics
- 1836–1843: Georgia legislature
- 1843: U.S. House of Representatives
- Friends with Abraham Lincoln in Congress, until they disagreed on the position of slavery

Stephens in the Confederate Government

- At first, Stephens was not in favor of secession. He envisioned that secession, and the inevitable war, would ultimately mean the end of slavery.
- Stephens actually wanted to be president of the Confederacy, but lost out to Jefferson Davis. So he was named vice president instead.
- Stephens was formally elected vice president in November 1861, having run unopposed.
- Stephens was inaugurated February 1862.
- Stephens helped draft the Confederate Constitution.

Criticizing Jefferson Davis

Stephens was certainly not a fan of the Confederate president. It's general knowledge that his opinion of Davis included such negative descriptions as "weak and vacillating," "timid," "petulant," "peevish," and "obstinate." Stephens opposed Davis's policies of:

- Conscription and the draft (he thought they were unconstitutional)
- Suspension of writ of habeas corpus
- Using former slaves as soldiers
- Attempting to create a controlling centralized government (he supported states' rights)

In fact, Stephens disagreed so much with everything Davis did that he left the capital in Richmond in 1862 and hardly ever returned.

The Hampton Roads Conference

- Scene: A steamboat at the mouth of the James River near Hampton Roads, Virginia.
- Date: February 3, 1865
- Participants from the Union: President Abraham Lincoln, Secretary of State William Seward
- Participants from the Confederacy: Vice President Stephens, ex-Supreme Court Justice John Campbell, former Secretary of State Robert Hunter

- Purpose: Talk about ending the war
- Stephens's Request: A cease-fire, followed by further talks between the two governments.
- Lincoln's Response: Lincoln said that calling a cease-fire would be the same as recognizing the Confederacy as a government, so he wouldn't do that.
- Lincoln's Counter-Request: Confederate soldiers should lay down their arms and acknowledge the Union's supremacy to end the war.
- Seward's Contribution: Southern states would get back all their constitutional rights.
- Lincoln's Further Contribution: Stressed that the Emancipation Proclamation was simply a war measure that could be reversed.
- The Result: They reached an impasse. Stephens wanted to stop fighting to discuss rejoining the Union. Lincoln insisted that the South had to rejoin the Union to discuss how they would stop fighting.

After the War
- May–October 1865: Arrested and imprisoned at Fort Warren in Boston.
- December 1865: Elected to his old Senate seat from Georgia, but he was denied his seat, along with all the other Confederate states.
- 1868–1870: Wrote the highly successful *A Constitutional View of the War Between the States*.
- 1873–1882: Returned to the U.S. House of Representatives— and was seated this time.
- 1882: Elected governor of Georgia.
- 1883: Died.

FAST FACTS:
GENERAL RICHARD TAYLOR

- He was President Zachary Taylor's son.
- He was the brother-in-law of Jefferson Davis, by Davis's first—doomed—marriage.
- Taylor was cited for his leadership capabilities both on the battlefield and in producing well trained, highly disciplined troops.
- Taylor's Louisiana Brigade was known for their perfect uniforms throughout the war. His more than three thousand men always showed up for battle looking better than any other brigade on either side.
- Once, Stonewall Jackson caught Taylor cursing during the heat of battle. The highly-religious Jackson was horrified, saying, "I am afraid you are a wicked fellow."
- Throughout his life, Taylor suffered debilitating attacks of rheumatoid arthritis, which left him crippled for days. Richard Taylor became violently ill on June 26, 1862, before the battle of Cold Harbor, and he gave command to a subordinate.

CIVIL WAR BATTLE TIMELINE: 1862

January 19: Battle of Mill Springs, Kentucky
February 6: Battle of Fort Henry, Tennessee (Forts Henry &
    Donelson Campaign)
February 8: Battle of Roanoke Island, North Carolina
February 13–16: Battle of Fort Donelson, Tennessee (Forts Henry &
    Donelson Campaign)
February 21: Engagement at Valverde, New Mexico Territory
March 6–8: Battle of Pea Ridge, Arkansas
March 9: U.S.S. *Monitor* vs. C.S.S. *Virginia* in Hampton Roads, Virginia
March 23: Battle of Kernstown (Stonewall's Shenandoah Valley
    Campaign)
May 8: Battle of McDowell (Shenandoah Valley Campaign)
May 23: Battle of Front Royal (Shenandoah Valley Campaign)
May 25: First Battle of Winchester (Shenandoah Valley Campaign)
March 26–28: Battle of Glorieta Pass, New Mexico Territory
June 8: Battle of Cross Keys (Shenandoah Valley Campaign)
June 9: Battle of Port Republic (Shenandoah Valley Campaign)
April 5–May 4: McClellan advances up the Virginia peninsula toward
    Richmond/ Siege of Yorkstown
April 6–7: Battle of Shiloh, Tennessee
April 7: Capture of Island No. 10, Tennessee
April 10–11: Bombardment and capture of Fort Pulaski, Georgia
April 18–24: Battle of Forts Jackson and St. Philip, Louisiana
    (Farragut's Mississippi River Operations)
April 25–May 1: Battle of New Orleans
April 29–May 30: Siege of Corinth, Mississippi
May 12–13: Battle of Natchez
May 15: Battle of Drewry's Bluff, Virginia
May 31–June 1: Battle of Seven Pines (Fair Oaks), Virginia
June 1: Robert E. Lee named commander of Army of Northern
    Virginia
June 6: Battle of Memphis, Tennessee

June 25: Battle of Oak Grove (Seven Days' Battles in Richmond, Virginia)

June 25–26: Battle of Mechanicsburg (Seven Days' Battles)

June 27: Battle of Gaines' Mill (Seven Days' Battles)

June 29: Battle of Savage's Station (Seven Days' Battles)

June 30: Battle of Glendale (Fraser's Farm) (Seven Days' Battles)

July 1: Battle of Malvern Hill (Seven Days' Battles)

August 5: Battle of Baton Rouge, Louisiana (Mississippi River Operations)

August 9: Battle of Cedar Mountain, Virginia

August 28–30: Second Battle of Manassas (Bull Run), Virginia

August 29–30: Battle of Richmond, Kentucky

September 1: Battle of Chantilly (Ox Hill), Virginia

September 12–15: Siege and capture of Harpers Ferry, West Virginia

September 14–17: Battles of South Mountain and Antietam, Maryland

September 14–17: Siege of Munfordville, Kentucky

September 19: Battle of Iuka, Mississippi

October 3–4: Battle of Corinth, Mississippi

October 8: Battle of Perryville, Kentucky

October 16–December 20: Grant's First Vicksburg Campaign, Mississippi

November 7: Burnside replaces McClellan

December 7: Battle of Prairie Grove, Arkansas

December 11–13: Battle of Fredericksburg, Virginia

December 11–January 1: Forrest's West Tennessee Raid

December 17–28: Van Dorn's Holly Springs Raid

December 27–29: Battle of Chickasaw Bayou, Mississippi

December 31– January 2: Battle of Murfreesboro (Stones River), Tennessee

FORT DONELSON

Ulysses S. Grant began building his reputation as a military leader during the early part of 1862, a time when Union forces delivered much-needed good news to the North with key victories in the western theater. The hot streak began with victories at Fort Henry and Fort Donelson. The former, located on the Tennessee River, and the latter, on the Cumberland River, represented key access points for moving goods and equipment through the South, though the Mississippi River remained the Holy Grail of Union designs for choking off Southern access and the region's economy.

Grant, leading a force of fifteen thousand men and supported by Commodore Andrew Foote's Union armada, took Fort Henry with ease. Twelve miles east along the Cumberland, Fort Donelson presented a much harder challenge. Donelson had been reinforced by troops from Fort Henry, and with a decided geographic advantage atop a bluff, made for a tougher task.

An initial maritime assault left Foote injured, as well as two of the six gunboats committed to the river's bottom. Grant began a siege as Confederate forces attempted an escape east to Nashville. Cavalry led by Nathan Bedford Forrest pushed the Union army, but hesitancy by other Confederate commanders left the opportunity wasted. Grant and his men rallied as several rebel leaders scurried away.

Forrest, a man who went on to frustrate Union leaders later in the war, dismissed talks of a Confederate surrender and opted to storm away with seven hundred men. Their escape succeeded.

That left Simon Bolivar Buckner of Kentucky to negotiate with Grant, a man Buckner considered a friend. No matter. Grant declined to negotiate, demanding "unconditional and immediate surrender."

Northern papers and citizens rejoiced over Grant's victory—and his steadfast resolve, coining a new nickname in the process: "Unconditional Surrender Grant."

CIVIL WAR JOURNALISM

Some estimate that almost five hundred members of the media (journalists, artists, and photographers) covered the war. With almost unlimited access to follow armies, attend battles, and interview commanders, the press provided a 360-degree view of the conflict. Their coverage was so complete that commanders often learned more from enemy newspapers than from their own spy reports.

Journalists found that watching and observing the war was as dangerous as fighting in it. Many members of the press were killed while covering the action, and those who survived sometimes were captured as prisoners of war.

Both in the North and South, newspapers were quick to criticize public officials, government policies, and military leaders. The worst criticism came after defeat in battle.

Newspaper and Magazine Illustrations

Periodicals such as *Leslie's Weekly*, *Harper's Weekly*, *New York Illustrated News*, and *London Illustrated News* employed illustrators to provide the timely depictions printed in their pages. "Special artists" quickly jotted down a pen-and-ink sketch of a battle's scene, hurried back to the office, and handed it over to be engraved on plates for printing. These brave reporters included Theodore R. Davis, Edwin Forbes, Thomas Nast, Winslow Homer, Henry Walke, and William and Alfred Waud.

Editorial Cartoonist and Caricaturist Thomas Nast

Bavarian emigrant Thomas Nast sketched battlefield and camp scenes for *New York Illustrated News* and *Harper's Weekly*. He also created the Democratic donkey, the Republican elephant, and the classic rounded-belly version of Santa Claus from Clement Moore's "A Visit from St. Nicholas."

SAY CHEESE! CIVIL WAR PHOTOGRAPHY

Photography during the Civil War obviously included inexpensive portraits for the soldiers to send home, called *carte de visite* because they were the size of calling cards. Photography also served another purpose: documenting the war.

Photographers followed the armies almost everywhere. For the first time, photographs using the new technology captured the reality of warfare in all its grim and gruesome truth. Because the art was barely twenty years old at the war's onset, any previous conflicts had been depicted in sketches and drawings.

Civilians back home wanted to know what was happening, and they looked forward to any information they could get about their sons, husbands, fathers, and sweethearts. Photographs provided a new window into that world.

Other photographers served an official army function, providing land and territory photographs for the Topographical Engineers Corps to map.

Taking photos back then sure wasn't as easy as choosing the "Auto." There was no such thing as an "action" shot. The lenses had one speed, too slow to freeze action. Anything moving in the picture would reproduce as a blur.

Photographers did their best to get a shot that showed the authenticity of battle, even if it meant "faking" the picture. They manipulated scenes, dragging and otherwise rearranging dead soldiers for more dramatic effect. Sometimes, they staged reenactments after the fact, in which soldiers struck a tableau pose and held still long enough for the camera to capture the scene.

PHOTOGRAPHS BY BRADY

The best known Civil War photographer was Mathew Brady of New York. He has been called the father of contemporary photojournalism. Brady and his staff gave historians more than 3,500 photographs of everything from camp life and military portraits to battle scenes and the horror of war. His photographs gave warfare a human face.

Brady began his career as a painter and a jewelry box craftsman, but soon turned to the new daguerreotype technology. In 1844, he opened a studio specializing in fashionable portraits, especially of celebrities. He was successful enough to open another studio in Washington in 1856.

At the beginning of the war, Brady felt a pull to document the conflict. His photography wagon was there from the First Battle of Bull Run, and it didn't take soldiers long to expect to see such a wagon at each battle site.

Brady's Secret: He did not take most of the photographs himself. By that time, his eyesight was almost completely gone, probably damaged by photofinishing chemicals. He hired a corps of assistants to work for his studio. While more wartime images are credited to Brady than to any other photographer, most of the "Photographs by Brady" were actually Photographs by the Brady Studio.

Many of Brady's photographers, including Alexander Gardner, James E. Gibson, and Timothy O'Sullivan, eventually struck out on their own and made names for themselves.

THE PROCESS FROM WET PLATE TO PHOTOGRAPH

The new wet-plate photographic process was mobile enough to take to the battlefields. Photographers traveled and worked out of specially-equipped wagons.

1. The photographer set up his big camera next to the wagon or as close as possible to the wagon.
2. Inside the wagon, the photographer's assistant carefully removed an 8" x 10" glass plate from its dust-proof box.
3. The assistant sensitized the plate in total darkness.
4. The plate was rushed to the camera before it could be exposed.
5. The photographer tripped the shutter, exposing the plate.
6. The assistant quickly ran the plate back to the wagon for developing.

Illustrator and Painter Winslow Homer

For about eight months during the Civil War, illustrator Winslow Homer worked as an artist for *Harper's Weekly*, providing interpretations of camp life. His *Sharpshooter on Picket Duty* was one of the most famous Civil War illustrations. After the war, he began painting landscapes and seascape, such as the popular *Breezing Up*.

THE BLUE AND THE GRAY

In 1867, New York lawyer and Yale graduate Francis Miles Finch read a *New York Times* article about Confederate women decorating the graves of fallen soldiers, both Northern and Southern. A former Union soldier himself, Finch was touched by their compassion for the dead of both sides and proceeded to write a poem to commemorate the country's healing process.

"The Blue and the Gray" soon became a standard in grammar school reading assignments throughout the country.

"The Blue and the Gray"

By the flow of the inland river,
Whence the fleets of iron have fled,
Where the blades of the grave-grass quiver,
Asleep are the ranks of the dead:
Under the sod and the dew,
Waiting the judgment-day;
Under the one, the Blue,
Under the other, the Gray.

These in the robings of glory,
Those in the gloom of defeat,
All with the battle-blood gory,
In the dusk of eternity meet:
Under the sod and the dew,
Waiting the judgement-day
Under the laurel, the Blue,
Under the willow, the Gray.

From the silence of sorrowful hours
The desolate mourners go,
Lovingly laden with flowers

Alike for the friend and the foe;
Under the sod and the dew,
Waiting the judgement-day;
Under the roses, the Blue,
Under the lilies, the Gray.

So with an equal splendor,
The morning sun-rays fall,
With a touch impartially tender,
On the blossoms blooming for all:
Under the sod and the dew,
Waiting the judgment-day;
Broidered with gold, the Blue,
Mellowed with gold, the Gray.

So, when the summer calleth,
On forest and field of grain,
With an equal murmur falleth
The cooling drip of the rain:
Under the sod and the dew,
Waiting the judgment-day,
Wet with the rain, the Blue
Wet with the rain, the Gray.

Sadly, but not with upbraiding,
The generous deed was done,
In the storm of the years that are fading
No braver battle was won:
Under the sod and the dew,
Waiting the judgment-day;
Under the blossoms, the Blue,
Under the garlands, the Gray.

No more shall the war cry sever,
Or the winding rivers be red;
They banish our anger forever
When they laurel the graves of our dead!

Under the sod and the dew,
Waiting the judgment-day,
Love and tears for the Blue,
Tears and love for the Gray.

Francis Miles Finch claimed to only dabble in poetry on the side from his profession as lawyer. However, his elegant poems were popular at the time, including a verse eulogy of Nathan Hale that said, "How proud and calm / A patriot could die, / With his last words, his dying words, / A soldier's battle-cry."

Smoking Songs

Near the end of the nineteenth century, at a time when pipes and cigars prompted thoughts of sophistication and power, Finch also wrote the college smoking song, "Smoking Away."

A few stanzas of his ode to pipe and cigar:

Floating away like the fountains' spray,
Or the snow-white plume of a maiden,
The smoke-wreaths rise to the starlit skies
With blissful fragrance laden. [. . .]
The dark-eyed train of the maids of Spain
'Neath their arbor shades trip lightly,
And a gleaming cigar, like a new-born star
In the clasp of their lips burns brightly.
It warms the soul like the blushing bowl,
With its rose-red burden streaming,
And drowns it in bliss, like the first warm kiss
From the lips with love-buds teeming.

Showdown of the Presidential Wives Mary Todd Lincoln vs. Varina Howell Davis

Mary Todd Lincoln (1818–1882)

Husband: Abraham Lincoln

Nation: United States of America

Lifestyle: Wealthy parents (banker father); well-educated; large social circle in Illinois

Southern Connection: Born in Kentucky

Northern Connection: Moved to Springfield, Illinois, in 1839 to live with her sister (the governor's daughter-in-law)

Love and Courtship: First wedding called off at the last minute due to groom's cold feet; Wedding successfully completed in 1842

Age at Marriage: Abraham – thirty-three; Mary – twenty-three

Husband's Temperament: Abraham was often moody, depressed, and absentminded

Children: Four sons – Robert Todd, born 1843; Edward Baker, born 1846; William Wallace, born 1850; Thomas "Tad," born 1853

First Lady: Mary tried to fit in with the Washington social scene, but her superior manner did not earn any votes in the popularity polls.

Rumors of Sympathy: Mary was a dedicated Unionist. Four of her brothers and three brothers-in-law served in the Confederate Army, making many suspect her of Southern sympathies.

Criticisms: Mary was criticized for trying to maintain a degree of social life during the war, although she was trying to lift everyone's spirits.

Tragedy: Three sons died before adulthood—Edward at age four, William at age eleven of fever, Tad at age eighteen of tuberculosis. Her husband was assassinated in 1865.

Sadness: She suffered a nervous breakdown after William's death. She was devastated by her husband's assassination and was too overcome with grief to attend the funeral.

Later Years: Mary was severely depressed after Tad's death. Her son Robert Todd committed her to a mental institution for several months.

Final Days: Mary quickly blew her sizable inheritance after Lincoln's death. Congress then approved a pension to support her for her remaining days.

Mary Todd Lincoln Oddities: Mary was known for her bad temper and wide jealous streak. In fact, Julia Dent Grant (wife of Ulysses S.) refused to be in the same room with Mary.

After William's death, Mary began experimenting with the supernatural. She held séances to contact his spirit and even claimed to have seen his and Edward's ghosts in the White House.

Varina Howell Davis (1826–1906)
Husband: Jefferson Davis
Nation: Confederate States of America
Lifestyle: Wealthy parents (plantation-owner father); privileged life; smart and energetic
Southern Connection: Born in Mississippi
Northern Connection: Grandfather was an eight-term governor of New Jersey; spent two years at Philadelphia finishing school
Love and Courtship: Met widower Jefferson Davis at seventeen years old; married in 1845
Age at Marriage: Jefferson: thirty-seven; Varina: nineteen
Husband's Temperament: Jefferson was often cranky and moody
Children: Six children—Samuel Emory, born 1852; Margaret Howell, born 1855; Jefferson, Jr., born 1857; Joseph Evan, born 1859; William Howell, born 1861; Varina Anne, born 1864
First Lady: After enjoying the Washington social scene as a congressman's wife, Varina adjusted to life as first lady of the Confederacy in Richmond.
Rumors of Sympathy: Varina supported her husband's new country. But, with such strong Northern connections, some accused her of Northern sympathies.

Criticisms: Varina was criticized for trying to maintain a degree of social life during the war. She was criticized for not doing enough to lift everyone's spirits.

Tragedy: Three sons died before adulthood: Sam at age two, Joe at age five after a fall from the president's mansion balcony, and William at age eleven. Her husband was imprisoned by federal troops in 1865.

Sadness: Spent two years petitioning for Jefferson's prison release, even meeting with President Andrew Johnson to discuss the situation.

Later Years: Varina and Jefferson lived in Mississippi until he died in 1889, when she moved in with her daughter Margaret in New York City.

Final Days: Varina published her memoirs in 1890 and contributed articles to magazines and newspapers.

Colonel Isaac G. Seymour

General Taylor handed over the brigade's command to Colonel Seymour before the Battle of Cold Harbor. For Seymour, the former mayor of Macon, Georgia, this was a dream come true. Unfortunately, it was a short dream. Seymour was shot and killed during his first day leading a brigade.

The Last Surrender

By 1865, Major General Taylor commanded the Department of East Louisiana, Mississippi, and Alabama. On May 4, he met with U.S. Volunteer Major General Edward R. S. Canby at Citronelle, Alabama, to discuss surrender.

According to Canby, Taylor surrendered on the fourth. But, Taylor says the surrender was on the eighth, the day his men accepted their terms. It makes a difference, because Taylor called it "the surrender of the last major Confederate force east of the Mississippi River."

BEAUVOIR
(JEFFERSON DAVIS'S HOME)

Beauvoir in Biloxi, Mississippi, was built by plantation owner James Brown in 1852 as a summer home and called Orange Grove because of the Satsuma oranges growing there. After Brown's death, Sarah Dorsey bought and named the home Beauvoir, French for "beautiful view," for the lovely front porch scenery.

When Dorsey learned that her family friend Jefferson Davis was looking for a retirement home to write his books and papers, she offered to let him stay on the property in a small cottage. On her death, Dorsey willed the property to Davis (in the end, he used the purchase price to pay off her estate's debts).

After Davis died in 1889 and his daughter Winnie died in 1898, his widow Varina sold the estate to the Mississippi division of the Sons of Confederate Veterans. She asked that they use it in two ways:

- A gratis home for Confederate veterans and widows
- A memorial to Jefferson Davis and Confederate soldiers

From 1903 forward, Beauvoir has been the memorial that Varina Davis requested. It also served as a Confederate Veterans home from 1903 until 1957, when the last three widows were moved to a private nursing home.

Beauvoir was seriously damaged by Hurricane Katrina in 2005. Almost half of the artifacts and all of the outbuildings were completely lost. After a lengthy renovation, the house itself has reopened to the public for tours.

The storm dumped four alligators into Oyster Bayou on the grounds. The two largest were named "General Beauregard" and "Beauregard Junior." The reptiles were relocated to ensure the safety of visitors to the national historic site.

CHOOSING THE PRESIDENT OF THE CONFEDERACY

At the Confederate Convention in Montgomery, Alabama, forty-three delegates represented six Southern states. (The delegates from Texas were on the way. They didn't arrive in time for the election. So much for "Don't Mess With Texas.")

Deliberating during the first week of February 1861, the delegates named Jefferson Davis the Confederacy's provisional president. The delegates also named themselves the Confederacy's provisional congress. Three other influential politicians, all Georgians, hoped to be considered for the position. They were given consolation titles:

1. Alexander Hamilton Stephens: Vice President
2. Howell Cobb: Provisional Speaker of the Confederate Congress
3. Robert Augustus Toombs: Confederate Secretary of State

While Stephens, Cobb, and Toombs all actively campaigned in Montgomery, Jefferson Davis stayed at home in Mississippi and let the other delegates do the work for him. He was inaugurated on February 9, 1861.

The Provisional Congress set about drafting a constitution, which was a lot like the U.S. Constitution. However, it limited the president to one six-year term, gave him a line-item veto, provided for state sovereignty and independence, and prohibited any laws denying the right to own slaves.

A general election was held in November 1861 for presidential and congressional appointments. Davis and Stephens both ran unopposed for their positions. Both were reelected and reinaugurated on February 22, 1862.

Alexander Stephens
Georgia House of Representatives 1836-1841
Georgia Senate 1842
U.S. Senate 1843-1859; 1873-1882
Confederate Vice President 1861-1865
Georgia Governor 1882-1883

Robert Toombs
Georgia General Assembly 1837-1843
U.S. House of Representatives 1844-1853
U.S. Senate 1853-1861
Confederate Secretary of State 1861
Confederate Army Brigadier General 1861-1863
Georgia Constitutional Convention 1877

Howell Cobb
U.S. House of Representatives 1843-1851
Georgia Governor 1851-1853
U.S. Senate 1855-1857
U.S. Secretary of the Treasury 1857-1860
Chairman of the Confederate Convention 1861
Provisional Speaker of the Confederate Congress 1861-1862
Confederate Army Brigadier General 1862-1865

Confederate Commanders: Patrick Ronayne Cleburne (1828–1864)

- A native of Ireland; relocated to Helena, Arkansas
- One of two foreign-born officers to become a Confederate Major General
- Known as a great combat officer, sometimes called the "Stonewall Jackson of the West"
- Often compared to General Nathan Bedford Forrest

Patrick Ronayne Cleburne

Military Career

Cleburne enlisted as private in Arkansas's Yell Rifles of Phillips. There, he was soon promoted to captain, then colonel of the 1st Arkansas. When General William J. Hardee took command in Arkansas, he promoted Cleburne to brigadier general.

Cleburne fought at Shiloh, was wounded in the mouth during the Kentucky campaign, and recuperated in time to fight in the Battle of Perryville. As the end of 1862 gave way to the New Year of 1863, Cleburne's service at the Battle of Murfreesboro earned him a promotion to major general. He even was specifically thanked by the Confederate Congress for saving trains for the Army of Tennessee.

In 1863, Cleburne saw combat in the Battle of Chickamauga, the Chattanooga Campaign, Missionary Ridge in Tennessee, and Ringgold Gap in Georgia. Throughout the Atlanta Campaign that raged through most of 1864, Cleburne showed his bravery and military strengths from the Battle of Resaca in May until the Battle of Jonesboro in September.

During Hood's Tennessee Campaign two months later, Cleburne's brigades backed up the Army of Tennessee in attacking Union fortifications at Franklin, Tennessee. Before the Battle of Franklin, on the night of November 29, 1864, Patrick Cleburne told his troops, "If we are going to die, let us die like men." During the suicidal strike, in what has been called "the bloodiest hours of the American Civil War," Cleburne was killed in action beside his men. He was buried near the battlefield.

Patrick Ronayne Cleburne Trivia

- Cleburne served as best man in William J. Hardee's second wedding to Alabama plantation owner Mary Foreman Lewis in January 1864.
- Cleburne's favorite horse, Dixie, was killed in the Battle of Perryville.

Controversy Over Freeing Slaves Who Fought for the Confederacy

Unlike many officers, Cleburne was one of the earliest advocates for using blacks as soldiers, not only as slave laborers building reinforcements. He recommended immediately training "the most courageous of our slaves" and offering freedom to those slaves who served the Confederacy in the war. Cleburne's idea was roundly criticized. Some called it "revolting," and others said it would demoralize the troops.

In fact, soldiers were about evenly divided on their thoughts for freeing slaves in exchange for their service in the army.

- Many said they were fighting to uphold slavery, and they would not agree to freeing slaves to aid in the fight.
- Others felt the cause was already lost, so they might as well free the slaves if it would mean reinforcing the troops to give them a chance to win the war and save face.
- Still others were simply tired and ready to pass on the burden of fighting—to slaves or anyone else who would take it on—and go home.

While a few small squads were formed, armed, and drilled, the war ended before any former slaves could actually join the Confederate army.

CONFEDERATE COMMANDERS: WILLIAM JOSEPH HARDEE (1815-1873)

Background: Georgia native, 1838 West Point graduate; veteran of the Mexican War
March 1861: Colonel in the Cavalry of the Confederacy
June 1861: Promoted to brigadier general; recruited soldiers from the Ozarks in Arkansas
October 1861: Promoted to major general; sent to Kentucky
February 1862: Helped capture Forts Henry and Donelson in Tennessee
April 1862: Wounded while fighting at the Battle of Shiloh
October 1862: Fought at the Battle of Perryville, Kentucky; promoted to lieutenant general; transferred to Mississippi under General Joseph Johnston
November 1863: Fought at the Battle of Chattanooga
July 1864: Hardee's infantry division, hoping to surprise Sherman, attacked Sherman's forces in Atlanta; the Confederates were outmanned and outgunned, losing more than 8,500 men.

Hardee's Tactics

When the U.S. infantry switched to new muskets with better accuracy and range in the 1850s, U.S. Secretary of War Jefferson Davis realized it was time to update the official tactics manuals. He employed Lieutenant Colonel William Hardee to incorporate skirmishing and fast marching into a new manual.

To account for the new rifles' long-range capabilities, Hardee taught increased tempos: quick time (110 steps per minute) and double-quick time (165 steps per minute). The book is divided into several parts, addressing arms and weapon carriage as well as individual and company movements.

In 1854, the new drill tactics were first tested at West Point before the book was published in 1855 and became the official manual of the U.S. Army. What this means is that any soldiers who came through West Point from about 1854 through the beginning of the Civil War had already become quite familiar with the tactics of the officer who would be leading troops for the Confederate side.

Training for War

When Confederates fired on Fort Sumter, they started a war no one was ready for. The Union army only had about sixteen thousand regular men. The Confederacy had zero.

Immediately, both sides called for soldiers from the various states' militia. President Lincoln asked the Northern states to provide seventy-five thousand of their "reserve" men.

While volunteers did have some experience in drill instruction, most of these men were amateurs with no combat training at all. Not only were they amateurs, they were youths: many were younger than the eighteen years they claimed when enlisting. They definitely had never worked together with other regiments.

Militia regiments before the war practiced from their drill books—almost all different. When they united as one army, many of these militia units had to forget what they had learned locally, and adapt to a new common drill.

The two most common drill books then:

- *Scott's Infantry Tactics*, known as the "heavy infantry manual," written in 1835.
- *Hardee's Rifle and Light Infantry Tactics*, published by the U.S. War Department in 1855, addressed the use of new muskets with greater accuracy and longer range.

Finally, in 1862, the Union army adopted *Casey's Infantry Tactics*, written by Brigadier General Silas Casey, for its updates in weaponry.

CONFEDERATE COMMANDERS: PIERRE GUSTAVE TOUTANT BEAUREGARD (1818-1893)

Background: Louisiana native, graduated second in his 1838 West Point class
Military Experience: Mexican War, chief engineer in New Orleans, superintendent of West Point
Rank: Brigadier general, promoted to full general, 1861

Comments on Beauregard's Civil War Achievements

Fort Sumter: Beauregard first offered to let Union Commander Anderson surrender. When Anderson elected to wait it out until his supplies were depleted, Beauregard then commanded the attack. Beauregard supposedly sent cigars and wine to the Union commanding officers while everyone waited on orders regarding how to proceed.

First Bull Run: The first significant meeting of the two armies. Beauregard was charged with holding the railroad junction at Manassas. Jefferson Davis criticized, saying he should have chased the Union soldiers all the way to Washington.

Shiloh: Confederate soldiers surprised woefully unprepared Union troops. But federal backups arrived the next day. Beauregard assumed command when General Albert Johnston was killed and blamed the loss on Johnston's strategy.

Corinth: With one-third of his troops on the sick list suffering from dysentery, Beauregard withdrew before Union troops arrived. Davis criticized Beauregard's loss of the city due to excessively elaborate military strategy.

Drewery's Bluff: Beauregard defeated Union General Butler and stopped the Union at Bermuda Hundred, Virginia. A Confederate victory was crucial in stopping the Union's advance on Richmond.

Petersburg: Beauregard led a successful defense in the opening assaults. Davis did not recognize the part Beauregard played at Petersburg and shipped him out west to an administrative position.

After the war, Beauregard served as a railroad president, then became superintendent of the Louisiana State Lottery, for which he was paid $30,000 per year. He turned down offers to command the Rumanian and Egyptian armies.

P. G. T. Beauregard Trivia

- Beauregard's lovely French name comes from his Louisiana Creole heritage. Born Pierre Gustave Toutant-Beauregard, at one point he went by G. T. Beauregard. By the time he gained fame as a war hero, he had reinstated the P to be known as P. G. T. Beauregard. But, his friends called him Peter.
- Beauregard was nicknamed "The Little Creole" and "Little Napoleon."
- As superintendent of the U.S. Military Academy at West Point, Beauregard resigned from the job after only four days to join the C.S.A. army.
- As commander of the attack on Fort Sumter, Beauregard was one of the first Confederate war heroes.
- It is said that Beauregard's troops were to first to use the famous "Rebel Yell" in battle after fighting Union soldiers for almost fourteen hours during the First Battle of Bull Run.
- Beauregard had four horses shot out from under him during the First Bull Run.
- Beauregard did not get along with President Jefferson Davis. So although he was a bold Confederate officer, he was not awarded the juicy command posts of some other, less heroic officers.

UNION COMMANDERS: WINFIELD SCOTT HANCOCK (1824-1886)

Background: Pennsylvania native; 1844 West Point graduate

Military Experience: Mexican War, Seminole War, Kansas border disturbances

Battles Participated In: Almost all major engagements in the eastern theatre—Gettysburg, Peninsula Campaign, Chancellorsville, Wilderness Campaign, Williamsburg, Frazier's Farm, Antietam, and Fredericksburg

Rank: Brigadier general, volunteers, 1861; brigadier general, regular army, 1864

In the Union Army: Hancock led the 2nd Army Corps to victory at Gettysburg, where he was wounded, and to devastating defeat during the Petersburg Campaign at Burgess Mill and Reams Station. In November 1864, Hancock resigned.

Battle of Spotsylvania Court House, May 1864: Grant wanted to get past Lee's fortifications to Richmond, vowing to bombard the Confederates until he could. Hancock led fifteen thousand men in an early morning ambush on the Confederate center, capturing the entire infantry, and splitting Lee's army in half. Hancock's corps pushed the Confederates back half a mile.

After the War: Promoted to major general in the regular army, Hancock fought in the Missouri Indian wars. As commander of the Fifth Military District during Reconstruction, Hancock disagreed with measures that he felt were offensive or unnecessary and refused to follow some orders. The 1880 Democratic presidential candidate, Hancock lost the election to James Garfield.

Winfield Scott Hancock Trivia

- Served under Winfield Scott in four major battles of the Mexican War.
- Known for showing up exactly where his troops were needed most.

- Joined the other commanders in a late lunch of stewed chicken during a break on the third day of Gettysburg.
- Conducted Ulysses S. Grant's funeral.
- A bit of a clean freak, Hancock took a dozen regulation shirts wherever he went. If a shirt was dirtied by gunpowder or blood, especially during a battle, he went straight to his tent and put on a clean shirt.

In 1863, black soldiers under Union Brigadier General Wild executed Georgia soldier Daniel Bright. In retaliation, Pickett hanged U.S. Private Samuel Jones, a black man. Then, Union troops seized Mrs. Phoebe Munden and Mrs. Elizabeth Weeks as hostages. North Carolina Governor Vance demanded the ladies' release. Union Major General Benjamin Butler allowed the women to be exchanged for their husbands.

Union Commanders: John Frederick Hartranft (1830-1889)

Background: Pennsylvania native; attended school in Virginia; graduate of Union College in New York

Experience Before the Civil War: civil engineer, lawyer, public servant

Civil War Participation: Battles of First and Second Bull Run, Fredericksburg, Vicksburg, Campbell's Station, Knoxville, Antietam, Spotsylvania, Fort Stedman (Petersburg); Sherman's Carolinas Campaign; Western Campaign; commanded the 3rd Division of the U.S. Army IX Corps

Rank: Colonel, 1861; brigadier general, brevet major general, 1865

Facing the Fight at Bull Run: In many units organized at the beginning of the Civil War, the soldiers volunteered originally for a ninety-day enlistment. Officers throughout both armies recognized that, if an engagement didn't get underway, their units would go home three months after signing up—without ever having seen battle.

This was the case with Hartranft's Fourth Pennsylvania regiment. The day before the First Bull Run was scheduled to finally heat up, Hartranft's comrades took a look at their calendars, realized their enlistments were up, turned around, marched to the rear, and went home.

Hartranft was embarrassed. He decided to stay and fight with the army. For his act of bravery, Hartranft earned the Congressional Medal of Honor—it was bestowed twenty-five years later, but he did get it.

Defending Knoxville: Charged with holding Knoxville, Hartranft tried a unique strategy based on his engineering background: he dammed up a millstream. The water pooled twelve-feet deep, effectively keeping the Southerners from progressing forward, at least not anywhere that Hartranft's men guarded.

Success at Fort Stedman: Hartranft's corps repelled the Confederate attack on Fort Stedman outside Petersburg. With Union success there, the doors were opened for Grant's army to move on to Petersburg and then to Richmond.

After the War: Hartranft was appointed special provost marshal during the trial of President Lincoln's murderers. He managed the prisoners and presided over their hanging. He also returned to public office in his home state of Pennsylvania, serving as: auditor general (1867-1873), governor (1873-1879), Philadelphia's postmaster and city port collector, and commander of the Pennsylvania National Guard, which he reorganized into its current form.

A statue of Hartranft on horseback stands on the grounds of the Pennsylvania state capitol building.

THE CONGRESSIONAL MEDAL OF HONOR

In 1886, John F. Hartranft was awarded a Medal of Honor. The citation read: "Voluntarily served as an aide and participated in the battle after expiration of his term of service, distinguishing himself in rallying several regiments which had been thrown into confusion." Ten other soldiers at Bull Run that day received the Medal of Honor as well.

The Medal of Honor was established by Congress in July 1862 to reward valor in action. The bill said it should go to "such non-commissioned officers and privates as shall most distinguish themselves by their gallantry in action, and other soldier-like qualities, during the present insurrection."

Since then, 3,467 Medals of Honor have been awarded; 1,522 were for service during the Civil War, 618 of which were awarded posthumously.

From 1890 to 1899 more medals were awarded for Civil War action than were given during the actual war. So in 1917, a committee reviewed all of the medals given for the Civil War against the stated criteria. They took back 911 of the honorary citations.

Finally, in 1963, guidelines were set for awarding the Medal:

- While engaged in an action against an enemy of the United States
- While engaged in military operations involving conflict with an opposing foreign force or while serving with friendly forces engaged in armed conflict against an opposing armed force in which the United States is not a belligerent party.

CONFEDERATE COMMANDER: BUSHROD RUST JOHNSON (1817-1880)

Background: Ohio native, Quaker religion, 1840 West Point graduate

Early Military Experience: Mexican War, Seminole War, colonel of Kentucky and Tennessee militias

Occupation Before the Civil War: Military Institute Professor

Battles Participated In: Fort Donelson, Shiloh, Murfreesboro, Perryville, Stones River, Chickamauga, Knoxville, Drewry's Bluff, White Oak Road, and Five Forks

Rank: Brigadier General, 1861; Major General, 1864

Battle of the Crater: You'll recall that "The Crater" was another plan hatched by thoughtful Northern commanders. To move the Siege of Petersburg along, Pennsylvania miners dug a shaft under the Confederate lines, and then blew it up. The explosion killed about three hundred Confederate soldiers and created a thirty-foot-deep crater. Union soldiers didn't get the exact plan, and instead of advancing around it, thought the crater would be an excellent stand to fire from.

In the meantime, Johnson's South Carolina troops were dug in at the trenches. They stood on the rim of the 170-foot-long crater and picked off the Union soldiers. They captured five hundred prisoners that day.

Last Days of the War: Johnson's division was shattered at Sailor's Creek on April 6, 1865. General Lee relieved him of his duties. After the South's surrender at Appomattox Court House, Johnson was paroled without a command.

After the War: He returned to teaching engineering, mechanics, and natural philosophy, and eventually he became chancellor of the University of Nashville. He then retired to a farm in Illinois and died.

Bushrod Johnson Trivia

- Johnson is an example of a Northerner who fought on the Southern side.
- Reports say Johnson resigned from the U.S. Army in 1847 when he was accused of selling contraband goods. (Maybe that's why he fought for the South: perhaps he couldn't go back to the Union Army?)
- Johnson was severely wounded at Shiloh by artillery shell.

Morgan Horses

Vermont was the native home of Justin Morgan, the original breeder of the American Morgan horse named for him. It is the first truly American-made breed of horse by bloodline.

At the time of the Civil War, the Morgan horse was known to be the lightest, toughest, and best cavalry horse available. By then, many Vermont natives had made their fortunes breeding and selling Morgans.

That's why the Union army went to St. Albans in October 1864 to buy seven hundred horses.

CONFEDERATE COMMANDERS: JOHN HUNT MORGAN (1825-1864)

Background: Alabama native; raised in Kentucky; expelled from Transylvania University for dueling
Military Experience: Mexican War
Rank: Captain (1861), Brigadier General (1862)
Early Civil War Service: Captain Morgan led the Lexington Rifles, Kentucky volunteers. Then, General Braxton Bragg sent Morgan to raid Union supply depots and take out transportation lines. Morgan's men cheerfully complied, destroying millions of dollars worth of supplies.
Morgan's Raiders: In July 1863, Bragg sent Morgan with two thousand soldiers to northern Kentucky. His mission was to cause confusion among Union forces. For what it's worth, Morgan brilliantly created turmoil for the United States Army. He grossly exceeded his orders, but, wow did he meet them!

Morgan crossed the Ohio River into southern Indiana, where his Raiders spent five days forcibly taking supplies and horses from Northern civilians.

Moving into Ohio, Morgan split his men into groups, who proceeded through eleven counties, on the way to the Ohio River. Looting along the way, he demanded business owners pay ransoms to save their establishments. An honorable man, he did spare the places whose owners paid up (more likely, he didn't have time to stop and torch them).

The Ohio governor called out the state militia, young men with no battle experience, to protect civilians from Morgan's Raiders. Union forces also headed to the rescue.

Near Buffington Island, Morgan's men started across the Ohio River. Some made it, but then Union gunboats and soldiers under Brigadier General Edward H. Hobson (remember that name!) arrived.

We know there was a battle after that. But, we don't know much else; Morgan didn't file a battle report and Hobson's report was vague. About three thousand Union men faced Morgan's Raiders, now down to 1,700. Around one hundred Raiders were killed with about one thousand captured, including Morgan's brother-in-law. Northern casualties: twenty-five.

The remaining Raiders headed northeast along the Ohio River, with Union troops in pursuit. At Salineville, Hobson (there's that name again) surrounded and captured Morgan and his Raiders.

The enlisted Raiders were sent to Camp Chase prison camp. Regarded as criminals, Morgan and his officers went to the Ohio Penitentiary in Columbus. They immediately planned escape. Morgan's sister visited, smuggling in $1,000 inside a Bible. After about eight weeks, the men tunneled into an airshaft, crawled to the prison yard, made a rope from their clothes, and climbed the wall. Morgan hopped on a train to Cincinnati and then hightailed it to Kentucky.

Morgan's Raid had no real impact on the war, other than instilling fear in Indiana and Ohio residents, giving them an even stronger resolve to defeat the Confederates.

Back with the Confederate army, Morgan led Tennessee and Kentucky cavalry units. Less than a year after being captured in Ohio, Morgan took Federal troops at Cynthiana, Kentucky. Their commander: Edward Hobson (aha).

On September 4, 1864, Morgan's luck ran out in Greenville, Tennessee. Northern soldiers surrounded the farmhouse where he was staying. While trying to slip away from the house, Morgan was fatally shot.

Morgan's Escape From the Ohio Penitentiary

On the train, Morgan confidently sat next to a federal officer. They engaged in friendly conversation, but didn't exchange names. The Fed even shared his brandy flask with Morgan. Passing the state prison, the clueless Yankee bragged, "That's where they've got old John Morgan."

Old John Morgan answered, "Yes, and I hope they always guard him as well as they do now!"

UNION COMMANDERS: PHILIP SHERIDAN (1831-1888)

Background: New York native, 1853 West Point graduate
Military Experience: Served in the U.S. Army in the West
Rank: Promoted to Major General, 1863
Battles Participated In: Perryville, Stone's River, Missionary Ridge, Chickamauga, Chattanooga, Wilderness Campaign, Cedar Creek, and Yellow Tavern
Shenandoah Valley Campaign: Sheridan's Shenandoah Valley Campaign lasted from August 1864 to March 1865. Sheridan's first goal was to stop Confederate General Jubal Early, who had been beating up on the Union soldiers near Washington, D.C. Sheridan ravaged the Virginia countryside in the process, destroying anything of value to the Confederates, including houses, food, crops, and livestock. Although Early enjoyed some minor victories, in the end, Sheridan decimated his troops and gained control of the Shenandoah Valley.
Petersburg: Grant sent Sheridan to destroy the South Side Railroad, the last Confederate supply route into Petersburg. Without the South Side Railroad, the Southern troops would be done for.

Sheridan's victory at Five Forks sealed the fate of Petersburg and Richmond, and led to the surrender at Appomattox Court House. Sheridan seemed obsessed with winning at Five Forks, pushing his men beyond their own capabilities.

It is said that one soldier next to him was struck in the throat. "I'm killed!" the soldier cried. Even though there was blood gushing from his throat, Sheridan urged, "Pick up your gun, man, and move right on!" The soldier did pick up his gun, took a few steps, and fell over dead.

Yellow Tavern: Sheridan had boasted that his cavalry could "whip Confederate General Jeb Stuart out of his boots," to which Grant challenged, "Let him start right out and do it." After the three-hour fight at Yellow Tavern, near Richmond, Sheridan's cavalry finally did. One Union soldier shot Stuart off his horse as the Confederate troops withdrew.

Appomattox: Confederate General Lee was desperately trying to get his troops to Appomattox Station, where they could get much-needed food and other supplies still loaded on trains there. Sheridan performed a veritable end-around at the train station, arriving before Lee and cutting off any hope of food for the Confederate Army. This disheartened the Confederate commander enough to offer surrender.

Knowing the poor state of Lee's army, Sheridan had already wired Grant the message, "If the thing is pressed, I think Lee will surrender." Grant shared the sentiments with President Lincoln, who said, "Let the thing be pressed." So, Sheridan was already preparing to attack the Southern troops one more time. Instead, one rebel soldier rode forward carrying a white flag and told him Lee was ready to meet General Grant to surrender.

After the War: Just one month after the South's surrender, Sheridan was again leading U.S. troops. This time, he was headed to defend the Mexican border from the military of that country. Later, he served as military governor of Texas and Louisiana during Reconstruction. Then, in 1884, Sheridan succeeded General Sherman as commander-in-chief of the U.S. Army.

Philip Sheridan Trivia

- Watching Lee and Grant agree on the terms of the Confederacy's surrender, the attending officers recognized the historical significance of the event. They also recognized the immediate value of the items in the home of Wilmer McLean, where the surrender took place. Sheridan offered McLean $20 in gold to buy the table on which Lee had signed the agreement. He then presented the table to George Custer as a gift for his wife.
- Sheridan changed the name of his favorite horse, Rienzi, to Winchester after his ride to that Virginia town. After Winchester/Rienzi died, Sheridan donated the stuffed body to the Smithsonian Institution.

Union Commanders: Gouverneur Kemble Warren (1830-1882)

Background: New York native, 1850 West Point graduate
Pre-War Work Experience: Corps of Topographical Engineers;
Math teacher at West Point
Battles Participated In: Big Bethel, Peninsula Campaign, Seven
Days, Gaines' Mill, Malvern Hill, Gettysburg, Bristoe Station,
Antietam, Fredericksburg, Chancellorsville, Second Bull Run,
Wilderness Campaign, and Spotsylvania Court House.
Rank: Lieutenant Colonel, 1861; Colonel, 1861; Brigadier General,
1862; Chief Engineer, 1863; Major General, 1863
Second Bull Run: Warren commanded the 5th New York Infantry,
a Zouave regiment, charged with holding the far left of the Union
line. This small regiment suffered about 60 percent loss when the
Texas Brigade surprised their position.
Gettysburg: Warren gained fame for quick thinking regarding the
strategic position of Little Round Top, which had been left
undefended. A topographer, chief engineer Warren recognized the
vulnerability of not having secured the position. There was potential
for disaster.

Warren quickly ordered a regiment to the hill; they took their
places just minutes before Confederates arrived with the same idea.
The Union soldiers were soon under intense fire from Confederate
lines to their fronts and sharpshooters at their backs, but they held
on. After that, Warren was called the "Hero of Little Round Top."
Petersburg Campaign: Warren commanded the U.S. Army V
Corps, which participated in most of the fighting around Petersburg.
Straight from the Wilderness Campaign, the V Corps headed toward
Spotsylvania Court House to cut off Lee's progress in defending
Richmond.

First they came upon a cavalry escort of Union Major General

George Meade and had to wait until the guard detail let them through. Then they encountered Confederate cavalry who were placed specifically to discourage the Union advance, so they arrived after the Union cavalry and the Confederate infantry.

After Spotsylvania, Warren's corps moved forward to dismantle the Weldon Railroad connecting Petersburg with Weldon, North Carolina. They succeeded in pulling up the tracks and destroying the rails, bending them so much that the Confederates would not be able to salvage them.

At Five Forks, Warren's corps provided the reinforcements Sheridan needed to win and open the way to Richmond.

Criticism and Dismissal: Sheridan, seething over Warren's late arrival at Spotsylvania, requested permission from Grant to fire him. It seems, with his engineer's mind, Warren took too much time to analyze each situation, or at least more time than Sheridan would allow him. So after Five Forks, Warren was removed from command.

After the War: Warren spent the final seventeen years of his army career as an engineer, building railroads and other structures along the Mississippi River. In the Corps of Engineers, he achieved the rank of lieutenant colonel.

Exonerated: Warren was truly upset by Sheridan's dismissal. He asked for a court of inquiry into Sheridan's charges. But it was not approved until after President Grant's term was over. President Rutherford B. Hayes ordered the inquiry fourteen years after the fact. In November 1882, the court cleared Warren of the charges—three months after he died.

FYI: A statue to Warren's memory was erected at Round Top, in Gettysburg. Another statue, with its base made of stone taken from Little Round Top, stands at the gateway to Brooklyn, New York's Prospect Park, in Grand Army Plaza.

What About That Name?

Warren was named for his father's friend, Gouverneur Kemble, a prominent local two-time U.S. Congressman and founder of the West Point Foundry.

UNION COMMANDERS: JOHN SEDGWICK (1813-1864)

Background: Connecticut native, 1837 West Point graduate
Early Work Experience: Teacher
Pre-Civil War Military Experience: artillery in Mexican War, Seminole War, Trail of Tears; cavalry in Bleeding Kansas, the Mormon Expedition, and Indian disturbances
Battles Participated In: Yorktown, Seven Pines, Seven Days, Antietam, Chancellorsville, Rappahannock Bridge, Fredericksburg, Gettysburg, Wilderness Campaign, and Spotsylvania
Rank: Major, Lieutenant Colonel, 1861; Colonel, 1861; Brigadier General, 1861; Major General, 1862, with most of this time in command of the Army of the Potomac
Antietam: Sedgwick's division marched into a trap and endured enemy fire from three sides. Half the men were lost.
Fredericksburg: Sedgwick broke through the Confederate line at Marye's Heights, trying to get into position to relieve Hooker's men. But Southern soldiers stopped Sedgwick's men at Salem Church, forcing them to retreat north.
Rappahannock Station: By capturing most of a Confederate division with its guns at Rappahannock, Sedgwick scored the only signal Union success in the Briscoe campaign.
Spotsylvania Court House: While placing his corps artillery in preparation for the fight, he was shot in the head by a Confederate sharpshooter. Sedgwick is known for his last ironic words, declaring that the Confederates couldn't fire accurately at that distance.

John Sedgwick Trivia

- In just a few weeks' time, Sedgwick replaced Robert E. Lee twice in the U.S. Army. The first time, Lee was promoted from the position, and the second, Lee resigned altogether.
- In 1861 Sedgwick took over General Charles P. Stone's division when Stone was arrested for the Union's failure at Ball's Bluff.

- Sedgwick was known affectionately by his troops as "Uncle John."
- In 1862, Sedgwick was wounded during the Seven Days' Battle, at Frayser's Farm, and again, twice, at Antietam.

Joint Committee on the Conduct of War

Before 1861 had drawn to a close, Congress had decided to do something about the embarrassing Union defeats at the Battles of Bull Run and Ball's Bluff. Republican radicals decided to form a joint committee, with members from both the House and Senate, to review issues arising as a result of the war—from bootlegging for the Confederate states, medical treatment for wounded soldiers, military contracts, to the causes of Union battle losses—as well as overseeing the president himself.

The panel included Senator Zachariah T. Chandler of Michigan, Senator Benjamin Franklin Wade of Ohio, Congressman George Washington Julian of Indiana, and Tennessee pro-Union Democrat Andrew Johnson.

Among other things, like emancipation and use of black soldiers, the Radicals hoped to push President Lincoln toward adopting more assertive war strategies and appointing more aggressive fighters to command the Union armies.

The Committee continued in existence until May 1865. During three and a half years, committee members held 272 meetings—all in secret.

The Committee's first target was General McClellan, who they didn't trust because he was a Democrat. They considered him a coward. Their plan was to get to McClellan by taking out his subordinates. McClellan was all too happy to offer up Stone as a scapegoat.

UNION COMMANDERS: CHARLES POMEROY STONE (1824-1887)

Background: Massachusetts native, 1845 West Point graduate
Military Experience: Served in the Mexican War under General Winfield Scott
Campaigns Participated In: Shenandoah Valley Campaign, Rockville Expedition, Port Hudson, Red River Campaign
Rank: Colonel, 1861
First Civil War Assignment: With the District of Columbia Volunteers in April 1861, Stone was charged with the safety of the capital and the president.
Under Military Arrest: Stone was blamed for the Union failure at Ball's Bluff. In October 1861, a Union recon team checking out Confederate strength was trapped on the banks of the Potomac. The Federal soldiers essentially had to choose death by close-range execution, falling off a cliff, or drowning in the river.

Stone was arrested under cover of darkness, at midnight on February 8, 1862, by the Committee on the Conduct of the War. He was not offered an explanation for the arrest. Stone spent fifty days in solitary confinement in New York's Fort Lafayette, and then was moved to Fort Hamilton. After being under arrest for 189 days, Stone was released in August 1862. He was never told the charges, and he was never cleared of them.

Negotiating Surrender: At Port Hudson, Louisiana, Stone was General Nathaniel Banks' Chief of Staff. As such, he was part of the Union commission Banks appointed to negotiate surrender of Confederate forces on July 8, 1863. Coupled with Grant's victory at Vicksburg, it secured the Union's control of the Mississippi River.
Leaving the War: Stone resigned from the Army in September 1864.
After the War: Stone worked as superintendent for a Virginia mining company. Then, he accepted an offer to join the Egyptian army as the chief of staff and general aide-de-camp of the khedive.

Stone was ranked lieutenant general and titled Ferik Pasha. After his stint in Egypt, Stone returned to America, eventually finding his way to an engineering job in New York City.

Charles Stone's Statue of Liberty Connection

Charles Pomeroy Stone was the chief engineer in charge of assembling the Statue of Liberty in New York Harbor. This is the same harbor where he had been held prisoner more than fifteen years earlier. Serving as grand marshal during dedication ceremonies on October 28, 1886, ultimately led to his death: he caught a chill during the festivities and died three months later.

Union Commanders: Nathaniel Prentice Banks (1816-1894)

Background: Massachusetts native, from a poor family

Early Work Experience: Cotton factory worker while very young; Mechanic apprenticed at the same factory; Edited several weekly newspapers; Admitted to the bar, 1839.

Family Life: Married factory co-worker Mary Theodosia Palmer, 1847.

Political Experience: Massachusetts House of Representatives (Free Soil party, 1849-1853, speaker 1851-1852); Massachusetts Constitutional Convention President (1853); U.S. House of Representatives (Free Soil/ Democratic and Know-Nothing parties, 1853-1857, speaker 1856-1857); Massachusetts Governor (1858-1860).

Nathaniel Banks had no military training or experience. He was a friend of President Lincoln, and from such connections, entered the Civil War in 1861 ranked major general of volunteers.

In the Shenandoah Valley: Banks was charged with detaining Stonewall Jackson's troops in the Shenandoah Valley so that they could not support Confederate forces while McClellan focused on taking Richmond. First, Jackson's speedy raiders lifted so many supplies from Banks that the Confederates referred to him as "Commissary Banks." Then Jackson's men pushed Banks out of Shenandoah Valley altogether, a Northern embarrassment.

At Cedar Mountain: Banks again faced Jackson's troops, and they enjoyed early success. But Confederate General A. P. Hill's reinforcements arrived to negate Banks' advantage. Then Union General John Pope showed up with his own reinforcements. The whole battle ended in a standoff.

Defending Washington, D.C.: Banks was moved to the capital's defense, building forts and digging trenches against potential Confederate attack.

Capturing Port Hudson: Lincoln asked Banks to pull his political strings and recruit thirty thousand volunteers from New York and New England. Banks sailed with the troops to Louisiana to replace Major General Benjamin Butler in New Orleans and open the Mississippi to Union gunboats. For perspective, in the meantime, General Grant was right up the river, taking on Vicksburg, Mississippi.

Banks' troops surrounded Port Hudson and assaulted the Confederate fort there for forty-eight days. When the Southerners in the fort learned that Grant had Vicksburg, they surrendered. Now, finally, the North controlled the entire Mississippi River.

Action in Texas: Banks sailed to Texas. His goal was to keep the French in Mexico from supplying troops to the Confederacy by way of Texas. He planned to quickly hit the Sabine River, moving on land to Houston and Galveston. The Battle of Sabine Pass was a Union disaster. Next, however, Banks sailed to the Rio Grande's mouth and captured the area.

Damming the Red River: The Union wanted to launch attacks on cotton land in Louisiana, Arkansas, and Texas from Louisiana's Red River. But, the North did not count on the Southern soldiers' tenacity under General Richard Taylor.

At first, Banks occupied Alexandria, Louisiana, and forced the Confederates to retreat. But, they didn't go far, and at Mansfield, the Confederates set up fortifications from which they defeated Banks' men. The next day, both sides restarted fighting at Pleasant Hill.

By this point, Banks was in trouble. Water and food for the men and horses were running low, and he had no idea where his supply boats were. So he retreated.

Without backup on land, Admiral David Porter's boats on the Red River were just sitting ducks. The river's water level was too low to float back down. Along with Lieutenant Colonel Joseph Bailey, Banks and his men worked around the clock to build a dam to raise the water level enough to float the fleet out of the area before Confederates could capture the whole kit and caboodle.

The Red River Campaign was a failure, and it was Banks' last command. President Lincoln put Banks on leave in Washington, where he applied his political clout lobbying for Congressional support of Lincoln's reconstruction plans.

CONFEDERATE COMMANDERS: BRAXTON BRAGG (1817-1876)

Background: West Point-trained Mexican and Seminole War veteran turned Louisiana sugar planter

Description: An "impatient, anxious soldier" suffering from bad temper, migraine headaches, chronic boils, and rheumatism

Rank: Promoted to Major General of the regular Army, September 1861; Replaced Pierre Beauregard as commander of the Confederate Army of Mississippi, June 1862.

Positives as a Confederate Commander: Bragg was good with military tactics.

Negatives as a Confederate Commander: Bragg repeatedly exercised paralyzing indecision on the battlefield, which proved fatal to many Confederate soldiers.

Examples of Indecisiveness: In the summer of 1861, Bragg was in charge of defending the Gulf Coast. President Davis had ordered him to take Fort Pickens on Santa Rosa Island near Pensacola. Bragg was not ready, so he did not proceed. Instead, the first major battle of the war was in Virginia, at Manassas.

In 1863, although Chickamauga was a Confederate victory, Bragg could have done things better:

1. As Union General William Rosecrans advanced around the city, his army had to divide up to get through. It would have been easy enough for Bragg's men to pick them off, but Bragg didn't get the order out.
2. As the Union forces retreated, Bragg did not pursue. This gave the Union the opportunity to regroup for what would be a Confederate disaster at Chattanooga.

Negatives as a Confederate Commander: Neither his superiors or the officers serving under him cared one bit for Bragg.

Examples of Discord Between Bragg and Others:

- In 1862, after Murfreesboro, Leonidas Polk argued with Bragg about tactics. Bragg tried to court-martial Polk. Jefferson Davis instead reassigned Polk to Mississippi.
- In 1863, after Chickamauga, Bragg blamed his indecision on his men. James Longstreet, Polk, Daniel Hill, and Thomas Hindman complained to the War Department, demanding his dismissal. Jefferson Davis visited Bragg's headquarters to review the troops and talk with the corps commanders. They all urged him to replace Bragg, but Davis left him in charge.
- Nathan Bedford Forrest refused to serve under him again, calling him a "damned scoundrel."
- In the spring of 1863, Bragg reduced his army's daily ration to only cornmeal and water. Mind you, Bragg didn't cut his own ration to simply cornmeal. To show their discontent, his men refused to fall in for drills. A few months later, they even stole one of their own supply trains with bacon, meal, and flour, so they could eat from it before Bragg denied it.
- In Chattanooga in November 1864, Bragg ordered a siege to cut off supply lines for Union forces fortified in the town, a strategy that depleted their food and arms. But Union General Grant showed up, opened the supply line, and planned an attack on Confederates at Missionary Ridge at about the same time Bragg sent a bunch of his troops off to West Virginia to help against General Burnside. Bragg did not communicate his strategic orders to all his men, so they didn't know what everyone was doing. Bragg's army was forced to retreat, and he blamed his own men for their cowardice and inability to hold the position. The defeat at Chattanooga left the door wide open for Sherman's Atlanta campaign. Bragg was removed from command.

In September 1862, Bragg was making progress in Kentucky, beating the Union at Munfordville and capturing Lexington. When he stopped to install a Confederate government at Frankfort, he lost valuable time, which led to a loss at Perryville to Union General Don Carlos Buell.

CONFEDERATE COMMANDERS: JOHN BELL HOOD (1831-1879)

Assessment of Military Skills: A courageous fighter who did not have the strategic thinking skills needed to successfully command an army.

Command: Hood's Texas Brigade; his men called him "Old Wooden Head."

Military Participation: Battles of Seven Days, Second Bull Run, Chickamauga, Gettysburg, Antietam, Atlanta, Nashville, Franklin

Battle Scars and Strong Drugs: At Gettysburg, Hood was badly wounded in the arm, leaving it useless. Then, at Chickamauga, he lost his right leg, almost all the way to the trunk. From that point, he wore a cork leg made in France, and he always carried a spare in case of emergency.

Hood had to be strapped to his saddle each morning, but he fought just as hard as he always had. He took quite a bit of laudanum for pain, and some say that his fearless bravery could have been the result of euphoria-induced overdosing.

Battle Experiences:

- **Antietam:** Before the battle started, Hood had been arrested, with A. P. Hill, for quarreling with superiors. Lee suspended the arrests when the fighting started so that his able leaders would be in place. During the battle, Hood's ferocious Texans, who would turn out to be Jackson's last reserves, broke the Union line, at a loss of 60 percent of their numbers.

- **Atlanta:** Late in the war, Hood replaced General Joseph Johnston as commander of the Confederate Army of the Tennessee in defending Atlanta from Sherman. Under Hood's leadership, trying (and trying and trying) to stop Sherman, the Tennessee division was all but wiped out. Hood and his men fought bravely, but they were grossly outnumbered. His retreating troops destroyed whatever they could to keep it from falling into the hands of the Federals, including factories and a railroad train, (all eighty-one cars) with cars and cars full of ammunition.

- **Franklin:** Hood's charge at Franklin has been compared to Pickett's Charge, the famous suicidal advance at Gettysburg. Some say that Hood was trying to discipline his army with this maneuver, and that he wanted to see what they were made of after what happened at Spring Hill. (And if you're wondering what happened at Spring Hill, the Confederate forces let the Union forces withdraw overnight to Franklin.) Hood lost six generals that day: John B. Carter, States Rights Gist, H. B. Granbury, John Adams, O. F. Strahl, and Patrick Cleburne.

  One of Hood's own Texas Brigade wrote of the Franklin debacle, "The wails and cries of widows and orphans made at Franklin will heat up the fires of the bottomless pit to burn the soul of General J. B. Hood for murdering their husbands and fathers at that place that day." Strong words.

- **Nashville:** This devastating December 1864 Confederates loss ultimately was the end of Hood with the Army of Tennessee. After the suicidal defeat at Franklin, he refused to retreat from Tennessee, hoping to retake the state, marching on to Nashville. Hood resigned his command after this loss.

Yellow Fever Takes Care of What the Union Couldn't Do: A yellow fever epidemic in New Orleans in 1878 ended Hood's life. His wife and one daughter also died. Ten remaining Hood children—including three sets of twins—immediately became orphans, but Confederate patriots across the South were all too happy to adopt the children of General Hood.

CONFEDERATE COMMANDERS: JAMES LONGSTREET (1821-1904)

Background: Born in South Carolina, raised on Georgia and Alabama cotton plantations

Military Experience: 1842 West Point graduate; veteran in the Mexican War

Battles Participated In: Blackburn's Ford, First Bull Run, Yorktown, Williamsburg, Seven Pines, Seven Days, Second Bull Run, South Mountain, Antietam, Fredericksburg, Wilderness, Gettysburg, and Chickamauga

Rank: Brigadier General, promoted to Major General to Senior Lieutenant General

Position in the Confederate Army: After Stonewall Jackson was killed, Longstreet became Robert E. Lee's most trusted aide. Lee even called him "my old war-horse." In fact, on April 7, 1865, when Grant sent a message to Lee requesting surrender, it was Longstreet who said, "Not yet." It was also Longstreet who, when Lee did ride to meet Grant on April 12, counseled him to come back and fight it out, if Grant's terms were not acceptable.

Ups and Downs of the Confederate Troops Under Longstreet's Command:

- **Antietam:** Longstreet and his colonels came across a Confederate cannon that had been abandoned. Longstreet jumped off his horse, and, with his colonels loading charges, aimed the gun and took control of firing.
- **Fredericksburg:** Longstreet participated in the worst defeat of the Union's Army of the Potomac in the history of the American army (to that point, anyway).
- **Battle of the Wilderness:** Longstreet's infantry almost overran Union General Winfield Scott Hancock's corps, but the Yankees rallied. Longstreet was accidentally wounded by one of his own men, shot through the throat and shoulder.

- **Second Bull Run:** Longstreet and Lee arrived on the second day of Bull Run to reinforce Jackson's troops and rout Union General Pope.
- **Gettysburg:** Longstreet's delay in reacting to a Union strategic gaffe was just what was needed for the Northerners to correct the error. (Do you want to know what the gaffe was? Union Major General Daniel Sickles had moved his men to an undefended position. But, before Longstreet could mobilize his Confederate troops, Union General Meade arrived to reinforce Sickles.) To his credit, more than once Longstreet suggested a large flanking attack, but Lee didn't want to follow his advice.
- **Chickamauga:** Longstreet reinforced Bragg's troops in the costly Confederate victory.

James Longstreet Trivia

- Longstreet appeared at the First Battle of Bull Run still wearing his U.S. Army uniform (he wasn't the only Confederate who showed up wearing the only uniform he had, even it was for a force he no longer fought for).
- Longstreet's men called him "Old Pete," which came from his childhood nickname "Pete," meaning "solid," or "a rock."

Longstreet the Scalawag

When you visit the Museum of the Confederacy in Richmond, Virginia, you won't find General James Longstreet represented among the portraits of the Confederate Generals. That would be because Longstreet:

1. Joined the Republican Party after the war. This was the party which enforced the hated Reconstruction policies. Democratic Southerners regarded Longstreet as a "scalawag."
2. Badmouthed Robert E. Lee after the war—in print, no less—suggesting the revered general had made tactical mistakes at Gettysburg.
3. Made friends with Ulysses S. Grant, and served as his minister to Turkey.

THE MERRIMAC AND THE MONITOR

An abandoned Union frigate, the *Merrimac*, became a top priority for the fledgling Confederate Navy early in the war. They aimed to build the first ironclad ship, a vessel that could pound the traditional wooden boats. Word spread in the North of the Confederate venture, sparking fears of an unstoppable attack—and spurring Secretary of the Navy Gideon Welles to tap inventor John Ericsson for an equally formidable answer.

Rather than converting a frigate, as the South had done, Ericsson delivered a one-of-a-kind design, a boat constructed out of nothing but iron—and with mobile guns made lethal because of their location in a revolving turret.

The *Merrimac*, renamed as the C.S.S. *Virginia*, debuted in March 1862, launching an attack on a fifty-gun Union ship at Hampton Roads, Virginia. The Union vessel, *Cumberland*, fired a barrage of shots at the Confederate ironclad, to no effect. The shots fell harmlessly from the ironclad. Then the *Merrimac* sank the *Cumberland*, set another Union ship on fire, and ran a third on to land.

The next morning, as the Confederates prepared to send the *Merrimac* out again, the *Monitor* arrived. Now the ironclads would square off, exchanging close-range fire for hours. Naval warfare would be forever changed by the two vessels, though their lone battle proved indecisive. Neither ironclad made an impact during the rest of the Civil War: The *Merrimac* was destroyed in May 1862 when the Confederates set fire to it while the *Monitor* sank in December 1862.

Nicknames

Lewis Addison Armistead: Nickname - Lo, short for "Lothario," which he was not

Nathaniel Prentice Banks: Nickname - Commissary Banks, was easily raided by Confederates for supplies

P. G. T. Beauregard: Nicknames - Little Creole, Little Napoleon

Maria Isabella "Belle" Boyd: Nickname - La Belle Rebelle, for espionage activities

Kady Brownell: Nickname - Daughter of the Regiment, by Colonel Burnside

Benjamin Franklin Butler: Nickname - Beast/Spoons, for treatment of New Orleans rebels/stealing Confederate property, i.e. silverware

Patrick Ronayne Cleburne: Nickname - Stonewall Jackson of the West, battle actions

John Lincoln "Johnny" Clem: Nickname - Johnny Shiloh, The Drummer Boy of Chickamauga, for outstanding bravery in action

George Armstrong Custer: Nickname - Armstrong, Audie, Fanny, Curly, by friends, West Point buddies, troops

Ulrich Dahlgren: Nickname - Ulrich the Hun, for despicable plans to murder the Confederate cabinet

Varina Anne "Winnie" Davis: Nickname - Child of the Confederacy, only child born under a sitting Confederate President

Bridget Divers: Nickname - Irish Bridget, Michigan Bridget, Irish Biddy, affection of the 1st Michigan Cavalry

Abner Doubleday: Nickname - Old Forty-Eight Hours, a deliberate manner

Jubal Anderson Early: Nickname - Old Jube, Old Jubilee, affection of his troops

Richard Stoddert Ewell: Nickname - Old Baldy, Old Bald Head, few hirsute characteristics

John C. Frémont: Nickname - The Pathfinder, travels as topographical engineer to northern frontier

Ulysses S. Grant: Nickname - Unconditional Surrender, for accepting no terms at Fort Donelson

Henry Wager Halleck: Nickname - Old Brains, Old Wooden Head, for great intellect/for poor Civil War leadership

John Bell Hood: Nickname - Old Woodenhead, affection of his Texas Brigade

Joseph Hooker: Nickname - Fighting Joe, from a media roster

Mary Anna Jackson: Nickname - Widow of the Confederacy, never remarried after Stonewall's death

Thomas Jackson: Nickname - Stonewall, for his stand at First Bull Run

William Edmondson Jones: Nickname - Grumble, for his disagreeable nature

Philip Kearny: Nickname - Kearny the Magnificent/The One-Armed Devil, for brilliant battle maneuvers, even after losing an arm

Hugh Judson Kilpatrick: Nickname - Kill Cavalry, for a high body count in battle

Edmund Kirby-Smith: Nickname - Seminole, for his home state of Florida

William Henry Fitzhugh Lee: Nickname - Rooney, Robert E. Lee's son

James Longstreet: Nickname - Warhorse, Old Pete, by Lee and by his men from a childhood nickname

John Bankhead Magruder: Nickname - Prince John, indulged his extravagant tastes

Dabney Herndon Maury: Nickname - Puss in Boots, because he was short of stature, his boots appeared to swallow him

Matthew Fontaine Maury: Nickname - Pathfinder of the Seas, discovered Gulf Stream and charted Atlantic Ocean floor

George McClellan: Nickname - The Virginia Creeper, bestowed by Phil Kearny for his indecision and inaction

John Singleton Mosby: Nickname - The Gray Ghost, by Union troops for his raids

Rose O'Neal Greenhow: Nickname - Wild Rose/Rebel Rose, by Union sympathizers/by secessionists

Lucy Pickens: Nickname - Lady Lucy, first lady of South Carolina

Alan Pinkerton: Nickname – The Eye, for ability to gather intelligence

Leonidas Polk: Nickname – Bishop, Episcopal Bishop of Louisiana

Sterling Price: Nickname – Pap, affection of his troops

William Rosecrans: Nickname – Old Rosy, Silly Goose, admiring soldiers and by McClellan

John Rowlands/Henry Morton Stanley: Nickname – The Rockbreaker, for his strong personality on explorations in Africa

Abram Joseph Ryan: Nickname – Poet-priest of the Confederacy, Catholic priest

Winfield Scott: Nickname – Old Fuss and Feathers, stickler for rules

John Sedgwick: Nickname – Uncle John, affection of his troops

Alexander Hamilton Stephens: Nickname – Little Ellick, The Great Commoner, by his friends and fellow Congressmen

Henry Warner Slocum: Nickname – Slow Come, didn't bring troops to the Gettysburg battlefield until the very end of the day

James Ewell Brown Stuart: Nickname – Jeb, from his initials

Mary Tepee: Nickname – French Mary, Vivandière of the 114th Pennsylvania Infantry

George Henry Thomas: Nickname – Pap/Rock of Chickamauga, by his soldiers and for his bravery

Harriet Tubman: Nickname – Moses, Underground Railroad work

Clement L. Vallandigham: Nickname – Valiant Val, by his friends

Earl Van Dorn: Nickname – Buck/General Damn Born, by friends, by soldiers who disagreed with poor leadership

Elizabeth Van Lew: Nickname – Crazy Bet, eccentric actions

Gouverneur Kemble Warren: Nickname – Hero of Little Round Top, for strategy at Gettysburg

Joseph Wheeler: Nickname – Fighting Joe, aggressive personality

A TALE OF TWO LEES

How's this for confusing? Robert E. Lee had a son named William Henry Fitzhugh Lee, and he had a nephew named Fitzhugh Lee.

Both younger Lees were almost the same age and each grew up on a Virginia plantation. Both were cavalry soldiers, commanded troops during the Civil War, and participated in many of the same campaigns (South Mountain, Chancellorsville, Petersburg, Appomattox). In fact, for a time, William Henry Fitzhugh's regiment was assigned under Fitzhugh's command.

Fortunately, the family gave the first cousins distinguishable nicknames.

Robert E. Lee's Son: William Henry Fitzhugh "Rooney" Lee (1837–1891)

Rooney Lee attended Harvard, and he was an excellent oarsman on the crew team. Instead of graduating, however, he joined the army in 1857 as a second lieutenant and saw fighting in Utah. He returned home to farming until the Civil War broke out.

In addition to action already mentioned, William Henry Fitzhugh participated in Fredericksburg, South Mountain, and Brandy Station. He missed Antietam because of an accident en route to the engagement. Covering the advance's rear, Lee's cavalry encountered Union horsemen. Of course, fighting broke out, Lee's horse was shot and fell on top of him. Lee was knocked unconscious and temporarily paralyzed. He spent the battle recuperating in a field hospital.

In 1863, Lee was wounded during Brandy Station and captured two weeks later as a prisoner of war. Several stories remain from his time at Fort Lafayette, New York.

1.   His horse had been stolen by Union captors. Union General Benjamin Butler—nicknamed "Beast" by the ill-treated New

Orleans residents under his military control—located the horse and returned it to Lee.

2. As the son of the great General Lee, Rooney was a valuable prisoner. In one situation, Union Captain W. H. Sawyer, who was being held in Libby Prison, had been sentenced to death as retaliation for execution of a Confederate captain. In turn, Lee was taken as a hostage in case Sawyer ended up being executed. The suspense was defused months later when the hostages on both sides were freed.

3. Rooney's release did not end with a happy homecoming. While he was confined in New York, his wife Charlotte had contracted tuberculosis. He was not allowed to leave prison to visit her, and she died before his release.

After his release, Lee was promoted to Major General, the youngest Confederate officer to reach that rank. He was with his father for the surrender at Appomattox the next year.

In his post-bellum career, William Henry Fitzhugh Lee served as Virginia state senator (1875–1878) and was elected a Democrat to the U.S. House of Representatives (1887–1891).

Robert E. Lee's Nephew: Fitzhugh "Fitz" Lee (1835–1905)

Fitz was the livelier of the two. He was known to be outgoing and fun-loving, a contrast to his more solemn cousin. A case in point is his well-known tenure at West Point. In danger of being expelled for bad behavior, Fitz convinced the superintendent to give him another chance (the superintendent happened to be Uncle Robert E). He did graduate in 1856, ranked forty-fifth in his class.

Upon graduation, Fitz Lee was commissioned into the U.S. cavalry and sent to the western frontier, where he was wounded while fighting the Comanches. By the time the Civil War started, Fitz Lee was back at West Point as the tactical officer. He enlisted as lieutenant colonel of the 1st Virginia Cavalry.

Along with the battles already listed, Fitz participated in First Bull Run, the Peninsula Campaign, Antietam, Kelly's Ford, Gettysburg, Overland Campaign, Spotsylvania, Shenandoah Valley, and the Carolinas Campaign. He suffered from inflammatory rheumatism so painful that he was sometimes forced to sit one out. At Winchester in 1864, three horses were shot out from under him, and he himself was severely wounded.

Fitz Lee achieved the rank of major general. After the war, he took up farming, writing, and some occasional soldiering. He served as Virginia's governor from 1886 to 1890, during which time he developed a successful plan to pay off the state's war debt. In 1894, Fitz Lee wrote a well-received biography of his famous uncle, *General Lee: A Biography of Robert E. Lee*. (He also wrote several other historical works.) Then he took a post as U.S. Consul General in Havana (1896–1898).

At the start of the Spanish-American War in 1898, Fitz Lee returned to the U.S. Army as a major general of volunteers. He retired from the Army as a brigadier general in 1902.

Some More Lee Boys

It bears mentioning that William H. F. Lee had an older brother, also a Confederate commander. Major General George Washington Custis Lee was also captured, on April 6, 1865, at Sayler's Creek, and held as a prisoner of war until his father surrendered to Grant later in the week. George Washington Custis Lee was the son who later regained control of his mother's family home in Arlington, Virginia.

Younger brother Robert E. Lee Jr. also participated in the Civil War, as artillery private and as an aide to the oldest Lee brother, George Washington Custis.

Finally, just to confuse everyone a little bit more, we'll share that middle brother William Henry Fitzhugh Lee had two sons, one of whom he named Robert Edward Lee.

Virginia Military Institute: The "West Point of the South"

The first state military college in the nation was founded in Lexington, Virginia, in 1839. Virginia Military Institute was responsible for turning out at least fifteen future Confederate generals as well as some equally-qualified Union soldiers. More than 1,700 graduates altogether served the Confederacy, and sixteen more fought for the Union.

Prior to the outbreak of the Civil War and receiving his famous nickname, "Stonewall," Thomas Jackson was a professor of natural philosophy there, and he is buried on the grounds. Before he was mortally wounded during the Battle of Chancellorsville, Jackson noticed the number of VMI alums on the field, saying, "The Institute will be heard from today."

Besides all its distinguished "sons," the Virginia Military Institute offers a couple of other Civil War claims to fame:

1. The Battle of New Market, May 15, 1864: The VMI Corps of Cadets marched from Lexington as a unit to join the battle. The corps claimed the hill with their own school flag. Their action turned the tide to a Confederate win. Of more than two hundred boys, aged eighteen or below—as the legend is retold, some claim as young as twelve—ten were killed or mortally hit, and forty-five were wounded.

   VMI is the only U.S. military college that sent cadets to fight as an independent unit. As such, it is the only school authorized to "fix bayonets" during parades.

   Today, the Virginia Military Institute holds an annual parade on May 15 to commemorate the bravery of the corps in battle. A solemn ceremony includes a roll call of the New Market cadets; designated students reply in the place of the casualties, "Dead on the Field of Honor, sir."

2. Burned by Union Soldiers, June 12, 1864. VMI was a valid wartime target, with its state arsenal and a military training school both on the grounds. Union General David Hunter ordered the barracks burned to the ground. Union soldiers proceeded to destroy the barracks, faculty residences, the library, and science labs. (They also stole a statue of George Washington, just for the fun of it.)

VMI moved to Richmond until the end of the war, temporarily suspended classes, and reopened in Lexington in October 1865. Washington's statue was returned in 1866, along with photographs of it in front of tourist sites across the country (just kidding about that last part).

By 1869, the barracks and other damaged buildings had been replaced. Former Confederate Naval Commodore Matthew Fontaine Maury, oceanographer and "Pathfinder of the Seas," joined the faculty teaching physics.

Notable Virginia Military Institute Alumni

- George C. Marshall, Class of 1901: World War II Five-Star General; U.S. Secretary of State, 1947–1949; U.S. Secretary of Defense, 1950–1951; Nobel Peace Prize, 1953
- Bobby Thomason, Class of 1949: NFL quarterback for eight seasons, six with the Philadelphia Eagles, 1952–1957
- Fred Willard, Class of 1955: American comedian and actor, known for his roles in each Christopher Guest movie, including *Best in Show* and *A Mighty Wind*—among many other parts

THE U.S. NAVAL ACADEMY

The U.S. Naval Academy was established in 1845 in Annapolis, Maryland, to provide a training ground for potential midshipmen before sending them to sea. Graduates refer to their alma mater as "Annapolis" or "The Academy," and affectionately call it "The Boat School" or "Canoe U." Sports and professional rivals take it down a notch, dubbing it "Shipwreck Tech."

At the beginning of the Civil War, the three upper classes were detached and sent to sea on the U.S.S. *Constitution*. The Academy moved the remaining students to Fort Adams in Rhode Island, where classes were held for the duration of the conflict. The Academy returned to Annapolis after the end of the war in 1865.

By mid-1865, 495 U.S. Naval Academy graduates had participated in the Civil War: four hundred in the Union Navy and ninety-five in the Confederate Navy. Of those, twenty-three were either killed or mortally wounded in battle.

Notable Alumni
- Rear Admiral William Thomas Sampson graduated in 1861 and took a job as instructor at the Academy. Later, he participated in the blockade, off the coast of Charleston.
- Rear Admiral Charles Dwight Sigsbee (1845–1923), graduated in 1863 and participated in the blockade. He is best remembered as Captain of the U.S.S. *Maine*, which exploded in Havana in 1898, setting off the Spanish-American War.
- James E. "Jimmy" Carter, Class of 1947: Thirty-ninth U.S. President
- Roger Staubach, Class of 1965: Heisman Trophy winner and Dallas Cowboys quarterback (1969–1979)
- David Robinson, Class of 1987: NBA 1990 Rookie of the Year and San Antonio Spurs center (1989–2003), known as "The Admiral"
- The U.S. Naval Academy has graduated fifty-two future astronauts, more than any other school in the country

UNION OFFICERS: JAMES WOLFE RIPLEY (1794-1870)

Upon West Point graduation in 1814, Connecticut native James W. Ripley immediately jumped into the fray of the War of 1812, defending New York's Sackett's Harbor. He then served under Andrew Jackson in the Seminole Wars and in Charleston Harbor during South Carolina's 1830s nullification crisis. Immediately thereafter, Ripley began his career in ordnance.

Ripley was nearing retirement age, having spent almost fifty years in the U.S. Army, when the Civil War began and he was appointed the Union's Chief of Ordnance. In 1861, he ran a small office with only sixty-four men to help supply the entire American Army.

Brigadier General Ripley was an old and old-fashioned artilleryman. He flat out opposed new weaponry. Coupled with the belief that the Civil War would be a short, ninety-day engagement, he didn't see any point in exploring new innovations. Imagine how this must have frustrated President Lincoln, who was fascinated by new technology!

First, Ripley felt that the Ordnance Department had plenty of weapons on hand to get the Union soldiers through the three months that it would take to end this conflict. But by fall of 1862, when it became clear that everything was far from over, the U.S. Ordnance Department had purchased more than 700,000 rifles.

Second, Ripley was opposed to the new repeating rifles. He argued that first of all, soldiers would waste too much ammunition trying to fire them (yes, you read that correctly), and secondly that there would be too much standardization required to implement different weapons (you read that correctly, too). As a result, many individual units bought repeating rifles with private money.

In 1863, James W. Ripley was forced to retire and was replaced by Brigadier General George D. Ramsay.

WAR SUBSTITUTES

While our modern fill-in teachers pelted with spit bombs might feel like they confront troops each morning, back in the 1860s, a substitute actually faced real life-threatening hazards for their pay.

In 1863, President Lincoln initiated the first draft, including every man between the ages of twenty and forty-five. Anyone compelled to serve could expect a three-year enlistment. Large loopholes made for quite a disparity between rich and poor. Lincoln provided that any man who paid a $300 commutation fee would be exempt from the draft.

Or you could send a substitute in your place. Thrifty or enterprising businessmen soon adopted this option. Some men who paid others to take their place:

- Theodore Roosevelt, Sr., father of the twenty-sixth U.S. President "Teddy" Roosevelt
- James Roosevelt, father of the thirty-second U.S. President, Franklin D. Roosevelt
- Andrew Carnegie, railroad and steel magnate, and prolific philanthropist
- J. Pierpont Morgan, banker and industrial tycoon
- John D. Rockefeller, oil mogul
- Grover Cleveland, later elected the twenty-second and twenty-fourth U.S. President
- George Templeton Strong, lawyer and co-founder of the U.S. Sanitary Commission

Abraham Lincoln's Substitute

John Summerfield Staples had already served one term as substitute when he went to war for President Lincoln. In early 1863, he served about six months in the 176th Pennsylvania Militia Infantry when he contracted typhoid fever and returned home to recuperate.

In 1864, while working with his father in Washington, Staples was asked to be Lincoln's representative. President Lincoln wanted to set an example by hiring the young man to go in his place and paid him $500.

For eleven months, Staples was stationed in Alexandria, Virginia, charged with defending Washington. His hairiest moments of the conflict occurred when he escorted Confederate prisoners to Columbus, Ohio.

Andrew Carnegie Pays a Substitute, Goes to War Anyway

Even though he paid a substitute to keep him out of the U.S. Army, Andrew Carnegie didn't entirely ignore the war efforts and even sustained an injury while in civilian service of the federal government.

It all started when he was employed as a telegraph operator for the Pennsylvania Railroad Company in the 1850s, working under Thomas A. Scott. At the beginning of the Civil War, Scott was appointed Assistant Secretary of War, and he was responsible for military transportation. Scott remembered Carnegie's brilliance at telegraph operation—Carnegie had learned to recognize the dots and dashes by their sound, so that he didn't have to write them down. Scott recruited the twenty-six-year-old Scottish native to serve as Superintendent of the Military Railways and maintain the government's telegraph lines in the East.

Working as a civilian, Carnegie's war effort contribution included establishing the telegraph office that President Lincoln visited for reports from the battlefields. Carnegie was injured by telegraph wire, not a bullet, leaving a scar on his cheek that he could call an old war wound, even though he was never quite on the front lines.

At the close of the war, Carnegie moved on from railroad endeavors to iron and steel. He founded the Carnegie Steel Company. At the turn of the century, Carnegie sold out his business interests to J. P. Morgan (who formed U.S. Steel), and channeled his funds toward charitable efforts.

Carnegie spent the rest of his life sharing his fortune of millions of dollars with the public, establishing outlets for the arts, such as Carnegie Hall in New York City, and libraries throughout the United States and the United Kingdom. In all, he supported about three thousand new libraries in forty-seven states.

"Lord, Help Us All!"

Some people figured out how to avoid "going to war," such as paying substitutes and bribing doctors to certify debilitating illnesses. In the South, wealthy planters could stay home to farm their plantations, based on the "Twenty Slave Rule." In addition, the Confederacy allowed certain occupations to avoid conscription, including postmasters, state legislators, blacksmiths, shoemakers, and ministers. The Confederacy even decreed in 1862 that chaplains taken as prisoners of war would be immediately released.

In the North, however, the War Department declared that clergy, although needed at home, were not exempt from the draft based on their occupation any more than any other profession was exempt. In fact, Reverend B. C. Ward, pastor of an Illinois Congregational church, tried to organize an entire infantry regiment of ordained clergymen, but he could not get enough interest in the idea for it to come to fruition.

Other Union Ministers Who Served in the Civil War

- John M. Chivington, Methodist minister. Chivington declined a chaplain's position, enrolling as major of the 1st Colorado Infantry, which later converted to a cavalry unit. Known as "The Fighting Parson," he conducted raids against Cheyenne Native Americans on the western front.
- John Eaton, Jr., Presbyterian minister and chaplain to the 27th Ohio. Eaton was promoted to brigadier general for organizing a black regiment out of contraband slaves.
- Arthur Buckminster Fuller, Unitarian pastor and chaplain of the 16th Massachusetts. Fuller was killed at Fredericksburg.
- Milton Lorenzi Haney, chaplain of the 55th Illinois Infantry, known as "The Fighting Chaplain." During the Battle of Atlanta, Haney "voluntarily carried a musket [. . .] and rendered heroic service in retaking the Federal works," according to the citation he received when awarded a Congressional Medal of Honor for his actions.

- Granville Moody, Methodist minister known as "The Fighting Parson." Moody organized and was appointed Colonel of the 74th Ohio Infantry.
- William Anderson Pile, Methodist Episcopal minister and chaplain of the 1st Missouri Light Artillery. Pile later transferred to the 33rd Missouri Infantry and achieved the rank of major general of volunteers in 1865.
- Albert A. von Puttkammer, German Baptist reverend. Captain von Puttkammer commanded the 11th New York Independent Battery, also called the "Havelock Flying Artillery," and was mindful to lead prayers three times daily.

Confederate Civil War Ministers
- Emmeran Bliemel, German chaplain of the 4th Kentucky, known as "Father Emery." While praying next to a dying soldier on the battlefield at Jonesboro, Father Emery was himself killed by cannon fire.
- T. L. Duke, chaplain of the 19th Mississippi. Duke was promoted to captain of scouts after grabbing a weapon and jumping into the fighting during the Battle of Chancellorsville. He was the only Confederate chaplain to be cited in the Official Records for gallant service.
- H. A. M. Henderson, Methodist minister. Henderson raised his own regiment in response to a Kentucky Methodist minister's sermons on Union superiority. He was commanding officer of Cahaba Prison Camp in Alabama.
- Edward H. Hudson, chaplain of the 6th Texas Cavalry. Hudson was wounded at Corinth, Mississippi, and again at Newnan, Georgia.
- William N. Pendleton, Episcopalian priest of Grace Church in Lexington, Virginia. A brigadier general in charge of Lee's artillery, Pendleton was called "Parson" by his troops. It is said that Pendleton named his cannon "Matthew," "Mark," "Luke," and "John."
- Leonidas Polk, former West Pointer who joined the ministry and rose to bishop of Louisiana. Polk resurrected his military experience to become a lieutenant general and was killed during the Petersburg campaign in 1864.

INFAMOUS FIGURES IN THE CIVIL WAR: KIT CARSON (1809-1868)

Missouri native Christopher Houston Carson had already made a name for himself long before he served the U.S. Army during the Civil War. He was known as a frontier explorer and friend of the Indians.

So, how did Christopher "Kit" Carson find his way from Boone's Lick, Missouri, to Taos, New Mexico? It all started after his father died unexpectedly when Carson was nine years old. To support his family, Kit began a saddle-making apprenticeship. While in the saddle-maker's shop, he had the opportunity to hear frontiersmen talk of their travels.

It wasn't long before young Kit decided to head out to Santa Fe, New Mexico. He settled near Taos and started leading fur-trapping expeditions. He became friendly with the Native Americans, who learned to trust him to keep his word.

On a visit back home to Missouri, Carson met John Charles Frémont, "The Pathfinder." Carson agreed to guide Frémont's explorations through the 1840s. Frémont's reports made the rugged mountain man "Kit Carson" into a national hero.

During the Mexican War Carson again acted as a guide, this time for U.S. Army forces. Then in 1853 he was appointed federal Indian agent for Northern New Mexico, which he held until the Civil War. New Mexico Territory was officially pro-slavery, but the land could not support the kind of plantation operations that required slave labor. So when the Civil War broke out, New Mexicans supported the Union.

In 1861, Carson became lieutenant colonel of the Union Army's First New Mexico Volunteers, about five hundred men.

In early 1862, Confederate forces under General Henry Hopkins Sibley invaded New Mexico with plans to raid gold fields in Colorado and add the captured gold to the Confederate budget. On February 21, 1862, Carson commanded his men in the Battle of

Valverde, with leadership that earned him a brevet promotion even though the Union lost the battle and the Confederates occupied New Mexico. The Southerners eventually abandoned the western territory due to lack of supplies.

In the meantime, Carson was sent to take care of relocating Navajo Indians in Arizona to a newly established reservation in New Mexico. With the "help" of other tribes who hated the Navajos, in 1864 Carson marched almost eight thousand Navajos on a three hundred-mile "Long Walk" to their new home.

After the Civil War, Carson settled in Colorado to a life of ranching. He died in 1868 of an aneurysm, a month after his wife died in childbirth.

Kit Carson Trivia

- Because he started working at such a young age, Kit Carson's formal education was entirely neglected. He did not learn to read and write until serving in the Civil War.
- Carson's first two wives were Native Americans: Arapahoe maiden Grass-Singing, who died of fever, and Cheyenne lass Making Out Road, who divorced him by throwing his saddle out of their tent.
- Carson married his third wife, the young Josefa Jaramillo of Taos, between his Frémont expeditions. He was thirty-four years old; she was not quite half that age.
- The legend of Kit Carson began to build even during his lifetime. He was the theme of many dime novels extolling his strength and bravado, with tales of whipping bears and Indians before breakfast. Kit Carson has also been portrayed through television shows, cartoons, comic books, and movies, including the Wonderful World of Disney's *Kit Carson and the Mountain Men*, starring Robert Reed (also known as Mike Brady) as John C. Frémont.

INFAMOUS FIGURES IN THE CIVIL WAR: JOHN THOMSON FORD (1829-1894)

John Thomson Ford owned Ford's Theater in Washington, D.C. when Abraham Lincoln was assassinated there. He was also, for a short time, considered a "person of interest" in the murder plot.

How did a Baltimore boy, who began his career in the family tobacco business, end up in theater management? After clerking in the family tobacco factory and dabbling in book sales, Ford finally found his calling when he wrote a farce about contemporary life in Richmond. The production of the play, *Richmond As It Is*, was fairly successful, and he was offered a position as business manager of an acting company, traveling with it throughout North America.

Then Ford built a theater on Tenth Street in Washington, D.C. In 1862, it burned down, but Ford built another theater. The new Ford's Theater opened in August 1863, with state-of-the-art equipment to lure top-name actors and productions. Ford's Theater was the venue for 495 performances until that fateful night on April 14, 1865, when John Wilkes Booth forever set his name down in the history books.

How was Ford implicated in Booth's plot? First of all, it was a well-known fact that Ford and Booth were good friends. So there was association there. Then to compound the accusations, at the time of the assassination Ford was away visiting Richmond, where many anti-Lincoln and anti-Union conspirators were known to meet. That would be the entire case against Ford.

Henry Rathbone was a distant cousin to actor Basil Rathbone, who was Margaret Mitchell's first choice to play the leading character, Rhett Butler, in the film version of *Gone With the Wind*. Basil Rathbone was best known for his onscreen portrayals of Robin Hood and Sherlock Holmes.

With that scanty "evidence," Ford was arrested on April 18, along with his brothers Harry Clay Ford and James Ford. John Ford did his best to cooperate and even offered his help in finding the real assassins. He was held in prison for thirty-nine days, then cleared of any charges and released because there was simply no evidence that he had been a part of Booth's plan.

According to Roy Chamlee in *Lincoln's Assassins: A Complete Account of Their Capture, Trial, and Punishment*, the only thing that came close to even being considered as a way of linking Ford to Booth's plot was a statement made by his brother Harry. Harry said that earlier on that historic April day, he had run into Booth on the street outside the theater and mentioned that President Lincoln and General Grant planned to attend a production of *Our American Cousin* that evening and sit in the Presidential box, though as we know, Grant didn't go to the show, after all.

After Ford's release, the United States government seized Ford's theater and gave him $100,000 in payment.

Today, Ford's Theater is again a functioning playhouse, administered by the Ford's Theater Society. It is furnished to look as it did on April 14, 1865, and even has the actual original red damask sofa where Major Henry Rathbone sat in the Presidential box with Lincoln.

The Lincoln Museum is located downstairs in the theater's basement. The collection includes items from Lincoln's visit to Ford's Theater on April 14, 1865, such as Lincoln's suit, Booth's pistol, and the flag that covered Lincoln's coffin.

John T. Ford also built the Academy of Music in Philadelphia, which is still a main concert hall in that city.

INFAMOUS FIGURES IN THE CIVIL WAR: ELIAS HOWE (1819-1867)

By the start of the Civil War, Elias Howe had already made his contribution to society and become a millionaire for patenting the first lock-stitch sewing machine in 1846. His sewing innovation meant that clothes could be produced in factories instead of by hand at home.

Howe used his considerable fortune to support a Union infantry regiment, the 17th Connecticut Volunteers. Howe himself served as a private in the regiment from August 1862 to July 1865.

During his Civil War service, Howe participated in Burnside's "Mud March" of January 1863. Trying to navigate around the Confederate army in Virginia, Burnside's command encountered an unbelievably deteriorated dirt road situation in which a winter storm left a sea of mud for navigation. Wagons mired down in it and some mules actually drowned in the muck.

Although his invention was so revolutionary and so popular that it was widely pirated in the United States and England, "Elias Howe" was not a household name, and "Private Howe" was able to enlist in virtual anonymity.

The Story of Elias Howe and the Sewing Machine

Massachusetts native Elias Howe began his career as a textile mill apprentice in the small town of Spencer. But, after the Panic of 1837 he moved to Boston to apprentice in a machinist's shop. This is how he got his "sewing" experience, then his "machine" experience.

As so often happens, Howe arrived at his groundbreaking innovation simply by following life's circumstances. To help support the family, Howe's wife began accepting hand-sewing work. Watching her stitch, Howe devised a two-thread system that could be automated to create a tightly locked stitch.

He put his system into action, assembling machines to carry out the lock-stitch motion. His workshop burned down, but he continued. His final product could lay down 250 stitches a minute, but it was quite expensive at about $300 per machine.

In 1845, Howe demonstrated the sewing machine in public. To show its capability, he employed five hand seamstresses who were known for their speedy work. Howe's machine out-sewed each of them. But, even with its great promise, the machine was too expensive, and he could not sell even one.

In 1846, Howe patented the lockstitch sewing machine. He headed over to England to try to sell the machine there. He wasn't much of a businessman, though, and ended up conned out of his blueprints and his royalties "across the pond."

So, he returned to America to find that the sale of sewing machines had really picked up in his absence. Unfortunately, he wasn't getting any of the profits—pirates were! One of these successful patent-ignoring entrepreneurs was Isaac Singer.

Howe sued all of the various sewing-machine bootleggers and won his case after a long uphill battle. In 1854, he finally received retroactive royalties from sales of his lockstitch technology. Then, he joined forces with the more marketing-minded Singer, a move that was certainly advantageous for Howe. By 1856, he had earned more than $2 million from sewing-machine sales. This is the money he used to support a regiment during the Civil War.

Howe died in 1867, at the age of forty-eight. That same year, his lockstitch sewing machine won a gold medal at the Paris Exposition. Howe was tapped for the United States National Inventors Hall of Fame in 2004.

Elias Howe did not invent the sewing machine. He devised the lock-stitch approach, and patented his method of mechanizing that technology. Others had built earlier primitive sewing machines, including Walter Hunt, who created an initial repeating rifle and the safety pin.

INFAMOUS FIGURES IN THE CIVIL WAR: PRINCE FELIX AND PRINCESS AGNES SALM-SALM

The Story of Prince Felix (1828–1870)

Prussian-born Prince Felix Constantin Alexander Johann Nepomuk Marie zu Salm-Salm was the youngest son of a minor ruling Prussian prince. Prince Felix received only the best education and entered the Prussian Army straight out of school as a cavalry officer. Consequences of his womanizing, dueling, and gambling compelled him to leave for the Austrian Army and then cross the ocean at the outbreak of the Civil War.

The Story of Princess Agnes (1842–1912)

Records vary on whether Agnes Elisabeth Winona Leclerc Joy was born in 1842 or 1844. They do show that she was an attractive, intelligent, strong-willed woman.

In her youth, the red-headed beauty lived in Havana, Cuba, performing as a stage actress. Later, mean-spirited society women expanded Agnes's myth to include work in the circus as a bareback horse rider.

Felix and Agnes Arrive in Washington, 1861

In America in 1861, Prince Felix was commissioned a colonel as General Louis Blenker's aide-de-camp in the 8th New York (1st German rifles) regiment. But, Blenker's staff didn't trust the foreigner.

In the meantime, Agnes had a habit of riding through the streets of D.C. on a barely-tame mustang, which could have led to the previously-mentioned uncharitable local sentiments. It was on one of these horseback adventures that she caught the eye of Prince Felix Salm-Salm, who arranged a meeting with the lovely young woman.

The Prince Finds His Princess

Felix and Agnes soon fell in love and eloped in a Catholic ceremony at St. Patrick's Church in 1862. Salm-Salm then took command of the 68th New York. When the new groom headed to Tennessee with the 68th New York, his bride went, too.

Soon, Agnes was elbow-deep in nursing assistance in the field hospitals, and she stayed with her husband throughout his Civil War career in the U.S. Army. She became a familiar and welcome face in the army hospital tents. The couple remained with the Union Army until the end of the war, when Felix was promoted to brigadier general.

Next Stop, Mexico

A career soldier, Prince Felix joined the forces of Emperor Maximilian in his attempt to rule Mexico. Princess Salm-Salm followed him there, too. As Maximilian's aide-de-camp, Felix was captured along with the emperor by Mexican republicans retaking government control.

Only by his wife's intervention was Prince Felix spared Maximilian's fate of execution. Agnes personally begged Benito Juárez for their release. Juárez promised to save her husband's life, and he did. She was not able to stretch the same luck to Emperor Maximilian.

The year after the ordeal, Prince Salm-Salm published *My Diary in Mexico* in 1867, including the *Last Days of the Emperor Maximilian, with Leaves from the Diary of the Princess Salm Salm*.

Back to Prussia

Prince Felix returned to his homeland and the Prussian army, rejoining as a major. Princess Agnes followed her Prince once more, where he joined in the fighting during the Franco-Prussian War. Again, Agnes found herself nursing wounded soldiers in field hospitals.

This time, Felix was not so lucky. He was killed in action during the battle of Gravelotte in the Franco-Prussian War in August 1870.

After Felix's death, Agnes remained in the service of the Prussian Army, and helped raise a hospital brigade. She never returned to the United States, but later remarried (and soon divorced). In 1875, Princess Salm-Salm published *Ten Years of My Life,* about her adventures as the wife of Prince Felix, and she died in present-day Germany in 1912.

NATIVE AMERICANS IN THE CIVIL WAR

About 3,600 Native Americans fought for the Union during the Civil War. Some joined as a tribe, such as the Confederacy's First Cherokee Mounted Rifles and the Union's 1st Michigan Company K. Others enlisted privately of their own accord, such as Pequot Austin George, who signed on with the Connecticut Colored Volunteers.

While their counterparts were doing their duty to preserve the Union, other Native Americans saw the Civil War as an opportunity to take back their own lands while federal troops were occupied elsewhere. This led to "Indian Trouble" in the West.

Two of the most well-known Native Americans in the Civil War were Colonel Ely Parker and Brigadier General Stand Watie.

Union Commander: Lieutenant Colonel Ely Parker (1828–1895)

Ely Parker was the highest-ranking Native American officer in the Union Army. A full-blooded Seneca Indian born on a New York reservation, Parker was educated in a Baptist Mission school, where he adopted his teacher's first name. As an adult, he lobbied in Washington for Native American tribal rights.

Although he had worked in government positions, including as a civil engineer on construction of the Erie Canal, when the Civil War began Parker was not allowed to enlist in the Union Army because of his heritage.

But, then, the need for soldiers increased, and the U.S. Army "reorganized" its enrollment requirements. Parker happened to be an old friend of Ulysses S. Grant from his civil engineering days, and Grant snapped him up as a military secretary. Parker was given a commission as a lieutenant colonel.

Parker participated in the Petersburg campaign and was chosen to transcribe the terms of Robert E. Lee's surrender to Grant at Appomattox Court House.

Confederate Commander: Brigadier General Stand Watie (1806–1871)

Georgia native and plantation owner Stand Watie was a leader of the Cherokee Nation and one of the Native Americans who had agreed to the treaty removing tribes to Oklahoma along the Trail of Tears.

Watie was a three-quarter blood Cherokee. He organized the largest Native American force in the Confederate Army, the First Cherokee Mounted Rifles, consisting of about eight hundred Native Americans.

The First Cherokee Mounted Rifles participated in many battles toward the end of the war, and when he was promoted to brigadier general in May of 1864, Watie became the only Native American in the Confederacy to achieve that rank.

One notable battle involving the First Cherokee Mounted Rifles was Pea Ridge, Arkansas, in 1862. In addition to Watie's regiment, other Cherokee tribes were recruited for help. Not all the Cherokee groups had friendly relationships, though, and at some point during the fighting, they turned their guns on each other rather than the advancing Union soldiers.

Watie holds the claim of being the last Confederate general to surrender. That's because when he heard that Lee had relinquished his sword, instead of doing so himself, Watie fled. He surrendered on June 23, 1865, to Union Lieutenant Colonel Asa Matthews.

1st Michigan Sharpshooters, Company K

Company K of the 1st Michigan was the largest unit of Native Americans in the Union Army. Made up mostly of Chippewa and Ottawa Indians from the shores of Lake Michigan, the group was known for their precision shooting, as well as their tough fighting and living.

Although they were first assigned to rear-line services such as patrolling prisoners of war, they finally saw real action during the Wilderness Campaign. During the Crater debacle outside of Petersburg, Company K of the 1st Michigan held their posts while most other Union soldiers ran or tried to run.

NOTABLE CIVIL WAR MOVIES

Almost as long as movies have been made, the Civil War has figured prominently in them. Here are some notable achievements in Hollywood's telling of various aspects from the war without end:

Gone with the Wind: It is safe to say that no book or movie has colored the perception (and misperception) of the Civil War with as much influence as this 1939 box-office smash starring Clark Gable and Vivien Leigh. Based on Margaret Mitchell's best-selling novel, it reaffirmed the false myth of cheerful slaves and servants in a South filled with grand mansions and plantations. Still, Gable's performance for the ages, the beautiful, lush cinematography, and epic sweep make it a must-see movie.

Birth of a Nation: This epic, released in 1915, introduced modern film techniques while glorifying the South's "Lost Cause" in infamous fashion. Director D.W. Griffith's historical perspective proves to be as flawed as his moviemaking sense is brilliant.

Gettysburg: Based on Michael Shaara's classic account ("The Killer Angels") of the war's seminal battle, this four-hour 1993 release stars Jeff Daniels as Union hero Joshua Lawrence Chamberlain.

Glory: Director Ed Zwick's 1989 account of the heroic 54th Massachusetts volunteer regiment of African-American soldiers stirs the heart—and the mind. Denzel Washington, who earned an Oscar for his performance, leads a cast that includes Matthew Broderick, Andre Braugher, and Morgan Freeman.

The Red Badge of Courage: Based on Stephen Crane's classic novel chronicling the soldier's terrifying experience, this John Huston-helmed film, released in 1951, starred World War II hero Audie Murphy.

Gods and Generals: Like *Gettysburg*, Ronald F. Maxwell directed this Civil War epic that clocks in right under four hours. Based on Jeffrey Shaara's novel depicting the battles of 1861-63, which serves as a prequel to his father's Killer Angels depiction of Gettysburg, Maxwell's film includes contributions from 7,500 war reenactors as well as Jeff Daniels and Robert Duvall.

Andersonville: Made for Ted Turner's cable network in 1996, this three-hour movie, directed by John Frankenheimer, offers an unsparing look at the notorious prisoner-of-war camp in southern Georgia. Frankenheimer steers a talented, but matinee idol-free cast. Character actor William H. Macy's is the lone name casual movie fans will recognize.

Cold Mountain: An uneven adaptation of Charles Frazier's popular literary best-seller, this 2003 film boasts strong performances from an all-star cast, including Jude Law, Nicole Kidman, Renee Zellweger (who won an Oscar for her role), Natalie Portman, and Donald Sutherland. Anthony Minghella (*The English Patient*) directs.

Ride with the Devil: Ang Lee's 1999 movie following the bloody Border Wars in Missouri and Kansas between the Bushwhackers and Jayhawkers stars Tobey Maguire and Skeet Ulrich.

North and South: A twelve-hour TV mini-series originally aired on ABC, this Emmy winner based on John Jakes' best-selling trilogy stars Patrick Swayze, Kirstie Alley, and David Carradine.

"Bloody Reality"

Until the Battle of Shiloh in Tennessee in spring of 1862, a fair number of military leaders, politicians, and citizens in both the North and the South still believed the war would be a quick one. They also expected minimal bloodshed, as they expected one side or the other would give up the fight.

So much for conventional wisdom.

The grim carnage that erupted in April 1862 followed Ulysses S. Grant's victories at Fort Henry and Fort Donelson in Tennessee. In pursuit of Albert Sidney Johnston and the Confederate forces who had headed for a key railroad supply line in Mississippi, Grant committed a colossal blunder—and was rescued by the man who would become his right arm through the rest of the war, William T. Sherman.

P. G. T. Beauregard, the lead commander during the attack on Fort Sumter and a key player at First Bull Run, became Johnston's second-in-command, sent west because of public critiques of Jefferson Davis. Grant, still under Henry Halleck, took forty thousand men to nearby Pittsburg Landing, Tennessee. His headquarters sat next to Shiloh Meeting House, a Methodist church. Shiloh, a Hebrew word meaning "place of peace," became the name of the battle after some of the heaviest early fighting took place near the church.

Grant, who arrived at Pittsburg Landing in March, had been told by Halleck to stay put until additional forces arrived.

The Union had little more than a prayer when Johnston and Beauregard surprised Grant and his men with an attack on April 6. Assuming the Confederates were regrouping, Grant never bothered with extensive fortifications or patrols. When the rebel army arrived with forty-four thousand men and a furious assault, Union troops fell into disarray. Men scrambled for cover. The Confederates routed the Union.

Gradually, though, the Union found some footing as the

Confederates became disoriented and entangled on the bloody, messy battlefield.

In the afternoon, Johnston was shot while leading a charge, hit by a bullet in the leg as he rode his horse. He initially ignored the wound—a decision that cost him his life. Johnston had been shot in the femoral artery. He turned pale and his men rushed to help him, but Johnston had already lost too much blood. He died that afternoon. Beauregard assumed command and sent a message to Davis in the evening that Johnston was dead, but the Confederates had won a key victory.

He was half-right.

Grant, ignoring his enemy's script, resumed the battle the following day. Overnight more Union troops had arrived, strengthening Grant's forces to fifty-four thousand men as Beauregard's shrank to thirty-four thousand. Sherman, regarded as little more than a hothead by most in the Union army, rallied the troops. Leading a counteroffensive, they eventually sent Beauregard and his men in retreat, turning an all but certain defeat into a standoff, if not outright victory. A month later, Beauregard would abandon his Mississippi position, giving the Union possession of a key strategic location.

More than anything, Shiloh delivered a strong message to political leaders, citizens, and both armies. This would be a long, bloody affair. The two armies suffered a combined 23,746 casualties, surpassing the number of casualties America had endured in all its previous wars combined. It was a sobering statistic, though Halleck used it to prove Grant as the opposite—that is, as a drunk.

Fearing Grant's rising stature and hoping to fuel critics who considered Grant too willing to sacrifice men in battle, Halleck maneuvered to have Grant reassigned. Grant had decided to quit the army in disgust. Instead, Sherman talked him out if it—setting the stage for a future partnership that would quash the Confederate rebellion and win the war for the Union.

As Grant led the miraculous turnaround at Shiloh, another Union victory was added in the western theater at Island Number 10, which was located on the Mississippi River at the northwestern extreme of Tennessee near the Kentucky border. Union commander

John Pope and Andrew Foote—the man who had helped Grant capture the two Tennessee forts (Henry and Donelson)—dug a path to and connected with an adjacent bayou to get around the Confederates. It worked and opened the river all the way to Fort Pillow, marking another advance in the Union's campaign to divide and conquer the South.

Johnny Surratt

The orders that Bennett H. Young supposedly followed when raiding St. Albans were hastily delivered to Montreal to provide the basis of his defense. They were couriered to Canada by "Little Johnny" Surratt.

The Surratt family owned a boardinghouse in Washington. They were known Confederate sympathizers. If the name sounds familiar, Johnny Surratt was Mary Surratt's son. That would be the same Mary Surratt who was hanged as part of the conspiracy trial for assassinating President Lincoln.

Prisoners of War and War Camps

More than 400,000 soldiers, Union and Confederate, were held as prisoners at some time during the Civil War. More than forty-five thousand of those died in prison. This is about a 14 percent mortality rate. Together, the two sides had more than 150 facilities to hold prisoners of war.

All prisoners who survived told of over-crowding, suffering from filth, hunger, insect infestation, and diseases. Men died from malnutrition, the elements, disease, and untended wounds. It was heartbreakingly common to see prisoners released at the end of the war weighing less than a hundred pounds.

Rations for prisoners were already sub-par, and some prison officials withheld food for punishment. For that reason, many captives ate anything they could get their hands on, including cats, dogs, rats, and bugs. Malnourished prisoners suffered from scurvy, diarrhea, pneumonia, and smallpox.

By 1864, everything was scarce in the South. Some of the reason for withholding food from Northern prisoners is because there wasn't much food for anyone. But, regardless, in 1864, U.S. Secretary of War Stanton ordered that Confederate prisoners of war held in the North would not get any more food than Northern prisoners of war held in the South were afforded.

Some prisons were established forts that had been converted, others were cheaply-built barracks, and still others were open land enclosed with an imposing stockade fences. As far as open stockades, some provided tents, while others left it to the captured soldiers to provide their own shelter the best way they could.

At times, prisoners used what they had brought with them to barter, trade, or buy supplies. At other times, there was nothing to be had. Officers fared slightly better than enlisted men. Both North and South housed captured officers in their own quarters, sometimes even in completely separate prisons.

GETTING OUT OF PRISON

Escaped Union soldiers relied on Union sympathizers to help get them back to Northern borders. They also found allies in Confederate deserters, who were relieved to help anyone who wasn't a conscription agent looking to take them back to the front. Those caught trying to escape risked punishment ranging from riding a rail, to hanging by the thumbs, to death.

Escape Attempts

- Confederate guards at Andersonville once discovered a prisoner-dug tunnel. One of the prisoners had probably turned informant, singing to the guards.
- Rock Island Prison, in the middle of the Mississippi River, posed special escape challenges. After tunneling out, escapees had to swim the four hundred-foot-wide river. Despite this, forty-one desperate men managed to escape and avoid recapture.
- When 107 Confederate prisoners found themselves transported on the side-wheel steamer Maple Leaf from Norfolk to Fort Delaware prison, they devised a plan. As soon as Union sailors let down their guard, the rebels took over the boat and headed south. Without enough coal to make the trip, seventy-one able prisoners abandoned ship, leaving behind those too wounded to survive. With federal agents in hot pursuit, the group navigated sixty miles of Virginia's Great Dismal Swamp—on foot—reaching Richmond and freedom seventeen days later.

Prisoner Exchanges

At first, there were no formal exchanges because Lincoln would not recognize the Confederacy as a separate nation. By 1862, the armies had agreed that all prisoners would be exchanged within ten days of capture. Enlisted men could be exchanged for an officer; a general was worth up to sixty privates, a major general worth forty privates, and on down, a noncommissioned officer for two privates. Privates were traded one-for-one.

About 200,000 soldiers from both sides were freed through prisoner exchanges. While most prisoners were released by exchange, there wasn't a lot of need for military prisons.

Paroles

"Parole" meant being released and agreeing not to take up arms again until officially exchanged for an enemy prisoner. Soldiers who returned to the field before they were exchanged risked being shot or hanged. Parole was an honor system that served to keep the prisons empty and gave the soldiers a reprieve until they were told to report back to duty.

For instance, rather than transport thirty-one thousand captured Confederate soldiers from Vicksburg to Union prison camps, Grant paroled the whole bunch. Some of these same men were recaptured at the next battle, which infuriated Grant. He decided to quit paroling Confederates until they agreed to honor the bargain.

The End of Paroles

The parole system changed in 1863 when Jefferson Davis declared that neither blacks nor whites serving in any colored regiment would be exchanged or paroled by the Confederacy. Lincoln responded by ending exchange and parole altogether.

Lincoln also hoped that keeping so many Southern soldiers off the battlefields would cripple the Confederate Army. In the process, he ended up damaging many Northern soldiers who were taken prisoner of war. Now, there was a need for a place to house prisoners. Both sides began designating makeshift prisons.

Hostages

Hostages started to be used when captured Confederate sailors were tried, convicted of piracy, and sentenced to death. Jefferson Davis and Secretary of War Judah Benjamin quickly informed the United States government that it would hold an equal number of Union inmates from Castle Thunder Prison as "hostages" until the Confederate sailors were safely released. Therefore, if any Confederate were executed, his designated "hostage" would also be executed in turn.

Union Soldiers Imprisoned in the South

Of 194,000 Union troops captured by the South, thirty thousand died. That's a mortality rate in Confederate prisons of about 15.5 percent.

Andersonville

With a death rate of 35 percent, Camp Sumter (as it was officially named) held the dubious honor of being the absolutely worst prison on either side of the war. Of forty-five thousand men imprisoned, almost fifteen thousand died; at one point, soldiers died at the rate of one hundred per day.

Originally a fifteen-foot tall stockade around sixteen acres of open land, it was designed for ten thousand men. Within four months, with four hundred new prisoners arriving daily, it was expanded to twenty-six acres. Within six months of opening, it held more than thirty-three thousand Union prisoners.

There were no shelters or relief from the Georgia summer sun or rain, no clothing, and no medical care. Prisoners were forbidden from building shelters. The only water came from a branch of Sweetwater Creek. It functioned as the drinking and washing water—and the latrine.

Andersonville's commandant, Henry Wirz, instituted the "dead line," a line fifteen feet from the stockade walls. Anyone crossing the dead line would be shot dead. Wirz was the only man tried, convicted, and executed for war crimes.

One Andersonville survivor, Union Sergeant Boston Corbett, was later in the party sent to track down John Wilkes Boothe after Lincoln's assassination.

Libby Prison

- A converted cotton warehouse that belonged to Libby & Son Ship Chandlers & Grocers, it was located near downtown

Richmond. Libby's three-story eight-room capacity held 1,200 officers.

- Libby's commandant, Lieutenant David H. Todd, was Mary Todd Lincoln's half-brother.
- One guard, Dick Turner, reportedly shot anyone who went to a window for light and air.
- The largest mass prison escape of the war was from Libby Prison. Union Colonels Thomas E. Rose and Abel Streight led 107 other prisoners out a tunnel they had dug from the prison's cellar. Of the men, forty-eight were recaptured.
- Union sympathizer Elizabeth "Crazy Bet" Van Lew visited Northern soldiers at Libby Prison to get troop information, deliver food and medicine, and even helped a few escape.
- New York Congressman Alfred Ely attended the First Battle of Bull Run as a spectator. At the end of the battle, he was captured and imprisoned at Libby.

Castle Pinckney

Located about a mile off shore from Charleston, it was the first Confederate prison camp. Union captives were treated well here at the beginning, but that didn't last long.

Castle Thunder

A large brick, converted tobacco warehouse near Richmond, it was used primarily for confining political prisoners. Prison guards here had a reputation for brutality.

Camp Ford

An open-stockade style prison near Tyler, Texas. Prisoners were responsible for building their own shelters. At its peak, Camp Ford held 4,900 men; about three hundred died.

Belle Isle Prison

A tent village located near Richmond in the middle of the James River. Although intended to hold only three thousand enlisted men, its population eventually reached double that number, and more. As many as thirty prisoners died here each day.

The island's location in the rapids of the James River made escape very dangerous. Many men who tried drowned before reaching safety.

Salisbury

An abandoned cotton factory in North Carolina, it consisted of open stockades. Designed for a capacity of two thousand, it soon held ten thousand prisoners. The mortality rate at Salisbury was 34 percent.

One Salisbury survivor was war correspondent Albert D. Richardson of *The New York Tribune*, captured at Vicksburg. After eighteen months, he managed to escape and walk four hundred miles to a Union camp.

Locations of other Confederate Prison Camps

Virginia	Danville
	Lynchburg
Louisiana	Shreveport
Georgia	Millen
	Macon
	Blackshear
Alabama	Mobile
Texas	Hempstead
South Carolina	Charleston
	Florence
	Columbia

Confederate Soldiers Imprisoned in the North

Of 214,000 Confederate soldiers held by the Union, twenty-six thousand died. That's a mortality rate in Union prisons of about 12 percent.

Elmira

Located in upstate New York. At 24 percent, it had one of the worst mortality rates; of the 12,123 Confederate men held here, 2,963 died. It was designed to hold five thousand men. Death came from starvation and diseases born of the terrible living conditions.

During a bitterly cold winter, guards deliberately withheld clothes and blankets sent by the prisoners' families. Hundreds of men froze to death. Survivors called it "Hellmira."

Point Lookout

The largest Union POW camp, located in Maryland, it was designed for ten thousand men to live in tents, as there were no barracks. It often held twice that number.

Old Capitol Prison

This Sixteenth Street building was actually the former capitol building of the United States converted into a detention house. Spies Rose O'Neal Greenhow and Belle Boyd were both held here.

Camp Chase

Near Columbus, Ohio, these barracks were meant to hold four thousand prisoners. By the war's end, more than nine thousand men were imprisoned here. As many as forty Confederate prisoners died each day.

Johnson's Island

Located in Ohio's Sandusky Bay, Lake Erie. An island three miles from land, guarded by a fifteen-foot stockade plus an eight-foot ditch. No matter, though. So many Confederates escaped from here that authorities offered an immediate $50 bounty to any citizen who captured escaped prisoners.

Ohio State Penitentiary

The State Pen in Columbus began housing Confederate prisoners when John Morgan's Raiders were captured and a truly secure confinement space was needed to hold them. Morgan's men were housed with the general prison population. Within a matter of months, all prisoners of war were transferred out to regular POW camps.

Camp Morton

Enclosed barracks near Indianapolis, Indiana, Camp Morton was regarded as one of the best-run prison camps, North or South. Nevertheless, more than 1,700 Confederates died here.

Camp Douglas

Barracks near Chicago housed more than thirty thousand Confederate prisoners. More than six thousand men died before it was destroyed by fire in December 1863.

The land where Camp Douglas was located is now the site of, among other things, Comiskey Park, home of the Chicago White Sox.

One Camp Douglas survivor was Confederate soldier Henry M. Stanley, famous for the "Dr. Livingstone, I presume?" quote.

Rock Island

It was located in the middle of the Mississippi River between Davenport, Iowa, and Rock Island, Illinois. With no medical attendants, 1,800 Confederate prisoners and almost two hundred guards died in one smallpox epidemic here. During Rock Island's nineteen months in operation, the mortality rate was more than 77 percent.

Fort Delaware

Located on Pea Patch Island in the Delaware River in view of New Jersey and built on a bog, the ground was too soggy to support the barracks, which were always close to tumbling over. This prison was the most dreaded by the South. More than 2,400 Confederates died there, many from typhoid fever.

Fort Monroe

Located in Virginia, Fort Monroe was the only federal installation in Virginia that was never controlled by Confederates. Confederate officers were held here.

Fort McHenry

Located in Baltimore Harbor, this is the same Fort McHenry where Francis Scott Key watched the rockets' red glare and wrote "The Star Spangled Banner" during the War of 1812.

Locations of other Union Prison Camps

Illinois	Illinois State Penitentiary in Alton
Massachusetts	Fort Warren in Boston Harbor
New York	Fort Lafayette
Missouri	Gratiot Street Prison in St. Louis

BANISHMENT AND DEPORTATION

Lincoln officially banished Clement Vallandigham from the United States. Many others, North and South, military and civilian, were also banished. Although deportation meant involuntary physical departure, it was not always from the nation; sometimes it was only from the home or state.

Most Civil War evictions were illegal. But when someone—or a whole troop—stands over you with loaded guns, it's hard to argue legality. Sometimes eviction was enforced against one particular person or family. At other times, a whole population was deported. While most evictions were not recorded, and the number of people relocated certainly weren't, some of them we know about:

- Brigadier General John Pope declared in Missouri that anyone taking up arms against the United States would be banished to Mexico.
- The Confederate Senate introduced a bill naming as "alien enemies" anyone loyal to the United States. It proposed ordering alien enemies to leave the Confederacy within forty days.
- Brigadier General James McPherson declared in Vicksburg that anyone insulting or disrespecting the president, the federal government, or the U.S. flag would be "fined, banished, or imprisoned."
- Brigadier General Thomas Ewing, Jr., ordered mass deportation of hundreds in Missouri counties known to harbor Southern sympathizers.
- Spy Rose O'Neal Greenhow was undoubtedly guilty of treason. Many federal officers shared secrets while "visiting" her. They all worried that if she was tried, then they would be implicated. So she was not tried, but instead simply banished.
- Union Major General Benjamin Butler was so upset when a New Orleans woman laughed at a Union officer's funeral, he exiled her to Ship Island off the Mississippi coast for "unpatriotic levity."

DETECTIVE AND SPY ALLAN PINKERTON (1819-1884)

Scotland native Allan Pinkerton settled in Chicago, working as a cooper (barrel maker) and an Underground Railroad stationmaster.

While cutting wood for barrels, Pinkerton happened on and captured a counterfeiting ring. Soon he was working with the Chicago police and became that city's first detective. With character descriptions like "born suspicious of his own parents," Pinkerton was a natural.

In 1850, he opened Pinkerton National Detective Agency, focusing on railroad security and train robbers. The Agency's logo was an "all-seeing eye," with the motto "We Never Sleep." Pinkerton's nickname, "The Eye," soon became associated with all detectives, or "Private Eyes."

Working on the railroad in 1861, Pinkerton warned Lincoln of an assassination plot brewing in Baltimore on the newly elected president's route to the White House for inauguration. So instead of joining a grand parade from Baltimore into Washington, Lincoln, escorted by Pinkerton, quietly slipped into the capital in the middle of the night. Many opponents criticized Lincoln for his anti-grand entrance into town.

Pinkerton became George McClellan's personal secret agent, known by the code name Major E. J. Allen. Pinkerton met the future general in 1857 while working for the Illinois Central Railroad.

As McClellan's source of information, Pinkerton claimed to spend days in disguise behind Confederate lines. Unfortunately, Pinkerton also relied on word-of-mouth from escaped slaves and put too much emphasis on redundant and incorrect reports. His faulty intelligence at Yorktown, grossly overestimating the number of Confederate troops, scared McClellan, who hesitated to attack after the First Bull Run.

Lincoln was frustrated with McClellan's caution, and removed the general from command. Pinkerton returned to his detective agency in Chicago and resumed his railroad security operations.

ANDREWS' RAIDERS AND THE GREAT LOCOMOTIVE CHASE

For about six hours on April 12, 1862, twenty-two Union soldiers captured a Confederate railroad.

Under Kentucky civilian James J. Andrews, who had made a name for himself smuggling quinine into the Confederacy and smuggling intelligence out, the band of men set out to cut off Chattanooga from reinforcements and supplies.

Their plan was simple. They would capture the General, a train on the Western and Atlantic line, burning bridges and destroying rails behind them as they traveled north.

While the Confederates botched early opportunities to impede everything before it happened, in the end, Andrews' men botched the whole enterprise worse (watch for examples of Confederate bungling as you read).

The men planned to meet in Marietta, Georgia, where they would board the wood-burning steam locomotive. Many planned to walk there, but some hopped on a Confederate troop train—and weren't even noticed (one).

To avoid suspicion, the raiders bought tickets for different stations along the line. When the train reached Big Shanty, present-day Kennesaw, it made a planned breakfast stop.

With most passengers and the conductor down the street eating, Andrews stole the General, with its fuel and water, empty boxcars, passenger cars, and a few passengers. Confederate guards happened to be training nearby. They saw this play out, but didn't do anything (two).

The General started pulling away. The train foreman alerted the conductor and crew, who were soon running the platform chasing their train. Confederates guarding the station finally, slowly, got off a few shots at the disappearing locomotive (three).

On board the General, the raiders stopped from time to time to tear up tracks and cut telegraph lines. Back at Big Shanty, the conductor hurriedly gave chase, and a valiant effort he made! He hopped on a push-car and pumped it until hitting destroyed tracks. He ran on foot for a while until he could hop another train.

This went on until he met the southbound locomotive, the Texas. All the Western and Atlantic crews knew each other, so it was easy enough for the General's conductor to flag down the Texas and explain the situation.

Remember, the General was heading north; the Texas was heading south. There wasn't time or a place to turn the Texas around, so she ran in reverse. And still she ran faster than the General.

Andrews realized the Texas was gaining on them; he stopped twice to unhitch boxcars in hopes of slowing down the Confederates. But, still the Texas chugged on. The high-speed chase continued; the two trains even approached the unbelievable speed of sixty miles per hour—and one of them was running backward!

The fun and games for Andrews' Raiders weren't destined to last. They didn't even reach the Tennessee state line before the General ran out of firewood and water. As little boys who play with trains can tell you, without steam, a steam engine won't go.

Andrews and his men did the best thing they could—they jumped off the train and ran like rabbits into the woods. Before long, they were all captured, not as prisoners of war, but because they were wearing civilian clothes, they were taken as spies. After a quick trial, they were found guilty and sentenced to hang.

PostScript: Of the raiders, nineteen were awarded the first Congressional Medals of Honor. Andrews, a civilian, was not one of them.

In the 1950s, Fess Parker portrayed Andrews in Disney's version of the escapade, *The Great Locomotive Chase*, also starring Slim Pickens.

CRESCENT CITY COLLAPSE

Before New Orleans suffered at the hands of Hurricane Katrina's destructive path in 2005, it endured the combined forces of David Farragut and Benjamin "Beast" Butler. The latter's nickname makes him sound more like a modern-day professional wrestler rather than a military leader in charge of a captured city.

New Orleans, located at the mouth of the Mississippi River, stood as the South's largest port and largest city. Farragut, an expert naval commander, assembled a thirty-eight-boat armada of frigates, gunboats, schooners, and sloops and began a fierce assault on two forts near the approach to the city. After a week of bombardment, Farragut and his fleet made it past the remaining, scattered Confederate opposition and claimed the city on April 25. During the course of his attack, Farragut lost one ship and suffered a light casualty total of 184 men.

Butler and his men marched into New Orleans and imposed onerous martial rule. When a citizen dumped a chamber pot on Farragut's head, Butler, in a fit of pique, heaped indignity upon the hapless New Orleanians. His most infamous decree was that any woman displaying hostile attitudes toward Union soldiers was to be considered a prostitute—and handled in a manner consistent with that designation.

Enraged residents took to calling Butler "Beast" and often put his picture inside of their chamber pots. The Union commander also was known as "Spoons," a snide reference to his predilection for seizing valuables from private homes. Butler, though, represented a small problem next to the South's devastating losses in the early part of 1862. Much of the Mississippi River rested in Union hands, as did the Cumberland and Tennessee Rivers and the largest port and city. The Union had cause for optimism.

Camp Life

My Dearest Martha:

It's awfully hot here in camp these summer days. We while away all the days and days between battles, trying to keep ourselves occupied. The guys have worked real hard to come up with things to do to pass all the free time.

We like to play cards. (I'm very sorry that I lost all my month's wages on the last poker game. I know that $13 would have helped you out a lot, Martha.)

The good news is that now I don't have any more money left to gamble on some of the many things we lay wagers against here. If I had any money, I could bet on boxing matches, horse races, and cockfights. I don't even have anything left to buy a pound of coffee (it's up to $12 now) or sugar from the sutlers, who follow our encampments around from place to place. They charge far too much for their wares, anyway.

The craziest thing you've ever seen would be the louse races. I hate for you to know this, but there's plenty of lice around here to find competitors for the races. We turn a tin plate upside down and put the tiny pests on top. Whichever louse runs off the plate edge first, wins. Tompkins always seemed to win, and we finally figured out his secret: he heats up his plate first, and his little critter runs right off.

We love to play a new game called "baseball." We use a board taken from a barrel as a "bat" to hit a "ball," which is usually a walnut with twine wrapped around and around it, and then we run from "base" to "base." All the enlisted soldiers here in camp are serious about winning and a game can be as bloody as battle some days.

Martha, a lot of the men here seek other entertainment with the "camp followers," pretty girls who hope to make some money. But, you know your loving husband is not interested in anyone but you. I leave the "horizontal refreshment" to the less-devoted men around here.

And, they're not the only people who keep up with us. Some wives and other civilians follow our camps and set up nearby, further from danger. Civilian women are not allowed in the military area unless they are escorted, and they go back to their nicer encampments at night to relax away from the crudeness that we have grown accustomed to here.

Even at night, it's so hot that we try to leave the flaps up on our tent to get some air. But, with the recent summer rains, we've had to keep the flaps down, to try to keep out the mud. And, Martha, let me tell you, a mighty powerful smell can build up overnight in our closed tent.

We're low on supplies, so we have about twenty men crammed into one twelve-man tent, which is shaped a lot like those Indian tepees that you see in your picture books. Between us all, none having bathed since I can't remember when, we can put off some awfully noxious odors.

Martha, you take care of yourself. I sure wish I could help out there at home, instead of spending all this time lolling around here doing nothing. I know you are working hard to run the farm, and I am going to try to get a furlough soon to come home to celebrate the baby's birthday.

I remain ever yours,
Johnnie

OTHER ENTERTAINMENT

Cyprians ★ *Fallen Angels* ★ *Daughters of Eve* ★ *Gay Young Chicks*

No matter what they called themselves, prostitutes were popular with lonely soldiers. Officers discouraged frequenting the oldest profession, but to no avail. For one thing, girls were readily available. In fact, soldiers had their own code for visiting women of ill repute: "horizontal refreshment."

Soldiers on leave often visited brothels, which they called "going down the line." Wherever they went on furlough, girls were ready, willing, and able in all the big cities. For instance, the many prostitutes in Richmond and Baltimore openly displayed their wares, hanging out boardinghouse windows to lure men in.

In Washington, D.C., by the second year of war, more than 450 houses of ill repute were in business, with names such as "the Ironclad," "Fort Sumter," "Madam Russell's Bake Oven," "the Haystack," "the Wolf's Den," and "Headquarters USA," all in an area within sight of the White House. This was called Marble Alley. By the end of the war, an estimated five thousand girls were working in the nation's capital.

In addition to Washington's "red-light district," Nashville and Memphis set up areas for prostitution in an effort to control spread of venereal diseases. Working girls could register with the health department, and with a clean bill of health and frequent follow-up exams, were allowed to practice their trade.

Prostitutes were also known to visit military camps in specially equipped wagons, with the impeccable timing to arrive on payday. The Light sisters—Kate, Anna, and Matilda—left their father's house of pleasure in Washington to follow the Union troops to Gettysburg. Other girls also followed troops, temporarily relocating to nearby towns where soldiers might be stationed for a while or where the boys were likely to go on furlough.

A WORD OR TWO ON CAMP TENTS

Sibley Tent

At first, both sides used the Sibley tent, named after Confederate general and inventor Henry H. Sibley. Shaped like the Plains Indian tepee, it was conical, with a center pole, about eighteen feet around and twelve feet tall. A circular opening at the top allowed ventilation and a cone-shaped stove provided heat. Men slept with their feet to the center and heads out along the walls.

Wedge Tent

Smaller and easier to carry, the wedge tent was a six-foot length of canvas draped over a horizontal pole and staked to the ground at the sides. Flaps closed over each end.

Dog Tent

Tents open at either end were known as "dog tents," because there was just enough room for two men and a dog (the forerunner of the smaller "pup tents" of World War I). Two soldiers each carried a piece of heavy canvas, one with a row of buttons, the other with buttonholes. The two pieces buttoned together to make one tent. The canvas was suspended from a center pole or line suspended between two tree branches with Y-shaped forks that served as uprights.

A-Frame Tent

The A-frame was larger and higher, with a front entrance that closed and secured with flaps. It was used by officers or as a general-purpose tent.

Wall Tent

The wall tent had short canvas walls at the ends for water runoff. In hot weather, the walls could be raised to allow a breeze.

CAMP MEDICINE: DISEASES, AILMENTS, AND WORSE

Diseases

Truly, soldiers had more to worry about from illness than the enemy. Disease, not bullets, was by far the biggest killer of all. For every one soldier killed in battle, two more died of disease.

A big problem in the field was proper sanitation. Clean drinking water was rarely found. In fact, all too often, drinking and bathing water became "commingled" with latrine water. Contaminated water along with poor hygiene invariably contributed to illness.

- Contagious diseases – Because army camps were close quarters, contagious diseases such as typhoid, diphtheria, and malaria could devastate a site within days.
- Childhood diseases – Many farm-boys-turned-soldiers had never before been exposed to measles, mumps, and chicken pox.
- Scurvy – Lack of fresh fruit and vegetables often led to outbreaks from vitamin C deficiency.
- Dysentery – In one year, 995 out of every one thousand Union soldiers contracted diarrhea and dysentery.
- Venereal disease – One in ten Union soldiers was treated for syphilis or gonorrhea (enough said).
- Blood poisoning – Improper sterilization during surgery led to sepsis.
- Pneumonia – Many soldiers recuperating from battle wounds developed secondary pneumonia.
- Homesickness – Not a diagnosable-and-treatable condition, homesickness was still a very real pain felt by the majority of soldiers. In fact, the Union desertion rate eventually reached two hundred a day.

WAR WOUNDS

Sadly, and almost unbelievably, surgeons of the early 1860s did not know about sterilization. Army surgeons would leave from attending one patient, go straight to the next wounded, and never stop to even wipe their hands or clean their instruments. Many soldiers who died from wounds in battle actually died from infection after surgery.

The quick solution to most limb wounds was amputation, often without morphine or chloroform. Surgeons of the day believed that anesthesia caused complications and even led to gangrene (whereas we now know that unsanitary conditions can lead to gangrene).

Therefore, instead of any anesthesia, either because none was available or the surgeon didn't believe in using it, soldiers were given a bullet or piece of cloth to bite while the procedure was performed. Understandably, surgeons perfected the art of speedy amputation, both for the patient's sake and because there were so many wounded to tend after a battle.

More than half of patients who underwent thigh amputation died, usually from blood loss and infection. The safest amputation was of the finger, with an almost 98 percent survival rate.

Even though use of anesthesia was not guaranteed, Army doctors did have some drugs of choice which they administered. Most of them, we now know, did more harm than good:

- Arsenic (now known as a poison)
- Strychnine (now known as a poison)
- Calomel (mercury!)
- Opium (now known as an addictive narcotic)
- Whiskey — to prevent shock (actually, a popular prescription with the troops)

WHAT SOLDIERS ATE

At the beginning of the war, as with many things, food rations started out on an even and more–than–merely–acceptable level. All things considered, soldiers for both sides ate well enough.

Union Soldiers

By virtue of support from an established government with enough funds to provision a war, Union soldiers fared (no pun intended) better in the category of food. Their rations included fresh or salted beef, salt pork, flour, sugar, salt, vinegar, dried fruit, and dried vegetables, usually beans. Sometimes they even had fresh vegetables, such as carrots and potatoes.

Confederate Soldiers

As it would prove to be with all supplies, Confederate soldiers were not as fortunate. They were rationed bacon and corn meal, tea, sugar or molasses, and fresh fruit or vegetables when they could get them. If available, they might even have fresh eggs for breakfast.

Coffee

Coffee was so important to the soldiers that we'll give it a separate heading. Soldiers drank it by the pot, and it was their most coveted mess item. They would gladly trade other foods for coffee beans. In a world of "make-do," they ground the raw beans with rocks or their rifle butts.

Again, Union soldiers had a better supply of coffee throughout the war's duration. Confederate soldiers needing a daily caffeine fix quickly learned to make substitutes out of peanuts, chicory, or other items limited only by their imagination, such as corn, okra, pumpkin seeds, and acorns.

Unsavorables

- Hardtack: No discussion of camp food is complete without an homage to hardtack, a hard★ cracker-like biscuit made of flour, salt, and water. While hardtack was nutritious and didn't spoil easily, it was clearly more of a favorite with weevils and other insects than it was with the soldiers. (On the bright side, any little critters that arrived with the hardtack meant an extra dose of protein with the meal.)
- Meat: Never at a loss for a colorful description, soldiers referred to spoiled meat as "salted horse."
- Substitutions: In the field, fresh meat and vegetables gradually became harder to come by. Soldiers were forced to eat a less tasty and varied diet of salt pork, dried beans, cornbread, and hardtack.

Later Years

As the war dragged on, food shortages became a serious problem. Both the Confederacy and even the Union found it harder and harder to supply adequate chow to all the armies in a timely manner. Eventually, soldiers began to take matters into their own hands, attempting to live off the land. They came up with some fresh meat by hunting wild game.

Sometimes soldiers—both Union and Confederate—were more aggressive in getting the necessary food from neighboring towns and homes. Their tactics ranged from asking for help from sympathetic citizens to stealing, looting, and pillaging out of pure desperation.

★When we say "hard," we mean that the soldiers called hardtack "teeth-dullers," and sometimes could only break it up with a swift hit of the rifle butt. Soldiers would soak the pieces in coffee, fry them in bacon grease, or crumble them in soup to try to soften the hardtack up enough to actually chew and eat.

CIVIL WAR RECIPES

Here's a sampling of what was cooking in the "good old days."

Southern Johnnie Cake
2 cups of cornmeal
2/3 cup of milk
2 tablespoons vegetable oil (lard)
2 teaspoons baking soda
1/2 teaspoon of salt

Mix ingredients into a stiff batter and form eight biscuit-sized "dodgers." Spoon batter into hot cooking oil in a frying pan over a low flame. Optional: Spread with a little butter or molasses.

Venison Soup (from *Godey's Magazine*, March 1861 issue)
4 pounds freshly-killed venison
One pound of ham
One onion, minced
Black pepper to taste
Water
One celery head, cut small (or celery seed)
Three blades of mace spice
1/4 pound butter, cut small and rolled in flour
1/2 pint port or Madeira

Cut venison off the bones; slice ham in small slices. Add onion and black pepper. Put only as much water as will cover meats and stew gently for an hour, keeping the pot closely covered. Skim well and pour in a quart of boiling water. Add celery and mace. Boil gently two hours and a half; then put in butter and port. Let boil a quarter of an hour longer and send to the table with the meat in it. This recipe also works well with a beef substitute.

WARTIME HOME REMEDIES

If reading about old-time recipes and soldier's rations hasn't already made you start to quiver inside, some of the home remedies employed during wartime will be enough to downright scare your sensibilities:

Soup for an Invalid

Cut one pound of beef or mutton, or part of both, into small pieces. Boil gently in two quarts of water. Skim off the scum. When reduced to a pint, strain. Use a little salt for seasoning. Take a teacupful at a time.

Drink for the Sick

Roast sour apples. Pour boiling water upon them. Drink apple tea when cold.

Draught for a Fever

Wash and dry a few sprigs of sage, balm, and sorrel. Then put them into a jug. Take off the yellow part of the rind of a small lemon; remove the white. Slice the lemon and put it into the jug with part of the peel. Pour in three pints of boiling water, sweeten it and stop it close.

Ease Pain of a Bad Bruise

Thoroughly mix together 1/4 pound of beeswax, 1/4 pound of pine resin, and 1/2 pound of lard. Apply with a soft cloth to the afflicted area. To return bruised skin to its natural color quickly, rub the area gently with oil.

Cure Irregularity

Before retiring, apply castor oil externally to the armpits, rump, backbone, and stomach, then go to bed. You will be cured by the next morning.

MUSIC OF THE CIVIL WAR

During the four long years of the Civil War, patriots and soldiers alike wrote many songs and ballads to publicize their cause. A lot of those pieces still survive and are recognizable today.

The songs of the Civil War lend themselves to a few different categories:

- Inspirational marching songs meant to boost the soldiers' morale.
- Negro spirituals and traditional slave songs for comfort.
- Sad songs that reminded soldiers of home.
- Patriotic songs to let families feel closer to loved ones away at war.

At camp, fifes, bugles, and drums were familiar instruments used both to issue commands and guide the soldiers. The shrill fife could be heard above cannon boom and other battlefield noises, and the deep drumbeats helped keep the soldiers in step while marching. Buglers played field commands to advance or retreat as well as the morning's reveille, the evening's taps, and other calls throughout the day.

Many tunes we know from the Civil War have two different sets of lyrics. That's because, if soldiers liked a song that they heard the enemy singing, they would filch the tune and write their own lyrics to sing. While some songs were more popular with Union soldiers, and others more popular with Confederate soldiers, just as many were sung by soldiers on both sides, such as "When Johnny Comes Marching Home."

POPULAR SONGS OF THE UNION

"The Battle Hymn of the Republic"
Mine eyes have seen the glory of the coming of the Lord;
He is trampling out the vintage where the grapes of wrath are stored;
He hath loosed the fateful lightning of his terrible swift sword,
His truth is marching on.

Glory, Glory Hallelujah,
Glory, Glory Hallelujah,
Glory, Glory Hallelujah,
His truth is marching on.

I have seen Him in the watch fires of a hundred circling camps;
They have builded Him an altar in the evening dews and damps;
I can read his righteous sentence by the dim and flaring lamps,
His day is marching on

"Billy Barlow"
Good evening, kind friends,
How do you all do?
'Tis a very long time
since I've been to see you.
I am a volunteer
For the Union I go;
And I'm down on Secession,
Is Billy Barlow

Oh! yes, I'm rough, I well know,
But a bully old soldier is Billy Barlow.

Since last I saw you,
To Richmond I've been,
And during my stay

Mrs. Davis, I've seen.
She treated me kindly,
And smiled on me so.
Old Jeff he got jealous
Of Billy Barlow

"The Battle Cry of Freedom"
Yes, we'll rally round the flag, boys, we'll rally once again,
Shouting the battle cry of Freedom,
We will rally from the hillside, we'll gather from the plain,
Shouting the battle cry of Freedom.

The Union forever,
Hurrah! boys, hurrah!
Down with the traitors,
Up with the stars,
While we rally round the flag, boys,
Rally once again,
Shouting the battle cry of Freedom.

We will welcome to our numbers the loyal, true and brave,
Shouting the battle cry of Freedom,
And although they may be poor, not a man shall be a slave,
Shouting the battle cry of Freedom.

"When Johnny Comes Marching Home"

When Johnny comes marching home again,
Hurrah, hurrah,
We'll give him a hearty welcome then,
Hurrah, hurrah!
The men will cheer, the boys will shout,
The ladies, they will all turn out,
And we'll all feel gay
When Johnny comes marching home.

Popular Songs of the Confederacy

"Dixie"

I wish I was in the land of cotton,
Old times there are not forgotten;
Look away! Look away! Look away, Dixie's Land!
In Dixie's Land where I was born in,
Early on one frosty morning,
Look away! Look away! Look away, Dixie's Land!

Then I wish I was in Dixie! Hooray! Hooray!
In Dixie's Land I'll take my stand, to live and die in Dixie!
Away! Away! Away down South in Dixie!
Away! Away! Away down South in Dixie!

"The Bonnie Blue Flag"

We are a band of brothers, and native to the soil,
Fighting for the property we gained by honest toil;
And when our rights were threatened, the cry rose near and far:
"Hurrah for the Bonnie Blue Flag that bears a single star!"

Hurrah! Hurrah!
For Southern rights, hurrah!
Hurrah for the Bonnie Blue Flag that bears a single star.

Then here's to our Confederacy, strong we are and brave,
Like patriots of old we'll fight, our heritage to save;
And rather than submit to shame, to die we would prefer,
So cheer for the Bonnie Blue Flag that bears a single star.

"Goober Peas"

Sittin' by the roadside on a summer's day,
Chattin' with my messmates, passing time away,
Lying in the shadow, underneath the trees,
Goodness, how delicious, eating goober peas!

Peas! Peas! Peas! Peas!
Eating goober peas!
Goodness, how delicious,
Eating goober peas!

Just before the battle, the Gen'ral hears a row,
He says "The Yanks are coming, I hear their rifles now!"
He turns around in wonder, and what do you think he sees?
The Georgia Militia — eating goober peas!

"Goober Peas" are peanuts.

SNAPSHOT: WALT WHITMAN

When the Civil War began, New York poet Walt Whitman had already self-published what became his seminal work, *Leaves of Grass*. It garnered effusive praise from the likes of Ralph Waldo Emerson even as critics chided its sexual overtones. Whitman soon found himself in an epic of another kind: the Civil War.

In December 1862, Whitman's brother George, a Union soldier, was listed in a newspaper among the injured. Walt Whitman set out in search of his brother, who, it turned out, had suffered a minor injury. The poet was touched by what he saw in the soldiers' camps and hospitals. He stuck around to nurse the injured and dying soldiers.

Soon after, Whitman found a job in the army paymaster's office in nearby Washington. In his spare time, Whitman visited local hospitals, meeting wounded soldiers. Whitman wrote about his encounters with battlefield victims for various newspapers.

George Whitman was captured by Confederate soldiers in September 1864. Five months later, he was freed and then released by the Union owing to injuries and poor health. Walt Whitman held other government jobs, and after Abraham Lincoln's assassination, he wrote a widely admired poem for the fallen president, "O Captain! My Captain!"

McClellan: Stop and Slow

George McClellan became a media darling of his day while earning the love of his men upon being named head of the federal troops. He brought order and discipline to his men as they drilled and trained for battle. McClellan had just one flaw. He was endlessly reluctant to engage in battle.

Lincoln, not to mention congressmen, journalists, and others, began to sour on McClellan after he spent an eternal eight months on various exercises with his soldiers. What began as an inspiring restoration of order and rigor had devolved into a parody of military preparation. In addition, "Young Napoleon" possessed a Rushmore-sized ego, characterizing himself as the nation's savior while dismissing Lincoln as "the original gorilla."

In March 1862, Lincoln stripped McClellan of his role as general-in-chief of all forces while leaving him in charge of the Army of the Potomac, the Union's main force in the eastern theater.

Growing ever more impatient, the president and others urged McClellan to move on the Confederate capital of Richmond in early 1862. Rather than making a straight approach from Washington, McClellan concocted a plan that Lincoln reluctantly supported. It centered on a massive logistical hurdle—moving 100,000 men with attendant supplies and ammunition by water—and then marching to Richmond after landing at Fort Monroe, Virginia. Buoyed by Montgomery Meigs' stellar planning, the landing succeeded. McClellan and his men arrived in soggy Virginia on April 4.

Matters unraveled quickly from there. Reports of Confederates leaving behind so-called "Quaker guns"—logs painted black to resemble artillery—provided a mocking reminder of McClellan's relentless overestimation of his enemies.

Known as the Peninsula Campaign, McClellan's strategy was to head for Richmond using the peninsula between the James and York rivers. Over and over again, McClellan blundered by not attacking and by hesitating out of fear that he was outnumbered by

Confederate forces. His wildly errant assessments of Confederate strength were comical and fueled by McClellan's paranoia as well as the sloppy work of his close friend Allan Pinkerton. A typical example: At Yorktown, where George Washington scored the decisive victory in the Revolutionary War, McClellan sank to the occasion. Despite having 100,000 men in tow—compared with John Magruder's fifteen thousand—McClellan refused to fight, convinced he was outmanned.

A month after landing in Virginia, McClellan finally pressed the issue. The Confederates abandoned their fortified position at Yorktown and headed for Richmond to receive reinforcements. Thus, McClellan claimed Yorktown, but only because Magruder had left it behind. McClellan also claimed Williamsburg, a minor skirmish of little value. Though the general was able to spin the story as a triumph for the North, Lincoln, among others, demurred. As an imminent series of bloody battles would prove, McClellan had wasted a precious opportunity with his hesitancy.

Greek Fire

President Lincoln was all about innovations, including chemical warfare using phosphorous, which produced a huge explosion when exposed to air. He even witnessed a trial of two thirteen-inch phosphorous shells as they spewed fire over an area about fifty feet in diameter. Lincoln was responsible for adding a few experimental "Greek fire" shells to the federal arsenal.

STONEWALL AND THE SHENANDOAH

Federal troops under George McClellan remained paralyzed in Virginia, but Confederate military leaders knew they needed to find a way to distract the Union as a means of evening the number of troops on both sides. Enter Stonewall Jackson, whose Shenandoah Valley campaign during the spring of 1862 ranks as one of the greatest maneuvers of the war.

The fiery, idiosyncratic Jackson, invariably called "Old Blue Light" by his men in homage to his glowing blue eyes on the battlefield, made the diversion of Northern troops his primary aim. His tactics emphasized feints toward Washington, a strategy designed to convince McClellan and other Union military leaders of a forthcoming Confederate attack on the capital city.

Though Jackson's initial engagement at Kernstown in late-March 1862 resulted in defeat and retreat, it served the larger purpose. McClellan's force sent thirty-five thousand men from the Peninsula Campaign to reinforce Washington in direct response to Jackson's action.

That move led McClellan to hesitate yet again—and gave the Confederates much-needed breathing room. As for Jackson, his troops frustrated three times as many Union soldiers while also spooking Northern politicians.

Notable and Quotable

The infinite needs of Union General George McClellan tried the patience of everyone in the Lincoln administration, including Edwin M. Stanton, the Cabinet member who presided over the War Department. After McClellan requested forty thousand more men, Stanton said, "If he had a million men he would swear the enemy has two million, and then he would sit down in the mud and yell for three."

SOME CIVIL WAR FIRSTS

- First state to secede from the Union: South Carolina
- First war documented in photographs
- First conflict covered by eyewitness journalists; first introduction of "war correspondents"
- First unit insignia patches: initiated by Phil Kearny
- First casualty of the Civil War: Private Daniel Hough, killed at Fort Sumter on April 14, 1861, during the Union soldiers' hundred-gun salute to the U.S. flag after surrendering to Confederate soldiers
- First man injured by hostile action: Nicholas Biddle, April 18, 1861, in Baltimore
- First Confederate general to be killed: Robert S. Garnett, shot at Corrick's Ford, Virginia, July 13, 1861
- First commander of any army to die in combat: General Albert Sidney Johnston, April 6, 1862
- First black regiment of the war: 1st South Carolina, April 1862
- First officially recognized black regiment: 1st Regiment Louisiana Native Guards, September 1862
- First black man to command a ship in the United States Navy: former slave Robert Smalls
- First Confederate shot of the war at Fort Sumter: traditionally attributed to Edmund Ruffin of South Carolina's Palmetto Guard (although others in history also claim that distinction)
- First Union shot of the war at Fort Sumter: fired by Abner Doubleday
- First engagement of the Seven Days Battles: Battle of Oak Grove, June 25, 1862
- First award of the Congressional Medal of Honor; the first recipients were the survivors of Andrew's Raid, of the Great Locomotive Chase episode
- First performance of the new lights-out bugle call: "Taps"
- First battle of the Civil War: Big Bethel, June 10, 1861

- First major engagement of the Civil War: First Bull Run, July 21, 1861
- First modern effort to strangle a nation by naval blockade
- First formal use of aerial observation by armed forces: observation balloons
- First aircraft carrier: to pull observation balloons
- First telegraph message ever dispatched from an aerial balloon: June 18, 1861
- First Republican president: Abraham Lincoln
- First president to wear a beard: Abraham Lincoln
- First president assassinated: Abraham Lincoln
- First war veteran to assume the presidency: Andrew Johnson
- First president impeached in office: Andrew Johnson, 1868 (acquitted by one vote in the Senate)
- First imposing of an income tax to fund war efforts
- First federal paper money printed: 1862
- First use of machine guns in battle
- First use of land mines in battle
- First Union submarine: the Alligator
- First Commander of the Union Army: Irwin McDowell
- First Rear Admiral: David Glasgow Farragut, July 1862; also, first Full Admiral, July 1866
- First use of ironclads in modern naval warfare: Battle of Hampton Roads
- First Confederate capital location: Montgomery, Alabama
- First woman assistant surgeon in the U.S. Army: Dr. Mary Walker
- First observance of Memorial Day national holiday
- First observance of Thanksgiving national holiday
- First acknowledged Jew elected to the U.S. Senate: Judah P. Benjamin, 1852
- First ranked in his class at West Point: George Washington Custis Lee (1854), James B. McPherson (1853)
- First Civil War officer commissioned by the State of Illinois: Benjamin Mayberry Prentiss
- First proclamation freeing slaves: August 1861, following the Battle of Wilson's Creek near Springfield, Missouri, by John Charles Frémont (rescinded by Abraham Lincoln, November 1861)

NAVAL TRIVIA

- When the war began, the U.S. Navy had sixty-nine ships, all of them wooden.
- At the outbreak of war, the U.S. Navy only had 7,500 sailors.
- During the war, the Union built seventy-four ironclads.
- The Federal blockade caught an average of one in every six blockade runners.
- The U.S. Navy captured 1,149 Confederate ships/blockade runners.
- The U.S. Navy reported more loss of ships—fifty-eight—from torpedoes than from all other causes combined.
- African-American sailors made up about 8 percent of the U.S. Navy during the Civil War.
- During the Battle of Mobile Bay, Union Admiral David Farragut tied himself to the mast of his U.S.S. *Hartford* so he could get a better look at the action without fear of falling.
- The Union's ironclad, *Monitor*, featured the first flush toilet onboard a warship.
- The Confederate merchant raider C.S.S. *Alabama* seized or sunk almost seventy Union merchant ships, with a total value of $6 million.
- The Union Navy employed twenty-four wooden sloops and gunboats plus nineteen mortar schooners to capture the Port of New Orleans in April 1862.
- Union sailor Charles Ellet, Jr., was promoted to colonel after the Battle of Memphis in June 1862. At the age of nineteen, he was the youngest person to hold that rank.
- The Confederate ironclad *Virginia* was actually a retrofitted version of the resurrected U.S.S. *Merrimack*.
- Six different Union vessels were christened Arizona.
- Although she sank in a storm off the coast of Cape Hatteras on December 31, 1861, the U.S.S. *Monitor* remained on the U.S. Navy fleet list until 1951.
- Under Confederate Admiral Raphael Semmes, the C.S.S. *Sumter* captured eighteen Union ships in a six-month span.

Union Commanders: Carl Schurz (1829-1906)

Background: German native, educated at universities in Cologne and Bonn

Military Experience: Junior officer in the German Revolution

Countries of Residence: Switzerland, France, England; Migrated to the United States in 1852, settling near family in Wisconsin

Antebellum Political Positions: Minister to Spain, 1861–1862; strong supporter of Lincoln and abolition

Political Backscratching: Lincoln appointed Schurz brigadier general of volunteers; this, in turn, gained the President German-American support in the Civil War.

Civil War Battles Participated In: Second Bull Run, Fredericksburg, Chancellorsville, Gettysburg, Chattanooga, and the Carolinas Campaign

Other Notables: Chief-of-staff to Major General Henry W. Slocum

Rank Achieved: Major General of volunteers, 1863

After the War: Schurz became a prominent political leader across the country. He particularly was influential with the German-American vote. Schurz supported black civil rights.

Political Positions: Missouri Senator (1869–1875), the first German-American in the U.S. Senate; U.S. Secretary of the Interior (1877–1881), received the appointment after supporting Rutherford B. Hayes in his successful presidential bid

Journalism Career: Chief Editor of the Detroit Post (1866–1867); Editor and co-owner of St. Louis's Westliche Post (Western Post) (1867–1869); Chief Editor and co-owner of the New York Evening Post (1881–1883); Editorial columnist for Harper's Weekly (1892–1898).

Carl Schurz Trivia

- Early in his career, young Joseph Pulitzer worked for Schurz at Westliche Post in St. Louis.

- Schurz's wife Margarethe founded the first kindergarten in America in 1856, on which the current kindergarten system is based.
- There are as many (if not more) monuments memorializing Schurz than any other similarly-ranked Civil War veteran, ranging from schools, parks, and streets to a German Army base and a mountain in Yellowstone National Park, and from New York, Wisconsin, and Wyoming all the way across the ocean to Germany.

A historic marker in Greencastle, Pennsylvania, commemorates the place where Ulric Dahlgren captured Confederate troops carrying a note from Jefferson Davis informing Robert E. Lee not to expect reinforcements at Gettysburg. Dahlgren shared this vital information with General George Meade. The marker reads:

Captain Ulric Dahlgren. Commanded a detachment of Union cavalry that made a surprise attack on a larger force of Confederate cavalry on this square, July 2, 1863. Important papers for General Lee were taken from the men who were captured.

Union Commanders: Abner Doubleday (1819-1893)

Background: A prominent upstate New York family
Family Ties: Grandfather fought in the Revolutionary War; father Ulysses F. Doubleday was a U.S. Congressman; two brothers fought for the Union Army
Military Education: 1842 West Point graduate
Military Experience: Mexican and Seminole Wars, artillery
Battles Participated In: Shenandoah Valley Campaign, Second Bull Run, Antietam, Fredericksburg, Chancellorsville, and Gettysburg
Rank Attained: Major General, 1862
Nickname: "Old Forty-Eight Hours," for a deliberate manner
Famous Claim: Doubleday was assigned to Fort Sumter in South Carolina. It is said that on April 12, 1861, he fired the first Union shot of the war in response to Confederate volleys.
After the War: Doubleday served as colonel of the 35th infantry until he retired from the Regular Army in 1873.
Abner Doubleday and Baseball: It seems that for a time, popular consensus was that Abner Doubleday invented modern-day baseball. There's even "evidence" in the form of a handwritten letter that he sat down one afternoon in 1839 while in Cooperstown, New York, and wrote down the rules of the game.

However, no less an authority than the Baseball Hall of Fame has uncovered documents that strongly hint at the existence of the game, in some form, long before 1839.

One Argument: If you'll scan back up to the top of the page, you'll see that Doubleday was actually at West Point in 1839. Now Cooperstown and West Point are only about 170 miles apart, so it's not unfathomable that Doubleday could have visited there and jotted down some notes. But back in those days you didn't just hop on I-87 to zip across the state for the weekend.

At any rate, Doubleday never actually made the claim himself, and while it's a lovely legend, there's not much truth to it.

CONFEDERATE COMMANDERS: HENRY "HARRY" HETH (1825-1899)

Background: Virginia native

Pronunciation of Last Name: Rhymes with "teeth"

Military Education: Was refused admission to Annapolis; Graduated dead last in West Point's class of 1847

Military Experience: Mexican War, promoted to captain

Distinction: The only person in the entire Army of Northern Virginia whom General Lee called by his first name

Early Civil War Service: Heth was commissioned colonel of the 45th Virginia, and served in West Virginia and then under Braxton Bragg in the West during the Kentucky Campaign. He didn't see real battle action until he was transferred back east in 1863.

Rank Achieved: Brigadier General

Battles Participated In: Chancellorsville, Gettysburg, Wilderness, Petersburg, Appomattox

Opening at Gettysburg: Heth's division started the battle on the first day of Gettysburg earlier than Lee had actually planned for the fighting to get underway. Heth did not exhibit heroic leadership, and his forces suffered heavy losses.

Wounded at Gettysburg: Heth took a bullet in the head that cracked his skull open and knocked him unconscious for twenty-four hours. It would've undoubtedly been fatal, except for the protection from his new felt hat.

No, the felt was not that resistant. It was just too big. To make it fit, Heth had folded up a handful of paper sheets and stuffed them inside the hat. The extra padding in his hat provided enough of a barrier to save his life. He was able to return to the field a few days later.

After the War: Heth sold insurance, worked as a government surveyor, and served in the Office of Indian Affairs.

Union Commanders: John Gibbon (1827-1896)

Background: Philadelphia native raised in North Carolina
Education: 1847 West Point graduate
Military Experience: Mexican and Seminole Wars; West Point artillery instructor and quartermaster, five years
Military Intelligence: Gibbon wrote *The Artillerist's Manual*. Not an official War Department publication, it proved to be a widely-referenced handbook by both sides during the war.
The Brothers' War: Gibbon's three brothers all fought for the Confederacy. He stayed loyal to the Union.
Battles Participated In: Second Bull Run, Antietam, Fredericksburg (severely wounded), Chancellorsville, Gettysburg (severely wounded), Wilderness, and Petersburg
Rank Achieved: Major general
Early Civil War Appointments: Stationed to desolate artillery posts out west, Gibbon transferred to the volunteers and was commissioned brigadier general.
"The Black Hat Brigade:" When given command of the I Corps Iron Brigade in 1862, Gibbon supplied the hats earning the brigade its colorful nickname.
After the War: Gibbon remained in the regular Army commanding the 7th Infantry. He served on the frontier for the next thirty years, became a noted Indian fighter, and retired as a brigadier general.
Memoirs: Gibbon's Personal Recollections of the Civil War was published in 1928.

Battles Notes
- Gettysburg: Gibbon commanded the troops at Pickett's Charge.
- Antietam: Gibbon had six cannon strategically placed on a knoll to protect the right flank. But he realized that the muzzles were aimed too high, and they were just firing over everyone's heads. So with Confederate troops charging the battery, Gibbon jumped

off his horse, ran to the guns, and quickly adjusted the elevations. Now repositioned, the cannon were far more effective, and Gibbon's daring action saved his battery from being completely wiped out, defenseless.

- Appomattox: Gibbon was one of the three commissioners to receive Lee's surrender.

The Other James Henry Lane

Virginia native James Henry Lane (1833–1907) fought for the Confederacy during the Civil War. A Mexican War veteran, he saw battle at Bethel Church, New Bern, Mechanicsville, Frazier's Farm, Cedar Mountain, Second Bull Run, Ox Hill, Harper's Ferry, Sharpsburg, Chancellorsville, Gettysburg, Bristoe Station, the Wilderness, and Spotsylvania Court House. Lane was wounded three different times.

It was actually a man from Lane's brigade who mortally wounded Stonewall Jackson at Chancellorsville. Lane reached the rank of brigadier general, and after the war turned to teaching, first at the Virginia Agricultural and Mechanical College and then at the Alabama Polytechnic Institute (now Auburn University).

UNION COMMANDERS: JAMES BIRDSEYE McPHERSON (1828-1864)

Q: What was James McPherson's background?

A: McPherson was born on an Ohio farm. When he was thirteen, his father was declared mentally incompetent, and young McPherson grew up quickly. He took a job as a store clerk to support the family. His employer recognized his potential and encouraged him to get an education from Ohio's Norwalk Academy.

Q: How did McPherson perform at West Point?

A: Because of his early work life, McPherson was twenty-one years old by the time he entered West Point. His maturity showed. McPherson graduated first in the West Point Class of 1853. He joined the Corps of Engineers and taught engineering at the Military Academy for a year. McPherson's West Point roommate was future Confederate General John Bell Hood.

Q: What did McPherson do after West Point?

A: He spent several years working on engineering projects, such as improvements to the Hudson River and building defense fortifications for the Harbor of New York. He also supervised the building of defenses at Alcatraz in San Francisco.

Q: How did McPherson get involved in the Civil War?

A: At the war's beginning, McPherson was stationed in California. He headed back east and lobbied to get appointed as aide-de-camp to Major General Henry Halleck. After that, he was chief engineer for Major General Ulysses S. Grant's Army of the Tennessee.

Q: What did McPherson do with the Army of the Tennessee?

A: First, he was instrumental in the capture of both Fort Henry and Fort Donelson. Then he participated in the Battle of Shiloh. After that he was named brigadier general of volunteers to lead a brigade of engineers.

Q: What did McPherson do next?

A: It wasn't long before McPherson was promoted again, to major general of volunteers. He was given command of the XVII Corps, and they participated in the Vicksburg and Atlanta Campaigns.

Q: Was McPherson a headstrong commander?

A: No. He was actually quite cautious and sometimes was criticized for his hesitation. Nevertheless, he was one of General William Sherman's favorite and most reliable commanders. Sherman often called on McPherson to execute his strategic maneuvers.

Q: What did Sherman think about McPherson?

A: Sherman once said of McPherson, "If he lives, he'll outdistance Grant and myself."

Q: What did others think about McPherson?

A: McPherson was well-liked by everyone, and generally regarded as "handsome," "warmhearted," and "intelligent."

Q: McPherson died in 1864. Was he killed in action?

A: Yes. During the Atlanta campaign, Sherman and Hood were playing peek-a-boo all around the Georgia town. McPherson expected his old roommate to pull something, but he didn't know when.

   On July 22, he happened to be away from his corps, meeting at Sherman's headquarters. The boom of cannon was a quick clue to Sherman and McPherson that Hood had made his move. McPherson and his orderly quickly galloped off to get back to the corps, but rode straight into a group of Confederates. Instead of surrendering, McPherson spurred his horse, and was shot in the back as he tried to escape.

Q: How did McPherson's death affect Sherman?

A: Sherman cried when he saw McPherson's body. Hood and Grant were both equally grieved.

Q: How old was McPherson when he was killed?

A: He was thirty-five years old

Q: Did McPherson leave behind any survivors?

A: Yes, his fiancée Emily Hoffman of Baltimore. They had planned to be married, but McPherson had not been able to get a furlough.

Q: What was significant about McPherson's death?

A: He was the highest-ranking Union officer ever killed in battle.

CONFEDERATE COMMANDERS: JOHN BUCHANAN FLOYD (1806-1863)

Virginia native John Buchanan Floyd's most significant contribution to the Confederacy actually took place in the days before any states seceded. But we'll get to that in a minute.

Floyd graduated in 1826 from South Carolina College and began a law practice. He then moved to Helena, Arkansas, where he managed a cotton plantation, poorly. Soon, he returned to Virginia and entered state politics, with better results.

Floyd served in the Virginia legislature (1847–1848 and 1855), was elected Virginia's governor (1849–1852), and was a delegate to the 1856 Democratic National Convention, where he backed James Buchanan for the presidential nomination. In March 1857, the new President Buchanan returned the favor and appointed Floyd as Secretary of War for his support.

This was when Floyd pulled some pretty sneaky moves for a government official. Floyd started hearing rumors of Southern secession, and he used his position as U.S. secretary of war to do what he could make sure the South would be prepared for any armed conflict that might result.

John Buchanan Floyd knew that if a war broke out, the Southerners would capture any federal supplies in their states, so he helped stack the deck in favor of the South. By 1860, Floyd had quietly transferred some 115,000 muskets and rifles from armories in the North to those in the South. For a little perspective, this was more than one-sixth of all military equipment the United States owned at the time and enough to arm at least ten infantry divisions.

Then, to put a little icing on the cake, Floyd transferred as many regular U.S. Army units as he could to remote assignments in the West—hoping that the eastern posts would be understaffed when a war broke out.

Floyd's plan did work, and it was a great help to the young Confederate nation. Most of the arms and ammunition used by the Confederate army in the first days of the Civil War came from the stockpiles he had arranged the previous year.

Floyd was duly rewarded for his foresight. Jefferson Davis appointed him brigadier general and gave him command of a brigade in the western theater.

Unfortunately, that was the highlight of Floyd's Confederate service. There were no more glory days for John Floyd. He was never able to top his great accomplishments while U.S. secretary of war. In fact, as a commander, he turned out to be pathetic.

In charge of Fort Donelson on the Tennessee River, Floyd really messed up. Holding Fort Donelson was extremely important to the Confederacy, because it meant maintaining control of the river. Grant knew this, and proceeded to besiege the fort.

When it became clear that the Confederates would be forced to surrender, Floyd didn't want to be the one to wave the white flag. Instead, he slipped away from Fort Donelson under cover of darkness. He left the dirty work of surrendering to General Simon Bolivar Buckner.

Later on, Floyd claimed that he was afraid to be captured. He just knew that he would be tried and executed for treason because of what he did as U.S. secretary of war. In any event, Confederate President Jefferson Davis didn't think Floyd should have deserted his post, and relieved him of his command, which is a nice way of saying, Floyd was fired.

Floyd retired to his Virginia home. We'll never know if he actually would have been convicted of treason at the war's end, because he died of natural causes in 1863.

THE SEVEN DAYS' BATTLES

These engagements led the Union and General George McClellan to abandon the Peninsula Campaign while also inflicting costly casualties on the undermanned Confederate army. The six battles between Richmond and the peninsula between the James and York rivers during the summer of 1862 ended as a victory for the rebels because they maintained their capital. It came at great cost.

Robert E. Lee took over as the field commander of the re-named Army of Northern Virginia on June 1. Lee's ascension resulted from General Joseph E. Johnston's wounding at the Battle of Seven Pines on May 31 and June 1. Johnston's injuries forced him to take leave from the war to recuperate.

Lee was a much more aggressive commander than Johnston. His first task was pushing McClellan and the Army of the Potomac away from Richmond. McClellan's Peninsula Campaign had been stalled for much of the spring. The Army of the Potomac landed at Fort Monroe, located at the tip of the peninsula between the York and James rivers, in April. McClellan's plan was to march northwest and take the capital.

Since arriving at Fort Monroe, though, McClellan had yet to secure a major victory. Much of the time the Union forces did little, hampered by McClellan's overcautious nature. He constantly believed the outnumbered Confederates had more troops than he did, and through his hesitation, McClellan allowed the rebel army to move reinforcements, bettering its odds when battle commenced.

By the time the Seven Days' began, on June 25 at Oak Grove, the Union had 104,000 troops to the Confederacy's ninety-two thousand.

The initial battle, along the Chickahominy River, went back and forth before the Union took a strong position as night fell and hostilities ceased. Like many of the Seven Days' engagements, it was hard to declare a conclusive winner and both armies (and their leaders) made significant mistakes.

A day later, at Mechanicsville, Lee's plan to trap Union troops on the Chickahominy fell apart. Stonewall Jackson failed to carry out a swift attack at the same time, and Confederate commander A. P. Hill went on the offensive alone, without Lee's approval. Though it ended in standoff, McClellan made a major error when he decided to relocate his men to a spot farther from Richmond.

The bloodiest battle came at Gaines' Mill. Confederate casualties reached 8,700 while the Union suffered 6,800. In this, the third of the Seven Days' Battles, the Confederacy absorbed heavy losses but saved Richmond. On the evening of June 27, following the bloodbath at Gaines' Mill, McClellan began the Union retreat in earnest.

Lee, eager to seize an opportunity to gouge the Army of the Potomac, kept pressing. Poor execution plagued Lee's plans. Union rear-guard actions allowed McClellan and his men to escape on the James River. Smaller battles at Savage's Station and Fraser's Farm along the way led to a final encounter at Malvern Hill.

Buoyed by clear topographical advantages—McClellan's forces manned an elevated position—the Union troops mowed down the Confederate offensives ordered by Lee. McClellan's men were so encouraged that they beseeched him to push on and go after the Confederates, but McClellan continued the retreat. With that, the Seven Days' Battles—and McClellan's Peninsula Campaign—ended.

The North inflicted twenty thousand casualties, while suffering sixteen thousand losses of its own, on an already undermanned Confederate Army, but Lee claimed the larger triumph by preserving Richmond. McClellan's retreat would lead Lee to begin planning for an invasion of the Union, first in Maryland and, later, in Pennsylvania.

Some Military Terms Explained

If it seems like Army officers held a lot of different ranks, that's because they did. If they had joined the army through their state militia, they could even have two different ranks at the same time: one would be their rank in the militia, while the other would be their rank in the army.

Army Military Ranks, Lowest to Highest

Confederacy	Union
Lieutenant	Lieutenant
Captain	Captain
Major	Major
Lieutenant Colonel	Lieutenant Colonel
Brigadier General	Brigadier General
Major General	Major General
Lieutenant General	Lieutenant General
General	

Navy Military Ranks, Lowest to Highest

Confederacy	Union
Master Lieutenant	Junior Grade
2nd Lieutenant	Lieutenant
1st Lieutenant	Lieutenant Commander
Commander	Commander
Captain	Captain
Admiral	Rear Admiral
Rear Admiral	Vice Admiral
	Admiral

Notes on Ranks

- In the Union Army, and even in today's armed forces, only the most senior of officers achieve the rank of lieutenant general. Civil War leaders Winfield Scott, Ulysses S. Grant, William Sherman, and Philip Sheridan all achieved the rank of lieutenant general.
- The Confederate Congress appointed seven full generals: Samuel Cooper, Albert Sidney Johnston, Robert E. Lee, Joseph E. Johnston, P. G. T. Beauregard, Braxton Bragg, and Edmund Kirby-Smith. John Bell Hood was temporarily named a full general, but reverted back to a lieutenant general six months later.
- In the Union Navy, David Farragut achieved the rank of vice admiral in 1864 and admiral in 1866, at which time David Dixon Porter was promoted to vice admiral.
- In the Confederate Navy, Raphael Semmes achieved the rank of rear admiral.
- In both the North and South, armies were divided up and similarly organized. From smallest to largest, the groupings are:

  - Squad
  - Platoon
  - Company
  - Battalion
  - Regiment
  - Division
  - Corps
  - Army

- Artillery refers to large weapons, like cannon, and the soldiers who fire them. Artillery was often used to discombobulate opposing forces before the troops launched an attack. The first cannon were called baby wakers.

- A battery is a unit of artillery, or a group of concentrated guns. When the guns or cannon were on wagons, thus being continually relocated and repositioned around the field during battle, they were called flying battery.
- Infantry were soldiers who fought on foot, although they could have used horses for riding between battles.
- Cavalry were soldiers who were trained to fight on horseback and were generally known for their speed and daring.
- A picket was a post in front of the army's camp to guard the front from enemy advances.
- A skirmish was a small-scale clash between troops apart from the entire army, either on scouting or defensive detail.
- The aide-de-camp was a personal assistant to high-ranking officers, which meant he had a lot of inside knowledge and as much of a responsibility to make sure things went smoothly. The position was also called the dog-robber, because the aide-de-camp would do anything, even robbing the family dog, to get the general what he requested.
- A brevet promotion was an honorary ranking, usually awarded for bravery. An officer could hold his brevet rank at the same time as his commissioned rank.

ADMIRAL FRANKLIN BUCHANAN, CONFEDERATE STATES NAVY (1800-1874)

We call Franklin Buchanan the "Two-Day Admiral," because, despite his experience and rank, he only saw two days of battle during the entire Civil War. We'll grant that they were two pivotal days, though.

Baltimore native Franklin Buchanan joined the U.S. Navy as a midshipman in 1815 and remained in the navy for his entire career. While commanding the warships *Vincennes* and *Germantown* in the 1840s, Buchanan progressed through the ranks from lieutenant to commander, and finally captain in 1855.

In the meantime, Buchanan consulted with Secretary of the Navy George Bancroft in organizing the U.S. Naval Academy at Annapolis, Maryland. It's not surprising, then, that Buchanan was the first superintendent of the school from 1845 to 1847.

He went back to active service during the Mexican War, and by the early 1850s, had joined Commodore Matthew Perry's expedition to the Far East, resulting in opening Japan to foreign trade. Buchanan topped off his four-and-a-half decade naval service as commandant of the Washington Navy Yard from 1859 to 1861.

Buchanan's U.S. Naval career ended, almost of by accident, when the Southern states seceded. Buchanan anticipated that his home state of Maryland would join the Confederacy, and he resigned his post with the U.S. Navy. However, Maryland did not secede, but stayed in the Union. Oops!

Buchanan tried to un-resign, but it was too late. The U.S. Navy dismissed him. So he joined the Confederate Navy as a captain in the fall of 1861. Buchanan's first responsibility was heading the Office of Orders and Detail. Soon he was assigned to defend the James River in Virginia.

Buchanan was the commander of the Confederate ironclad

C.S.S. *Virginia* (formerly the U.S.S. *Merrimac*). He was aboard the Confederate ship the day it rammed the Union's *Cumberland* and *Congress* in Hampton Roads.

Buchanan suffered a dangerous thigh wound and had to leave the ship to be treated, and he remained away throughout the long road to recovery. He was not present for the memorable ironclad showdown the next day between the C.S.S. *Virginia* and the U.S.S. *Monitor*.

Buchanan was promoted to admiral, making him the ranking, senior officer in the Confederate Navy. This lasted until Raphael Semmes was promoted to rear admiral in 1865.

After he was healed, Buchanan went to Mobile Bay to oversee construction of the C.S.S. *Tennessee* in the shipyards of Alabama. Once the ship was completed, Buchanan was given command of the ironclad as it joined in the defense of the Bay.

When Union Rear Admiral David Farragut came along in August 1864 and disregarded the torpedoes mining the Bay to sail "full steam ahead," Buchanan was on board the *Tennessee*. The ironclad gave a good fight as its fellow Confederate ships were sunk or captured, but eventually it was forced to surrender. Admiral Buchanan was again seriously wounded, shot in the thigh.

Buchanan spent the rest of the war out of pocket; six months as a prisoner of war until his exchange in February 1865, and three more months recovering from his injury.

Because he was wounded in both actions on the *Virginia* and the *Tennessee*, Buchanan was engaged in combat during only two days of the Civil War.

Three destroyer-class U.S. Navy ships were named in honor of Admiral Franklin Buchanan, the last being decommissioned in 1991.

America Picks Up Two New States

Number 35: West Virginia, June 20, 1863

When the state of Virginia voted to secede from the Union on April 17, 1865, it was not a unanimous vote. Many of the delegates from the western counties in the state cast their ballots against leaving the United States.

So after Virginia seceded from the Union, delegates from these western counties met and voted to refuse to secede with Virginia. In fact, they set up a "Restored Government of Virginia," claiming to govern the entire state. This meant that, for a while, Virginia was operating as a Confederate state with Confederate government officials at the same time that delegates from the western counties were operating as if Virginia was a Union state with Union government officials.

By August of 1861, these western delegates began talk of carving a separate state out of Virginia and passed a dismemberment ordinance. They discussed what to call the new state, considering such names as "Kanawha," for the Kanawha River; "Allegheny," for the Allegheny Mountains; "Augusta;" "Columbia;" "New Virginia;" "Vandalia," the name of a British colony once planned for establishment in that area; "West Virginia;" and "Western Virginia."

Local voters approved the creation of a new state, and in November delegates met to draft a constitution for the state, which they decided to call "West Virginia."

In the meantime, the citizens began acting like a state. They formed the 3rd West Virginia Cavalry, Company A, in October of 1861. All total, West Virginia sent about thirty-two thousand sons to fight in the Union Army and about ten thousand to the Confederacy.

Next began the long road to statehood, which included voter approval of the new Constitution and U.S. Senate approval of the new state, and ended eighteen months later, when West Virginia was admitted to the Union.

Arthur I. Boreman of Parkersburg was elected the first governor. The young state suffered some growing pains, starting with a resolution in 1866 to deny citizenship and voting rights to anyone who had supported the Confederacy. This was finally reversed in 1871. The capital also relocated a few times, from Alexandria to Wheeling and finally to Charleston on the banks of the Kanawha River.

As a postscript, the state of Virginia later challenged the legality of the new state in a case that went to the U.S. Supreme Court in 1870. The Supreme Court decided in favor of West Virginia, and that was that.

Number 36: Nevada, October 31, 1864

At the end of the Mexican War, the United States ended up with the land that became the Utah Territory, which included almost all of present-day Nevada. Some of the first explorers to visit the Nevada lands were Kit Carson and John C. Frémont in the mid-1840s.

For the next decade or so, Nevada was only a place gold prospectors had to travel through on their way to the mines of California. Then at the end of the 1850s, the famous Comstock Lode of silver was discovered near present-day Virginia City, and a rush to Nevada was on.

Congress declared Nevada a separate territory from Utah in 1861, which gave the U.S. government more power to enforce laws. In 1862, the territory was enlarged, but not to the size we know today.

On October 31, 1864, Nevada was admitted as a state with Carson City as the capital and Henry Goode Blasdel as the governor, even though the territory did not meet the population requirements for statehood. Some people say this is because Lincoln needed more votes to pass the upcoming Thirteenth Amendment.

The state name comes from the Sierra Nevada mountain range. "Nevada" is Spanish for "snow-covered." Nicknames include the "Silver State," for its silver mines; the "Sagebrush State," for its sagebrush; and the "Battle-Born State," as it came to statehood during the Civil War.

The state of Nevada finally reached the shape we know today in 1866 when the southern tip was added from the Utah Territory.

FLORIDA: A CONFEDERATE STATE WITH MIXED FEELINGS

Under Governor Madison Starke Perry, Florida became the third state to secede on January 10, 1861. But Florida proved to be less than 100 percent sympathetic to the Southern cause.

Like in other states, one of the first things Perry did was capture a federal arsenal at Chattahoochee and Fort Marion in St. Augustine under Confederate control. But, what the Confederates in Florida never did was gain control of Fort Pickens in Pensacola, Fort Jefferson in the Dry Tortugas, and Fort Taylor in Key West. These were strategic positions that would remain in Union hands throughout the war. This amount of Union control in a Confederate state was indicative of public sentiment.

Clearly, there were plenty of Unionists living in Florida, as evidenced by the Unionist newspapers that continued to be published there. Certain areas in the state even became known as havens for Confederate deserters.

In fact, there were so many Confederate deserters and Union sympathizers, that the U.S. Army formed two Union regiments in Florida: The 1st Florida U.S. Cavalry, operating in the panhandle, and the 2nd Florida U.S. Cavalry, operating on Florida's west coast. Deserters also formed their own little bands of outlaw raiders and spies.

"Homer's Sharpshooter"

A *Harper's Weekly* illustration by Winslow Homer is one of the most memorable—and most collected—images of the Civil War. Published on November 15, 1862, and titled "The Army of the Potomac - a Sharp-Shooter on Picket Duty (from a painting by W. Homer Esq.)," it is often referred to as "Homer's Sharpshooter."

CIVIL WAR SHARPSHOOTERS

The word sharpshooter refers to a marksman, someone skilled in shooting. It is not the same thing as a sniper. A sniper is a marksman who specializes in shooting from a concealed position over long ranges, often with a special weapon.

Sharpshooters on both sides were less used as snipers, more used as special soldiers. Trained marksmen were often at the front of an advance and first to meet the enemy.

Sharpshooters used a variety of weapons, including the breech-loading Sharps rifles, British Whitworth rifles, sporting arms, and their own custom-made weapons.

Rather than entire regiments of only sharpshooters, most of the time they were included as small companies within larger regiments and given special assignments in action. Many marksmen provided their efficient and effective service throughout the war, particularly at Yorktown, Gettysburg, Vicksburg, Chattanooga, Atlanta, Spotsylvania, the Wilderness, and Petersburg.

Although it seems a logical conclusion, the term sharpshooter is not derived from the rifle designed by Christian Sharps. Instead it comes from being a "sharp-eyed" shooter, and has been recorded in use as early as 1802. Sharps first manufactured his weapon in 1848.

Some Especially Notable Civil War Sharpshooter Units
- 1st United States Volunteers Sharpshooter Regiment—formed under Hiram Berdan of men from New York City, Albany, New York, and the states of New Hampshire, Vermont, Michigan, and Wisconsin
- 2nd United States Volunteers Sharpshooter Regiment—formed under Hiram Berdan of men from New Hampshire, Maine, Pennsylvania, Michigan, Minnesota, and Vermont
- 1st Michigan Sharpshooters, Company K—an all-Native American company, primarily Chippewa and Ottawa Indians from northern Michigan

- 1st Texas Sharp Shooters, Burnet's Battalion
- 1st Battalion United States Sharpshooters—formed from men in New York and Pennsylvania by Major W. S. Rowland in October 1862, consisting of four companies, the 6th, 7th, 8th, and 9th

Hiram Berdan's Sharpshooters

At the outbreak of the Civil War, New York City mechanical engineer and inventor Hiram Berdan was thought to be the best amateur marksman in the country. Naturally, he began recruiting volunteers.

Berdan gathered enough men for two regiments, the 1st United States Volunteers Sharpshooters and the 2nd United States Volunteers Sharpshooters, called "Berdan's Sharpshooters." To qualify, prospective soldiers had to prove their precision by placing ten shots in a ten-inch circle from two hundred yards, using any rifle and any position of their choice.

Berdan's Sharpshooters were probably the most memorable units of their kind, both for their accomplishments and appearance. They marched into battle wearing green coats and caps with black feathers.

Berdan's Sharpshooters claimed that they "took out" more Southern soldiers than any other similarly-sized regiment. They were involved in constant action from the war's beginning to its end; of the 2,600 men who enlisted, more than a thousand were killed or wounded.

Some have speculated that Berdan—thought to be "thoroughly unscrupulous and unreliable" by his Northern contemporaries—originally organized the sharpshooting regiments as a way to market and sell his inventions. Whether that was truly his motive or not, Berdan proved to be an effective leader. He led the sharpshooters himself to the front lines at Chancellorsville and Gettysburg. At the war's end, Congress awarded Berdan an honorary major general ranking.

COURTS-MARTIAL

The published numbers of courts-martial range from eighty-thousand to 100,000 cases throughout the war years—and this is only for the Union Army, as the Confederate records aren't as easily available. Charges varied from stealing supplies and deserting to disobeying orders and murder.

Violations of military law were tried in general court-martial. The justice system also included courts of inquiry to investigate the necessity of a court-martial. Finally, misbehavior by private citizens could be addressed by a military commission.

One of the most common charges for court-martial was desertion. A conviction for deserting was often sentenced to execution by shooting or hanging. On appeal, the sentence could be commuted to dishonorable dismissal.

Another common charge was insubordination. In one instance where an intoxicated private assaulted a first lieutenant, the private was sentenced to one year in prison at hard labor with a twenty-four-pound ball and chain.

Some examples of court-martial cases, ranging from the most well-known to almost completely forgotten:

- Clement L. Vallandigham, private citizen—found guilty by military commission of treason by urging Union soldiers to desert; sentenced to banishment from the United States
- Major Henry Wirz, commander of Andersonville Prison Camp—found guilty of maliciously damaging the health of Union prisoners of war and of murder; sentenced to death by hanging
- Major General Fitz-John Porter—tried for failing to obey the orders of Major General John Pope to attack Stonewall Jackson's army at the Second Battle of Bull Run, contributing to the Union defeat; found guilty of "disobedience, disloyalty, and misconduct in the face of the enemy" and dismissed from military service

- Brigadier General James G. Spears, Army of the Ohio—as a slave-owning Tennessee Unionist, spoke against the legality of the Emancipation Proclamation; found guilty of charges including "using disloyal language," and dismissed from service
- Brigadier General Ivan Turchinoff (Americanized to John Turchin)—brought to trial for allowing his troops to burn and loot the town of Athens, Alabama; after his wife appealed to President Lincoln, he was pardoned and promoted
- Brigadier General of Volunteers John H. Martindale—charged with preferring surrender rather than retreat at Malvern Hill; cleared by a Confederate court of inquiry and promoted to major general
- Major General Lafayette McLaws—charged by Confederate General James Longstreet of noncooperation and poor preparation before the engagement at Fort Sanders; guilty findings were overturned by Jefferson Davis
- Major General William Edmondson "Grumble" Jones—court-martialed by Confederate General Jeb Stuart for insulting him; although found guilty, Robert E. Lee managed to reduce his sentence to a transfer
- Sergeant William Walker, 3rd South Carolina Colored Infantry—accused of leading his company in mutiny for equal pay for African-American soldiers; despite overwhelming evidence that his claims were warranted, Walker was convicted and executed before President Lincoln could consider his case
- Major John Henry Gee, commander of Salisbury, North Carolina, prison camp—charged for cruelty and murder because thousands of prisoners died from starvation and disease while awaiting exchange; with evidence showing Gee's heroic efforts to improve conditions, a U.S. military commission unanimously acquitted Gee of all charges
- Lieutenant General Leonidas Polk—quarreled with Confederate General Braxton Bragg after the battles of Stones River and Murfreesboro; Bragg tried to court-martial him, but Polk was merely relieved of command

UNION COMMANDERS: JOHN POPE (1822-1892)

Claim to Fame: Lincoln's choice to lead the Army of the Potomac between McClellan's first and second attempts at that task

Background: Kentucky native, related by marriage to Mary Todd Lincoln, 1842 West Point graduate, served in the Mexican War

Rank achieved: Major General of Volunteers; Brigadier General

Early Civil War Service: Pope was first assigned command in Missouri. He excelled in a coordinated effort with the Union Navy to capture Island Number 10 in the Mississippi River near New Madrid, Missouri. This was important in opening the river to the Union all the way to Memphis.

Civil War Career Highlight: Lincoln appointed Pope to replace George McClellan to command the Army of Virginia. Pope started off on the wrong foot with the troops, bragging that in the West his men had seen only their enemy's backs.

Things Head Downhill for Pope: In August 1862, Confederate General Robert E. Lee targeted Pope. Stonewall Jackson beat him at Cedar Mountain. Jeb Stuart raided his headquarters at Catlett's Station, taking some $35,000 in cash and gold, Pope's dress coat, horses, and strategy documents. At the month's end, Jackson looted Pope's supply depot at Manassas Junction, taking food and ammunition.

Pope Hits Rock Bottom: When Pope discovered Jackson's troops near Bull Run, the Union commander announced his intentions to "bag the whole crowd." In an unorganized and uncoordinated attack, Pope's army advanced on the Confederates. Jackson's troops held fast, throwing rocks when ammunition ran out.

Pope thought he had the upper hand and went to bed expecting to claim victory the next day. But in the meantime, General Longstreet arrived with Confederate reinforcements, which Pope knew nothing about. The next morning, as Pope hoped to "crush" Jackson, Longstreet surrounded Pope's men.

Pope blamed the Second Bull Run loss on his subordinates and saw to it that Major Fitz-John Porter was court-martialed and dismissed from the Army. But no matter who was blamed, it didn't change the Union loss.

Pope Gets Demoted and Sent into "Professional Exile:"
Lincoln sent Pope to Minnesota to deal with the Sioux Indians and reinstated McClellan. Pope stayed in the Department of the Northwest until the end of the war.

Post-War Accomplishments: Pope remained a career soldier, and established Fort Hays, Kansas, then commanded the Department of California. He retired in 1886.

The Personality of Pope

Pretentious, boastful, and harsh, Pope was far from likable. His U.S. Army contemporaries took their potshots where they could. When Pope earned command of the Army of Virginia, he bragged that he would be a frontline leader with his headquarters in the saddle. That led to varied comments about the difference between his headquarters and his hindquarters.

When trying to say something nice about Pope, usually it was only offered that he was a good horseman (essential for operating out of the saddle), soldierly (whatever that means), and handsome. Notice the lack of mention of likability or leadership skills.

Southerners cared for him even less than his own colleagues, and for good reason. He required the Virginia citizens to take an oath of loyalty to the United States, upon threat of suspicion of espionage and deportation. He even encouraged his men to seize food and supplies from the farms of Virginia rebels, deeming it fair punishment for their insurrection.

Robert E. Lee regarded Pope as "a miscreant" for his treatment and opinions regarding punishment of the Southerners. Even George McClellan stated that he would not be able to stand serving under Pope if the braggart were promoted above him.

UNION COMMANDERS: FRANZ SIGEL (1824-1902)

Background: German-born, 1843 graduate of Germany's Karlsruhe Military Academy

Homeland pre-Civil War Military Career: Lieutenant Sigel entered the German army but resigned after killing another officer in a duel over a political disagreement. The next year, he joined German rebel forces against the royal family; this didn't end well. He fled to Switzerland, was deported to England, and arrived in America in 1852.

American Antebellum Career: Sigel taught school in New York City, then moved to Missouri to become director of St. Louis City Schools in 1857.

The American Civil War: Against slavery, Colonel Sigel was happy to command the 2nd Missouri Brigade. He probably was commissioned by virtue of his heritage, as Lincoln needed to get German-American support of the war. It worked; most Missouri German-Americans followed Sigel in supporting the Union. More than any battle tactics, this was probably Sigel's biggest contribution to the Civil War.

After the Union loss at Wilson's Creek, Sigel was promoted to brigadier general for his heroics. Then the Union victory at Pea Ridge gave the North control of Missouri and northern Arkansas. It also gave Sigel a promotion to Major General of Volunteers.

Sigel was part of Grant's four-part plan to destroy the Confederacy. Sigel's job was to advance up the Shenandoah Valley, but he was routed at New Market. Next, he led his corps against Jubal Early's advance toward Washington.

Relieved nevertheless from command for "a lack of aggression," Sigel withdrew from active duty due to "ill health." After the war, he worked in various positions including editing a German-language newspaper.

Union Commanders:
George Stoneman
(1822-1894)

Infamy: The highest-ranking Union officer captured in the war
Background: A western New York native, grew up on the family farm
Military Education: 1846 West Point graduate
Trivia: Stonewall Jackson was his roommate
Military Experience: Mexican War, and other Southwestern outposts, fighting Indians
Physical Description: Six feet, four inches; quiet and serious

The Ups and Downs of George Stoneman's Civil War Career
DOWN: At the outbreak of the Civil War, Stoneman was posted at Fort Brown, Texas, on the Rio Grande. Opposed by Confederates looking to capture the garrison, Stoneman escaped with most of his men to Union lines.
UP: McClellan promoted his former classmate Stoneman to brigadier general over the Army of the Potomac cavalry.
DOWN: Under McClellan, Stoneman's cavalry was limited and ineffective.
UP: Stoneman led a corps in battle at Fredericksburg and performed well. Joe Hooker again gave Stoneman command of the Army of the Potomac cavalry. This time, Stoneman had more support and performed to expectations.
UP AGAIN: In the Chancellorsville Campaign, Hooker sent Stoneman's cavalry behind Southern lines in Virginia to occupy the Confederate cavalry. "Stoneman's Raid" succeeded in disrupting Confederate lines of communication, upsetting the government in Richmond, and raising Northern morale.
DOWN: When Hooker lost at Chancellorsville, he blamed Stoneman as his scapegoat. Stoneman was replaced and transferred to Washington for "medical reasons."

BUMMER: Stoneman really didn't have any medical problems, unless you count hemorrhoids, which could be an issue for anyone who rides horses often. But that's sort of a personal problem, and Stoneman didn't make an effort to publicize it himself.

WE'LL CALL THIS FLAT: For the last six months of 1863, Stoneman held the administrative position of head of the Cavalry Bureau in Washington. His job was to supply horses and provide for training new cavalry.

UP: Stoneman was "back in the saddle," leading the Army of the Ohio during the Atlanta Campaign. He participated in several skirmishes against Confederate General Joe Wheeler.

DOWN: In February 1864, Sherman sent Stoneman's cavalry on a raid to cut Hood's supply line. Stoneman extended their plans to include the Andersonville prison camp. But he got into trouble and was captured with seven hundred of his men by the Georgia state militia.

UP: Stoneman was exchanged several months later and returned to Virginia. He continued conducting destruction raids for Sherman. In April 1865, Stoneman went on his last cavalry raid, destroying Confederate railroad lines.

DOWN: Stoneman joined in the hunt to find Confederate President Jefferson Davis, who had fled Richmond. Another Union cavalry unit led by James H. Wilson captured Davis and collected the $100,000 reward offered by President Johnson.

UP: After the war, Stoneman helped with Reconstruction in occupied Memphis, Tennessee, and then in Petersburg, Virginia. The Southerners there regarded him as a fair administrator.

UP: Stoneman returned to the Regular Army and commanded troops in Arizona. He retired from the army to California in 1871. But his career wasn't over yet. In that western state, he served as the railroad commissioner (1876–1878) and governor (1882–1886).

DOWN: Stoneman's ranch in California burned in 1885. Some say it was torched by political rivals. Suspecting his wife of adultery, he left her and returned to his family home in New York. Stoneman died of a stroke in 1894.

UNION COMMANDERS: JAMES HARRISON WILSON (1837-1925)

Background: Born in Illinois to a pioneer family from Virginia; 1860 West Point graduate; Posted to Fort Vancouver, Washington, as a topographical engineer

Civil War Rank Achieved: Major General

Participated in all of the War's Theaters: Port Royal, Fort Pulaski, South Mountain, Antietam, Vicksburg, Chattanooga, Knoxville, Shenandoah Valley, the Wilderness, Franklin, Nashville

Wilson Enters the Civil War: As an engineer, Wilson fought on the battlefield in the West and served as McClellan's aide-de-camp. He was soon recommended by Grant to head the new Cavalry Bureau in Washington.

Wilson took charge of the Bureau in February 1864 as a brigadier general. In the three months he spent behind a desk, he utilized his leadership and organizational talents to their best. Wilson's best-remembered innovation in cavalry operations was providing Spencer repeating rifles for soldiers fighting on horseback.

In April, Wilson moved from engineering to active cavalry duty, commanding a cavalry division first in the Shenandoah Valley, then in the Department of the Mississippi. This is when he conducted one of the Civil War's most successful cavalry raids.

Wilson's Raid: On Sherman's direction, Wilson led his cavalry through Alabama and Georgia in the spring of 1865. Historians note a distinction from similar raids—Wilson controlled his troops and did not allow them to participate in the "total warfare" of looting and burning that is still strongly remembered from Sherman's March to the Sea.

During the twenty-eight-day raid, Wilson targeted the armory, gun manufacturing plant, and warehouses in Selma, one of the last war supply manufacturing cities still under Southern control.

Confederate General Nathan Bedford Forrest—aided by about 2,500 men including Brigadier Generals James Chalmers, James T. Croxton, and even the one-eyed Daniel W. Adams—led his cavalry in repeated attempts to cut off Wilson's three divisions advancing across the state. But, Wilson out fought and outlasted the considerably smaller Confederate cavalry at every turn.

Finally, on April 2, the Confederates retreated and abandoned the important town. After capturing Selma, Wilson headed east. Along the way, he captured Montgomery, Alabama, on April 12 and Columbus, Georgia, on April 16 (Most people consider this the last battle of the Civil War). On April 20, Wilson captured Macon, Georgia.

The Capture of Jefferson Davis: New president Andrew Johnson offered a $100,000 reward to anyone who caught Jefferson Davis. Wilson's units took on the chase. Before they went down in the history books on May 10, 1865, in Irwinsville, Georgia, and split the cash among them, Wilson's regiments suffered a small, but definite, tragedy.

Two different regiments, thinking they were closing in on Davis, were actually closing in on each other. Each group fired on the other. Before anyone realized the mistake, two men were dead and many were wounded. They did reach their target, though, and claimed the reward.

Wilson After the War: Wilson remained on active duty in the U.S. Army Corps of Engineers until 1870. He served in Puerto Rico and Cuba during the Spanish War and joined in China's Boxer Rebellion in 1901.

Old Soldiers: When he died in 1925, Wilson was the last living member of his West Point class. Only three Union Civil War generals survived him.

UNION QUARTERMASTER GENERAL: MONTGOMERY C. MEIGS (1816-1892)

Born in Augusta, Georgia, Montgomery Meigs was raised in Philadelphia, Pennsylvania. He graduated in 1836 from West Point and began his long service in the U.S. Army Engineer Corps.

By virtue of his Army connections, Meigs was appointed quartermaster general of the U.S. Army in June 1861. What does that mean? Other than food and ordnance (weapons), Meigs was in charge of purchasing and distributing all the supplies for the entire army. You name it, and he was in charge of making it happen: horses, tents, vehicles, clothing, canteens, and medicine.

It turns out, Montgomery Meigs had great talent for this, and it has been said that without his considerable contribution to the war effort, the Union Army would not have had anywhere close to the success that it did. He was described as "remarkably" efficient and scrupulous, as well as a budgetary wizard. Union soldiers were always better equipped than Confederates, even though the bulk of the war was fought on Confederate soil.

One example of Meigs's genius is the organization required to sail the Army of the Potomac to Fort Monroe during the Peninsula Campaign. In addition to various pontoon bridges, tents, and telegraph wire, he spent three weeks delivering the following to the island at the mouth of Hampton Roads:

- Four hundred ships
- 121,500 men
- 14,592 horses and mules
- 1,150 wagons
- Forty-four batteries of artillery
- Seventy-four ambulances

Arlington National Cemetery exists where it does today as a result of Meigs's suggestion to locate it on the abandoned property owned by Robert E. Lee. The land was first used to bury Union soldiers in the spring of 1864, when other local Washington military cemeteries had become completely full of fallen soldiers. Meigs's own son was buried there less than a year later, and it is also Meigs's final resting place.

Even after the Civil War, Meigs held his position as quartermaster general until he retired in 1882. More than a hundred years later, Meigs was inducted into the Quartermaster Hall of the Fame in the program's first year, 1986.

Thanks to Montgomery Meigs

We can thank Montgomery Meigs for many of his military innovations that eventually became a part of civilian life. He introduced standard "sizing" to make uniforms fit better—and now we can order clothes online based on size charts.

Meigs also encouraged the practice of machine-sewing shoe uppers to the sole—and today we can't imagine buying hand-sewn shoes.

WHY MEIGS CHOSE LEE'S LAND FOR ARLINGTON NATIONAL CEMETERY

What we're about to tell you amounts to rumor. We don't repeat gossip, so you better pay attention the first time.

As the war progressed, Meigs hated the Southerners fighting against the Union more and more. He especially hated his old Corps of Engineers colleague Robert E. Lee.

So in 1864, when Secretary of War Edwin Stanton asked Meigs to find land for a new army cemetery, Meigs immediately thought of a way to make sure Lee could never return to his Virginia home in Arlington.

You'll recall that Lee and his wife had abandoned the land early in the war. They were unable to pay the property taxes, because laws required payment in person, and the U.S. government seized the land.

Meigs personally oversaw the burial of twenty-six Union soldiers next to Mary Custis Lee's rose garden. Later, Meigs had a Tomb of the Unknown Dead from the Civil War built in the middle of the garden, marking the burial site of more than 1,100 unidentified Union soldiers.

CONFEDERATE OFFICERS

Daniel W. Adams
Laurence S. Baker
P. G. T. Beauregard
Braxton Bragg
William L. Brandon
John C. Breckenridge
Franklin Buchanan
Matthew C. Butler
John C. Cheves
Charles Clark
Patrick Ronayne Cleburne
James Connor
Stapleton Crutchfield
Jubal A. Early
Thomas T. Eckert
Nathan Evans
Richard Ewell
William H. Forney
Nathan Bedford Forrest
Birkett D. Fry
John Brown Gordon
Wade Hampton
William Joseph Hardee
A. P. Hill
Daniel Harvey Hill
Theopohilus H. Holmes
John Bell Hood
Albert Sidney Johnston
Joseph E. Johnston
John Kerr
James Longstreet
William W. Loring

John B. Magruder
James G. Martin
Dabney Maury
Matthew F. Maury
John S. Mosby
Francis R. Nicholls
George Pickett
Edmund Kirby Smith
Marcellus A. Stovall
James Ewell Brown Stuart
Stand Watie
Henry Wirz
Felix Zollicoffer

SECOND BULL RUN

Vexed yet again by a general who would not do what was asked of him, Lincoln—provoked by McClellan's latest request for more men—installed General John Pope as lead commander in the East. Pope became head of the newly named and consolidated Army of Virginia while Henry W. Halleck took over as general-in-chief of all Union forces. Halleck, knowing McClellan's hesitant tendencies, sent the Army of the Potomac north from Harrison's Landing in Virginia to combine forces under Pope's command at Chesapeake Bay.

As Pope awaited McClellan in late-August, the Confederates stirred up trouble with a series of daring raids by Jeb Stuart as well as Stonewall Jackson's successful attack on the Union supply station at Manassas, site of the First Battle of Bull Run. Frustrated by Jackson and Stuart circling the Union men, Pope was ready to fight, which the Union and Confederacy did, beginning on August 29.

Pope and the Northern troops unleashed a barrage on Jackson, whose men eventually withdrew. The Confederates had been turned back. Pope assumed victory.

It wasn't to be. The other half of Robert E. Lee's Army—under General James Longstreet—had arrived on the twenty-ninth but did not participate in the first day's fighting. The next day, Longstreet's men tore into the left flank of the Union army, inflicting severe, damage.

Longstreet wreaked havoc on the Union troops, leading Pope to retreat under cover of darkness. The Union ended the battle with more than fourteen thousand casualties, while the Confederates lost eight thousand men. For Pope, it was a speedy end to a brief rise to prominence. Lincoln sent him to Minnesota and McClellan once again assumed command.

HOSPITAL HELL

Medical conditions during the Civil War were, to understate things, dreadful. Armies on both sides endured awful care facilities that lacked doctors, nurses, and equipment. As the Union army surgeon general famously remarked, the Civil War took place "at the end of the medical Middle Ages."

Medical training in the United States at the time the war began lagged in comparison to European standards. Harvard University acquired its first stethoscopes and microscopes only after the Civil War was over—a clear indication of how primitive the medical environment in America was at the time.

Wounded soldiers were far more common than dead soldiers. The wounded no doubt often envied their fallen comrades. Makeshift hospitals lacked sanitation standards and equipment. Almost without exception, they were understaffed as well. At the start of the war, the Union had a medical staff of about a hundred, four times that of the Confederates. Four years later, that disparity remained, with the Union using twelve thousand doctors and the Confederates eight thousand. Neither side had enough doctors or medical equipment, though conditions improved as the war went on.

Battlefields and encampments worsened the situation. Latrine water routinely was located nearby or even in the camps, while discarded food, trash, and other unsavory items piled near where the men ate and slept. It was a predictable prescription for illness and disease, giving constant life to bacteria and viruses.

The principal maladies included diarrhea and dysentery, typhoid and pneumonia. Doctors were unsure how to cure diarrhea and dysentery, and around 27,558 soldiers died from these maladies. Sixty thousand Union soldiers died from malaria. Attempted cures included laudanum, opium, castor oil, turpentine, and whiskey. Doctors used flannel wraps for the body and opiates to alleviate pain. Disease was the leading cause of death for Civil War soldiers.

Poor diets—bread, coffee and little else—worsened the illnesses borne by soldiers.

According to historian James M. McPherson, "Disease reduced the size of most regiments from their initial complement of a thousand men to about half that number before the regiment ever went into battle."

In other words, Pepto-Bismol could have earned a fortune—and prevented tens of thousands of deaths along the way—if it had been available during the Civil War.

Snapshot: Jeb Stuart

A dashing figure known for tactical acumen and a flair for the dramatic, James Ewell Brown "Jeb" Stuart became a celebrity during the Civil War. Stuart led his cavalry on a series of daring reconnaissance missions, delivering key information about the Union to Confederate commander Robert E. Lee while, not insignificantly, burnishing his colorful reputation.

Stuart, in fact, personally dispatched accounts of his battlefield derring-do to various newspapers as a way to relax after his military rides. He also became known for his sartorial splendor, sporting a red-lined cape and a plumed hat in the saddle. Stuart's exploits included a spectacular 1862 spying mission on Union General George McClellan's Army of the Potomac, during which Stuart circled the entire Northern army and gleaned details for Lee's battle plan. Later in 1862, Stuart even managed to snatch the dress uniform of Union commander John Pope from Union camp headquarters, an audacious feat by any measure.

In May 1864, Stuart was killed in battle.

WOMEN IN THE WAR

Nurses

One way women contributed was volunteering as nurses, either in the Northern hospitals, or the many Southern homes opened to the battle-wounded. At the time, army nurses were all men, as it was considered scandalous for women to experience such horrors as were seen in army hospitals. This sense of propriety was dropped as the casualties and injuries began to so far outnumber the doctors available.

Women clung to the belief that offering comfort and relief to another woman's man when he was far from home would mean another unknown sympathetic woman might offer the same level of care to their own men.

Relief Efforts

Women provided supplies, knitted socks and mittens, sewed shirts, raised money for relief, and made bandages for the wounded. They held sewing bees, food drives, and benefits to raise money and collect medicine.

Going to War

Some wives couldn't bear to be separated from their husbands and followed behind the troops, setting up in the civilian camps that were always near the army encampments. They cooked, sewed, laundered, and otherwise offered support as if everyone were still at home.

Other women even enlisted. It was unbelievably easy for a woman to dress in pants and act as a man. Passing the most basic physical exam, she could easily join the army without her secret being detected.

Spies

It was also surprisingly easy for women to move among opposing troops, gather intelligence, and pass it on to their own men.

WOMEN AS CONFEDERATE SPIES: BELLE BOYD

Maria Isabella "Belle" Boyd was probably the best known of all Southern spies. Before her eighteenth birthday, she watched Union soldiers pillage her father's Front Royal, Virginia, home, and then resolved to spy for the Confederacy.

Stonewall Jackson's Aide-de-camp: An attractive young girl, Boyd used her feminine ways to wrangle valuable information from Union soldiers, who had no idea that her flirting was more than girlish fun. Thus Boyd was able to provide Generals Turner Ashby and Stonewall Jackson with valuable information about Union troop movement in the Shenandoah Valley in early 1862.

While other spies employed operatives and servants to deliver messages, Boyd carried reports in person, making dangerous nighttime rides through Union territory to the Confederate officers. For her daring, Jackson appointed her a captain and honorary aide-de-camp on his staff. She soon became known as "La Belle Rebelle."

Arrested and Imprisoned: Having made a pastime of bewitching men, Boyd was bewildered when one lover betrayed her identity. She was arrested in mid-1862—the first of at least six times she was detained—and held for a month in Washington's Old Capitol Prison.

Prison guards could not grasp the concept of pretty women as spies, and spent too much time talking to the pretty Belle. She listened carefully, then immediately revealed their secrets to Confederate sympathizers outside the jail by hiding messages inside rubber balls, then pitching them out her cell window.

Released and Rearrested: Boyd spent a month in jail, and less than a year later, was arrested again in Martinsburg. Six months later, suffering from typhoid, she managed to get released from prison.

Travels to England: Boyd claimed she was going to Europe to recuperate. But, many believe she was actually taking secret papers from Jefferson Davis to Confederates overseas. To return to America,

Boyd traveled on a blockade runner that could get her past Union ships and into Southern harbors. But, that landing never happened.

Belle Meets Sam: The blockade runner was intercepted by Union Captain Samuel Hardinge. A war romance followed, and Hardinge helped Boyd escape to Canada. From there, she went back to England. Hardinge was dismissed from the U.S. Navy for neglecting his duty by letting his captive escape, and he headed across the Atlantic, too. In England, Sam married Belle.

Belle Loses Sam: Sam left to return to Richmond. Unfortunately, he was captured by Union soldiers and imprisoned in New York. He died shortly after his release, without seeing his young bride again.

The Widow Belle Boyd: After her husband's death, Belle wrote *Belle Boyd in Camp and Prison* in 1865 in hopes of raising money. She also began acting on the English stage. She married an English soldier and moved to Stockton, California. They divorced, and six weeks after, she married an actor seventeen years her junior. She toured the western United States, publicly speaking about her Civil War adventures.

Belle Boyd's Feminine Wiles

While riding with two Confederate officers near Union lines, Belle's horse bolted. The Confederate soldiers knew better than to follow within striking distance of the Union soldiers, lest they be shot.

Belle, however did not worry. Upon gaining control of her horse, she found herself in Union territory. Two unsuspecting Union soldiers made a gallant move to escort who they thought was a helpless woman back to Confederate territory.

Once they arrived, Belle made a big show of delivering two Union prisoners to the Confederates; nevertheless, the Southern soldiers let the Northerners go.

WOMEN AS CONFEDERATE SPIES: ROSE O'NEAL GREENHOW

A Flower of Washington Society: Born in Maryland, Rose O'Neal spent her teenage years with her family in Washington, D.C., society. An all-around lovely woman, O'Neal was known to be friendly, smart, outgoing, social, beautiful, and any other superlative you want to apply here. Her years in Washington were spent increasing an ever-widening social circle that would prove to matter greatly in later years. Her association with John C. Calhoun would later identify Rose as a Southern loyalist.

Of her many Washington suitors, Rose O'Neal married Dr. Robert Greenhow, and they had four daughters. By the time Dr. Greenhow died in 1854, he had attained a post in the U.S. State Department. By virtue of her husband's position, Rose Greenhow numbered among her friends many high-ranking officials who would play parts (witting or not) in her role as Confederate spy.

Rose Leads the Spy Ring: The story goes that Thomas Jordan, Philip Sheridan's old West Point roommate, was responsible for setting up a network of spies in Washington to further the South's cause. He put Rose in charge, gave her a quickly devised coding system for messages, and then fled to the safety of the Confederacy. As it turned out, Jordan's "secret" code was so poor that pretty much anyone who intercepted Rose's papers could easily crack it.

Rose O'Neal Greenhow was a thirty-six-year-old widow. She must have still been quite a looker, because her suitors included President James Buchanan, New York's Senator William Seward, future Secretary of War Edwin Stanton, and Massachusetts Senator Henry Wilson.

Rose Influences the Battle of Bull Run: It's Henry Wilson who turned out to be of most use. He provided Greenhow the means to gather intelligence for the Southern troops. It was good intelligence, indeed, that Greenhow provided to General P. G. T. Beauregard, resulting in huge Union losses at First Bull Run.

Union General George McClellan later said it was almost like the rebels knew the orders even before some of the other Union commanders heard them. Wilson denied giving any information to Greenhow, although she had letters signed, "Yours ever, H," written on U.S. Senate stationery of the thirty-sixth Congress.

Operating from Old Capitol Prison: Suspected of espionage, Greenhow was held in Old Capitol Prison along with her youngest child, Little Rose, in 1862. While imprisoned, she continued gathering and forwarding information to Confederates, knitting presents for her friends with code messages included in the design. She even sent a message by carrier pigeon to Jefferson Davis. Finally, claiming her daughter was sick, Greenhow convinced guards to let her go and was deported to Richmond.

From Richmond, Jefferson Davis sent Greenhow to Europe to relay information to Confederate agents there. In 1864, she returned from Europe with urgent information for Davis, as well as $2,000 in gold intended for aiding the Southern cause. Neither reached their destination.

The Blockade Runner Captured: Traveling on a blockade runner to get to North Carolina's shore, Greenhow's party met with danger. A Union ship forced the smaller boat aground on a sandbar. Greenhow did not want to risk capture and another stay in prison, so she and two other men attempted to row ashore in a lifeboat. Rough waters capsized the little boat. Weighed down by the gold tied around her waist, Rose drowned.

Her body washed ashore, and the lucky person who first found it made off with the gold. The second time it was found and identified, she was buried with honors in Wilmington. In Washington, she was known as "Wild Rose." In Richmond, they called her "Rebel Rose."

WOMEN AS UNION SPIES:
PAULINE CUSHMAN

New Orleans native Pauline Cushman began as an actress in New York City at the age of eighteen. You would expect actors to be good spies, but by the Civil War, it was apparent that Cushman wasn't a great actress. One role, however, propelled her into espionage.

In 1862, she was performing in an unmemorable play in Louisville. The script required her character to give a toast. One night she answered a dare to toast Jefferson Davis on stage. It certainly made her look like a Southern sympathizer, and she was banned from the theater and banished beyond Confederate lines.

This put her in place to spy for the Union. She dressed in her finery to attract Confederate officers, and joined other camp followers in Kentucky and Tennessee. It worked. She gleaned valuable information about troop movements and fed it to Union General William Rosecrans.

Then her acting skills failed. Confederate soldiers near Shelbyville, Tennessee, caught her with drawings from their army engineers. Cushman was taken to General Braxton Bragg, court-martialed, and sentenced to hang. She broke down (perhaps she was acting then), and her sentence was delayed.

Cushman got lucky. Before Bragg could send her to the gallows, he had to retreat out of Shelbyville—and quickly. So quickly, in fact, that they left her behind. Northern forces rescued her, and she helped the Union one last time, relaying information on Confederate strength and their plans.

For her accomplishments, President Lincoln made Cushman an honorary major. She traveled the country, giving speeches about her adventures as a Confederate spy. The novelty of a female spy doesn't last forever, though, and soon there was no interest in her tales. She returned to acting, and eventually committed suicide with an opium overdose. She was buried with military honors in San Francisco.

Women as Union Spies: Elizabeth Van Lew ("Crazy Bet")

Remembered as an effective Union spy, Richmond-native Elizabeth Van Lew gained her strong abolitionist views while attending school in Philadelphia. By the beginning of the Civil War, she was a middle-aged spinster and set in her ways, some of which were decidedly kooky.

Crazy Bet: The neighbors all called her "Crazy Bet" for her eccentric actions that ranged from bizarre dress to wandering the streets singing nonsense songs. She was known to be rebellious (her home was a stop on the Underground Railroad) and outspoken. In fact, her running off at the mouth proved to be a great cover for spying; who would suspect someone to be so transparent? Spies kept their loyalties to themselves to avoid discovery, so surely someone who so openly pledged allegiance to the Union could not be a spy, right?

Libby Prison: Van Lew accomplished quite a lot of espionage just by visiting Union soldiers held at Libby Prison. She brought baskets of food, medicine, and books to the imprisoned men.

- She talked to new arrivals to get information about the strength and location of Confederate troops they had seen while en route to the prison.
- She eavesdropped on prison guards, who thought she was too crazy to understand the things they were saying about military plans.
- She helped prisoners escape.
- She taught the Union prisoners to communicate with her in code through the books they exchanged, either by underlining words or pricking under letters with a pin.

- She delivered supplies and messages in pie pans that had false bottoms. (Once, a suspicious guard asked to inspect a dish to be delivered to a prisoner. She gladly placed the heated pan, which she had been holding with her shawl, in his bare hand.)

Infiltrating Jefferson Davis's Home: "Crazy Bet" was crazy like a fox. She loaned one of her former slaves to Jefferson Davis himself. Unbeknownst to the Davis family, the servant, named Mary Elizabeth Van Lew Bowser, had been educated in Northern schools and was able to read confidential papers. Like other Southerners, the Davis family assumed that Mary Elizabeth could not read, and were careless about leaving important papers out in the open.

Delivering the Intelligence: In the beginning, Van Lew Bowser simply mailed letters to federal officials (yeah, that one makes us laugh, too). Then, she devised a more covert system: She sent household servants northward with baskets of eggs to sell. Some of the eggs had been hollowed out, with papers of encoded messages replacing the whites and yolks.

Not only did Van Lew Bowser have good sources and foolproof delivery methods, she also provided timely intelligence. In fact, she is known to have sent flowers to General Grant from her garden, undoubtedly a note of some kind attached, which arrived still "fresh as a daisy." Grant later said, "You have sent me the most valuable information received from Richmond during the war."

When he was elected President, Grant repaid Van Lew Bowser's efforts by naming her postmistress of Richmond, a position she held from 1869 to 1877. By this point, her exploits to the Union's favor were well-known among her neighbors, who snubbed her thoroughly and without ceasing. She died in Richmond.

Edgar Allan Poe is said to have recited his poem "The Raven" during a party at the Van Lew mansion in Richmond.

WOMEN MASQUERADING AS MEN DRESSED AS WOMEN, PART I

Fast Facts About Confederate Spy Loreta Janeta Velázquez

- Loreta claimed that her ancestor was Diego Velázquez, who was the conqueror and first governor of Cuba.
- Originally from Cuba, Loreta Janeta Velázquez married a U.S. army officer in 1856. They settled in New Orleans.
- Velázquez asked to accompany her husband to battle, but he refused to let her.
- Velázquez decided to participate in the war anyway. She used some of her own great personal wealth to design a uniform with a wire frame that would hide her female figure and make her look masculine.
- Her disguise included the special uniform and a realistic moustache and beard. Her self-description: "an uncommonly good-looking fellow."
- After fashioning her disguise, by the time she reached her husband at camp, she only had a short time with him. His gun misfired, killing him.
- She took her husband's place and made up the name Lieutenant Harry Buford. She paid for her own supplies and equipment.
- As Buford, Velázquez traveled with a black servant named Bob, who apparently did not know her true identity.
- Assigned to a reserve unit, she participated in the Battle of Bull Run, where she acted as courier for Confederate General Bernard Bee.
- She claimed to have temporarily commanded a company during the Battle of Ball's Bluff (Virginia) when the officers disappeared and were assumed dead. After the battle, the first lieutenant mysteriously reappeared, saying he had been captured by Yankees but escaped. Velázquez wondered if he had not just been hiding.
- Velázquez offered her services as a Confederate spy. Her disguise was as a female. She borrowed the clothes from a slave.

- According to her own claims, she once traveled to Washington and met Abraham Lincoln.
- Velázquez fought in the Battle of Fort Donelson in Tennessee.
- At the Battle of Shiloh, she was wounded. Rather than risk discovery by an army surgeon, she slipped away to New Orleans to heal.
- As her disguise was war-battered and had seen better days, she looked suspicious enough that Confederate soldiers detained her for being a Union spy. She challenged the guards to make any specific charges against her, which they could not. They let her go, arrested her the next day on suspicion of being a woman, which she soon confessed to.
- After a short some time in prison, she headed back to Tennessee to reenlist as Buford.
- Helping to bury dead soldiers near Corinth, Mississippi, she was wounded in the arm by shellfire. This time, an army surgeon all but discovered her secret. She retreated to New Orleans, and hung up her soldier's uniform to work as a female spy.
- From New Orleans, she operated as a blockade runner to Cuba, bringing back supplies and medicines. Under threat of discovery, she moved toward Richmond.
- In Richmond, she was discovered as a woman and imprisoned at Castle Thunder for being a Union spy. She befriended the prison superintendent's wife and wangled a release to continue her Confederate espionage.
- Moving to Atlanta, she met up with an old friend of her late husband's. They were married (she wore a dress to the ceremony). Velázquez also lost this husband in the Civil War.
- After the war ended, she married for the third time, then the fourth time, had a child, and traveled throughout the southwest.

WOMEN MASQUERADING AS MEN DRESSED AS WOMEN, PART II

Union Spy Sarah Emma Edmonds

In April 1861, Sarah Emma Edmonds enlisted in the United States Army as male nurse Franklin Thompson. She cut her hair, dressed in a man's suit, and passed the army physical by answering questions. There was no medical examination.

Emma heard that McClellan needed a spy for the Virginia campaign. She studied weapons, tactics, local geography, and military personalities, and thus excelled in the interview for the position.

The Many Disguises of Sarah Emma Edmonds

Cuff: Emma decided to disguise herself as a black man. She used silver nitrate to darken her skin, put on a black wig, called herself "Cuff," and set out for the Confederate front. "Cuff" was sent to help build the ramparts to hold McClellan. Her hands were so blistered after the first day that she switched assignments with another slave. The second day, working in the kitchen, she heard about the size of the army, weapons available, and even the "Quaker guns" (logs painted black to look like cannon from afar) to be used at Yorktown. She delivered the information in a personal interview with McClellan.

Bridget O'Shea: Edmonds dressed as a fat Irish peddler woman to sell wares at the Confederate camps and garner as much information as she could.

Mammy: Edmonds dressed as a black mammy laundering uniforms in a Confederate camp, again blacking her face and wearing a bandanna head-wrap. She struck "gold" while cleaning an officer's coat—a packet of papers fell out of the pocket. Edmonds scooped them up and quickly delivered them to Union officers.

Charles Mayberry: Edmonds assumed the role of a young man with Southern sympathies to infiltrate the Southern spy network in Louisville.

Problems for Private Thompson

Before the battle of Vicksburg, Edmonds contracted malaria. Afraid to admit herself to the hospital where her true identity would be discovered, she decided to leave camp for awhile and recover in private. She traveled to Cairo, Illinois, donned ladies' dresses, and checked herself into a hospital.

While in Cairo, Edmonds read an army bulleting listing Private Frank Thompson as a Union deserter. She decided that it would be best not to assume that disguise again. So, she traveled to Washington and worked as a—female—nurse until the end of the war. Private Frank Thompson had completed eleven successful missions.

After the War

Edmonds published the popular best-seller *Nurse and Spy in the Union Army,* and in 1867 married Linus Seelye with whom she had three sons. But although she had a happy life, she was bothered that her career as Frank Thompson, after all her contributions, had ended on such an unpleasant note.

Emma petitioned the War Department to review the case. In 1884, a special act of Congress granted Emma Edmonds, alias Frank Thompson, an honorable discharge from the army, plus a bonus and a veteran's pension of $12 a month.

Final Days

Sarah Emma Edmonds Seelye died in Texas in 1889. She is buried in the military section of Washington Cemetery in Houston.

WAR IS HELL ON THE HOME FRONT, TOO

With their menfolk gone, women found themselves taking over roles normally reserved for the male gender. Women excelled at them, too, learning quickly how to barter for goods and services, as well as how to pay bills and balance accounts. Northern women stepped into positions in mills and factories. Southern women began managing the farms, cultivating crops, and even defending their homes and valuables from enemy raids.

Women suffered emotionally, though. They missed their men, writing letter after letter telling them how much they cared and worried. Many women went so far as to petition the government to get their men released from service, both by letter and by personal visits to Presidents Lincoln or Davis.

Particularly in the South, where the ports were blockaded against imported goods, women struggled to feed their families, teetering on the brink of starvation. To add insult to injury, Southern women faced raids for food and supplies, both by Union forces and by desperate Confederate renegades. Especially the case at farms located far from cities and other nearby neighbors, women on the home front feared pillaging by Union forces of their already scant food stores. Union soldiers ruthlessly burned farms to prevent Confederate troops from potentially benefiting from any crops there.

To protect themselves against pillaging and other personal crimes, women learned to load, aim, and shoot guns. We've all heard tales about women burying silverware to hide it from the Yankees; others were known to conceal it in the hoops of their skirts.

In the final years of the war, Union forces advanced across the South. Many women fled their homes with what little they could carry, moving from one refuge to the next ahead of the Northern army.

EXTREME MAKEOVERS OF THE DESPERATE KIND

As in all wars, goods became scarce and prices for those still available skyrocketed. The situation was especially dire in the South, where Northern blockades prevented ships from importing goods. Even if there had been money to purchase supplies, simply put, there was nothing to buy.

Creative Southern women practiced extreme self-reliance that would make today's "green" movement pale in comparison. They resorted to natural substitutes for everything from food ingredients to medicines to clothes-making materials.

Newspapers published recipes for alternative soap, along with information on how to get the materials for making all the substitutions. For candles, Confederate ladies sewed together rags, dipped them in liquid wax, or if beeswax was not available, used boiled berries with cow fat.

Instead of . . .	Women used . . .
lemonade	maypop seed pulp juice
ink	pomegranate rind and poke berries
kerosene	distilled turpentine
insecticide	ox-eyed daisy
wine	blackberry, wild grape, and elderberry wine
soda	seaweed and corncobs
sugar	honey
candles	dried corn husks
purple cloth dye	maple and sweet gum bark, black oak galls in a vitriol solution
dove color cloth dye	maple, red oak, and copperas

brown cloth dye	maple and walnut
black cloth dye	sweet gum and copperas, smooth sumac, root and bark, berries, walnut root and leaves
yellow cloth dye	peach tree leaves and alum, artichoke and black oak bark, alum and alder
bright yellow cloth dye	black oak bark and alum
pale yellow to bright orange cloth dye	tin oxide
green cloth dye	hickory bark and alum
brown cloth dye	white oak and alum
olive cloth dye	hickory bark and copperas

Snapshot: Clara Barton

Known as the "Angel of the Battlefield," Clara Barton, a school teacher and patent clerk, began volunteering to help wounded and dying soldiers soon after the Battle of Bull Run.

Barton's early involvement included gathering and taking supplies into the field for wounded men, whom she tended to with legendary care. Commanders allowed Barton to ride in Union army ambulances and she worked amid chaos and bloodied men during campaigns around Richmond and other parts of Virginia.

Just after the war ended, Barton went to the notorious Confederate prison site in Andersonville, Georgia, where she identified and marked the graves of Union soldiers who died there, giving them a proper final resting place. Barton's reputation was enhanced after the war. She worked for women's suffrage and, at the behest of Frederick Douglass, backed the cause of civil rights. Her legacy was secured with the successful establishment of the American Red Cross in 1881.

HELL ON EARTH: ANTIETAM

The battle of Antietam in western Maryland, fought in September 1862, remains the bloodiest single day of warfare in American history. Confederate and Union forces waged a devastating twelve-hour battle that left twenty-three thousand casualties among the 100,000 soldiers who participated.

The battle took its name from nearby Antietam Creek. Sharpsburg, Maryland, was the main site of the battle. Though it is commonly referred to as Antietam, Southerners often refer to it as the Battle of Sharpsburg.

The battle marked the end of Robert E. Lee's first foray into the North. Known as the Maryland Campaign, Lee's strategy focused on moving the war out of Virginia—home of the Confederate capitol— and into enemy territory. The gambit was also aimed at geographically separating Maryland from the Union, a reasonable notion considering its role as a border state that included slaveholders and a significant number of Southern sympathizers.

Lee made plans to embark on the attack soon after winning the Second Battle of Manassas in late-August. He crossed the Potomac and sent half of his forces with General Stonewall Jackson to seize control of Harpers Ferry, an important supply link for the Confederates. Lee's movements prompted President Lincoln to order Major General George B. McClellan to gather the dazed Army of the Potomac and fight the invading Southerners.

The armies first met on September 14, 1862, on South Mountain in Maryland. It led to a Confederate retreat, prompting Lee to consider crossing the Potomac back into Virginia. Instead, Lee went for the throat at Sharpsburg, buoyed in part by news of Stonewall Jackson's successful capture of the Union garrison at Harpers Ferry.

McClellan moved his men into position during the next two days. As dawn broke after a rainy night on September 17, soldiers enshrouded in fog tore into one another. The Union launched several major attacks on the left side of the Confederate Army as Lee adjusted constantly in an effort to stave off defeat. Cruel, fierce fighting haunted every corner of the battle. So much blood was spilled on a farm road, then known as the Sunken Road, that it would thereafter be known as "Bloody Lane." On the right side of the Confederate forces, Union General Ambrose Burnside attacked and captured a bridge, later dubbed the Burnside Bridge, but he delayed his follow-up engagement, thus allowing the Confederates time to gather much-needed reinforcements from Harpers Ferry.

Six generals were killed at Antietam or died from mortal injuries suffered during the battle. Three of the fallen generals were from the North and three from the South.

On September 18, the bloodied, decimated armies buried their fallen comrades and tended to the thousands of wounded soldiers. The Battle of Antietam was over.

While neither army gave ground, the battle marked a major turning point for the Union, because Lee ended his Northern invasion and headed back to Virginia with his army. That move allowed Lincoln the opening he had been seeking to publicly issue a so-called preliminary Emancipation Proclamation on September 23— less than a week after the battle at Antietam. It stated the slaves would be freed in all states outside the Union as of January 1, 1863.

UNION COMMANDERS: BENJAMIN FRANKLIN BUTLER (1818-1893)

Character Descriptions

- Balding, overweight, cross-eyed, incompetent
- Known throughout the Confederacy as "Beast Butler"
- Rode a horse named "Almond Eye"

Baltimore Skirmish: Butler was in an early skirmish in April 1861. His 6th Massachusetts Militia headed to defend Washington. Marching through Baltimore, the militia was verbally harassed by secessionists called "Plug Uglies." Things escalated, and the mob started throwing bricks and rocks.

The militia fired on the Plug Uglies. Butler swore he did not order the troops to fire, and no one ever admitted who took the first shot. The point is, federal troops armed with weapons fired on civilians armed with clubs and stones. At least twelve civilians and four soldiers were killed.

To Coin a Phrase: In May 1861, Butler was charged with holding Fort Monroe in Virginia, the one installation that never fell under Confederate control. Escaped slaves began coming to the fort for amnesty. Butler tried returning them to their homes, but things got out of hand.

Completely unauthorized, he declared those people as "contraband of war." Technically, slaves were not free, but they were confiscated property. Congress passed a Confiscation Act, and runaway slaves were called "Contrabands."

No Popularity Contests in New Orleans: After the Union captured New Orleans in 1862, Butler was named military governor. He ordered that any woman who insulted any U.S. officer would be treated as a prostitute, after one "lady" emptied her chamber pot over Admiral David Farragut's head. (Before indoor plumbing, people kept little pots under the bed to use when nature called in the night.) No wonder, then, that the ladies took to lining the insides of their chamber pots with Butler's picture.

Butler also threatened to impose a $25 fine on anyone he heard singing "The Bonnie Blue Flag."

"Spoons" Butler: Butler earned himself an even less-complimentary nickname, from a nasty little habit of stealing Confederate property, including silverware, from local houses and churches.

Going From Bad to Worse: Thankfully, Butler's superiors in Washington recognized the levels of bribery and corruption he had reached. He was removed from his position and later sent to command troops in Virginia. While there, he attempted to reroute the James River and carry out other equally preposterous military plans.

After the war, Butler joined Radical Republicans and led the attempt to impeach President Johnson. He remained on the political scene in Congress, as Governor of Massachusetts, and even ran for president in 1884. (If you've studied your American history, you know he lost.)

Get This: During the 1860 election, Jefferson Davis considered running for U.S. president. It didn't go far. But Benjamin Butler put Davis up for nomination at the Democratic convention in Baltimore and voted for him on every ballot—more than fifty times.

Three years later, after Butler's famous "Woman Order" in New Orleans, Davis put out standing orders to have him hanged on the spot if ever caught.

Plug Uglies

Plug Uglies were a Baltimore street gang of pro-secession civilians. They liked to think of themselves as a political club, but they were mostly just thugs. They were named after the plug hats they wore. They also wore studded spikes in the fronts of their boots to really make an impact when kicking someone.

Contrary to what you've been told in historical fiction movies or books, the Plug Uglies were not a gang of New York.

CONFEDERATE COMMANDERS: ALBERT SIDNEY JOHNSTON (1803-1862)

Background: Kentucky native, 1826 West Point graduate (eighth in his class)

Home Life: Widowed in 1836

Description: Handsome, a six footer

Military Experience: Black Hawk War, Brigadier General in the Republic of Texas, Secretary of War in Texas

Union Assessment of Johnston's Leadership Potential: Grant said he "expected him to provide the most formidable men that the Confederacy could produce."

Confederate Assessment of Johnston's Leadership Potential: Davis said, "I hoped and expected that I had others who would prove generals, but I knew I had one, and that was Sidney Johnston."

Johnston was known, then, to be a skilled commander. At the beginning of the Civil War, both sides offered him a high commanding position. Johnston was a close friend of Jefferson Davis, so he accepted an appointment as full general commanding the Confederate Department of Mississippi.

Davis gave Johnston free rein in building his Confederate Army in Mississippi. Things were going well until Johnston faced Grant's army at Pittsburg Landing, Tennessee, on April 3, 1862. Grant thought the Confederates would stay in Corinth after the showdown, so he did not order adequate fortifications around the encampment.

Johnston took advantage of this, and the Confederates attacked the poorly defended Union camp. The Northern soldiers broke and ran, and the entire battlefield was chaos.

The fighting was bloody and intense in the little peach orchard near Shiloh church. Riding his horse, FireEater, Johnston led a charge to capture an important position. He thought he had made it through safely, even though his clothes were riddled with bullet holes. There was even evidence of a shot through his boot sole.

"They didn't trip me up that time," he told his aide.

But, as a matter of fact, Johnston was more than just tripped up. He was hit in the leg. Blood was pouring into his boot. Johnston thought it was only a flesh wound, and waved off the surgeon's offer of medical care, sending the doctor to tend to other wounded.

Johnston passed out, still in the saddle. His aides got him off FireEater, but by then it was too late. Johnston had bled out from a severed artery behind his knee. He died right there, in the middle of the afternoon, at age fifty-nine.

When the surgeon returned to Johnston's dead body and looked at the location of the wound and the angle of the shot, the doctor determined that it was likely Johnston had died of an accidental shot from one of his own men.

Without letting the troops know their leader was dead, General P. G. T. Beauregard quickly took over. Confederate forces held the upper hand that day. The hungry Confederate soldiers rushed into the abandoned Union camp and looted the tents, eating what they could find. But Union reinforcements arrived in the night, and the Battle of Shiloh ultimately went on the books as a Confederate loss.

When Jefferson Davis heard of Johnston's death, he openly wept. Davis said, "The cause could have spared a whole state better than that great soldier."

Albert Sidney Johnston was not related to General Joseph E. Johnston.

UNION COMMANDERS: WINFIELD SCOTT (1786-1866)

- Virginia native, a Southerner who remained loyal to the Union
- Nicknamed "Old Fuss and Feathers," as a stickler for rules
- A true war hero, served in every American military action since the War of 1812
- The second Lieutenant General in the U.S. Army after George Washington
- Whig candidate in the 1852 presidential election

By 1861, seventy-five-year-old Scott was too old and overweight to ride horseback, let alone command soldiers in the field. Although suffering from gout, he could advise, which he was happy to do as general-in-chief of the United States Army.

Scott counseled Lincoln to appoint Robert E. Lee as U.S. Army commander. Lee declined and resigned.

Scott opposed volunteer soldiers, knowing the problems surrounding untrained, unskilled troops. Yet, at the war's beginning, Lincoln called seventy-five thousand militia for a three-month tour. Scott tried to train the new soldiers quickly. However, political pressures to get the war going meant that Scott's U.S. Army went into battle ill-prepared. (Most of them also had one foot out the door: First Manassas started around day eighty-nine of the three-month enlistments. Some soldiers simply went home rather than risk battle.

Scott's proposed first a blockade of the South's ports, in order to cut off imports and exports. The planned blockade would then be followed by a naval expedition down the Mississippi River to New Orleans to split the Confederacy in two. The media mocked Scott in the newspapers, calling it the "Anaconda Plan." Most people wanted a more aggressive approach, although Lincoln did order the blockade.

President Lincoln soon tired of Scott's advice, replacing him with General George B. McClellan, who thought of Scott as an old "dotard."

CONFEDERATE COMMANDERS: JOSEPH WHEELER (1836-1906)

- Georgia native, West Point graduate, major general
- Robert E. Lee considered Wheeler one of the two best Confederate cavalry leaders.
- Sixteen horses were shot out from under Wheeler.
- Wheeler's cavalry battled hard against Sherman during the March to the Sea.
- Wheeler's raiders were captured near Atlanta. Trying to pass himself off as a "contraband" slave and avoid imprisonment, Wheeler switched clothes with his valet. His ruse was discovered, and he was sent to Fort Warren Prison anyway.
- After the Civil War, Wheeler served in Congress as a U.S. Representative from Alabama.
- In 1898, Wheeler rejoined the federal army as brigadier general of volunteers to participate in the Spanish-American War.
- Fighting in Cuba, Wheeler sometimes lost track of himself, urging his troops to fight harder against the Yankees.
- Wheeler appeared in the silent film, *The Surrender of General Toral*, which portrayed the surrender of Santiago at the end of the Spanish War.
- With his part in the Spanish-American War, Wheeler served as a war-time general for two opposing forces.
- Wheeler is one of the few Confederate soldiers buried in Arlington National Cemetery.

National Statuary Hall

In 1864, Congress approved a National Statuary Hall and invited each state to send two statues of esteemed citizens for national commemoration. Joe Wheeler was designated by the state of Alabama for bronzed recognition in the United States capitol.

CIVIL WAR OFFICERS TRAINED AT WEST POINT

You're probably catching on that many of the commanders you've read about here graduated from (or at least attended) the U.S. Military Academy at West Point. Established in 1802 to teach the arts and sciences of warfare, West Point has been known ever since to turn out the best military strategists and officers.

That was certainly the case for the Civil War. West Pointers commanded troops on both sides of the conflict, with 151 Confederate and 294 Union generals. In fact, when the war began, of all the graduates living then, 259 took up arms for the Confederacy and 638 for the Union.

In more recent history, well-known West Point graduates include Douglas MacArthur, Dwight D. Eisenhower, George S. Patton, and H. Norman Schwarzkopf.

We've compiled a handy list to show you some of the most recognizable names of the Civil War:

South	North
Jefferson Davis	Ulysses S. Grant
Robert E. Lee	William T. Sherman
Thomas "Stonewall" Jackson	George McClellan
James Longstreet	George Meade
George Pickett	Irvin McDowell
P. G. T. Beauregard	Robert Anderson
Joseph E. Johnston	Herman Haupt
Joseph Wheeler	Montgomery C. Meigs
Jubal Early	Ambrose Burnside
Barnard E. Bee	George Henry Thomas
Joseph Reid Anderson	Gouverneur Kemble Warren
John Clifford Pemberton	Oliver Otis Howard
Josiah Gorgas	George A. Custer
Braxton Bragg	Ranald Slidell Mackenzie

William Hardee
Benjamin Hardin Helm
Leonidas Polk
John Henry Winder
Earl Van Dorn
J. E. B. Stuart
Dabney Herdon Maury
Edmund Kirby Smith
George Washington Custis Lee
Fitzhugh Lee
Albert Sidney Johnston
John Bell Hood
A. P. Hill
Daniel Hill

George Crook
John Sedgwick
Abner Doubleday
William Rosecrans
Benjamin Stone Roberts
Fitz John Porter
James Birdeye McPherson
Alfred Pleasonton
Edmund Kirby
Hugh Judson Kilpatrick
Joseph Hooker
Winfield Scott Hancock
Henry Halleck
Don Carlos Buell
Edwin Stoughton

The "Fighting Joes"

Union General Joseph Hooker was known as "Fighting Joe." Stories say he got his nickname from a media roster that listed "Fighting - Joe Hooker" (as in, "Joe Hooker fought in this battle today").

The Confederacy's "Fighting Joe," General Joseph Wheeler, came by his nickname based on personality. He exhibited a "dogged aggressiveness."

PERRYVILLE

Kentucky worked hard to maintain a neutral stance when the war began in 1861, a fitting response since both Abraham Lincoln and Jefferson Davis were natives. While both North and South initially left the Bluegrass State alone in fear of pushing it into the arms of the enemy, it became clear that this trend would not continue for long. By summer 1861, a small number of Union and Confederate soldiers had arrived in the state.

In 1862, the South had decided to launch a more ambitious invasion in an attempt to get Kentuckians on their side. If successful, Confederate strategists hoped support from residents would help push the Union soldiers out of Kentucky and preserve it for the South.

Edmund Kirby Smith and Braxton Bragg led Confederate soldiers into Kentucky in the summer of 1862. Bragg turned his attention toward Louisville, hoping to take possession of a major city strategically located on the Ohio River. He abandoned that track soon after crossing into Kentucky, allowing Don Carlos Buell and his Union forces to reinforce their hold on Louisville.

Bragg opted instead for the state capital at Frankfort, where he installed a Confederate government on October 4, 1862. Immediately Bragg and the Confederates were confronted by Buell and his soldiers, prompting Bragg to retreat to Lexington. The Confederates then headed for Harrodsburg to join forces with Smith and his men. On October 8, at Perryville, the armies collided, unleashing an intense battle that led to a combined seven thousand casualties.

The Confederates retreated to Tennessee, leaving Kentucky to the Union. Soon after, the North would claim Tennessee as well. Both represented two key victories for the Union forces in the western theater.

END OF THE ROAD

In the wake of Antietam, Abraham Lincoln grew frustrated—yet again—with General George McClellan and his incessant refusal to fight. McClellan's failure to pursue Robert E. Lee and the Confederate army after Antietam cost the Union a prime opportunity to end the war.

Instead McClellan allowed Lee and his army, battered but intact, to retreat back to Virginia. Their escape set off a sequence of events that extended the war by nearly three years and cost both North and South hundreds of thousands of lives.

Two weeks after Antietam, on October 1, 1862, McClellan had failed to move. Lincoln, angered by his army's lack of action, ordered McClellan to cross the Potomac River and take the fight to Lee and the Confederates. McClellan chose to ignore the orders and stayed put. Another week passed. Lincoln, now furious over McClellan's recalcitrance, asked the general why he still had not taken action. McClellan's blamed cavalry fatigue, which included horses suffering from hoof-rot and other maladies.

At last, in late-October, McClellan and the Army of the Potomac set out, but only after Jeb Stuart's latest foray into Union territory created derisive headlines in the North. McClellan had waited too long to get going. The constant delays allowed Lee to regroup the Confederate troops and cut the Union forces off well before they threatened Richmond.

On November 5, the inevitable occurred, and Lincoln relieved McClellan, replacing "Young Napoleon" with Ambrose Burnside.

FREDERICKSBURG

The 120,000-man Army of the Potomac was camped near Warrenton, Virginia, when Ambrose Burnside assumed command in November 1862. Burnside favored an attack on Fredericksburg, forty miles away. His strategy was to put the Union forces in line for a direct march to Richmond.

Lincoln approved Burnside's plan, and on November 15, the Army of the Potomac moved out. Two days later, Burnside's troops were in place.

After Antietam two months earlier, Robert E. Lee had divided his seventy-eight thousand-man Army of Northern Virginia. Stonewall Jackson had taken half of the men into the Shenandoah Valley, leaving Lieutenant General James Longstreet with the other half. Longstreet arrived in Fredericksburg on November 19, a day after Burnside. The Union's opportunity vanished while Burnside, instead of searching for alternative crossing routes, waited for army pontoon bridges to arrive instead.

The delay gave Longstreet time to take up defensive positions, including positions in the hills beyond town. Bureaucratic bungling and other factors locked Burnside in place for a week, still waiting for the pontoons. In the meantime, Lee had united his troops, costing the Union a chance to crush half of his army.

On December 11, the pontoon bridges were ready. Burnside's men started across the Rappahannock, but Confederates complicated his plans, firing on the federal troops trying to assemble platoons. By December 12, the Union forces made it to Fredericksburg and proceeded to waste valuable time looting the town.

The battle's primary action took place the next day. Confederate soldiers had taken up positions in the hills and elsewhere, including Marye's Heights, which was located along the main road to Richmond.

Despite the looming potential for disaster, Burnside sent his men into the maw of misery, ordering more than a dozen suicidal charges on the Confederates. At one point, the Army of the Potomac lost three thousand men during a single hour of assaults on Marye's Heights. Burnside continued ordering additional charges, all but guaranteeing a trip to the morgue. The Union's devastating losses prompted Lee's famous remark, "It is well that war is so terrible, else we should grow too fond of it."

The next day, Burnside began a retreat executed more deftly than anything else the Union attempted during the Fredericksburg Campaign. In all, the Union suffered thirteen thousand casualties, more than double the Confederates' five thousand. Six weeks later, Lincoln accepted Burnside's resignation, the latest casualty among Union commanders. Decisive as the Confederate victory had been, it failed to shift the momentum of the war toward the South. It did, however, delay the inevitable follow-up Union campaign to take Richmond.

Lee endured losses he could ill afford, and the North quickly replenished what it had lost. As Lincoln knew all too well, to win, the Army of the Potomac had to find a general who was willing to fight.

KADY BROWNELL:
"DAUGHTER OF THE REGIMENT"

Kady Brownell was a strong-willed woman. When her husband Robert enlisted, Kady refused to be left behind. She was one of the few women who went to war without putting on a disguise or dressing as a man. Her enthusiasm could have been because she left a dusty position in the textile mills at home.

At camp, Kady cooked, washed clothes, and did other chores. In her regiment, she was surrounded by sharpshooters and worked with them to perfect her own shot. She became the official color bearer for the company and was nicknamed, "Daughter of the Regiment."

Kady fought in the Battle of Bull Run in 1861. While helping attend the wounded on the field, she was near the flag-carrier when he was hit. She quickly grabbed the flag, and was wounded herself while carrying it.

Kady is best known for heroic actions that saved her Rhode Island regiment from friendly fire during a battle in New Berne, North Carolina, in 1862. Other Union troops mistook her company for the enemy. Kady grabbed their flag, ran to high ground, and waved it until the other soldiers realized they were on the same side.

Unfortunately, Robert Brownell was seriously wounded during that same battle. Kady spent the rest of her life caring for him. Beginning in 1884, Kady received an army pension of $8.00 per month for her service.

Flag Bearers

Flag-carriers had an important but dangerous job. Important, because the other soldiers looked to the flag as a landmark to make sure they knew where their own company was. It was a dangerous task, because flag-carriers couldn't manage both a flag and a gun. Since opponents hoped to disorient and scatter enemy troops by downing the flag, they were constantly targeted.

BRIDGET DIVERS

- Called by the soldiers "Irish Bridget," "Michigan Bridget," and "Irish Biddy"
- Rode with her husband's company, the 1st Michigan Cavalry
- Served as soldier, nurse, messenger, guard, scout, raider, and handywoman
- Enlisted openly as a woman
- Known for her bravery and endurance
- Stepped in to take the place of wounded soldiers in the heat of battle
- Exhibited her skills as horsewoman and rider; three different horses were shot out from under her during her service
- Slept on the ground alongside the men, enduring snow, rain, and stifling heat
- Acted as unofficial oral historian for the regiment to the U.S. Christian Commission
- Liked military life so much that she stayed with the army after the war as a laundress and went west with a frontier detachment

Heroic Action

Bridget is known to have retrieved the body of the unit's captain after a failed raid. Her troop having already retreated, she turned around and rode fifteen miles into enemy territory, placed the officer on her horse, and brought him back to camp. Then she returned to the field with ambulances to collect the wounded. Next, she purchased a coffin and shipped the captain's body home to his family.

"Albert Cashier"

We list "Albert Cashier's" name in quotes because "he" was actually a "she." Many things have been written about the woman who became Albert, but no one can agree on how to properly spell her birth name—perhaps because she never went back to her female identity. Jennie Hodgers (or Hodges) was an Irish immigrant who is now known for her lifelong masquerade as a man.

- Jennie devised "Albert D. J. Cashier" several years before the war, living and working as "him" in Illinois.
- When "Albert" enlisted, passing the medical exam was not an issue. All that was asked was to display the hands and feet.
- No other soldier ever suspected that "Cashier" was really a woman.
- "Albert" served in the 95th Illinois Infantry Volunteers regiment from August 1862 until August 1865.
- "Albert" participated in the battles of Vicksburg, Nashville, and Mobile, and in raids in Tennessee.
- In June 1863, Jennie became ill and was hospitalized. She still managed to conceal her sex.
- "Albert Cashier" was honorably discharged.
- Jennie continued her male disguise after the war.
- "Albert Cashier" received a veteran's pension and joined the Grand Army of the Republic.
- In 1911, at age sixty-six, Jennie was hit by a car and broke her leg. Taken to the veteran's hospital for treatment, her secret was discovered. Jennie convinced the doctor not to tell so that she could continue to receive her veteran's pension.
- After the accident, "Albert" was admitted to the Soldiers and Sailors Home.
- When Jennie died in October 1915, she was buried with full military honors wearing her soldier's uniform.

THE BELL COUSINS: MOLLY AND MARY

Cousins Molly and Mary Bell grew up together on a Pulaski County mountainside farm in southwestern Virginia, living with an uncle who abandoned them to join the Union army. The girls, Southern sympathizers, were irate at his action and wanted to do something about it.

They hatched a scheme to counter his federal enlistment by offering their own services to the Confederate forces. Molly and Mary decided the best plan of action would be disguising themselves as men.

The cousins cut their hair, put on men's woolen work shirts, and practiced lowering their voices and swaggering in their walk. Being from a small farm, they already had experience riding and working hard. Ready to enlist in a cavalry regiment, Molly took on the identity of "Bob Morgan" and Mary became "Tom Parker."

The girls had the misfortune of joining troops who were soon all—every last one of them—captured and headed to a Union prison. Within hours, General John Hunt Morgan rode in with reinforcements, overtook the Yankees, and liberated the Confederate troops.

Then the cousins joined Confederate General Jubal Early's infantry, where they served for two years. While under General Early:

- Bob Morgan and Tom Parker earned the respect of their comrades for their bravery.
- Bob Morgan killed three Union soldiers while guarding the picket and was promoted, for his gallantry, to corporal.
- Bob Morgan was slightly wounded in the arm by a piece of shell, but refused medical attention for fear of discovery.
- Bob Morgan and Tom Parker participated in the Battles of Chancellorsville, Gettysburg, and Spotsylvania Court House.
- Tom Parker was promoted to the rank of sergeant.

Molly and Mary were able to keep their true identities hidden by confiding in their captain. He had been impressed by their accomplishments in battle and kept their secret. When the captain was captured in 1864 at Belle Grove during the battle of Cedar Creek, fighting with Sheridan's regiments in Shenandoah Valley, the cousins made a quick decision to involve their lieutenant in the deception. This was a mistake, as he was more interested in gaining favor with Early than with protecting the girls. The secret was quickly out.

General Early was not amused. Their military service notwithstanding, the girls were accused of being camp followers and prostitutes and generally of demoralizing the troops. Early ordered them taken to Richmond.

Molly did manage to get off a parting shot—figuratively—to Early, before she was taken away, though. She told him that she knew of six other women in disguise in the army. But she wouldn't tell him who they were. She left Early to puzzle out who she might mean. Whether she was right or just reaching for straws, it was a sly final volley.

Molly and Mary were committed to Richmond's Castle Thunder prison in October 1864 to await further decision on their situation. The cousins were released three weeks later and told to go home, which they did, still wearing men's uniforms. For the Bell girls, the war was over.

Julia Grant
(Wife of Ulysses S.)

Born in St. Louis, Julia Dent was the child of a fur trader-turned-farm-owner. (Translation: she grew up on a Southern plantation that profited from slave labor.) By virtue of her family wealth, she attended boarding school in St. Louis, and her brother, Frederick, attended West Point.

This last point is important because one day Frederick brought home his West Point classmate, First Lieutenant Ulysses S. Grant. Grant soon asked Julia to wait for him as he headed off to the Mexican War. She agreed.

Four long years later, in 1848, they were finally married at the Dent house, and Julia began the life of an army wife, moving with her husband from post to post. In short order, the Grant family grew to include four children. After his tour, Ulysses brought his family back to his Galena, Illinois, home to work in his father's leather goods store.

At the outbreak of the Civil War, Ulysses joined his state volunteer militia, wearing a uniform that Julia had hand-sewn for him. With her husband's return to the military, Julia returned, too. Throughout the war, Julia joined Ulysses in camp whenever she could to make sure he ate "good home-cooked food."

At the end of the war, Julia and Ulysses enjoyed a hero's reception all throughout the North. They were showered with gifts for the War hero, including a new house in Galena.

Then Ulysses was elected president of the United States. Julia took full advantage of her position as first lady, entertaining extensively, throwing lavish parties and expensive receptions dressed in fine jewels, silks, and laces.

Upon leaving the White House in 1877, the Grants took a two-year world tour that turned out to be not terribly prudent. When they got home, they had no money. To provide for his wife, Grant wrote his personal memoirs, which he finished just four days before he died of cancer. Julia was so devastated that she could not even attend the funeral.

Grant's memoirs served their purpose and made Julia a wealthy woman, which was fortunate, as she lived another seventeen years after her husband. She is buried alongside him in Grant's tomb in New York City.

Julia Grant Trivia
- Grant's family refused to attend the wedding because the Dent family owned slaves.
- Julia was cross-eyed. She wanted to have the problem corrected, but Ulysses refused to hear of it. He said he liked her eyes just the way they were.
- After the Mexican War, Grant "resigned" from the Army because of drinking problems. It is speculated that Julia's presence in the Civil War camps kept him away from alcohol and contributed to his sober leadership successes.
- Julia is believed to be the only wife of a Union major general to be taken Confederate prisoner. In December 1862, she was one of the civilians captured by Confederate Brigadier General Nathan Bedford Forest at Holly Springs, Mississippi. As soon as he found out who she was, he sent her right back through the lines (he probably cussed a little bit, too).
- During the war, Julia owned three slaves. She hired out two of them, but kept one with her. That slave was with Julia when she visited her husband during the siege of Richmond. At that time, this one servant—also named Julia—was probably the only slave in Richmond. All other blacks were free. This is because the Emancipation Proclamation freed all slaves owned in rebelling states, but not slaves owned in the states of the Union.

THE SHORT HAPPY LIFE OF HETTY CARY AND JOHN PEGRAM

Hetty Cary

Baltimore native Hetty Cary was a Southern sympathizer caught in the North. She was known to wave a Confederate flag from her window as federal troops marched past. Beautiful and of high social standing, she could get away with it—for a while, anyway.

As the war heated up, the Cary family decided to leave Baltimore before they ended up in prison for their Confederate support. Hetty and her sister, Jennie, smuggled medicine and clothes through the blockade to Richmond, where they stayed with their cousin Constance. The three young ladies soon focused all their efforts on providing necessities for the Confederate soldiers.

John Pegram

Virginia native John Pegram was a West Point graduate and former U.S. Army officer commissioned as a lieutenant colonel with the Virginia Infantry. By the time Hetty's volunteer work activities caught the eye of thirty-two-year-old John, he had already been captured and released by Union soldiers.

Hetty and John

In 1862, at a party in his mother's home, John met the lovely Hetty Cary and fell in love. John asked Hetty to marry him, knowing he was asking one of the most beautiful women in the South. Hetty said "yes" to one of Virginia's most eligible bachelors.

The Wedding

Finally, Hetty and John were married on January 19, 1865. The wedding was a welcome social affair during a trying time; even President and Mrs. Jefferson Davis attended the ceremony in the historic St. Paul's Episcopal Church.

Afterward, the couple settled at Pegram's headquarters near Petersburg. On February 6, while leading a charge at the Battle of Hatcher's Run, John took a minie ball to the chest, near his heart.

The Funeral

Hetty returned to Richmond on the same train with her husband's body. The funeral was held in the same church and presided over by the same minister, Dr. Charles M. Minnegerode, who had performed the wedding three weeks earlier. General Robert E. Lee personally wrote a letter of condolences to the new bride/widow.

Hetty Carries On

Later, while traveling in Europe, Hetty met Henry Newell Martin, a physiologist and Johns Hopkins University professor. They were married in 1879.

The Vivandière

Some say that Bridget Divers accompanied her husband's unit as a *vivandière*, which is sort of like a female "sutler," or vendor.

Unlike the camp followers and prostitutes, the vivandière had the respect of the unit. She was allowed to take canteens to the wounded, as well as carry a pistol or rifle and liquor for wounded soldiers. She was often the wife or daughter of one of the unit's men. She usually wore a uniform of a knee-length skirt over trousers, a tunic blouse, a white apron, and hat.

HETTY CARY AND THE SOUTHERN CROSS FLAG

During the First Battle of Bull Run, soldiers were confused by too-similar flags for the Union and the Confederacy. To avoid friendly fire, Confederate General Beauregard proposed changing the Confederate flag.

The Confederate battle flag featured the X-shaped cross of St. Andrew, the patron saint of Scotland. It had thirteen stars (representing the eleven states in the Confederacy, plus Kentucky and Missouri), three white stars on each leg of the X and one in the center. Square-shaped, the flag's field was red, the cross was blue edged in white, and the entire banner was fringed with gold. Called the Southern Cross, it served as the battle flag for the cavalry, infantry, and artillery in the Army of Northern Virginia.

It is pretty clear that Hetty Cary had a part in creating one of the first Southern Cross battle flags. How much depends on who you ask. By her own account, the Cary girls—sisters Hetty and Jennie and cousin Constance—were personally asked to make the first three battle flags for General Joseph Johnston, General Beauregard, and General Earl Van Dorn. By other accounts, the Cary girls, having caught wind of the new design, took it upon themselves to quickly make the first flags for the three generals.

Either way, we do know that the girls sent their flags to the troops, who celebrated the new silk banners with unofficial ceremonies.

Mrs. Paul: "A Saucy Woman"

We're not sure if Gabriel Paul was much of a soldier, but we couldn't pass up telling you about the woman who Abraham Lincoln called "saucy."

Gabriel Paul was a legacy soldier, with both his father and grandfather fighting under Napoleon. Gabriel, a West Point graduate and U.S. Army lieutenant colonel, fought in the Mexican War.

During the Civil War, he served in the Southwest, and participated in the Battles of Fredericksburg and Chancellorsville. During the 1862 Confederate invasion of New Mexico, federal troops held Fort Union under Paul's leadership, as he had temporarily been granted command in the interim absence of ranking officers.

As a career soldier, Paul felt slighted to see others often promoted even though their service had not been lifelong. He thought this was unfair to career officers, namely himself. This point of contention was one of increasing discussion between Gabriel and his wife.

After talking and talking about it with her husband, Mrs. Paul had a good grasp of what he thought was wrong with the Army's seniority system. She decided that it was time to take action. In August 1862, Mrs. Paul made the long trip from New Mexico to Washington to lobby President Lincoln for her husband's promotion.

After their meeting, the president said, "She is a saucy woman, and I am afraid she will keep tormenting till I may have to do it."

In September, Paul was nominated for promotion to brigadier general, but not confirmed by the Senate. Finally, in April 1863, he was nominated again and confirmed. Mrs. Paul did get what she wanted for her husband.

Post Script: Three months later, Gabriel Paul was wounded at Gettysburg. A minie ball entered his right temple and exited from his left eye, leaving the general permanently blind.

VIRGINIA TUNSTALL CLAY: SOUTHERN BELLE, LOBBYIST

Virginia, the Belle: Virginia Tunstall's mother died less than a year after she was born in 1825 in North Carolina. Her father, Dr. Payton Randolph Tunstall, sent her to live with relatives in Tuscaloosa, Alabama. This wasn't an "ugly stepsister" situation; the aunts and uncles she lived with were local elite and took good care of her:

- Mary Ann and Henry Collier (chief justice of the state supreme court)
- Millicent and Alfred Battle (a merchant and one of the town's wealthiest men)

As a guest in their homes, Virginia learned the importance of being flexible and gracious—traits of any successful belle. By the time she graduated from the Female Academy in Nashville at the age of fourteen, Virginia already had attracted many male suitors.

Clement Claiborne Clay, the Lawyer: Clement Claiborne Clay was the son of Clement Comer Clay, one of the most prominent men in the state and owner of a 2,700-acre plantation with at least seventy slaves. Father Clay had been the first chief justice of the state supreme court and governor of Alabama. Clement Claiborne graduated from the University of Alabama and earned a law degree from the University of Virginia.

Virginia Meets Clement: In December 1842, Tuscaloosa was the state capital. At the time, the Colliers took Virginia to a round of parties to celebrate the new legislative season. As a new member of the Alabama legislature, Clement Claiborne Clay attended these same parties. He soon fell in love with the energetic, attractive, sociable Virginia.

Love and Marriage: Clement courted Virginia with candy, books, and romantic verses for two months. On February 1, 1843, Virginia was eighteen when she married twenty-six-year-old Clement. They spent the first years of their marriage living with her in-laws in Huntsville, Alabama. Virginia occupied herself with visiting, sewing, gardening, and playing piano. They never had children.

A Political Career in Washington: In 1853, Clement was elected to the U.S. Senate, and the Clays moved to Washington. Virginia burst onto the Washington social scene, calling herself "a belle of the fifties." She also deeply indulged her favorite pastime, shopping, even traveling to New York and Philadelphia on sprees.

Clement was reelected to the Senate four years later. By this time, Northern and Southern sectionalism was apparent, and Virginia would only socialize with Southerners and their sympathizers.

The Civil War: Alabama seceded in January 1861, and the Clays returned home from Washington. Clement won a seat in the Confederate Senate, but he was not reelected in 1864. Jefferson Davis appointed him to a Confederate diplomatic mission to Canada.

In May 1865, federal forces arrested Clement for treason and conspiring with Davis to assassinate President Lincoln, in part because of his trips to Canada. He remained in prison for eleven months.

Virginia, the Belle, Again: Virginia dusted off her "belle" characteristics to put her talents to work on her husband's behalf. She borrowed one hundred dollars and enough silk to make a new dress. Then she hopped on the train to Washington, where she planned to call on President Johnson.

And call on him she did. Virginia visited Johnson's office repeatedly over the next two months, each time lobbying to have her husband freed. Finally, in April 1866, Clement Clay was released.

Post Script: Virginia later applied her powers of persuasion to the cause of women's right to vote. From 1896 to 1900, she served as president of the Alabama Equal Suffrage Association.

KATE CLARKE

William Clarke Quantrill was a Confederate guerrilla soldier given to raiding Union homes and ambushing Union troops. His ruthless band of marauders did not abide by the codes of war.

Kate Clarke was Quantrill's wife, or common-law wife, or lover, depending on what you believe. She undoubtedly was "his woman."

In 1863, Sarah Katherine King met William Quantrill at her father's farm. She was about thirteen years old to his twenty-six. Sarah's father naturally thought she was too young for him. So Sarah began to meet William in secret. They supposedly eloped and were married in a church near her parents' farm.

To hide her true identity and protect herself from Quantrill's enemies, Sarah changed her name to "Kate Clarke," combining Quantrill's and her own middle names.

After their marriage, Kate settled into the life of an outlaw's wife, following her husband from camp to camp. An experienced horsewoman, she rode with her husband and his men and benefited from their looting.

In 1864, Quantrill headed to Washington, D.C. on a mission to assassinate President Lincoln. He didn't get past Kentucky, where he was fatally wounded by federal troops. In the twenty days that he lived after being shot, Quantrill purchased a cemetery plot and headstone.

The young widow Kate Clarke inherited $500 in gold. She promptly used the money to start a house of ill repute in St. Louis (some kind people call it a "boardinghouse").

Before she died at the age of eighty-two, Kate had been married five times. She met her last husband, Walter Head, while both were living at the Jackson County Home for the Aged (i.e., the "poorhouse").

The James and Younger brothers both rode with Quantrill at one time or another.

THE ONLY WOMAN OFFICER OF THE CONFEDERATE ARMY: SALLY TOMPKINS

Robertson Hospital in Richmond ("Aunt Sally's")
- Staff: 6
- Capacity: 21
- Treated: 1,333 wounded
- Survivors: 1,260
- July 31, 1861–June 13, 1865

Miss Sally Louise Tompkins
- Age 28 (1861)
- Single
- 5'0"

After the First Battle of Manassas, Sally Tompkins opened the private Robertson Hospital in the home of Judge John Robertson, who had moved his family to the country for the duration of the conflict.

Sally Provided What Was Needed
- Equipped the building at her own expense
- Enlisted townspeople to supply bandages and linen
- Borrowed her mother's cook to handle the kitchen
- Purchased food herself
- Obtained medicine and drugs from blockade runners
- Solicited donations from patriotic friends
- Nursed the wounded
- Read the Bible aloud
- Accepted no arguments from patients
- Charged nothing for patient care

The Dilemma

Because of rampant corruption, the Confederate government closed all private hospitals. All soldiers would be transferred to hospitals under an officer ranked captain (that is, assistant surgeon) or higher. To keep "her boys," Sally personally visited President Davis with evidence of her exemplary patient treatment:

- Only seventy-three fatalities, a record unmatched by any other Civil War hospital, North or South.
- Number of soldiers returned to their army commands was greater than any other Richmond hospital.
- Many wounded soldiers from distant places begged to be taken there.

The Solution

The Confederate secretary of war commissioned Sally Tompkins as captain of cavalry. As a captain, she could issue orders. She declined to draw army pay.

Sally Tompkins was buried with full military honors in 1916. Even before her death, the Sally Tompkins chapter of the United Daughters of the Confederacy was formed in her honor.

EMMA SANSOM

Teenager Emma Sansom saved the Confederate Railroad from Union destruction. Her bravery led General Nathan Forrest's troops to capture General Abel Streight's raiders before they could dismantle the railroad in Chattanooga.

On May 2, 1863, Union soldiers reached the Sansom household about three miles from Gadsden, Alabama. They burned the bridge over Black Creek to slow the Confederates down. The Sansom women watched in horror as the Yankees used their fence ties to kindle the blaze.

When General Forrest arrived in hot pursuit, he found the bridge demolished and the creek high from spring rains. He could see Union soldiers waiting on the opposite bank ready to shoot if he tried to cross.

Forrest asked the location of the nearest bridge. Emma said it was more than two miles away, but that she could show him a nearby ford where she had seen cows cross in low water.

Without wasting time for Emma to saddle her own horse, Forrest insisted she ride behind him on his. This was not ladylike at all—either sitting behind a man on a horse or riding off with a stranger—and Emma's mother protested. Forrest assured the widow he would bring her daughter back safely.

Under enemy fire, they rode across a cornfield, and Emma pointed out the crossing. Forrest delivered her home then quickly went after Streight. He soon captured the Union soldiers. The Confederate railroad was spared.

Because she helped Forrest's forces stop the Union soldiers, he credited the victory to Emma and wrote her a personal "thank you" note.

Emma became a local heroine. The people of Alabama City honored her in 1907 with a marble-relief monument and in 1929 with the new Emma Sansom High School.

MARY ANNA JACKSON, WIDOW OF THE CONFEDERACY

Lieutenant General Thomas "Stonewall" Jackson married Mary Anna Morrison in 1857 (Jackson's first wife, Elinor Junkin Jackson, had died in childbirth).

Known as Anna, Jackson's wife was happy to report her pregnancy shortly after their wedding, but their first daughter died as an infant. This tragedy only strengthened the bond between Thomas and Anna.

Four years into their marriage, war broke out and Thomas joined the Army of Virginia. Anna often visited her husband in camp. Soon, the Jacksons welcomed another baby, a daughter born in 1862. Jackson named the little girl "Julia," after his mother.

Baby Julia Jackson was just five months old when her father died of wounds sustained during the Battle of Chancellorsville in 1863. Anna and Julia were at Jackson's side as he died, with Anna reportedly singing hymns in his last moments.

Mary Anna Jackson became known as the "Widow of the Confederacy." She did not remarry and continued to wear the black crêpe of mourning for the rest of her life. After Jackson's death, Anna returned to her native North Carolina with Julia. After the war, Anna attended Confederate veterans' reunions throughout the South.

Julia grew up, married William E. Christian, and with the birth of her own son and daughter, made Anna a grandmother twice over. But tragedy struck again when Julia died of typhoid fever in 1889 at the age of twenty-seven. Anna took on the task of raising her two grandchildren.

In 1898, Anna established and became the first president of the Stonewall Jackson Chapter of the United Daughters of the Confederacy in Charlotte. She directed the chapter's activities until old age and remained the chapter's honorary president until her death in 1915. Anna was buried next to her husband in Lexington, Virginia.

STONE'S RIVER

Fredericksburg sent a crushing blow to Northern morale as 1862 ended. Lincoln, readying for the enactment of the Emancipation Proclamation on January 1, longed for good news to share with the country. He received some from the western theater at the Battle of Stones River.

Though considered a tactical draw, it gave the North control of Middle Tennessee and removed a crucial supply source from the Confederates.

The two armies suffered nearly twenty-four thousand combined casualties—ranking, on a percentage basis, even higher than the casualty rates at Shiloh and Antietam. It pitted Confederate commander Braxton Bragg against the Union and William S. Rosecrans.

Bragg and the Confederate Army of Tennessee had staked a position just northwest of Murfreesboro, Tennessee, on the Stones River. Rosecrans and the Union were in Nashville, thirty miles away. The campaign began on December 26, when Rosecrans, began pursuit of the rebel army.

Bad weather and persistent disruptions by Confederate cavalry raids delayed the Union forces. On December 30, the two armies were across from each other at Stones River. Both commanders came up with similar battle plans, to attack the enemy's right side and separate the opposing force from its supplies. Confederates surprised the Union with an early morning attack on New Year's Eve.

As the Confederates hammered the Union, subsequent attacks designed to hold the Union in place for the final, crushing blow started. Only the heroics of Union General Philip Sheridan prevented a complete massacre. Union forces delayed the Confederates for two hours.

A crucial strategic position in an area known as the Round Forest, located between the Nashville Pike and the Stones River, led to a Union rally. Colonel William Hazen's brigade would be the only one that held its position. The brigade battled the Confederates in what was dubbed "Hell's Half-Acre." On January 2, fighting resumed. The Union troops delivered a decisive blow, leading Bragg and the Confederates to retreat a day later.

By a Whisker

Ambrose Burnside and George McClellan shared at least two traits. Both men were beloved by their soldiers, and both were considered dashing figures. Burnside's defining feature, mutton-chop whiskers, was oft-imitated and led to the coining of a slang term still in use today—sideburns.

Though Burnside bore none of the haughty demeanor displayed by McClellan, he also disappointed Lincoln as a commander. He had twice turned down earlier offers to lead the Union army, believing the job to be beyond his talents. Burnside lived up to his own suspicions, leading a foolhardy attack on Fredericksburg, Virginia, in December 1862. On January 26, 1863, the president accepted his resignation.

UNION COMMANDERS: JOHN C. FREMONT (1813-1890)

Background: Georgia native, attended Charleston College (though expelled before graduation for "inattention to studies" but later awarded his degree), U.S. Navy math professor

Antebellum Career: Long before the Civil War, Frémont made his name as the explorer of the West. A U.S. topographical engineer, he traveled extensively in the land between the Missouri and the northern frontier, earning the nickname, "The Pathfinder."

In the 1840s, Frémont made several trips with Kit Carson to map the Oregon Trail to the Pacific Ocean. In the process, he reached the highest peak in the Wind River Mountains, now called Fremont's Peak.

Frémont also reached Great Salt Lake; it was his reports that the Mormons relied on when settling that region.

Life in California: In 1846, American settlers in California revolted against the Mexican government and established their own Bear Flag Republic. Frémont was present there with the U.S. Army, and he got caught in a struggle with General Stephen W. Kearny, the Washington-appointed governor of California.

Frémont refused to give up the office, which was given to him by Commodore Robert F. Stockton, and was arrested for mutiny and insubordination, and was court-martialed in Washington. He was found guilty and sentenced to dismissal, but President Polk rejected the conviction. Frémont resigned anyway.

Pre-War Political Aspirations: Frémont stayed in California, though, and represented the state in the United States Senate for seven months in late 1850, one of the first two senators from the new state of California.

In the 1856 Presidential campaign, Frémont ran as the first Republican candidate under the slogan "Free Soil, Free Speech, Free Men, Frémont." Republicans carried all eleven Northern states but received less than 1 percent of the Southern vote. Frémont lost to Buchanan.

Civil War Controversy: Frémont entered the U.S. Army as major general in the Western Department at St. Louis. In August 1861, he proclaimed martial law in Missouri and arrested secessionists. President Lincoln was pleased.

But, this is where he got on Lincoln's bad side: Frémont issued what was actually the first emancipation proclamation freeing slaves owned by those opposing the Union.

Lincoln was afraid this proclamation would push any fence-sitting border states toward secession. So, he "took back" the proclamation and fired Frémont. Lincoln made his Emancipation Proclamation a year later.

Other Civil War Achievements: There weren't many. In the Shenandoah Valley, Frémont's troops chased Confederate General Stonewall Jackson up and down the land but ultimately let the Southern commander go.

When his troops were absorbed into the Army of Virginia under Pope, Frémont resigned for personal problems with the commanding officer.

Post-War Political Aspirations: In the 1864 Presidential campaign, Frémont accepted the nomination from a Republican splinter group, the Radical Republicans. The platform:

- Equality under the law for all men regardless of race
- Protection of civil liberties in areas not under martial law
- Congressional (not presidential) control of Reconstruction
- Distribution of confiscated land to soldiers and former slaves
- Constitutional amendment abolishing slavery

His candidacy didn't go far. The Republican party urged Frémont to withdraw. They were afraid that with Frémont in the race, Republican votes would split between him and Lincoln, opening the way for a landslide Democratic election of George McClellan.

UNION COMMANDERS: GEORGE GORDON MEADE (1815-1872)

Personal Background: Born to Philadelphia-native American parents in Cádiz, Spain; 1835 West Point graduate; worked as a civil engineer in the private sector

Military Background: Served for a year in 1835; rejoined the U.S. Army in 1842; fought in the Seminole War and Mexican War

Civil War Action: Mechanicsville, Gaines's Mills, White Oak Swamp (badly wounded), Second Bull Run, Antietam, Fredericksburg, Chancellorsville

Character Description: a blunt, bookish man; fondly remembered as a "damned old goggle-eyed snapping turtle."

Meade's Big Promotion: It came about because Union General Joseph Hooker argued with his superior, Major General Henry W. Halleck, over the most efficient use of troops. Hooker was so mad that he resigned. President Lincoln replaced Hooker with George Meade as commander of the Army of the Potomac just days before the Battle of Gettysburg. Meade was shocked by the sudden announcement, but he accepted the position, sending Lincoln a telegraph: "As a soldier, I obey it, and to the utmost of my ability will execute it."

The Battle of Gettysburg: Meade's appointment gave the tired Union troops some much needed oomph. Fast forward to the third day of the battle, and by this time, Meade expected the Confederate advance. After lunch (stewed chicken, by the way), Confederates stormed the Union lines with a massive artillery bombardment. Meade had his men hold fire to conserve ammunition and to draw the Confederates out into the open field between the lines.

The Confederates took the bait, thinking they had destroyed the Union batteries. Pickett's division charged the wall, only to be decimated.

Meade and his men, however, were exhausted after three days at battle, and they did not attack Lee's retreating army. Meade wired

Lincoln that he had pushed "from our soil every vestige of the presence of the intruder."

This frustrated Lincoln to no end. "Is that all?" was Lincoln's response; his objective was the total destruction of Lee and his army.

The Wilderness Campaign: In 1864 in the Wilderness, according to Grant's plan, Meade was to lead the Army of the Potomac, 110,000 strong, as they headed south to take on Lee. Grant's simple plan, as he told Meade, was, "Wherever Lee goes, there you will go also." That is what Meade did.

The Battle of the Crater: Remember, in this battle, miners tunneled from their lines all the way under the Confederate camp, then filled the tunnel with explosives and created a huge crater where the rebel tents had been.

The original plan was to send trained and combat-proven black soldiers in the front lines through the breach immediately after the explosion. These soldiers were aware of the tactical plans for maximizing the "crater."

Meade made a last-minute change, afraid that if the black soldiers were annihilated, it would make for bad press. So he sent another, white, division to lead the attack. Unfortunately, as they had not been training for weeks to complete this strategy, they didn't know the plan, and advanced right into the crater instead of around it. They were easy targets, like "fish in a barrel," for the Confederates to pick off.

Immediately After the War: On May 23, 1865, Meade led his Grand Army of the Potomac as they marched in review from the Capitol down Pennsylvania Avenue for President Lincoln and Secretary of the Navy Gideon Welles. On the second day of celebration, Meade joined Grant and Sherman on the review stand.

Later After the War: During Reconstruction, Meade oversaw the military district of Alabama, Georgia, and Florida. He died of war wounds complicated by pneumonia in 1872.

George Meade received the Thanks of Congress in January 1864.

CONFEDERATE COMMANDERS: JOHN SINGLETON MOSBY (1833-1916)

Early Life: Virginia native John S. Mosby was expelled from the University of Virginia for shooting a classmate. While cooling his heels in jail, Mosby began reading his attorney's law books and decided to become a lawyer himself. Virginia's governor later pardoned Mosby after three hundred of his friends and family mounted an impressive letter-writing campaign. Mosby passed the bar and began a career as an attorney. He met Pauline Clarke, daughter of Kentucky Congressman Beverly Leonidas Clarke, and married her in a ceremony attended by future President Andrew Johnson.

Political Sentiments: Actually a staunch unionist, the pint-sized attorney kept his allegiances with his mother state when Virginia seceded and decided to support the Confederacy.

Early Civil War Action: As a private in the Virginia Cavalry, Mosby fought at First Bull Run. During the Peninsula Campaign, he volunteered to scout Union General McClellan's troops, reporting back to Confederate Brigadier General Jeb Stuart.

Partisan Ranger: Mosby found that he liked scouting detail, and asked Stuart to let him put together a group of rangers. Mosby and his men proved to be effective at tearing up rail lines, blowing up bridges, robbing trains, and capturing supplies and prisoners of war. Union troops called him "The Grey Ghost." During the course of the war, Mosby was wounded seven times.

Northern Reaction to Mosby

- General George Custer justified executing six of Mosby's men as "guerrillas." Mosby then executed six captured Union soldiers. Custer got the message and dropped his vendetta.
- General Ulysses Grant gave standing orders to hang Mosby without trial if he was captured. Mosby himself claimed to have almost captured Grant once.

- General Philip Sheridan sent a hundred soldiers to hunt down Mosby with Spencer repeating rifles. Mosby's Rangers killed or wounded ninety-eight of them and captured their fancy weapons.

No Surrender: Instead of surrendering to Union forces at the end of the war, Mosby simply disbanded his unit. This meant they negotiated no terms for peace with the federal government.

Rank: Promoted to captain (1863), to major (1863), to lieutenant colonel (1864), and full colonel (1864). If you read Robert E. Lee's dispatches, you'll find Mosby mentioned more often than any other Confederate officer.

Mosby as Scalawag: Mosby's wife petitioned Grant for a pardon, so Mosby supported Grant as presidential candidate. Mosby's return to unionist politics and Republican policies after the war led other Southerners to regard him as a "scalawag."

Friends with Grant: As unlikely as it seems, Mosby and Grant became friends. The president favored the former ranger with appointments, and Mosby served as consul to Hong Kong from 1878 to 1885. Returning to America, Mosby learned that Grant had appointed him to a job with the Southern Pacific Railroad in San Francisco—just one day before the old Union general died.

Pauline Clarke Mosby

When she married John Mosby, Pauline chose a skinny, unhealthy, unionist lawyer as her husband. Was she in for a shock with the coming of the Civil War!

Pauline traveled with her husband as much as possible during the war years. Because Mosby's Rangers did not stay in normal camps, they tended to bunk in houses with local townspeople who hid them from Union soldiers.

One night, Northern soldiers broke into the house where Pauline and John were sleeping. They found Pauline, in her nightclothes, alone in bed. She declared that she was alone, and the soldiers left. Truly, she was alone—John had jumped through the bedroom window to hide among the limbs of the walnut tree outside.

MOSBY'S RANGERS

Who They Were: The Forty-Third Battalion of Virginia Cavalry, in existence from early 1863 until April 1865

Where They Were: Based in Virginia's Fauquier and Loudoun counties, known as "Mosby's Confederacy"

Who Helped Them: Mosby relied on local civilians for food, covert shelter, and intelligence. Mosby's Rangers dressed as normal civilians for their daytime disguise.

What They Did: Targeted Union camps toward Washington, D.C., past the Blue Ridge Mountains to the Shenandoah Valley and across the Potomac River into Maryland

Their Operations: Success depended on the element of surprise and Mosby's clever planning. Mosby took a couple dozen men with him on a raid, which could last two or three days. The men struck swiftly, usually after dark, then returned to base to divide the spoils among themselves and the Confederacy (which got most of it).

Their Goals: The rangers crossed Union supply and communication lines to attack wagon trains, railroad cars, outposts, and troop detachments.

The value of their actions came not only the spoils of their raids, but also from diverting Union manpower. Federal officers soon realized that they would have to include rear guards against Mosby's Rangers in all of their advancement and encampment plans.

Consequences: Mosby's Rangers were notorious during the war, and their legacy still lives on. Success did not come without a price, though. Mosby estimated 35 to 40 percent of his men were killed, and almost five hundred were captured and imprisoned.

Capture of Edwin Stoughton

On a March 9, 1863, raid of Fairfax Court House in Virginia, Mosby's Rangers started by cutting telegraph wires as they rode along. Clever, but it gets better: They walked right up to the headquarters of Brigadier General Edwin Stoughton and knocked on the door.

General Stoughton was sleeping off a hangover and was therefore easily captured. Mosby's Rangers also netted two captains, thirty privates, and fifty-eight horses.

When he heard about the raid, President Lincoln was upset about losing the steeds, saying, "For that I am sorry, for I can make brigadier generals, but I can't make horses."

The Greenback Raid

On October 14, 1864, Mosby's Rangers destroyed a section of railroad tracks in Quincy's Siding, West Virginia, and waited. It wasn't long before a Baltimore and Ohio Railroad passenger train came barreling through and derailed.

The Rangers had a specific target in mind when they set the trap, since they had heard that U.S. Army paymasters would be riding on the train in the baggage car. Mosby's men went straight for that car, pried open the door, and collected about $172,000 in a matter of minutes. Then they burned the train for good measure.

Back at base camp, they celebrated while splitting up the cash. Two fiddlers provided background music, playing the only song they knew, "Malbrook Has Gone to the Wars."

"Malbrook Has Gone to the Wars"

This was a popular song in eighteenth century Paris and London about John Churchill, the Duke of Marlborough, which was mangled in the translation from French to "Malbrook" in English. It is sung to the tune of "For He's a Jolly Good Fellow."

If you're curious, the general story is that Marlborough went to the crusades. His lady waited patiently for his return, watching from the tower window each day. Then one day a page returned from the wars to tell her that he had been killed in battle.

UNION COMMANDERS: FITZ-JOHN PORTER (1822-1901)

Q: True or False: Fitz-John Porter was a New Hampshire native.

A: True

Q: True or False: Porter was the son of War of 1812 naval hero David Porter.

A: False. He was David Porter's nephew. Fitz-John was the son of a naval officer, and cousin to Civil War naval heroes David Dixon Porter and David Farragut

Q: True or False: Porter was an 1845 West Point graduate.

A: True. He also served the U.S. Army in the Mexican War.

Q: True or False: Porter was ranked major general.

A: True.

Q: True or False: Porter fought in the Peninsula Campaign, Yorktown, the Seven Days' Battle (at Gaines's Mill), Glendale, Malvern Hill, and Second Bull Run

A: True.

Q: True or False: Porter was a Union spy.

A: True, sort of, if you count accidentally. First of all, you need to know that Union strategists had figured out how to use hot air balloons for reconnaissance. To be fair, the Confederates eventually figured it out too, but they never launched as effective an operation as the Union did. For the most part, balloons were kept tethered so that they could run a supply of gas to the crafts, and they could telegraph back their findings.

During the siege of Yorktown, which lasted almost a month, Porter found himself one day on an accidental cross-country hot air balloon ride. He had taken a ride up, more because he was bored than anything else, when the tether ropes gave way.

Before he was able to snag the valve rope and ensure his descent, Porter used his spyglass to get a good look at Confederate encampments and troops.

Q: True or False: Porter was involved in two court-martials.

A: True. For the first, he accused John H. Martindale for surrendering at Malvern Hill rather than retreating. Martindale was tried in court-martial, cleared, and promoted to major general.

For the second, Porter himself was tried for refusing to obey Pope's order to attack Stonewall Jackson's men at the Second Bull Run. The outcome for Porter wasn't nearly as good as it was for Martindale.

Q: True or False: Porter was honorably discharged from the U.S. Army.

A: False. Porter was charged with disobedience, disloyalty, and misconduct by the Joint Committee on the Conduct of War. It seems Porter was an avid supporter of that committee's main target, General McClellan, and they used him as their scapegoat to get at McClellan. He was found guilty and dismissed by dishonorable discharge.

Q: True or False: Porter reenlisted under a false name to continue serving his country during the Civil War.

A: False. Porter did not go back to war, but he did spend the next couple of decades trying to clear his name. Finally, in 1878, an inquiry determined that the attack was apparently impossible and completely exonerated Porter. In 1886, he was reinstated as an infantry colonel—retired—but denied back pay. Two days later, he resigned from the Army.

Q: True or False: Once Porter's good name was restored, he was able to resume his career in public service.

A: True: Porter later served as New York City commissioner of public works, New York City police commissioner, and New York City fire commissioner.

UNION COMMANDERS: WILLIAM ROSECRANS (1819-1898)

- Ohio native, 1842 West Point graduate
- Called "Old Rosy" by his admiring soldiers
- Called "a silly fussy goose" by less-admiring General McClellan
- Received Thanks of Congress, March 1863

Rosecrans in Tennessee
- By 1862's end, the Union Army of the Cumberland under Rosecrans had done their best to push the Confederate Army out of central Tennessee.
- At Stone's River, the South seemed to be winning. Rosecrans rode along the line to rally his men, apparently unafraid of the shell that blew off his aide's head right next to him. After three days, it was a standoff.
- For six months, the two armies picked at each other. Lincoln demanded that Rosecrans do something. Rosecrans asked for more troops, more supplies, and more time.
- Finally Lincoln threatened to remove him from command. That lit a fire under Rosecrans. He ordered swift banking maneuvers in a steady rain, driving Confederate General Bragg eight miles to Chattanooga. The Union occupied the city.
- Then the Confederates lured the Union army out of town and attacked along Chickamauga Creek.
- On the second day at Chickamauga, Rosecrans really messed up. He couldn't see a large section of his troops, and so he thought there was a break in the Union lines. Rosecrans ordered troops to close up the nonexistent hole, opening up a new gap instead. Southern troops poured through.
- Rosecrans's corps staggered to Chattanooga in retreat. Lincoln described Rosecrans as "confused and stunned, like a duck hit on the head."
- Grant replaced Rosecrans with George Henry Thomas.

- Strong criticism such as this from Assistant Secretary of War Charles Dana said of him: "His mind scatters; there is no system in his use of his busy days and restless nights. There is no courage against individuals in his composition." Thus, Rosecrans lost his command.

Maggots and Gangrene

Confederate prisoners of war discovered, quite by accident, the Maggot Debridement Therapy that had been used by physicians since about AD 1000. It is still used in twenty-first century medicine, albeit today under sterile conditions. In essence, maggots eat only dead flesh. So when the POWs were unable to obtain bandages from their captors, maggots infested their dirty wounds, providing an unexpected service by removing decay and leaving healthy skin on the way to recovery.

UNION COMMANDERS: GEORGE HENRY THOMAS (1816-1870)

The Rock of Chickamauga

At Chickamauga, after Rosecrans retreated to Chattanooga like a "stunned duck," Thomas remained on the field to lead what was left of the Union forces. His stubborn troops refused to withdraw. Thomas rallied the men, who formed a strong line on the ridge of Snodgrass Hill.

Try though they might, the Confederate forces could not penetrate Thomas's men. A witness said, "Thomas had placed himself with his back against a rock and refused to be driven from the field."

Thomas finally realized that holding the position was futile, and at nightfall withdrew his men to Chattanooga. Historians agree that, thanks to Thomas, the Union loss at Chickamauga was a lot less severe than it could have been.

This brave action earned Thomas the new nickname, "The Rock of Chickamauga." (Thankfully not "The Rock of Snodgrass!") It also earned him the command of the Army of the Cumberland, as Grant replaced Rosecrans with Thomas immediately after Chickamauga.

Success at Chattanooga

Next, at Chattanooga, Grant asked Thomas's Chickamauga veterans to make a limited (remember this word) attack on the first line of Confederate trenches below Missionary Ridge. Thomas's men moved toward the hill, settled into the trenches at its bottom, and waited for orders.

That is, until the Confederates ignited the fuse of Irish-blooded Phil Sheridan's temper. Suddenly, Sheridan—followed by the rest of Thomas's men—made his way up the ridge. Ultimately, they took what seemed impregnable Confederate lines, capturing four thousand prisoners.

States' Rights or Rites by State?

This story gives us some insight into Thomas's personality. The day after the Battle of Chattanooga, Thomas had a Union cemetery laid out on Orchard Knob hill, where the fighting had been especially heated. The chaplain in charge asked if he should administer the burial rites by state. "No, no. Mix 'em up," Thomas said. "I'm tired of States' Rights."

Decimating the Confederacy

By May of 1864, Thomas's Army of the Cumberland had joined Sherman's Grand Army of the West. Thomas participated in Sherman's unrelenting march through Georgia. Then in December 1864, Thomas's troops were sent to dispatch what was left of Confederate General John Bell Hood's men in Nashville. In a battle fought in sleet and rain, Thomas shattered the rest of Hood's troops.

Interesting Tidbits about George Thomas

- In 1861, Thomas had forbidden the reception of fugitive slaves into his camp. By the end of the war, he had changed his mind and became an advocate of using black soldiers, for which he received high commendations.
- Thomas and Sherman were the generals who finally formally recognized the medical qualifications of Dr. Mary Walker and awarded her a commission as assistant surgeon with the 52nd Ohio. She, in turn, engaged in espionage for their benefit.
- Thomas received the Thanks of Congress recognition in March 1865 for crushing Hood in Nashville at the end of the previous year.
- A native Virginian, Thomas was a unionist who stayed in the U.S. Army after the outbreak of Civil War.
- Thomas was known to his men as "Pap."
- Thomas had a bay horse named "Billy," after General Sherman.
- Thomas made a lifelong career of his military service, dying of a stroke at his desk.

RAIDERS OF THE LOST CAUSE

Croxton's Raiders

A Kentucky native and son of a wealthy plantation owner, John T. Croxton opposed slavery and states' rights, siding with the Union when the Southern states seceded. He joined the Union Army early in the war, and by all accounts showed a knack for military strategy and tactics. He made a name for himself near the end of the war when he led a group of about 1,500 men in a sweep of the state of Alabama.

Croxton's Raiders were charged with disabling the University of Alabama in Tuscaloosa, where many Confederate officers had graduated and a number of cadets were still training. Croxton's goal was to destroy the bridge spanning the Black Warrior River and take out any structures that would aid the South's war effort, such as factories, mills, and the college.

The cadets tried to defend the town, but ultimately they were young boys. University President Landon Garland decided not to risk their lives. The town surrendered.

By the time Croxton's Raiders marched on toward Georgia, they had leveled stores in Bessemer, destroyed ironworks and a tannery at Tannehill, burned the bridge in Tuscaloosa, skirmished with the University cadets, looted stores and businesses, harassed and robbed civilians, captured two cannon, burned the Pickens County Courthouse, and looted and destroyed a Pleasant Ridge mill. They torched whatever they could, including a hat factory, niter works, a cotton factory, warehouses, and more than two thousand bales of cotton.

Croxton achieved his main goal, which was to level the state university. His raiders exploded the school's ammunition supplies to set the campus ablaze. All but four of the University's buildings were burned. Those four included an observatory, faculty houses, and a small guardhouse, the only campus structure with specific military purpose.

One other building was spared, the President's Mansion. Croxton's Raiders did set it on fire. The official line is "due to the bravery of [the president's wife], the fire was extinguished and the house allowed to remain." But every University of Alabama student knows the legend: Mrs. Garland scolded the Northern soldiers, telling them, "Gentlemen don't act this way." She made them snuff the fire and rearrange the furniture.

Croxton's Raiders rejoined their cavalry corps in Georgia three weeks after Lee's surrender at Appomattox.

The First and Second Florida Cavalry

It seems that the First and Second Florida Cavalry were known for welcoming unhappy Confederates into their Union ranks.

For instance, southeast Alabama native Joseph Sanders started out fighting for the Confederacy in Stonewall Jackson's corps and was an avid defender of the cause. But at some point, he got tired of it all and deserted, fleeing to Florida's Gulf Coast. There he was able to hide with Union forces, and soon became a lieutenant in the First Florida Cavalry. With that corps, Sanders led numerous raids into south Alabama, capturing prisoners, horses, mules, and weapons, as well as looting plantations and battling Confederate forces. They even burned the county courthouse just down the road from Sanders' hometown.

Another disillusioned former Confederate, Tampa Bay native Milledge Brannen, succumbed to the Union's East Gulf Blockading Squadron recruitment into the Second Florida Cavalry. Brannen participated in raids against plantations, railroads, and Confederate supplies. With the Second Florida, Brennan even helped Union troops capture Tampa.

THE LOUDOUN RANGERS

Several special units were formed specifically to oppose Confederate rangers in Virginia: Blazer Scouts, Jesse Scouts, Cole's Maryland Cavalry, and others. The group that should have been the most distinctive was the Loudon Rangers.

Why? Because they were Union sympathizers, the only organized unit of Virginians who fought against the Confederacy. They knew the land, and they knew the people, so it stood to reason that they would be successful.

The Loudoun Rangers were from the town of Waterford, near Leesburg. They were all German, Quaker, or Scotch-Irish. Unfortunately, they were poorly trained, and all of them seemed to have a fondness for the liquor they collected in their raids.

As unionist Virginians, they often found themselves literally fighting brother against brother. In August of 1862, a Confederate company of men led by Elijah White attacked the Loudoun Rangers at Waterford Church. The Rangers eventually ran out of ammunition and surrendered.

One of White's Comanches, as they were called, William Snoots, tried to shoot his captive—and brother—Loudoun Ranger Charles Snoots. It took several Comanches to forcefully remind William of the rules of civilized warfare before he spared his brother. The Loudoun Rangers were later paroled.

The fate of the Rangers was ultimately settled by another group of rangers, those led by John S. Mosby. In April 1865, the Loudoun boys were lolling around camp, figuring that the Confederates didn't pose much of a threat anymore. They were indeed surprised by Mosby's Rangers, who captured the entire group of Unionists and all their horses.

When General Winfield Scott Hancock received a telegram informing him of the attack, he simply laughed, wadded up the paper, and said, "Well, that's the last of the Loudoun Rangers."

McNeill's Rangers

After being wounded at Lexington, seeing his son killed in battle, suffering capture, and imprisonment, Captain John Hanson McNeill decided to take another approach to serving the Confederacy.

"Hanse," as he was known, formed the McNeill Rangers, operating in the western regions of Virginia and West Virginia. They became a well-known thorn in the Union's side, capturing wagon trains, supplies, and prisoners of war, as well as scouting for intelligence and foraging for food to provide to Confederate armies.

McNeill's Rangers were a group of brave, talented men known for their precise strategy and military discipline in conducting raids. Their numbers included a precision military mathematician, strategists, and invaluable scouts.

The Rangers focused their frequent raids on the towns of Piedmont, West Virginia, and Cumberland, Maryland. They achieved their three main objectives:

1. **Objective:** Create havoc among federal troops in the area
   Achievement: Federal commanders diverted more than twenty-five thousand troops to guard the B&O against McNeill's Rangers
2. **Objective:** Disrupt traffic and communications on the Baltimore and Ohio Railroad
   Achievement: Constantly under attack, the B&O main line suffered damages of hundreds of thousands of dollars service interruptions that could last for days
3. **Objective:** Supply cattle for beef for the Confederate armies
   Achievement: Scores of cattle were relocated from unionist farms to army mess provisions

PIEDMONT

McNeill targeted the small town of Piedmont often. Its mountain location provided easy access to the B&O, and several machine shops and railroad supply warehouses were there. It took a couple of unsuccessful raids, but McNeill finally destroyed the railroad and burned the Piedmont factories.

Court Martial: Hanse McNeill was court-martialed in 1864 for not handing over members of his band who had joined him after deserting the regular army. He was acquitted.

Springfield, June 1864: One summer afternoon, the Rangers were on a raid to gather cattle, and they came up on the South Branch River. There they found about sixty Union soldiers skinny-dipping and taking a break. The Rangers captured every one of the startled soldiers—and their horses and equipment—without firing a shot.

Mount Jackson, October 1864: When McNeill led his men in a raid to take a bridge near Mount Jackson, Virginia, he expected an easy victory over the Union guards. What he didn't expect was to be shot by one of his own men. Some say it was an accident; others say the fellow ranger was unhappy with his leader. Hanse McNeill died weeks later from a postoperative infection. After John Hanson McNeill's fatal injury, his son Jesse took over command of McNeill's Rangers.

General Kelley: Union Brigadier General Benjamin F. Kelley tired of McNeill's increasing hits to his command. Kelley requested more men to guard against the Rangers, but to no avail. In fact, the raiders would embarrass Kelley further before the war was over.

Jesse knew that his father had wanted to capture Kelley, and on February 21, 1864, he proceeded to carry out Papa McNeill's wishes. Riding through Union territory, braving guards on the pickets, the Rangers managed to outsmart or out-handle all the Northern soldiers they encountered. They walked right into the hotel where Kelley and General George Crook were sleeping in Cumberland, Maryland, and essentially captured them in their beds. Then they rode out of town, back across the Union lines, and into Confederate territory. Later they learned that they left three other Union generals back in Cumberland, including future President Rutherford B. Hayes. What a coup that would have been!

At the close of the Civil War, Jesse McNeill surrendered on May 8, and McNeill's Rangers disbanded.

U.S. Sanitary Commission

Union camps were often regulated by the United States Sanitary Commission, which was formed by private citizens for the soldiers' relief. Commissioners (including Central Park designer Frederick Law Olmsted) visited and inspected Union camps and hospitals, cleaning up, improving food rations, distributing care packages, and providing blankets, shoes, and medicine.

STREIGHT'S RAIDERS

In early 1863, former lumber merchant and publisher Abel D. Streight had an idea to take his 51st Indiana Infantry into the South on a raid. With General Rosecrans' permission, Streight planned to disrupt the Western & Atlantic Railroad from Chattanooga to Atlanta and effectively cut off supplies to Confederate General Braxton Bragg's Army of Tennessee.

Streight's circuitous route would take him from Nashville, to Memphis, to Eastport, Mississippi, then across the northern half of Alabama to Rome, Georgia, where he hoped to destroy their foundries and machine shops.

When the Union army started looking for ways to cut costs when outfitting the raid, there were signs of trouble to come. Streight suggested that it might be more economical to use mules instead of horses. Then he spent some time justifying the silly notion to himself, reminding himself that mules are smart animals, plus they would be better suited to the mountains of northern Alabama and Georgia than horses would be.

The mules quickly proved how smart they were when they broke out of their makeshift pens before the adventure even got underway. And while mules are smart, they're also notorious for being stubborn, and they definitely weren't trained for combat.

So the Indiana boys started out on their mission. Streight used advance scouts and rear details, and he thought they made it all the way to the Appalachian Mountains without the Confederates knowing what the raiders were up to. But he should have known better than to get too comfortable.

As it turned out, Confederate General Nathan Bedford Forrest knew exactly where Streight and his men were. Although Forrest was almost doubly outnumbered, he used his own brand of strategy and tactics to make Streight think he was surrounded by a mass of rebel soldiers.

Instead of engaging with Forrest head-on, Streight's men took off with the Confederates in pursuit. For three days, Streight's men (and their war-novice mules) rode without stopping to eat or sleep, fighting off Forrest's men in the rear. Forrest, on the other hand, let his men attack in shifts so that they could get some rest.

To be fair, a skirmish at Day's Gap went down in the Union victory column because Streight captured two of Forrest's favorite cannon. The weapons were actually Union-issue that Forrest had captured in Murfreesboro, Tennessee. But soon the Indiana troops were delirious from lack of sleep.

The raiders almost made it to Rome, but they couldn't get across the Oostanaula River. Streight surrendered, and Forrest found himself with more than 1,500 prisoners of war.

Streight and his men were sent to Libby Prison, where many of them later took part in the largest mass prison escape of the war. Union Colonel Thomas Rose masterminded the plan using homemade tools to dig a tunnel from the prison's cellar.

Although it was Rose's plan, Colonel Streight declared that since he was the senior officer, he should to be the first to go. Other prisoners created a diversion to occupy the guards, and 109 Northerners made their way through the tunnel and out into the Richmond night. Straight and fifty-eight others got back safely to Union lines to rejoin their regiments. Two escapees drowned at stream crossings, and forty-eight others, including Rose, were recaptured.

Streight was promoted to brigadier general. After the war, he served in the Indiana State Senate from 1877 to 1878, and again from 1889 to 1890.

THE MUD MARCH

The crushing loss at Fredericksburg left Union commander Ambrose Burnside determined to give Lincoln and the North some much-needed cause for hope. On January 20, 1863, as the Army of the Potomac remained encamped in Virginia, Burnside launched a planned offensive that called for an attack on Lee and the Confederates at a ford located ten miles above Fredericksburg.

If successful, Burnside would be in position to destroy Lee's flank. To stave off Burnside and the Union, Lee began reinforcing his left flank. This led Burnside to reconsider and instead set his sights on a nearer crossing as the sources of his attack.

When the Army of the Potomac moved into position, a deluge of rain followed. For the next several days, it never stopped. Pontoons, supply wagons, and the men all labored forward, to no avail. Instead, they sank deeper.

Horses and mules dropped dead on the spot, felled by the exertion of trying to drag supplies through the muck. Confederate soldiers looked on with glee from across the river, brandishing signs bearing messages such as, "This way to Richmond." The attack was scuttled. On January 26, Burnside resigned his command. Lincoln replaced him with General Joseph Hooker, the beleaguered president's latest attempt to find a satisfactory commander.

CIVIL WAR BATTLE TIMELINE: 1863

January 1: Lincoln issues Emancipation Proclamation

January 1: Battle of Galveston, Texas

January 9–11: Battle of Arkansas Post, Arkansas

January 19–23: Burnside's Mud March

January 26: Hooker succeeds Burnside

March 29–July 4: Grant's Second Vicksburg Campaign, Mississippi

April 7: Federal Ironclads attack Charleston, South Carolina (Operations against Charleston)

April 11–May 3: Streight's Raid, Tennessee/Alabama

April 11–May 4: Siege of Suffolk, Virginia

April 16–22: Union fleet passes Vicksburg river batteries

April 29: Battle of Grand Gulf, Mississippi (Grierson's Raid)

April 29–May 8: Stoneman's Road (Chancellorsville Campaign, Virginia)

May 1: Battle of Port Gibson, Mississippi (Grierson's Raid)

May 1–4: Battle of Chancellorsville (Chancellorsville Campaign, Virginia)

May 3: Second Battle of Fredericksburg (Chancellorsville Campaign)

May 3–4: Battle of Salem Church (Chancellorsville Campaign)

May 10: Stonewall Jackson dies at Guiney's Station, Virginia

May 12: Battle of Raymond, Mississippi (Grierson's Raid)

May 14: Battle of Jackson, Mississippi (Grierson's Raid)

May 16: Battle of Champion Hill, Mississippi (Grierson's Raid)

May 17: Battle of Big Black River Bridge, Mississippi (Grierson's Raid)

May 19–July 4: Siege and surrender of Vicksburg (Grierson's Raid)

May 21–July 9: Siege and surrender of Port Hudson, Louisiana

June 9: Battle of Brandy Station, Virginia (Gettysburg Campaign, Pennsylvania)

June 13–15: Second Battle of Winchester, Virginia (Gettysburg Campaign)

June 7: Battle of Milliken's Bend, Louisiana (Grierson's Raid)

June 23–July 4: Tullahoma Campaign, Tennessee

June 28: Meade replaces Hooker

July 1–3: Battle of Gettysburg (Gettysburg Campaign)

July 2-26: Morgan's Raid, Kentucky/Indiana/Ohio

July 10–11: Fort Wagner (Operations against Charleston)

July 10–16: Siege of Jackson, Mississippi

July 16: Secessionville (Operations against Charleston)

July 17: Battle of Honey Springs (Elk Creek), Indian Territory

July 18–September 7: Fort Wagner/Morris Island (Operations against Charleston)

August 17–August 23: Fort Sumter/Charleston Harbor/Morris Island (Operations against Charleston)

September 7–8: Charleston Harbor/Battery Gregg (Operations against Charleston)

September 8: Battle of Sabine Pass, Texas

September 18–20: Battle of Chickamauga, Georgia

October 14: Battle of Briscoe Station, Virginia

October 28–29: Wauhatchie Night Attack (Chattanooga Campaign, Tennessee)

November 6: Battle of Droop Mountain, West Virginia

November 7: Engagement at Rappahannock Station, Virginia

November 17–December 4: Siege of Knoxville

November 19: Lincoln delivers Gettysburg Address

November 23–25: Battle of Chattanooga (Chattanooga Campaign)

November 26–December 2: Mine Run Campaign, Virginia

BY HOOK OR BY CROOK

In January 1863, President Lincoln threw in his lot with "Fighting Joe" Hooker as the latest leader of the Army of the Potomac. Joining a list that had grown to encompass Irvin McDowell, George McClellan, and Ambrose Burnside, Hooker offered yet another attempt at a Union commander. He was known for back-biting and piling on the back of a faltering superior while also being a self-promoter, as well as given to heavy drinking.

Under Burnside's command, Hooker had openly opined that both the army and the government needed a dictator to take charge. In his January 26, 1863 letter to Hooker naming him as commander, Lincoln offered a sternly humorous response: "Only those generals who gain successes can set up dictators. What I now ask of you is military success, and I will risk the dictatorship."

Hooker rallied the troops upon assuming command of the Army of the Potomac. He streamlined operations, improved the quality of food—adding servings of fresh bread and vegetables. He managed to also improve uniforms for the soldiers and honed their training.

He pronounced himself satisfied in the spring of 1863 after a winter spent rebuilding the army. "I have the finest army the sun ever shone on," Hooker said. "If the enemy does not run, God help them."

Hooker fell prey to politics, a penchant for boozing, and of course, the tactics of Robert E. Lee. Hooker presided over a major loss at Chancellorsville in spring 1863 and bungled his way through Lee's Northern invasion soon after. He resigned on June 28, three days before the pivotal Battle of Gettysburg began. His replacement was George Meade.

EMANCIPATION AND ANTICIPATION

How free is free? Casual observers often make the mistaken assumption that the Emancipation Proclamation enacted by President Lincoln on January 1, 1863, set all slaves free.

Not exactly.

Instead, it freed only the slaves living in any region controlled by the Confederacy.

Although Lincoln believed the practice of slavery to be immoral, his proclamation hewed to strict legal interpretation. Lincoln feared that the Union border states, since they allowed slavery, would be alienated and leave to join the Confederacy.

The Emancipation Proclamation failed to completely satisfy abolitionists and even irritated some Northern soldiers and others who considered the war a battle to preserve the Union rather than a conflict over slaves' freedom. Despite these misgivings, Lincoln's political acumen proved shrewd.

The proclamation ensured the Confederacy would never win support from European nations, a major blow to Southern hopes. More practically, it put added pressure on the Southern war effort, because any slaves who were lost or fled left the heavy burden of labor behind. Without slaves to drive the home front economy while white men went to war, the Confederacy's already meager finances and fighting forces were depleted further.

As for the fate of the slaves everywhere, full emancipation did not arrive until after Lincoln's death in 1865. The Thirteenth Amendment to the Constitution took effect in December—eight months after John Wilkes Booth assassinated Lincoln.

RYE FOR AN EYE

The Richmond Bread Riots occurred in the spring of 1863, a direct result of soaring inflation and a shortage of basic goods like flour and salt. As the war went on, economic conditions worsened in the capital and across the Confederacy.

Suffering was even more acute in Richmond. The city struggled to cope with its surging population even as Union blockades and nearby battles severely limited production and delivery of crops. In other words, more people had less to eat while everyone became steadily poorer and hungrier.

Basic necessities became luxury items. By 1863, for example, a barrel of flour cost $100—a result of an 1862 shortage that tripled prices, followed by another doubling, to tripling in the following year. In 1864, flour reached $250 per barrel, thirty times its pre-war cost, according to the Federal Reserve Bank of Richmond. By the end of the war, inflation across the South reached an astounding 9,000 percent.

In April 1863, several hundred women marched across town to Richmond's Capitol Square chanting and demanding bread. They called for flour and bread at government cost—a direct response to rumors that a similar campaign in North Carolina had led to better prices from the local government.

In Richmond, the frustrated and hungry women broke into stores and shops and took whatever provisions they could find. They also took anything else handy. Jefferson Davis personally came down to cool the flaring tempers, and under threat from the local militia, the crowd dispersed. Southern papers downplayed the incident and the Confederates later tried to hide any record of the it.

LUCY HOLCOMBE PICKENS: QUEEN OF THE CONFEDERACY

Born in 1832 in Fayette County, Tennessee, and educated at a Quaker school in Bethlehem, Pennsylvania, Lucy Petway Holcombe was known to be not only a classic beauty, but also a gracious and intelligent woman.

Cuban Policy: In fact, she was so politically savvy that her interests in Cuban affairs led her to write a historical romance novel about the exploits of General Narciso López. Titled *The Free Flag of Cuba, or the Martyrdom of Lopez: A Tale of the Liberating Expedition of 1851*, the book was a thinly veiled story of her fiancé and his death fighting for the Cubans.

The Mississippi Legislature: To satisfy her political curiosity, in 1850, Lucy visited the Mississippi legislature while on a family visit to that state's governor, John Quitman (Lucy and Quitman agreed on the position of liberating Cuba). The attractive, captivating Lucy so distracted the policymakers that they quickly adjourned in her honor.

Colonel Pickens: The Holcombe family took their annual summer vacation to White Sulphur Springs, Virginia, in 1856. That year, Lucy met Colonel Francis Wilkinson Pickens, a twice-widowed lawyer and secessionist. He was also twice her age.

Lucy was attracted to Pickens' power and agreed to marry him if he would secure a diplomatic post and take her overseas.

Life in Russia: In 1858, Pickens was appointed ambassador to Russia. He quickly married Lucy at her father's plantation home in Marshall, Texas, and they sailed for Russia.

In St. Petersburg, Lucy became a favorite of Russia's Czar Alexander II and his Czarina. They offered her gifts of diamonds and emeralds; she cooked them sweet potatoes and mayhaw jelly. When Lucy became pregnant, the Czarina arranged for her royal physicians to attend the birth in the imperial palace. Eugenia Frances Dorothea Pickens was born in 1859 with a built-in set of godparents in Russia's royal couple. The Czarina even christened the baby Olga Neva and called her "Douschka" (meaning "little darling"), by which she was always known.

Return to the Confederacy: The South moved closer toward secession. Colonel Pickens returned home to support the Southern cause. In 1860, he was elected governor of South Carolina. Lucy Pickens contributed to the Confederate effort, selling the jewels she had received from the Russian royal family to supply the "Lucy Holcombe Legion" of soldiers. She became known as "Lady Lucy."

After the war, Francis Pickens died in 1869 at his Edgewood Plantation in South Carolina. Lucy never remarried and continued to live there until her death in 1899.

Rumor: Lucy Holcombe Invents Iced Tea

Legend says that Lucy invented iced tea. Trying to imitate the Southern gentleman's mint julep, which is basically whiskey tempered with a little bit of sugar-water and mint sprigs, Lucy put mint into sugar-laced tea. To cool the beverage, she used ice imported by steamboat from Jefferson, Texas, to New Orleans.

Lucy Pickens and Confederate Currency

Lucy Pickens is one of the few women whose image has appeared on national currency—she was pictured on Confederate one-dollar bills and one-hundred-dollar bills. Because most nations only picture heads of state on currency, Lucy Pickens has sometimes been called the "uncrowned Queen of the Confederacy."

MOTHER BICKERDYKE

Bickerdyke: The name alone is stern enough to understand why William T. Sherman allowed only her of all women into his camps. In fact, when an officer complained of her brusque administrations, the general who burned his way across the entire Southern geography and brought the Confederate nation to its knees simply said, "She outranks me."

Ulysses S. Grant once counseled an unhappy surgeon, "My God, man. Mother Bickerdyke outranks everybody, even Lincoln. If you have run amuck of her, I advise you to get out quickly before she has you under arrest."

Who Was Mary Ann Bickerdyke?
- An Ohio-native, Oberlin College-trained, widowed nurse and mother of two sons.
- Entrusted by residents of Galesburg, Illinois, to deliver medical supplies to Union soldiers, Bickerdyke established a military hospital for the Northern men.
- A Sanitary Commission Agent, Bickerdyke cleaned the hospitals top to bottom, ordered bathtubs made from barrels, set up decent kitchens, and disciplined anyone in her way.
- She traveled with the Union army through four years and nineteen battles (including Shiloh), establishing more than three hundred field hospitals.
- Bickerdyke did whatever needed to be done: assisting at amputations, brewing barrels of coffee, washing clothes, rounding up meat and eggs to feed the men, scrounging together supplies, and helping run army field hospitals.
- During battles, Bickerdyke often risked her life by searching for wounded soldiers, even by lantern-light after dark.
- She earned a reputation for sidestepping bureaucracy and outting officers who provided poorly for their men.
- She solicited contributions from the civilian population.

- When a surgeon once asked on whose authority she acted, she responded, "On the authority of the Lord God Almighty. Have you anything that outranks that?"

Bickerdyke After the War

- General Sherman invited Mother Bickerdyke to participate in a grand review in Washington. She led an entire corps down Pennsylvania Avenue. But she refused Sherman's offer of a seat on the reviewing stand, instead passing out water to soldiers after the parade.
- Bickerdyke provided legal assistance to Northern veterans seeking pensions from the federal government and helping with other legal issues.
- She also helped secure pensions for more than three hundred women nurses, but she did not receive a $25 per month pension herself until the 1880s.
- Bickerdyke moved to Kansas where she helped veterans to settle and begin new lives by securing donations to buy land, tools, supplies, and free transportation to that state.
- Bickerdyke later opened a boarding house in Salina, Kansas.
- She spent four years campaigning to clean up the slums in New York City
- Hoping that a change of climate would restore her declining health, Bickerdyke relocated to San Francisco, where she accepted a position at the United States Mint.
- She died in Kansas on November 8, 1901, and was buried with full military honors in Galesburg, Illinois, next to her husband.

A United States hospital ship named in her honor, the S.S. *Mary A. Bickerdyke*, was launched in Richmond, California, in 1943.

DR. MARY EDWARDS WALKER

- The only woman graduate of Syracuse University Medical School, Class of 1855
- The only female doctor commissioned during the Civil War
- The first woman assistant surgeon in the U.S. Army

The Surgeon General's office denied Dr. Walker's 1861 application for military surgeon because she was a woman. She refused a nursing position, working instead as an unpaid volunteer in the Patent Office Hospital in Washington.

In 1864, General George Thomas ignored the Board of Surgeons' objections and commissioned Walker as assistant surgeon. Dr. Walker worked as a Union field surgeon, attending wounded from Bull Run, Fredericksburg, Chickamauga, and Atlanta.

Walker also engaged in espionage for General Thomas and was captured by Confederates. She was a prisoner of war in Richmond's Castle Thunder for four months. She was traded for a Confederate surgeon during a prisoner exchange. This act meant the Union recognized her position as a surgeon.

Mary Walker's Congressional Medal of Honor

For heroism on the battlefield and caring for other prisoners, Mary Walker was awarded the Congressional Medal of Honor in 1865. She is still the only woman to have ever received the "purple heart."

In 1917, Congress reviewed the number of Medals of Honor, and determined that more than nine hundred too many had been awarded. Mary's medal was revoked, with almost one thousand others, because it had not been awarded for combat. But she would not give it up, and in 1919 was buried with the decoration in her hand.

In 1977, President Jimmy Carter posthumously restored the medal to her.

FANNY RICKETTS:
PRISONER OF WAR

With her husband, Union Captain James Ricketts, fighting in Manassas, Fanny anxiously awaited word of the battle's outcome. The regiment returned to Washington without him, presenting his sword and telling her he had been wounded and was near death.

Fanny, determined to find him, got a pass from Lieutenant General Winfield Scott to go through Union lines to Bull Run. But beyond Union pickets and at Confederate lines, the Union officer's pass was worthless. She could not proceed any farther.

Thinking quickly, Fanny remembered that her husband had earlier served in the Southwest with J. E. B. Stuart. She sent a note to the Confederate colonel in Fairfax, who returned a pass allowing Fanny onto the battlefield among the victorious Confederates.

After four days, Fanny found James in a makeshift hospital, a private home where the wounded were delivered. This was her first experience with field surgery; the horrors she witnessed in the house led her to refuse amputation of her husband's leg in the following days.

Within weeks, Captain Ricketts was transferred to Libby Prison in Richmond. Fanny stayed with her husband the entire time, almost five months.

While a prisoner of war, Captain Ricketts was named as a "hostage" for Confederate prisoners. This meant he could be exchanged for a specific prisoner of war in a Northern prison. But if that person were executed instead of released, then Rickets would be executed in turn. Hostages were chosen based on their rank.

Fanny stayed with her husband until he was exchanged for Confederate seaman Julius A. de Lagnel in January of 1862. Later that spring, Captain Ricketts was promoted to brigadier general.

Malinda and Keith Blalock

North Carolina couple Keith and Malinda Blalock may have been the only husband-and-wife team to fight for both the Confederates and the Union.

Q: Who were they?

A: William McKesson "Keith" Blalock and his wife Sarah Malinda Pritchard Blalock

Q: Where did they live?

A: In western North Carolina on Grandfather Mountain, near the Tennessee and Kentucky borders

Q: What side were they really on?

A: Keith and Malinda were both Union sympathizers.

Q: What did they do?

A: Either under pressure from friends, or by draft, Keith enlisted in Company F of the 26th North Carolina Infantry. Malinda didn't want to be left behind, so she cut her hair and enlisted as his sixteen-year-old brother, "Sam."

Q: Did anyone suspect "Sam" of being a woman?

A: Some men in the regiment noticed that Sam and Keith seemed to have an unusually close relationship. But, "Sam" was respected for being a good shot, and no one discovered "his" secret.

Q: What were they really trying to do?

A: Keith's plan was to join the Confederate troops so that he could get as close as possible to the Union troops. Then he was going to desert to the North when an opportunity presented itself.

Q: What happened to Keith's plan?

A: By the time Keith and his wife reached the 26th North Carolina, the troops had marched far enough away from Union lines that skipping out was not an immediate option.

Q: What did they do when they found out they wouldn't be able to easily desert?

A: Keith and "Sam" fought as Confederate soldiers in three battles.

Q: Why didn't they stay with the regiment?

A: Malinda was wounded in the shoulder. A surgeon discovered her secret when removing the bullet. The surgeon would not agree to keep quiet, but he did agree to be slow to talk.

Q: What was Keith's solution to the problem?

A: Keith got himself discharged. He rolled around in poison oak for a first-class allergic reaction. Within hours he was blistered and swollen with a high fever. It looked alarmingly like smallpox to the surgeon, and Keith was given an immediate medical discharge.

Q: What did Malinda do after Keith was discharged?

A: She instantly told Colonel Zebulon Vance her secret. He didn't believe "Sam," and he called in a physician to confirm the claim. In short order, Malinda was discharged, too.

Q: What did Keith and Malinda do after they went home to North Carolina to recuperate?

A: First of all, they had to be careful about not being recalled to the Confederate army. Next, they decided to see what they could do for the Union cause.

Q: How did Keith and Malinda help the Union?

A: Keith and Malinda became outlaws in the Blue Ridge and Great Smoky Mountains of western North Carolina and east Tennessee.

Q: What were some of the guerrilla tactics the Blalocks used?

A: They harbored Union sympathizers and escaped Union prisoners, and then guided them safely through the mountains to the North. They also led a band of raiders against Confederates' family farms in the area.

Q: Did Keith and "Sam" ever join another regiment?

A: Before the end of the war, they served as scouts and raiders for the 10th Michigan Cavalry, Company T. For this service, Keith later applied for a veteran's pension from the U.S. Army.

New York Times best-selling historical romance author Sharyn McCrumb's 2003 novel, *Ghost Riders*, weaved the tale of Malinda and Sam Blalock, Colonel Vance, and their adventures.

HOMES FOR CONFEDERATE WOMEN

Richmond, Virginia

In 1897, several destitute widows pooled their meager resources to live together in Richmond. The Ladies Auxiliary of the Confederate Veterans of Camp Pickett recognized their need and held a bazaar to raise $1,000 for their benefit.

In 1898, the Virginia Legislature voted to establish a Home for Needy Confederate Women to care for female relatives (wives, widows, sisters, and daughters) of Confederate sailors, soldiers, and marines. The General Assembly granted $1,000, and charity groups raised another $7,500 for the cause.

The Home for Confederate Women opened in 1900 in downtown Richmond. The first ten incoming residents surrendered their estates in exchange for lifelong care. The Home was administered by Virginia's first lady, Elizabeth Montague, and Robert E. Lee's daughter, Mary Custis Lee.

The admission requirements:

- All applicants must be free from mental derangement, contagious diseases, morphine or alcohol habits, and epilepsy.
- No gossip or tale-bearing will be tolerated.

Throughout the home's history, funding changed from public support to private donations and back again. By 1904, the population had doubled, and the facility moved to a larger building that had once been used as the Office of the Confederate Treasury.

In the 1920s, President Calvin Coolidge's wife, Grace, visited the home, where she learned how to knit a counterpane bedspread pattern. She sold the pattern to *McCall's* magazine and donated the proceeds back to the home.

After this house was destroyed in a fire, a new, hundred-room building opened in 1932 for about eighty residents. The women loved to gather around the old piano, which had belonged to

Jefferson Davis' daughter, and sing songs from the old days, such as "Dixie" and "Sewanee River."

After the board of trustees ruled against admitting granddaughters of veterans, the last daughter entered the home around 1980. By 1989, the house was in disrepair, and the board closed the building, auctioned off its contents, and relocated the seven remaining women into their own wing of a new nursing home. The last resident died in 1997 (the daughter of a veteran, she was born in 1898 to his second wife). The building now belongs to the Virginia Museum of Fine Arts.

Residents of the Confederate Home for Women included Captain Sally Tompkins, a great-niece of Thomas Jefferson, a cousin of Chief Justice John Marshall, and three nieces of President John Tyler.

Austin, Texas

In 1903, the United Daughters of the Confederacy established a Wives and Widows Home Committee to raise funds to care for widows and wives of honorably discharged Confederate soldiers and other women who aided the Confederacy. As in Virginia, support came from both public and private sources throughout the funds' administration.

In 1908, the Confederate Woman's Home opened in Austin, Texas. The two-story, fifteen-bedroom facility housed three women. The requirements:

- Residents must be at least sixty years of age
- Residents must be without means of financial support

Admittance grew. Sixteen women lived in the home in 1909, and the population expanded to eighteen in the next two years. So in 1913 a two-story renovation added twenty-four new bedrooms, and in 1916 a hospital was constructed, too.

The institution peaked from 1920 to 1935, when anywhere from eighty to 110 women called it their home. By 1945, only fifty-five women remained. In 1963, the last three residents were moved to a private nursing home. The facility was closed, and the property sold in 1986. During its fifty-five years in operation, more than 3,400 women made a home at the Confederate Woman's Home.

THE SOUTHERN BELLE

There really were Southern belles in pre-Civil War times, and they really were considered a "catch" by the gentlemen of the day. First and foremost, a belle was pretty, and she was single. She also came from a wealthy family with a good name. She was what we now call "fun and fearless," turning on the famous Southern charm while flirting mercilessly and without satisfactory resolution, at least for her target.

While her goal was to marry a gentleman of wealth and high social standing, she had to bring a lot more to the table than a flair for fashion. The ultimate trophy wife, a classic Southern belle was expected to be able to hold up her end of a conversation, play a musical instrument, draw, do needlework, write legibly and coherently, understand mathematical figures and geography, and have at least studied the French language.

The belle's training and skills not only served to attract a potential mate, but they also prepared her for the duties of wife and mother, such as bearing children, caring for her family, and managing the household.

The Famous Belle, Octavia Le Vert

A Georgia native, Octavia Walton Le Vert was one of the most sophisticated and celebrated belles in the South.

Family Name and Wealth: Grandfather George Walton signed the Declaration of Independence; Father George Walton was Governor of Florida.

Education: Octavia studied science and spoke Greek, Latin, Italian, French, and Spanish.

Gentleman Husband: Dr. Henry Le Vert, son of a fleet surgeon under General Rochambeau in the Revolutionary War

Feminine Tactics: After the war, Octavia lobbied in Washington for her friend General Beauregard's pardon.

Intelligence: Octavia named the capital of Florida, choosing the spelling of the Seminole word Tallahassee, meaning "beautiful land."

CHANCELLORSVILLE

Despite being outnumbered by more than a two-to-one margin, the Confederate army managed to defeat the Union at the Battle of Chancellorsville in May 1863.

The South walked away worse for wear, if jubilant, in victory. The battle claimed one of the Confederacy's most valued military leaders in Stonewall Jackson, as well as a higher percentage of casualties—about one-quarter of the Confederate men involved in the battle—than the Union.

The Confederates were sixty thousand strong at Chancellorsville, while Union forces numbered 120,000. Confederate commander Robert E. Lee devised a brilliant strategy to defeat the Union and Joseph Hooker. Lee's maneuvers leading into and during the battle, working against an enemy with superior numbers and supplies, became known as Lee's masterpiece.

Hooker's spring offensive aimed to force Lee to give up the Confederate entrenchments at Fredericksburg. To do so, Hooker sent ten thousand cavalry toward Richmond to disrupt communication lines between Lee and the Confederate capital. He sent the bulk of the Union infantry across the Rappahannock and Rapidan rivers to move against Lee's left flank. The final piece would be a head-on attack at Fredericksburg.

By the end of April, Union forces had crossed the Rappahannock, leaving Lee little choice but to fall back and avoid Hooker's pincer movement. Instead, Lee divided his army. This time he sent Jubal Early and ten thousand men to fight from the Fredericksburg trenches. Lee took the rest of his men toward the Wilderness—a dense area of tree thickets—and Hooker's flanking column. Once there, Lee divided his forces again, sending Stonewall Jackson through the Wilderness with thirty thousand men to take a circuitous path to the Union's exposed right flank. Meanwhile, Lee would use the remaining fourteen thousand men at his disposal to distract Hooker to give Jackson time to attack the Union.

Skirmishes along Jackson's twelve-mile march led the Union to believe the Confederates were in retreat. Warnings of a Southern attack were dismissed, and Hooker's depleted cavalry left little possibility for uncovering exactly where Jackson and his men were located in the thick cover of the Wilderness.

Late on May 2, Jackson attacked the vulnerable Union flank and scored a surprise blow. As evening fell, the attack was halted. Fighting continued for the next two days, with the Confederates taking control despite the severe disadvantage in soldiers and equipment. Hooker pulled back the next day, allowing Lee to reunite his divided army and avoid Union counterattack.

The Confederates won the battle as Hooker ordered a retreat back across the Rappahannock. Hookers' men were frustrated at the decision. Historians believe that Hooker, had he decided to stay and fight Lee, could have reversed the battle's results. Instead, the North absorbed another disappointing loss, paving the way for Lee's invasion north into Pennsylvania in the summer of 1863.

Jessie Frémont

In 1840, fifteen-year-old Jessie Benton met John C. Frémont in Washington, D.C. Her father, Missouri senator Thomas Hart Benton, understandably resisted his young daughter's declarations of love. Jessie and John married in 1841.

Jessie figures in the debacle of her husband's emancipation proclamation in Missouri. She visited Lincoln to plead her husband's case and was granted at least two audiences with the president. It seems that she did more harm than good.

"MY RIGHT ARM"

The high point for Confederate military leadership occurred at Chancellorsville, a tribute to Robert E. Lee's strategic genius and the expert performances of Stonewall Jackson and cavalry leader Jeb Stuart.

Jackson, after leading some thirty thousand men on a winding twelve-mile march through the Wilderness to a brilliant attack of the Union flank late on May 2, was killed at this scene of storied triumph. As he made his way through the woods on horseback during the evening of the first day's battle, Jackson was shot in the dark by Confederate soldiers s as he and his staff made their way back to the camp.

His injuries included his left arm, hand, and wrist. As with so many others in the Civil War, the wounds didn't kill him, infection did. On May 10, suffering from pneumonia, Jackson died in an outbuilding located on Thomas Chandler's 740-acre plantation, where he arrived after a twenty-seven-mile ambulance ride with his doctors. These included his chief surgeon, Dr. Hunter McGuire, who had amputated Jackson's left arm and removed a bullet from his right hand before the lengthy ride.

McGuire kept watch over Jackson for his six-day stay at the outbuilding, ending with his death on May 10. After deliriously barking out orders in his last breaths, Jackson stopped and offered his final words: "Let us cross over the river, and rest under the shade of the trees."

MISSISSIPPI MUD

Ulysses S. Grant knew the importance of controlling the Mississippi River. After all, choking off Confederate access to the massive river had been a strategic goal from the start of the war. With the Union controlling more and more of the top half of the river, as well as having taken New Orleans, the remaining obstacle was the bluff-top town of Vicksburg.

Beginning in December 1862, Grant turned his sights on finding a way to take Vicksburg despite its impregnable position. After seven months, thousands of deaths and casualties, and repeated abandoned campaigns, he managed to take Vicksburg in a crucial triumph for the North and a backbreaking defeat for the Confederacy.

Grant started the lengthy campaign with a joint land-naval approach, hoping to circumvent the Confederate guns trained on anything that moved below Vicksburg's bluffs. The Union set up a forward base at Holly Springs, with Grant hoping to unite his forty thousand men by railroad with William Sherman's thirty-two thousand soldiers traveling by water.

Earl Van Dorn and Confederate soldiers destroyed those well-laid plans with a surprise attack at Holly Springs, wreaking havoc on Union supplies along the way. A companion railroad raid under the direction of Nathan Bedford Forrest's expert cavalry charges left sixty miles of train tracks in tatters. Grant and Sherman scrapped their attack plans.

During the winter of 1863, Grant carried out a series of failed canal campaigns aimed at finding alternative water routes to Vicksburg. Each attempt failed. Grant plowed ahead in spite of repeated disappointment. Later attempts included a short-lived campaign to find a water route, an attempt that traversed hundreds of miles of swamps and bayous in neighboring Louisiana to try and reach Vicksburg south of town. That, too, was scuttled, as was a naval expedition through the Yazoo Pass.

The Union fleet in Mississippi narrowly avoided virtual

extinction during a pass through Steele's Bayou in March 1863. After navigating eleven boats through a tricky, treacherous path above Vicksburg, Confederate forces blunted the procession. Only Sherman's heroics and his marching soldiers saved the Union from naval devastation.

Grant next blew off an assignment that would have united him with Nathaniel Banks' men at Port Hudson, just outside Baton Rouge. Instead Grant turned his attention to Jackson, the Mississippi capital. In mid–May, the Union captured Jackson. Two days later, Grant led a triumphant but blood-soaked battle at Champion's Hill as the Union absorbed 2,400 casualties and inflicted 3,800 on the Confederates.

There was nothing left but to attack Vicksburg. Confederates repulsed Grant's assaults on May 19 and 22, costing the Union thousands of casualties and ceding no ground.

Assault failed, so Grant turned to siege and starvation, taking the fight to the citizens and the soldiers alike in Vicksburg. The harrowing six-week siege began in May. Union soldiers hammered Vicksburg with constant mortar and artillery barrages. Citizens dug caves and scrambled for scraps of food amid ceaseless shelling and rampant sickness.

Despite their resilience, the people of Vicksburg flagged, at last, on July 4—one day after the Confederate army endured its crushing defeat at Gettysburg. How painful was the siege of Vicksburg for the beleaguered Mississippians? Vicksburg ignored the Fourth of July national holiday for decades afterward, finally recognizing Independence Day again at the tail end of World War II. Yes, World War II. Now that's a grudge.

In a thirty-mile-per-hour wind, the Washington Monument sways 0.125 of an inch.

THE WASHINGTON MONUMENT DURING THE CIVIL WAR

If you've ever toured Washington, D.C., you've seen the monument memorializing our first president. You've probably noticed the difference in the color of the marble at the 150-foot mark.

You may have read the brochure explaining that the monument's construction was halted around the time of the Civil War. When the work restarted, the same vein of stone was no longer available. A slightly different color of marble was used.

Many people think the construction stopped because of the Civil War. The truth is a bit more complicated than that.

It was decided, to economize, to invite groups to provide memorial stones for the interior walls. Every donated stone was one less to buy. Almost two hundred stones were donated from groups as varied as American Indian tribes, professional organizations, and foreign countries. Needless to say, some inscriptions were not about Washington at all.

This led to political arguments about how to spend the money. Financial support for the monument dwindled. About the time the money ran out and construction stopped, the country's focus shifted to funding the Civil War.

Construction was completed under Civil War veteran and Corps of Engineers Lieutenant Colonel Thomas Lincoln Casey.

Washington Monument Timeline

1833: The Washington National Monument Society is organized.

1847: $87,000 is collected to construct a monument to George Washington.

1848: With great ceremony, the cornerstone is laid, using the same trowel used to lay the Capitol cornerstone in 1793.

1854: Construction is halted for lack of funds.

1876: President Grant approves taking federal responsibility for completing construction.

1880: Work begins again on the monument.
1884: Construction is completed.
1885: The Washington Monument is dedicated.
1888: The Monument opens to the public.

"Father" figure

In August 1863, President Lincoln wrote a letter that included an admiring nod to the fall of Vicksburg the previous month. In his characteristically muscular, elegant prose, the president noted that the "Father of Waters again goes unvexed to the sea." The reference to Ulysses Grant's successful siege had just one slight problem—it furthered a mistaken notion that the word Mississippi literally means "Father of Waters." The erroneous translation first popped up in the early-1800s and was promulgated by many others in subsequent years, including James Fenimore Cooper. Its actual translation is "Big River." But that doesn't sound as good as Lincoln's phrase, does it?

THE OTHER JEFFERSON DAVIS

Indiana native Jefferson Columbus Davis (1828–1879) was still a seminary student when, at the age of eighteen, he decided to head off to the Mexican War under the command of General Zachary Taylor. Davis exhibited skill in battle and was promoted to first lieutenant.

In 1858, Davis was sent to Fort Sumter as the first commander of that military installation. He was still there when Confederates fired on the garrison in 1861.

Promoted to captain, Davis led an Indiana squad at Wilson's Creek, Pea Ridge, and Corinth.

Then in September 1862, Davis got into an argument with his former commanding officer Major General William Nelson in Louisville's Galt House hotel. It seems that Nelson had relieved Davis of duty, which Davis saw as a personal insult. Davis cornered Nelson in the hotel, demanding an apology. Nelson refused, slapping Davis in the face. Davis followed him outside, and right there in the street, shot the unarmed Nelson in the chest at point-blank range. Davis was arrested and held for twenty days. He was released without standing trial for the action, in great part due to the influence of the Indiana governor.

Davis returned to duty, participating in the battles of Murfreesboro and Chickamauga and Sherman's March to the Sea.

Davis was involved in another particularly ugly event at Ebenezer Creek, near Savannah, Georgia, toward the end of 1864. At this point in the war, about five hundred slaves were following behind the Union troops, in hopes of gaining freedom by association. After the Union soldiers crossed the creek, Davis pulled away the pontoon bridge, knowing full well that he was stranding the slaves between the water and Joseph Wheeler's advancing Confederate cavalry. Many of the refugees drowned trying to swim across the river.

CONFEDERATE COMMANDERS: DABNEY HERNDON MAURY (1822-1900)

Born in Fredericksburg, Virginia, to a family of influence, Dabney Herndon "Dab" Maury originally wanted to be a lawyer and enrolled in the University of Virginia. But once there, he found he didn't like that course of study and decided to change majors.

Maury transferred to West Point, where one of his classmates was future Confederate commander George Pickett, known for his ill-fated charge at Gettysburg. Graduating in the class of 1846, Maury served in the Mexican War as a lieutenant in the Mounted Rifles. During that time his left arm was maimed.

After the Mexican War, Maury returned to West Point to teach military tactics, geography, history, and ethics. Next, he accepted a position as superintendent of the cavalry school in Carlisle Barracks, Pennsylvania.

In 1860, "Dab" was appointed assistant adjutant general of the Department of New Mexico, but he left the position when Virginia seceded from the Union. He didn't quite resign, though. He later learned that he had been accused of "treasonable designs" against the United States. This is important because it meant he could never again rejoin the U.S. Army.

In the Confederate Army, as a cavalry captain, Maury fought in a number of important victories. He was most famous for his heroics in the West. In 1862, he had been promoted to colonel as a chief of staff under General Earl Van Dorn, commander of the Trans-Mississippi Department.

Maury fought in the battles of Pea Ridge, Iuka, Corinth, and Hatchie Bridge, then was charged with defending the District of the Gulf. Unfortunately, he was eventually forced to surrender Mobile to the Union. By the war's end, Maury had attained the rank of major general.

Maury must have been short. His men called him "Puss in Boots" because he seemed to be swallowed in his cavalry boots. They also said he was "every inch a soldier, but there were not many inches of him."

After the war, Maury taught at the Classical and Mathematical Academy of Fredericksburg, which he founded. He began to doubt his qualifications as a teacher, and then moved to New Orleans. During a cholera epidemic, he volunteered as a nurse in the city's hospitals.

Maury accepted an appointment as minister to Colombia from 1885 to 1889. He also wrote his memoirs, magazine articles, and books.

The Southern Historical Society

Dabney Maury founded the Southern Historical Society in 1868 to document Southern viewpoints from the Civil War. He accepted papers from military figures (soldiers, officers, politicians) and civilians alike, and then collected them into the *Southern Historical Society Papers*.

This fifty-two-volume set of materials, ranging from congressional minutes to personal correspondence, even today is valuable to historic researchers, both professional and amateur. The papers are now housed by the Virginia Historical Society.

Dabney Maury's Uncle

After Maury's father died, he was raised by his paternal uncle, Commodore Matthew Fontaine Maury. Matthew Maury was himself an accomplished Naval officer and oceanographer who also operated in the service of the Confederate Navy.

Through his research on ocean currents—using messages in weighted bottles—Commodore Maury was the first man to determine the existence of the Gulf Stream. Known as "the Pathfinder of the Seas," Matthew Maury pioneered the study of the world's largest bodies of water, including charting the Atlantic Ocean's floor.

CONFEDERATE COMMANDERS: LEWIS ADDISON ARMISTEAD (1817-1863)

North Carolina native Lewis Armistead is known for his last battle, leading a group of Virginians to sure death at Gettysburg. Armistead was expelled from West Point for hitting Jubal Early over the head with a plate in the dining hall. He did, however, serve in the Mexican War. After he joined the Confederate Army, Armistead eventually reached the rank of brigadier general.

Thinking they had routed the Northerners, Confederate troops advanced to take the wall. The Union waited to open fire until they were at close range. Southerners reached the Union line only at one place, called "the Angle." They were led by Armistead, who encouraged his men, increasing to double time. He jumped the stone wall, waving his hat on his sword, calling "Virginians! With me!" and seized a Union battery. Then he was mortally shot.

Several similar stories circulate involving his old friend and Union General Winfield Scott Hancock, commanding at the Angle that day.

- The night before battle, Armistead packaged his Bible to send to Hancock's wife, Mira, if he didn't make it. With the unreliable war-time mail service, it arrived months later.
- Armistead gave his West Point ring—which he still wore, even though he didn't graduate—to George Pickett for Pickett's wife.
- Before he died, Armistead sent his watch to Hancock for safekeeping.
- Armistead's dying wish was for Hancock to send his personal effects home to his family.

Other Battles Participated in: Peninsula Campaign, Seven Pines, Seven Days, Second Bull Run, Antietam (wounded), Fredericksburg, and Malvern Hill.

CONFEDERATE COMMANDERS: RICHARD STODDERT EWELL (1817-1872)

Nicknamed "Old Baldy" or "Old Bald Head," Ewell was born in Georgetown and raised near Manassas. He graduated from West Point in 1840 and reached the rank of lieutenant general.

Ewell served under Stonewall Jackson during the Shenandoah Campaign and took over command of Jackson's troops after his death.

Controversy at Gettysburg: You know the story: Barefoot Southerners heard that a shoe shipment was stored in Gettysburg, and they needed new footwear. Of course, both armies were already moving into place for battle, so it wasn't over shoes. But some say it was Ewell's men who sparked the first day's action.

Here's where things get sticky: Most accounts say General Lee gave Ewell an ambiguously-worded order to secure the high ground before nightfall, if practical. And most accounts say Ewell considered it, decided his men needed rest, and determined it not practical.

This leads to one of those great fifth-quarter "what if" questions: What if Ewell had moved forward to get the early advantage? Some historians recently said that Lee never gave that order, or it wasn't worded that way, or it was given but about another position.

Later, while retreating from Richmond after the Confederate capital fell to Union hands, Ewell and most of his men were captured at Sayler's Creek days before Lee's surrender. He was imprisoned for three months, then returned to his Tennessee family farm to live out the rest of his days.

Other Battles Ewell Participated In: First Bull Run, Seven Days, Cedar Mountain, Second Bull Run (wounded), Second Winchester, Chancellorsville, Wilderness, and Spotsylvania.

While Ewell was home recuperating from leg amputation, he renewed his fondness for his cousin Lizinka Campbell Brown, a wealthy widow. They were married before he returned to action.

Confederate Commanders: Leonidas Polk (1806-1864)

An 1827 West Point graduate, Polk turned to missionary work and was later named the Episcopal Bishop of Louisiana.

Columbus, Kentucky, 1861-1862: Confederate troops under Polk invaded from Tennessee into the border state of Kentucky, taking the town of Columbus. Polk battled back and forth over the city with the Union, including Grant's first Civil War action at Belmont. Polk eventually lost control of Columbus and evacuated in early 1862.

Belmont, Missouri, November 1861: Union soldiers under General Grant pushed back the Confederates under General Gideon Pillow. The Northern soldiers began looting the Confederate camp but were scattered by cannon fire from a high bluff across the Mississippi River from Polk's troops. With Polk's help, Grant was pushed back.

Chickamauga, Georgia, September 1863: As Union Major General William Rosecrans retreated, Confederates under Polk and General James Longstreet repeatedly attacked Union General George Henry Thomas's remaining men defending Snodgrass Hill. This battled earned Thomas the nickname "Rock of Chickamauga." Union troops were finally forced to withdraw.

General Braxton Bragg failed to attack the retreating Union forces, and Longstreet and Polk demanded his dismissal. Bragg, in turn, tried to court-martial Polk. Jefferson Davis, a longtime friend of Polk's, quickly reassigned him.

Pine Mountain, Georgia, June 1864: Polk and Joe Johnston joined William Hardee in trying to stop Sherman's advance toward Atlanta. The troops were dug in at Kennesaw, waiting out a summer rain.

From a distance, Sherman noticed several Confederate officers on a hilltop in discussion, apparently surveying the lay of the land. Sherman ordered his artillery to harass them. Johnston and Hardee ducked, but Polk was hit and shattered.

Other Battles Polk Participated In: Shiloh, Corinth, Perryville, Stones River, and Murfreesboro.

LEE MOVES NORTH

After his remarkable victory at Chancellorsville in May 1863, Robert E. Lee felt compelled to lead the Confederate army north. The combination of inept Union commanders and successful military chances taken and converted by Lee had preserved Richmond, but Lee knew it was only a matter of time before President Lincoln found the right combination for the Union army and conquered the Confederate capital. The Union had men and guns and supplies to spare, while the Confederates, even in triumph, became more threadbare and desperate as the staggering costs of the war continued to accrue.

Lee sought to provide a boost of confidence to his men and the Confederacy as a whole. Invading the North, if successful, could deal a double shot of momentum by rallying Southern hopes and demoralizing the North.

More problems loomed for Lee, though. The imminent Union takeover of the Mississippi River—pending Ulysses S. Grant's siege on the city of Vicksburg—spurred Lee to land a decisive blow before Union forces from the western theater were brought east, thus putting even longer odds on the Confederacy's chances.

Joseph Hooker and the Army of the Potomac remained in Virginia in the wake of their embarrassment at Chancellorsville. Now, several weeks later and upon word of Lee's plans to move north, Hooker favored an assault on Richmond to possibly take the capital with minimal resistance, with the idea of forcing Lee to abandon his planned northern invasion. Instead, Lincoln balked and told Hooker to concentrate only on Lee.

That led to the first skirmish in the campaign, a twelve-hour battle between the armies' cavalries at Brandy Station. Hooker had revamped and reinvigorated the Union cavalry, an afterthought previous to his command. Alfred Pleasanton demonstrated the fruit of those efforts at Brandy Station, as Confederate hero Jeb Stuart and his men struggled for a narrow victory over Pleasanton. The battle provided Hooker with much-needed information—Lee was definitely on the move—and caught Stuart flat-footed, a rare moment of comeuppance for the flamboyant Confederate cavalryman.

By mid-June, Lee and his men had made it across the Potomac River into Maryland. Matters began to go awry for the Confederates. Stuart, still stinging from the Brandy Station affair, persuaded Lee to let the cavalry take a longer route around Hooker's army to gather intelligence.

That led to Stuart's unexpected ten-day disconnect from Lee, an eternity for a commander to be without reconnaissance. Lee mistakenly assumed Union troops had yet to cross the Potomac when, in fact they had, leaving Lee's vulnerable. At the same time, on June 28, Lincoln replaced Hooker with George Meade, the latest in the Army of the Potomac's long-running managerial saga.

Lee in George Washington's Family Tree

1. Martha Custis had a son, John Parke Custis from her first marriage
2. Martha Custis married George Washington
3. John Parke Custis had a son, George Washington Parke Custis
4. George Washington Parke Custis had a daughter, Mary Anna Randolph Custis
5. Mary Anna Randolph Custis married Robert E. Lee

SNAPSHOT: JOSHUA LAWRENCE CHAMBERLAIN

This unlikely hero built his legend on the battlefields. Joshua Lawrence Chamberlain, a college professor from Maine, won acclaim for his role defending the strategic position of Little Round Top during the Battle of Gettysburg in July 1863. Leading the 20th Maine Infantry, Chamberlain, despite being outnumbered and having a depleted regiment, successfully defended and then defeated a Confederate attack on his position. By the end of the fighting, as Chamberlain's men ran short on ammunition, they resorted to a long-shot tactic that surprised and overwhelmed the Confederates. Reports and accounts described his derring-do. Chamberlain earned the nickname "Lion of the Round Top."

For those actions, Chamberlain won the Congressional Medal of Honor. He worked his way up to become a major general despite lacking any military education. Chamberlain left his job as a professor of rhetoric and languages at Bowdoin College in Maine to enter the war. His brother Tom also served as an officer in the 20th Maine.

Chamberlain went on to distinguished service in later battles of the war. In 1864, at Petersburg, he suffered a gun shot to his hip and groin. The battle wound aggravated him for the rest of his life, requiring numerous surgeries. Chamberlain was thought to be dying after this wound, but he recovered and returned to battle in the fall of 1864.

In April 1865, he earned the honor of overseeing the Confederate infantry surrender at Appomattox. When Chamberlain had his men align in military salute to the defeated Confederates, General John Gordon of the Confederates returned the somber tribute and later described Chamberlain's gesture in heroic terms.

After the war, Chamberlain returned to Maine. His post-military career included four terms as governor of Maine and teaching and administrative posts at Bowdoin College. Chamberlain returned to Gettysburg in 1913 as part of the fiftieth celebration of the battle. He died the following year at age eighty-five.

THE BIG ONE: GETTYSBURG

It's gotta be the shoes. Right?

The epic battle of Gettysburg began soon after a Confederate reconnaissance mission into the small southern Pennsylvania college town. Legend has it, the mission included a search for shoes for some of the rebel soldiers.

Whatever the impetus, there is little doubt that the Confederates discovered Union cavalry in the town of Gettysburg on June 30 and decided to push them out the following day.

On July 1, small-scale fighting began around 9:00 a.m. It marked the start of a three-day battle that turned the tide against the Confederates for good—and cemented Gettysburg in military annals forever. Gettysburg was the first of two titanic blows absorbed by the Confederacy during the first week of July 1863. A day after Robert E. Lee and his bedraggled army hobbled across the Potomac in retreat from Gettysburg, Vicksburg surrendered to Ulysses S. Grant, giving the Union control of the Mississippi River and cutting the Confederacy in half.

In the summer of 1863, about 2,400 people lived in Gettysburg, a railroad junction made up of a local college, a seminary, and farms.

The small early skirmishes between Union and Confederate soldiers spurred both armies to swarm into Gettysburg, setting the stage for the gruesome full-scale battle. Union General John Buford, in charge of cavalry, managed to take possession of hills and high ground surrounding Gettysburg, a crucial early turning point that occurred before both armies had even gotten in position. Buford's aggressive stroke allowed him to beat the Confederates to the punch and preserve his spot until reinforcements arrived under Major General John Reynolds, who performed heroically as the 1,800-man "Iron Brigade." Reynolds died at Gettysburg the same day, felled by a shot to the head.

As the first day's battle continued—and after Reynolds was lost— Confederates gained control, eventually pushing the Union from McPherson's Ridge. Union soldiers sought refuge in town. Lee had ordered one of his corps commanders, Richard Ewell, to press his advantage "if practicable." The vagueness of the wording led Ewell to believe he had a choice of fighting or resting his men. He chose the latter, to the everlasting dismay of Lee and the Confederates. Historians remain intrigued with the notion of what might have happened had the Confederates forced the issue. Could they have destroyed the Union army? We'll never know.

At the end of the first day of fighting at Gettysburg, both armies controlled high ground around the town, with farm fields and some wooded areas in between. By midnight, Meade and the rest of the Army of the Potomac occupied a three-mile stretch outside of town.

James Longstreet had become Lee's top confidante in the wake of Stonewall Jackson's death at Chancellorsville. A pessimist or realist, depending on your point of view, he was known as "Gloomy Old Pete." Longstreet had frowned on the invasion of the North. Now he believed the Union positions around Gettysburg to be impenetrable. Lee disagreed.

The second day of fighting, July 2, began with Longstreet and Ewell attacking the left and right sides of the Union army. Though Longstreet urged withdrawing and attacking Meade behind his army, Lee preferred a characteristically bold approach. Lee plotted battle strategy despite his personal illnesses—Lee was suffering from diarrhea and, likely, angina, as well. The Union's ninety thousand men looked on at an enemy numbering seventy-five thousand.

On the left end of the Union "fishhook," the notorious Major General Dan Sickles exposed the Union flank with an unauthorized movement. It was a dumb move, but it worked. The Confederates hesitated, failing to launch an immediate attack. As Sickles' corps began retreating in the face of Confederate volleys, the Union army's chief engineer frantically took note of the abandoned, but crucial, hilltop position known as Little Round Top.

It would be saved by a college professor from Maine, Joshua Lawrence Chamberlain. He pushed his 385 men to defend their position—the last hope for preserving Little Round Top. When they ran out of bullets, Chamberlain convinced them to charge with bayonets, somehow managing to not only hold the position, but also to defeat the Confederate opposition.

Similarly intense fighting went on nearby at the Wheatfield, Devil's Den, and the Peach Orchard. Humble Pennsylvania farmland suddenly turned into strategic territory (and a cottage industry of study for future historians). At the end of July 2, the Union had retained most of its positions.

On July 3, Lee was again ready to press an aggressive attack, convinced he had come close to victory each of the previous two days. On a scorching summer afternoon, Lee set in motion the destruction of the Confederacy.

Preceded by an intense artillery exchange, Lee ordered a large-scale assault. Twelve thousand Confederate soldiers began a one-mile charge from their position at Seminary Ridge toward the Union army at Cemetery Ridge. Named for Major General George Pickett, commander of three of the nine brigades involved, what became known as "Pickett's Charge" is one of the most spectacular failures in American military history. Less than half of the Confederate soldiers made it back to Seminary Ridge. Pickett later accused Lee of ordering his men "massacred." Lee was equally as harsh in self-judgment. "It is all my fault," he told his men.

Gettysburg produced a combined fifty-one thousand casualties: twenty-three thousand Union, twenty-eight thousand Confederates. Meade counted it a great victory but Lincoln, as ever, found himself vexed over lost opportunities when Meade allowed Lee and the Confederates to escape back to Virginia.

The president sputtered, "My God, is that all?"

It was.

Snapshot: Dan Sickles

Dan Sickles could never be described as a hero, but he ranks as one of the most intriguing characters in a war filled with them.

Sickles was dubbed a "political general," one of many in the Union army who earned a high military rank from political patronage rather than strategic ability. Before he even reached the battlefield, Sickles carried a controversial reputation.

In 1859, Sickles, then a Congressman from New York, murdered Philip Barton Key, the U.S. Attorney for the District of Columbia. Key, the son of "Star-Spangled Banner" lyricist Francis Scott Key, was involved in a torrid public affair with Sickles' wife at the time Sickles killed Key in Lafayette Park near the White House. The murder led to one of the most notorious criminal trials of its time. Sickles was acquitted in a precedent-setting defense that cited "temporary insanity" as the cause of his crime. Edwin M. Stanton, President Lincoln's future secretary of war, represented Sickles in the murder trial.

As a general, Sickles served with better results than many of his political brethren, a backhanded compliment if ever there was one, turning in commendable service at the Seven Days. He became a corps commander under Joseph Hooker in February 1863, a controversial move because of Sickles' lack of credentials.

At Gettysburg in 1863, Sickles committed a blunder that made many observers wonder whether his insanity was more than a temporary condition. He moved the corps he was commanding a half-mile or so from the rest of the Union line, creating and exposing a vulnerable flank to the Confederates. That he made this move without any orders demonstrated poor judgment in the field.

The inevitable Confederate attack against such a vulnerable corps devastated Sickles' men. Sickles was shot in the right leg with a cannonball. Despite a jaunty exit from the battlefield that included the general puffing on a cigar from his stretcher, Sickles lost the leg to amputation. Soon after, he donated his leg and the cannonball to a new medical museum in Washington, where Sickles paid regular visits to his personal battle monument.

An intensely political creature, Sickles spent much of his postwar life excoriating Meade for criticizing his movement at Little Round Top. Beyond that, Sickles held a whirlwind of appointments and roles, including a stint as a diplomat and an influential position in the preservation of the Gettysburg battle site. Three decades of lobbying led to a medal of honor for Sickles' role at Gettysburg on the day he was wounded.

He died in 1914 and was buried at Arlington National Cemetery.

Stonewall Jackson Shrine

Fredericksburg and Spotsylvania National Park include the Stonewall Jackson Shrine in the building where he died after being fragged during the Battle of Chancellorsville. Following the accident, Jackson was relocated behind the lines to Guinea Station, Virginia. Today, the office outbuilding on the 740-acre Chandler farm, "Fairfield," is the only structure still standing from the entire plantation.

THE GETTYSBURG ADDRESS
GIVEN NOVEMBER 19, 1863

"Four score and seven years ago our fathers brought forth on this continent, a new nation, conceived in liberty, and dedicated to the proposition that all men are created equal. Now we are engaged in a great civil war, testing whether that nation, or any nation so conceived and so dedicated, can long endure. We are met on a great battlefield of that war. We have come to dedicate a portion of that field as a final resting place for those who here gave their lives that that nation might live. It is altogether fitting and proper that we should do this. But in a larger sense we cannot dedicate, we cannot consecrate, we cannot hallow this ground. The brave men, living and dead, who struggled here, have consecrated it far above our poor power to add or detract. The world will little note, nor long remember what we say here, but it can never forget what they did here. It is for us, the living, rather to be dedicated here to the unfinished work that they who fought here have thus far so nobly advanced. It is rather for us to be here dedicated to the great task remaining before us, that from these honored dead we take increased devotion to that cause for which they gave the last full measure of devotion; that we here highly resolve that these dead shall not have died in vain; that this nation, under God, shall have a new birth of freedom, and that this government of the people, by the people, and for the people shall not perish from the earth."

GETTYSBURG GREATNESS

"Four score and seven years ago . . ."

Along with Thomas Jefferson's Declaration of Independence—
"We hold these truths to be self-evident, that all men are created
equal"—and FDR's defiant call for courage—"The only thing we
have to fear is fear itself"—Abraham Lincoln's words at Gettysburg
stand among the most revered in American history. Lincoln delivered
his remarks on November 19, 1863, at the battlefield cemetery. His
appearance and speech were initially thought to be superfluous—a
last-minute addition of little note. Instead, the president delivered a
graceful, forceful tribute to the fallen soldiers while also outlining the
justification and necessity for continuing a bloody war. Lincoln spoke
for two minutes, but his words have echoed for more than a century.
His speech proved so eloquent and influential that later generations
remain largely ignorant of the day's featured speaker, politician and
intellectual Edward Everett, who delivered a two-hour address at
Gettysburg the same day. Everett, and everyone else, was eclipsed by
Lincoln's stirring, elegiac oratory that resonated for the ages.

NOT-SO-QUIET RIOTS

Less than two weeks after the North collected two dramatic military triumphs—at Gettysburg and Vicksburg—riots exploded in New York City. The violence stemmed from the draft, as well as racial mistrust and class resentment. Over four days in July 1863, Irish immigrants wreaked havoc on the draft board along with blacks, who were beaten and lynched in the streets. Mobs even attacked an orphanage and cheered its destruction. President Lincoln and Congress approved a draft for men in the eighteen to forty-five year-old range earlier in 1863. Each man drafted would serve three years.

The draft began without incident on July 11, with officials drawing names from a box, but anger flared two days later when hundreds of angry Irishmen erupted at the second drawing. Several factors led to the violent uprising. The Irish immigrants living in New York struggled to make new lives in thankless, but scarce, jobs. The Irish feared the war would only serve to bring competition for work in the form of freed slaves migrating from the South. The draft represented a call for immigrants to risk death to help bring about further economic hardship for their section of the population in particular. If they were lucky enough to survive, their reward would be economic oblivion, as they saw it. Resentment festered beyond these uncertainties and prejudices roiled the working class. Adding insult to injury, aristocrats could buy their way out of military service, even if drafted. So-called commutations sold for $300 each, allowing anyone drafted to be relieved of all military obligations. The commutation fee represented the better part of a year's pay for most workers—wages averaged $400 to $500 a year at the time—making a commutation an option afforded only to the wealthy classes. Draftees could also enlist replacements, another way of avoiding mandatory military duties. About fifty thousand of the 750,000 men drafted in the North became Union soldiers, ample evidence that conscription provided a small portion of the North's soldiers.

Beyond New York, similar violence and unrest rippled through other parts of the city as well as Massachusetts, New Hampshire, and Pennsylvania. Estimates of the death toll from the riots in New York vary widely, with a safe estimate being in the hundreds. Soldiers who had just fought at Gettysburg were among the regiments brought in to quell the riots. Soldiers used their weapons to stem the violence, and the draft resumed a month later without further incident.

Labor Gap

Rosie the Riveter, and her anonymous working sisters during World War II, dominate discussions of how women began to prove themselves beyond the home.

In truth, labor shortages created by the Civil War marked the first sustained shift for women as workers—as well as recognition of their skill. Men streamed out of towns and cities in the North and South by the hundreds and thousands, leaving farms to be tended, factories to be manned and much more.

This worker deficit was solved by women drawn into the workforce, by the hundreds of thousands of immigrants who arrived on American shores during the war, and by technological advancements that improved efficiency while replacing manual labor with machinery.

THE COLOR LINE

Several early attempts to make blacks part of the Union army were nullified by Lincoln and his administration. Various reasons were cited, from fear of rallying Southern morale to concerns over outrage in the Union border states. Many Union soldiers and officers struggled to make peace with the notion of waging war to free blacks—one of the chief reasons Lincoln delayed the Emancipation Proclamation as long as he did—much less having them as fellow soldiers on the battlefield. Pervasive racism also led many in the North to question whether blacks possessed the bravery and intelligence needed for war.

Frederick Douglass, the escaped slave who prodded the North in matters of racial recognition at every step of the way before, during and after the war, pushed for integration in the army. "Once let the black man get upon his person the brass letters, 'U.S.,' let him get an eagle on his button, and a musket on his shoulder and bullets in his pocket, and there is no power on earth, or under the earth, which can deny that he has earned the right to citizenship in the United States," Douglass said.

As the war went on, and casualties mounted, the notion of blacks serving in the military started to gain acceptance. In January 1863, soon after the Emancipation Proclamation, the push finally succeeded. Blacks still faced significant prejudice and hardship after gaining admittance to the army, though. They were invariably led by white officers and assigned the most menial duties, manual labor, in most cases. In addition, blacks earned less money for serving and made do with inferior uniforms and equipment.

"The government of the United States will give the same protection to all its soldiers, and if the enemy shall sell or enslave anyone because of his color, the offense shall be punished by retaliation upon the enemy's prisoners in our possession." —Abraham Lincoln, July 30, 1863, in a government order to ensure fair treatment of black soldiers if captured by Confederates

Glory Days

Blacks accounted for 10 percent of the active troops by the end of the war. Casualties and attrition dictated that blacks would begin to see the battlefield, and they did.

The best-known black company was the 54th Massachusetts Infantry led by Robert Gould Shaw. The twenty-five-year-old Shaw was a dashing figure from an affluent Boston family who supported abolition. Shaw's regiment was the first black unit assembled in the North. Sent to South Carolina, on July 18, 1863, Shaw led his men into battle on the beaches near Charleston with an attack on an impregnable position manned by Confederates at Battery Wagner. The suicide mission led to predictably grim results, as nearly half of the six hundred-man 54th Massachusetts became casualties of war that day.

Shaw was among the fallen, shot and killed in the battle. Enemies stripped Shaw and buried him among his soldiers, an implied slap in the face, particularly for a white officer whose men were black.

Shaw's family dismissed that notion out of hand and proclaimed his burial among members of the 54th as the greatest honor he could have received as a proud leader of the regiment.

Sergeant William Carney received the Congressional Medal of Honor for his actions at Battery Wagner, becoming the first black man so honored in American military history. In 1990, the movie *Glory*—starring Matthew Broderick, Morgan Freeman, and Denzel Washington—brought renewed attention to the plight of black troops while demonstrating the courage of the men who made up the 54th Massachusetts.

CONFEDERATE COMMANDERS: EDMUND KIRBY-SMITH (1824-1893)

- Born St. Augustine, Florida
- 1845 West Point graduate, Mexican War veteran
- Nicknamed "Seminole" because of his home state
- West Point assistant professor of math, 1849–1852
- Eventually achieved the rank of full general; when he died in 1893, Kirby-Smith was the last surviving full general of the Confederate Army

The Hyphenated Name: Born Edmund Kirby Smith, at some point our war hero decided that his last name did not stand out in a crowd. So, he added a hyphen to completely change his name. This is how he signed his name. The general never legally changed his name, but since it was his personal preference, we're sticking with "Kirby-Smith" here. Today when you research the commander of the Trans-Mississippi Department, you are as likely to find him listed under "Kirby-Smith, Edmund" as "Smith, Edmund Kirby."

The Trans-Mississippi Department: Kirby-Smith was put in charge of the areas of Arkansas, western Louisiana, and Texas, called the Trans-Mississippi Department. Once the Union captured Vicksburg, then Port Hudson, and took control of the Mississippi River in 1863, Kirby-Smith was cut off from the rest of the Confederate States of America.

Suddenly Kirby-Smith found himself not only commanding the Confederate forces, but running the economy and taking care of securing ordnance and other supplies. Without any way to communicate with Richmond, Kirby-Smith was practically running his own mini-country. The area became known as the "Kirby Smithdom."

Kirby-Smith made his own administrative decisions about such options as running the blockade from Mexico and burning cotton and other equipment that didn't need to fall into Union hands.

The Last to Fight, the Last to Surrender: Again, Kirby-Smith was out of communication with Richmond. So he didn't hear about Robert E. Lee's surrender at Appomattox Court House on April 12, 1865. As far as he knew, the war was still on.

Thus, the last battle of the Civil War was fought in western Texas under Kirby-Smith's command on May 12–13, 1865. Smith won, overpowering more than twice as many Union soldiers under Theodore Barrett at Palmito Ranch.

Then, on May 26, Confederate General Simon Buckner surrendered the Trans-Mississippi Department for Kirby-Smith, in absentia. This was the last surrender of armed forces in the Confederate States (although Stand Watie was the last Confederate general to surrender).

Kirby-Smith accepted the surrender terms on June 2, and then fled to Mexico and Cuba to avoid serving time in a POW camp.

After the Civil War: Kirby-Smith engaged in several varied enterprises. Then, from 1875 until his death in 1893, he held the position of professor of mathematics at the University of the South in Sewanee, Tennessee.

Battles Kirby-Smith Participated In: First Bull Run (wounded), Richmond (Kentucky), Perryville, Murfreesboro, and Red River.

The Lost Gold of the Confederacy

It sounds a movie title, doesn't it? There are no secret, underground caves or snake pits in this story.

It's been told that Kirby-Smith was in charge of $5,000 in gold that had been earmarked for Jefferson Davis's personal expenses, namely escaping from Union troops. However, the Confederate president was captured on May 10 before Kirby-Smith even knew it was time to trot out the funds.

Since his men had not been paid lately, Kirby-Smith took out enough money to divide between them as salary. Then he sent the rest of the "secret service fund" to Union military governor General Edward Canby in New Orleans.

UNION COMMANDERS: LEW WALLACE (1827-1905)

- Indiana native, Mexican War veteran
- Newspaper reporter, lawyer, and state senator
- First commanding appointment was due to political connections
- Achieved the rank of major general
- Loved to read anything he could get his hands on

Controversy at Shiloh: Everyone agrees that, on the first day of battle, Wallace was stationed miles away from the battlefield, told to guard the supplies. According to Wallace supporters, on the second day, Grant gave him vague orders, and he ended up doing a lot of marching back and forth before finally showing up at the battlefield, late enough to miss all the fighting.

According to Wallace critics, he got lost in the woods. Was Wallace hopelessly bad with directions, or was he Grant's fall guy for the horrendous Union loss?

Union general Henry Halleck was no fan of Wallace's. He generally regarded Wallace as incompetent. If you asked Halleck, he would definitely come down on the "lost" side. Two different times, Halleck removed Wallace from command, but first Abraham Lincoln himself, then General Grant, stepped in on Wallace's behalf.

Other Civil War Action: Wallace was at Corinth when the Union soldiers took the deserted town. Wallace led the troops who finally stopped Jubal Early in his relentless advance toward Washington in July 1864.

Most Memorable Civil War Contributions: Having had questionable success as a commander, Wallace remains best known for his achievements after Lee's surrender. He presided over two trials directly related to the Civil War:

1. The eight conspirators involved in the plot to assassinate President Abraham Lincoln. Three were sentenced to hard labor

for life, and one was sentenced to six years in prison. Of the four sentenced to swift hanging, Mary Surratt became the first woman ever executed by the United States.

2. Henry Wirz, the sadistic commander of Andersonville prison camp. Convicted for atrocities against Northern prisoners of war, Wirz was the only Confederate officer executed after the war. He was hanged for war crimes.

The Other Life of Lew Wallace

It was no secret that General Wallace was an atheist. So it came as some surprise when in 1889 he published *Ben-Hur: A Tale of the Christ*. It seems that during the time Wallace served as governor of the New Mexico territory (1878–1881), he had a religious conversion (in addition to meeting Billy the Kid). This change of heart led to his writing one of the most popular novels of the nineteenth century.

In 1959, the epic movie *Ben-Hur* was filmed with a cast of thousands, starring Charlton Heston and Stephen Boyd. The movie won a record eleven Academy Awards, which has been equaled by other films, but never topped. It was ranked second in the American Film Institute's top ten epic movies of all time.

Wallace also served as the U.S. Minister to Turkey (1881–1885), and continued his writing career, producing:

- *The Fair God: or, the Last of the 'Tzins*, 1873
- *The Life of Ben Harrison*, 1888
- *The Boyhood of Christ*, 1888
- *The Prince of India*, 1893
- *Lew Wallace: An Autobiography*, 1906 (completed by his widow Susan)

CONFEDERATE COMMANDERS: WILLIAM BARKSDALE (1821-1863)

Background: Tennessee native, moved to Mississippi to practice law
Military Experience: Mexican War veteran
Highest Rank Achieved: Brigadier General
Political Experience: Mississippi Representative in the U.S. House
Brigade: 13th Mississippi, known as "Barksdale's Mississippi Brigade"
Battles Barksdale Participated In: First Bull Run, Savage Station, Seven Days, Malvern Hill, Antietam, Peninsula Campaign, Fredericksburg, Chancellorsville, and Gettysburg

Without any military training, Barksdale came by his appointment by virtue of his political connections. Nevertheless, he was an enthusiastic leader, always at the head of a charge, always ready to jump into the middle of it, and always confident.

"The Grandest Charge" at Gettysburg

At Gettysburg, on July 2, 1863, Barksdale led the "grandest charge ever made by mortal man," to repeat an oft-quoted line from an unknown Union commander. He urged his men straight to the Peach Orchard, where Union soldiers were positioned. The brigade broke the Union line and kept moving.

By the time they reached Plum Run, the men were exhausted, and it began to show. Barksdale was wounded once (hit above the left knee), then again (severing his foot), and finally a third time (in his chest). The third hit was hard enough to knock him out of the saddle.

Barksdale was taken to a Union field hospital and died the next morning.

CONFEDERATE COMMANDERS: RAPHAEL SEMMES (1809-1877)

Background: Maryland native, orphaned at age ten
Naval Experience: Joined the U.S. Navy at age fifteen, Mexican war veteran
Ranks Achieved: Rear Admiral; Brigadier General

Stationed in Mobile, Alabama, Semmes joined the Confederate Navy. He was soon able to use what he had learned about foreign waters against the U.S. Navy, eluding blockade ships. More importantly, Semmes began a successful run of preventing U.S. ships from importing and exporting goods that could aid the Union Army.

Semmes captained the C.S.S. *Sumter* for about six months before the ship reached an unseaworthy point of disrepair. During that time, he captured eighteen federal ships.

Then Semmes took command of the C.S.S. *Alabama*, making a name for himself with the single-most successful Confederate merchant raider on the seas.

After losing the *Alabama* in one of the most famous Civil War maritime engagements, Semmes and his sailors were reassigned to the Confederate Army. Brigadier General Semmes was responsible for blowing up the Confederate fleet in the James River as the Union advanced into Richmond. The force of the explosion shattered window glass across the city.

Semmes Takes Prisoners of War: Semmes was known for his humane treatment of captives. In fact, after the war, he was tried for cruelty to prisoners of war, but was cleared of charges after many Union captains testified in his favor.

Union Commanders: Don Carlos Buell (1818-1898)

Background: Ohio-born, Indiana-raised, West Point Class of 1841
Military Experience: Seminole and Mexican Wars veteran
Rank Achieved: Major General
Civil War Assignment: The West, covering Kentucky, Tennessee, Ohio
Most of Buell's Civil War action took place during 1862:

- In Tennessee, Lincoln expected Buell to encourage the numerous Union loyalists there. Buell followed his own plans and captured Nashville in early 1862, with very little resistance.
- At Shiloh, the plan was for Buell's Army of Ohio to join Grant's troops at Pittsburg Landing, Tennessee. Then they could move forward together into Mississippi to attack the Confederate railroad center in Corinth.

   However, the Confederates attacked Grant's troops before Buell got there. The first day was decidedly a Southern success. But with Buell's arrival late in the afternoon and into the night, Grant's reinforced army counterattacked on the second day.

   The battle went down as a Union win, for which Buell gave himself credit, although historians don't necessarily always agree.
- In Kentucky, Buell's forces were able to stop a second Confederate advance into the Northern states. The Battle of Perryville served that purpose, but not much else.

   Buell did not attack the retreating Confederates, because he claimed not to have had enough supplies to do so. Nevertheless, he was relieved of his command, and the incident was reviewed by a military commission that never made a decisive judgment on the issue. The upshot, though, was that Buell was never given another command or any further orders.

> Buell was one of the few federal officers who owned slaves. They were inherited from his wife's family.

UNION COMMANDERS: BENJAMIN MAYBERRY PRENTISS (1819-1901)

Background: Born in Virginia, relocated to Missouri, then to Illinois
Military Experience: Mexican War veteran
Rank Attained: Major General
Civil War Claims: Prentiss was the first Civil War officer commissioned by the State of Illinois. He was instrumental in blockading the Mississippi River at Cairo, Illinois.
The Battle of Shiloh: Prentiss's troops defended the "Hornet's Nest" long enough to gain the Union valuable time to reorganize and renew their attack. The "Hornet's Nest" was a heavily contested spot, with so many bullets whizzing back and forth that it was said to sound like a buzzing hive.

Prentiss's men held the position for six hours under relentless Confederate fire. Grant asked Prentiss to hold the road until sundown at all costs. It is said that for the rest of the day, Prentiss repeatedly looked to the sky to track the movement of the sun, which at times seemed to have stopped its tracks. Prentiss was finally forced to surrender at 5:30 p.m., and all of his men were captured and imprisoned.

Prentiss spent eight months in a Confederate prison camp, then went on to lead a Union win at Helena, Arkansas, on July 4, 1863. After that, he resigned his commission and returned to civilian life.

Benjamin Prentiss Trivia

- After the war, Prentiss was appointed Postmaster in Bethany, Missouri, by both Presidents Benjamin Harrison and William McKinley.
- Prentiss fathered twelve children by two successive wives.
- As a civilian before and after the war, Prentiss worked in rope-making, known at the time as "cordage manufacturing."
- Prentiss ran unsuccessfully for U.S. Congress in 1860. After the war, he was a Republican Party leader in Missouri.

U.S. PRESIDENTS AND THEIR ROLES IN THE CIVIL WAR

John Tyler (1790-1862): Member of the Confederate House of Representatives

Millard Fillmore (1800–1874): Opposed President Lincoln and supported President Johnson during Reconstruction

James Buchanan (1791–1868): Sitting President when Southern states seceded, and the Fort Sumter resupply crisis began

Abraham Lincoln (1809–1865): President during the Civil War

Andrew Johnson (1808–1875): Union sympathizer; Military governor of Tennessee; President during Reconstruction

Ulysses S. Grant (1822–1885): Union General who accepted Robert E. Lee's surrender at Appomattox; President during the end of Reconstruction

Rutherford B. Hayes (1822–1893): Major General – the only future president to be wounded in action (four times); had four horses shot out from under him; participated in battles of Cloyd's Mountain, Opequon, Fisher's Hill, and Cedar Creek

James A. Garfield (1831–1881): Major General of Volunteers; Led the 42nd Ohio Volunteer Infantry; Saw action at the battles of Shiloh and Chickamauga

Chester A. Arthur (1829–1886): Quartermaster General of the State of New York militia, recruiting volunteers and providing supplies for their military service

Benjamin Harrison (1833–1901): Brigadier General; Led the 70th Indiana Volunteer Infantry in Kentucky against Confederate General Braxton Bragg; Participated in Sherman's Atlanta campaign

William McKinley (1843–1901): Enlisted as private in the 23rd Ohio Volunteer Infantry under Rutherford B. Hayes; Exhibited bravery under fire at Antietam; Rose to rank of Major of Volunteers

MORE BLOOD IN KANSAS

Murder and mayhem marked the life of William Clarke Quantrill. An itinerant former teacher, Quantrill left Kansas in 1860 for Missouri, set on the run by charges of horse theft and murder. Tensions along the Kansas-Missouri border raged in the decade before the Civil War, and as Quantrill's actions demonstrate, during it.

Quantrill supported the Confederacy in the war and harbored deep resentment toward the free-soil Jayhawkers, pro-Union sympathizers who carried out attacks on pro-slavery bushwhacker gangs. A ragtag band of guerrillas, Quantrill's Raiders, formed in 1861. Soon after, killers and criminals signed on.

In August 1863, Quantrill carried out his most notorious attack. Quantrill led 450 men into Lawrence, Kansas—the hub of Jayhawkers and home to ardent abolitionist U.S. Senator James Lane. The men burned and looted the town and killed between 183 unarmed civilians. Lane survived the attack, taking refuge in a nearby cornfield. Quantrill's strike followed the collapse of a temporary Union jail in Kansas City a week earlier.

Union soldiers had captured a group of women with ties to Quantrill's gang and held them in Kansas City. The building that housed the women collapsed, killing several of the prisoners and injuring others. Bloody Bill Anderson, one of Quantrill's top lieutenants, lost one sister to death while another suffered injuries.

Whether in retaliation or not, Quantrill's attack decimated Lawrence. It also infuriated Union General Thomas Ewing, Jr. Four days after the attack on Lawrence, Ewing crafted General Order Number 11. It called for residents to abandon the majority of four Missouri counties on the Kansas border. Union soldiers then torched and killed all that remained, from buildings and houses to food supplies and livestock. Ewing and the Union hoped to remove any and all vestiges of support for Quantrill and other pro-slavery gangs. The Union's carnage and destruction bequeathed a grim nickname to the area—the "Burnt District."

Quantrill and his men headed for Texas. Infighting soon splintered the gang of raiders, diminishing their effectiveness. In the spring of 1865, during a raid in Kentucky, Quantrill was shot. He died several weeks later at the age of twenty-seven.

Presidential Tragedy

Both Abraham Lincoln and Jefferson Davis suffered a parent's worst nightmare during the Civil War. Davis and his wife, Varina, lost their five-year-old son, Joe, when he died after falling from the veranda of the Confederate White House in 1864. Abraham and Mary Todd Lincoln could empathize with their devastation. In February 1862, the Lincolns' third child, eleven-year-old Willie, died of a fever at the White House. He was viewed as the child most like his father, and his fast departure shattered both parents for the days—and years—to come.

CHICKAMAUGA

Military action all but halted following the Union's pivotal victories at Gettysburg and Vicksburg in July 1863. The next significant battles came two months later, in Georgia and Tennessee.

Ulysses Grant wanted to plow through Mississippi and Alabama after claiming Vicksburg, but his Union boss, Henry W. Halleck, nixed that notion. Instead Halleck ordered Grant to send segments of his army across several Southern states to occupy recently conquered territories.

Those maneuvers left William Rosecrans and the Union's Army of the Cumberland to wage battle in Tennessee. His first assignment came in the spring and early summer of 1863, as Rosecrans maneuvered to prevent Confederate General Braxton Bragg and his Army of the Tennessee from providing assistance to besieged Vicksburg.

Rosecrans carried out a skillful campaign, employing a range of tactics to push Bragg into a steady retreat. A masterful march through the gaps of Lookout Mountain—located just outside Chattanooga—forced Bragg out of Chattanooga. The Union forces claimed Chattanooga with minimal losses.

Rather than rest and reorganize, Rosecrans pushed his men onward. Bragg and the Confederates, now based twenty miles south of Chattanooga in Georgia, soon gained much-needed reinforcements. With his army restocked, Bragg moved back toward Chattanooga and the Union troops. The armies' collision course occurred near the midway point between their respective positions—at Chickamauga Creek. Chickamauga, an Indian word that roughly translates to "river of death," lived up to its name.

The battle began on September 18. Momentum swung back and forth, though the South's superior numbers—seventy thousand compared with fifty-seven thousand federal troops—began to give the Confederates an edge.

On September 20, fierce fighting resumed. Confederates took charge behind a superb, if lucky, assault by James Longstreet on an unexpected gap in the Union defenses. The Battle of Chickamauga took place in thick woods and on tricky terrain made worse by soupy conditions from recent rainfall, conditions that led to suffering among both armies.

Longstreet's thrust spurred a Union retreat toward Chattanooga. The lone exception was Union Major General George H. Thomas, soon to become known as the "Rock of Chickamauga."

Thomas' courageous stand prevented the Confederates from finishing off Rosencrans' battered troops. Instead, Bragg and the Confederates claimed a hollow victory, one that failed to make the most of tactical and numerical advantages. Bragg suffered more casualties with 18,500, compared with the Union's sixteen thousand, and began a siege around Chattanooga that led to Rosencrans' dismissal.

He Builds Machines

Richard J. Gatling was both a doctor and an inventor during the Civil War era, with the latter talent proving most lasting. His tinkering laid the foundation for the future development of machine guns. Gatling created a crude version of a repeating weapon—the aptly named Gatling gun—in 1862. The Union made minimal use of Gatling's invention, but the U.S. Army adopted it a year after the war ended.

THE BATTLE ABOVE THE CLOUDS

The Confederates took up positions around Chattanooga and laid siege after winning the Battle of Chickamauga in late September. On October 19, the Union relieved Rosencrans of duty. His replacement was George H. Thomas, the "Rock of Chickamauga."

Bragg planned to starve the Union army by cutting it off from all supplies inside Chattanooga. The plight of the Union troops prompted action from military headquarters in Washington.

Reinforcements came from George Meade's Army of the Potomac in early October. At the same time, William Sherman and his men began marching from Memphis in the east, toward Chattanooga. Grant, now with expanded authority in the western theater, established a much-needed supply connection into Chattanooga—the so-called "Cracker Line."

Thomas' Union troops regrouped with the aid of Grant's successful supply line; the Confederates found themselves in dire straits. Jefferson Davis visited Bragg's troops around Chattanooga and heard entreaties for provisions from the soldiers.

On November 23, the Battle of Chattanooga began. Joseph Hooker, whose disastrous loss at Chancellorsville led to his demotion, now served under Grant. Hooker's task was to conquer Lookout Mountain. Beginning on November 24, Hooker's men battled all day and most of the night, finally claiming victory atop the 1,100-foot mountain early on November 25. The victory earned a lasting nickname: the "Battle above the Clouds."

November 25 also marked the long-awaited emergence of the Army of the Cumberland under George Thomas. Furious over needing reinforcement from Grant and Sherman, Thomas' men chomped at the bit to fight.

Grant sent Thomas and his men to take Missionary Ridge from the Confederates. Originally ordered to take the rifle pits at the base of the ridge, Thomas' men stormed up the ridge of their own volition and drove the Confederates into full retreat. With that, the Union took control of the western theater—and never let go.

By the end of 1863, Union victories in the eastern and western theaters put the Union in position to finally win the war, though more than a year of additional bloody fighting would be required. As Grant's supply line mission at Chattanooga demonstrated, no one could match his zeal for taking the fight to the enemy. President Lincoln soon realized that, at last, he had found the relentless military commander he and the North had so long sought.

Soldiers' Pay

Ulysses S. Grant led the Union to ultimate victory over the Confederacy in the Civil War—and later served two terms as president of the United States. But his ascension to greatness was shocking to almost everyone, perhaps even to himself. When the war began, Grant's command was hardly an indication of future greatness—he was colonel of the 21st Illinois Infantry. Despite such humble origins, Grant quickly distinguished himself on the battlefield and, with William T. Sherman, became a military hero with victories at Vicksburg and, later, over Robert E. Lee's Army of Northern Virginia.

Civil War Battle Timeline: 1864

February 3–14: Capture of Meridian, Mississippi
February 20: Battle of Olustee (Ocean Pond), Florida
February 22: Battle of Okolona, Mississippi
March 9: Grant appointed commander of Union armies
March 23–May 2: Camden Expedition, Arkansas (Red River, Camden Campaigns, Louisiana and Arkansas)
April 8: Battle of Mansfield, Louisiana
April 9: Battle of Pleasant Hill, Louisiana
April 12: Fort Pillow, Tennessee
April 30: Battle of Jenkins' Ferry, Arkansas
May 5–6: Battle of the Wilderness, Virginia
May 8–21: Battle of Spotsylvania Court House, Virginia
May 9–24: Sheridan's Richmond Raid
May 13–15: Battle of Resaca (Sherman's Atlanta Campaign)
May 15: Battle of New Market, Virginia
May 16: Battle of Drewry's Bluff, Virginia
May 25–26: New Hope Church (Sherman's Atlanta Campaign)
May 23–26: Battle of North Anna River, Virginia
May 26–June 1: Dallas (Sherman's Atlanta Campaign)
May 27: Pickett's Mill (Sherman's Atlanta Campaign)
May 31–June 12: Battle of Cold Harbor, Virginia
June 5–6: Battle of Piedmont, Virginia
June 10: Battle of Brice's Cross Roads, Mississippi
June 11–12: Battle of Trevilian Station, Virginia
June 15–18: Battle of Petersburg, Virginia
June 17–18: Battle of Lynchburg, Virginia
June 27: Battle of Kennesaw Mountain (Sherman's Atlanta Campaign)
July 9: Battle of Monocacy, Maryland (Early's Washington Raid)
July 12: Battle of Fort Stevens, near Washington (Early's Raid)
July 14–15: Battle of Tupelo, Mississippi
July 20: Battle of Peachtree Creek (Sherman's Atlanta Campaign)
July 22: Battle of Atlanta (Sherman's Atlanta Campaign)

July 24: Second Battle of Kernstown, Virginia (Early's Raid)

July 28: Battle of Ezra Church (Sherman's Atlanta Campaign)

July 30: Battle of the Crater (Siege of Petersburg, Virginia)

August 5: Battle of Mobile Bay, Alabama

August 18–21: Battle of Weldon Railroad and Ream's Station (Siege of Petersburg)

August 29–December 25: Price's Raid, Arkansas/Missouri/Kansas/Indian Territory/Texas

August 31–September 1: Battle of Jonesboro (Sherman's Atlanta Campaign)

September 2: Union troops occupy Atlanta (Sherman's Atlanta Campaign)

September 19: Third Battle of Winchester (Opequon Creek) (Sheridan's Shenandoah Valley Campaign)

September 22: Battle of Fisher's Hill (Shenandoah Valley Campaign)

September 29: Engagement at New Market Heights (Siege of Petersburg)

September 29-30: Battle of Fort Harrison (Chaffin's Farm) (Siege of Petersburg)

September 29–October 2: Battle of Peebles' Farm (Siege of Petersburg)

October 19: Battle of Cedar Creek (Shenandoah Valley Campaign)

October 27–28: Battle of Burgess' Mill (Boydton Plank Road) (Siege of Petersburg)

November 8: Lincoln reelected president of the United States

November 22: Engagement at Griswoldville, Georgia (Sherman's March to the Sea)

November 29: Affair at Spring Hill (Hood's Tennessee Campaign)

November 30: Engagement at Honey Hill, South Carolina (Sherman's March to the Sea)

November 30: Battle of Franklin (Hood's Tennessee Campaign)

December 13: Capture of Fort McAllister, Georgia (Sherman's March to the Sea)

December 15–16: Battle of Nashville (Hood's Tennessee Campaign)

December 22: Savannah, Georgia (Sherman's March to the Sea)

FORT PILLOW MASSACRE

Led by the notorious, brutal, and brilliant Nathan Bedford Forrest, this Confederate attack left more than half of the Union forces—under 557 men—as casualties. On April 12, 1864, Forrest and his band of cavalrymen surrounded Fort Pillow, a former Confederate garrison located forty miles north of Memphis. Built in 1862, the fort had been claimed by the Union later that same year.

Forrest and his men seethed with an appetite for destruction. The Union forces at Fort Pillow were split evenly between black and white soldiers. These racially-combined forces, in this case, earned enmity among Confederate troops beyond the typical hostilities—the whites included a significant number of unionist Tennesseans, and many of the blacks were freed slaves from Memphis.

Tensions mounted when William Bradford, the Tennessean in charge of the Union garrison at Fort Pillow, launched a campaign to seize supplies from the countryside. Bradford's men took food, and anything else that came in handy, from civilians.

Forrest demanded the Union surrender after surrounding Fort Pillow with 1,500 men. The Union stalled for time as Bradford hoped to receive reinforcements before being forced to capitulate. Forrest suspected as much and demanded an immediate answer.

The answer came back: No surrender. Forrest and the Confederates attacked immediately, sending the Union troops scrambling to the riverbank. The federals hoped to reach a gunboat, located just offshore to provide protection.

Now in disarray and headed for the river, Union soldiers attempted to surrender to Forrest's cavalry. Instead, they were massacred—especially the black Union soldiers. The Confederates killed two-thirds of the black troops, often with shots fired at point-blank range.

Historians and other war experts still debate whether Forrest ordered a massacre, but at minimum, it is clear that he fostered an attitude among his men that made such an action palatable.

ALL ABOUT THE BENJAMIN

Few characters were as colorful as Confederate Cabinet member Judah P. Benjamin (1811–1884). Born in the West Indies, Benjamin later came to the United States and attained his citizenship. He attended Yale Law School as a teenager, but later dropped out. At twenty-one, Benjamin moved to New Orleans, where he met and married the daughter of a wealthy Creole family. That provided him with the means to head a sugar plantation and begin dabbling in politics. Benjamin moved up the ranks and, eventually, became a member of the U.S. Senate, where he befriended a Mississippi colleague (and future Confederate president): Jefferson Davis. Under Davis, Benjamin became known for his sharp mind and deft political maneuvers while serving stints as attorney general, secretary of war, and secretary of state.

Benjamin in Popular Literature

Poet Stephen Vincent Benét wrote a Pulitzer-Prize-winning book-length poem in 1928 narrating the entire Civil War, from Harper's Ferry to Appomattox. *John Brown's Body* included a widely-held description of Judah Benjamin:

Seal-Sleek, black-eyed, lawyer and epicure,

Able, well-hated, face alive with life, [. . .]

Perpetual smile he held before himself

Continually like a silk-ribbed fan.

John Brown's Body was adapted for stage as a three-man show and produced on Broadway in 1953, starring Tyrone Power, Jr. A 1989 revival starred Christopher Reeve.

POWs

Cruel conditions extended beyond the battlefield for Civil War soldiers. Soon-to-be infamous prisoner-of-war camps sprung up in both the North and South.

As the war grew bloodier and grimmer, so did the POW camps.

The most infamous was Andersonville, located in Sumter County, Georgia. Its official name was Camp Sumter, but the prison became known as Andersonville in deference to the village located near the POW ground.

Captured Union soldiers first went to Andersonville in early 1864, when Richmond prison space for captured enemy troops became too cramped.

Built as a stockade with capacity for ten thousand men, Andersonville bulged with thirty-three thousand captured Union soldiers by August 1864.

Conditions were deplorable at the start and deteriorated further under the prison's sadistic leader, Henry Wirz. He became the only Civil War soldier executed after the war, convicted of causing ten thousand deaths at Andersonville. Of the forty-five thousand Union soldiers held at Andersonville during the war, at least thirteen thousand—29 percent—died at the notorious prison camp. Historians believe the toll was likely much higher than that.

A second Confederate prison, in Salisbury, North Carolina, supplanted Andersonville for the dubious distinction of having the highest mortality rate (34 percent), though it was a much smaller prison. In both prisons, the captured soldiers suffered from diarrhea, malaria, lice, and infinite other horrors. Fetid water and unsanitary conditions were routine. Starvation and malnourishment raged rampant.

In the North, conditions proved little better for captured Confederates. A prison camp at Elmira, New York, known as "Hellmira" among Southern POWs, produced an equally gruesome 25 percent mortality rate among its twelve thousand prisoners.

Rather than stifling heat, Elmira offered the opposite. Freezing temperatures enfeebled and killed Confederate prisoners. Many were routinely denied warm clothes, coats, blankets, and proper shelter. Despite plentiful food supplies in the North, Confederate POWs received paltry provisions. Those orders came straight from the secretary of war, who sought to make captured Southern soldiers suffer as much as their comrades on the battlefield who had to make do with meager portions as the North starved out the Confederacy's dwindling supplies.

Happy Fourth of July

For the Union, that is. On July 4, 1863, two pivotal military victories came to a close for the Union armies and a jubilant North. A day earlier, George Meade's Army of the Potomac defeated Robert E. Lee at Gettysburg, considered the turning point of the conflict. And on the nation's birthday, as the Gettysburg victory was celebrated, more good news followed as the final Mississippi River stronghold—Vicksburg—fell. After a months-long siege, the city surrendered to Ulysses S. Grant after enduring repeated shelling and horrid living conditions. To say Vicksburg held a grudge would be a vast understatement. The Fourth of July would not be celebrated again in the Mississippi city until World War II.

"I Can't Spare This Man"

The year 1864 brought President Lincoln and the Union what they had long needed—a worthy commander.

After burning through general after general, on March 9, 1864, Lincoln promoted Ulysses S. Grant to lead the Union armies. Grant would finish the job started (but never completed) by Winfield Scott, George McClellan, John Pope, Henry W. Halleck, Ambrose Burnside, Joseph Hooker, and George Meade.

Each of Grant's predecessors had shown glimpses of promise— from McClellan's revamped and expertly trained Army of the Potomac to Meade's triumph at Gettysburg—before, inevitably, disappointing Lincoln. The specter of Robert E. Lee loomed over the Union's mounting casualties and errant strategy, and thus doomed each man to military quagmire—or worse.

Grant was different. His victory at Shiloh in 1862 made that clear. The Union suffered thirteen thousand casualties in that battle, and at the time, such losses were unthinkable. Rumors raged over Grant's alleged heavy drinking and as his penchant for meat-grinder tactics on the battlefield.

Lincoln cut through those criticisms with a blunt assessment of Grant. "I can't spare this man," Lincoln said. "He fights."

With that, the unlikeliest of commanders took the reins. A disappointment at West Point, Grant floundered after leaving the military in 1854. His subsequent failures included real estate, agriculture, and an infamous stint clerking in the family tannery business.

Unlike his predecessor, Henry W. Halleck, Grant favored a strategy of taking the fight to the Confederates instead of capturing strategic cities. He recognized that the quickest and most effective path to victory was by taking advantage of the North's larger population and pool of fighting men. In other words, Grant knew the horror of war and was willing to sacrifice his men in order to bleed and ravage the Confederates.

His strategy, mapped out upon Lincoln's promotion, made that clear. Grant reset the Union agenda by putting constant pressure on both Confederate armies, Robert E. Lee's Army of Northern Virginia and the Army of the Tennessee led by Joseph E. Johnston. Grant showed an unwavering commitment to endure staggering casualties as the Union suffered fifty thousand to fifty-five thousand during a month of carnage in Virginia. Grant believed with grim certainty that only intense suffering would force a Confederate surrender.

Grant's strategy ultimately won the war for Lincoln and the Union—and it began with Grant's promotion in 1864. His initial moves proved prescient when Grant installed William Sherman as head of the western troops and placed the equally hard-nosed Philip Sheridan at the head of the Union cavalry.

Home Sweet Home

For President Lincoln, that description rang false for the White House during Washington's hot, humid summers. Lincoln often sought to beat the heat with treks to the Soldiers' Home during the muggy season. The Lincolns made frequent daily trips back and forth between the White House and the cottage at the Soldiers' Home— located three miles from Washington. It was the Camp David of its day and used by other presidents, though it became historic because of Lincoln's frequent forays. At the Soldiers' Home cottage Lincoln contemplated the Emancipation Proclamation and conducted numerous high-level Cabinet meetings to plot war strategy. Little known to many contemporary Americans, the cottage and Soldiers' Home opened to the public in 2008 after decades of neglect—and after receiving a seven-year, $15 million facelift.

THE WILDERNESS: BEGINNINGS

The Union and Confederate armies engaged in bloody, costly battles during the spring of 1864. Known as the Wilderness Campaign, this series of clashes led Northern critics to refer to Union commander Ulysses S. Grant by a harrowing nickname: "Butcher."

Grant's army absorbed a staggering fifty thousand to fifty-five thousand casualties, far more than the Confederates' thirty-two thousand. It would still be considered a Union victory, because of its strategic importance. Grant asserted his determination to bleed the Confederates (literally and otherwise) of any will to fight while forcing Robert E. Lee to assume the unfavorable position of defending Petersburg—under siege, no less.

Soldiers from the Union and the Confederacy were drenched in blood and fought amid mountains of corpses strewn across the battlefields of Virginia during the Wilderness Campaign. Despite the staggering toll, Grant kept ordering more attacks. He would have no mercy—on his own men or the enemy.

Grant had 120,000 men in the Army of the Potomac, almost double Lee's Army of Northern Virginia. On May 4, the Union troops crossed the Rapidan River with plans to head south and battle the Confederates. Lee, being Lee, sought to shift the military landscape by launching a Confederate attack on Grant and the Union in the dense woods and thickets of an area known as the Wilderness.

Creeks, streams, and tangled, impenetrable patches of bushes and trees made the area a dreadful place for battle. Lee chose it for just that reason. With half as many men as Grant, he needed a way to level the battlefield; an unlevel battlefield was it.

Blankets of thick smoke and intense forest fires sparked by constant shooting and savage fighting haunted the two-day battle. By its end on May 6, the Union suffered nearly eighteen thousand casualties, more than twice the Confederates' 7,500. The latter's toll included Lee's trusted aide, James Longstreet. Longstreet, like

Stonewall Jackson before him, was killed by Confederate guns. Unlike Jackson, Longstreet made a full recovery.

Grant withdrew during the evening of May 6, but chose to sidestep and head for Spotsylvania Court House on the road to Richmond. That sent a strong message that no matter the carnage, Grant would press the fight to the rebel army. Even if he lost, Grant planned to keep the pressure on Lee's army.

Despite staggering casualties, Grant maintained his unwavering determination. He knew that the North could withstand the losses whereas the South had no means to replenish its dwindling forces. Simple, if gruesome, mathematics drove Grant's strategy.

Lee deciphered Grant's intentions and beat him to Spotsylvania. On May 8, the two armies engaged in a brief sparring session. Over the next eleven days, relentless clashes ravaged both sides. The federals and rebels battered one another while the Union cavalry, under Philip Sheridan, embarked on a separate push aimed at drawing out Jeb Stuart. Sheridan's ten thousand-man cavalry—stretching thirteen miles—drew the attention of Stuart and his renowned Confederate cavalry, as intended. Outnumbered by more than two-to-one the Confederate cavalry took up a defensive position just north of Richmond at Yellow Tavern, an abandoned inn.

Sheridan's men failed to break the Confederates, who fought with keen determination in defense of their nearby capital city. Despite the Confederates' successful stand, Sheridan claimed quite a consolation prize in Stuart. A Union private named John Huff, glimpsing a Confederate officer in colorful garb some thirty feet away, took aim and fired. Huff's shot found its target—Stuart, the dashing, daring cavalryman who had caused the Union ample embarrassment and discomfort. Stuart died the next day. Lee, as he had been the previous year with the loss of Stonewall Jackson, was devastated.

The final bout of significant fighting at Spotsylvania took place at a Confederate stronghold known first as the Mule Shoe, and later as the Bloody Angle. The Mule Shoe took its name from the shape of the Confederate entrenchments. Grant sent twenty thousand men to attack the Mule Shoe. Intense fighting led to the nickname Bloody Angle. An early morning Union attack on May 12 led to a major breakthrough—including the capture of four thousand Confederates—before devolving into a stalemate amid a heavy downpour.

Mississippi Maverick

The first African-American U.S. senator came from Mississippi during Reconstruction—and inherited the seat last occupied by Confederate President Jefferson Davis. Hiram Revels (1822–1901), a man of mixed ethnicity, grew up in North Carolina as a free man and later attended college in Indiana.

He became a pastor and established himself at a church in Natchez, Mississippi. Revels dabbled in local and state politics during the 1860s. In 1870, Revels, with some controversy, was seated in the U.S. Senate and served a one-year term, fulfilling the final year of Davis' term. He proved himself an eloquent speaker and fought for racial equality, though he had scant support from colleagues. Upon returning to Mississippi, Revels accepted a post as the first president of a fledgling college now known as Alcorn State University.

WORDS OF WAR

There are tens of thousands of books on the Civil War, from histories, to novels, to coffee table keepsakes, and everything in between. There are no signs that the flood of titles will slow any time soon, as Drew Gilpin Faust's highly acclaimed history, *This Republic of Suffering: Death and the American Civil War*, proves.

There are dozens of stellar titles left off this list simply because of space limitations, but the following are a good start for any Civil War library:

Nonfiction

A Stillness at Appomattox by Bruce Catton (1953): The final volume in Catton's Army of the Potomac trilogy won the Pulitzer Prize and the National Book Award.

The Civil War: A Narrative by Shelby Foote (1974): This three thousand-page trilogy turned Foote into the authority on the war, though he insisted he was a novelist and not a historian. No matter, since Foote's twenty-year project paid off. The three doorstop volumes require diligence and dedication from the reader. Those willing to invest in the trilogy will be well rewarded.

Battle Cry of Freedom by James M. McPherson (1988): Regarded as the best single-volume historical account ever written on the subject.

April 1865 by Jay Winik (2001): This acclaimed history of the war's turbulent, decisive final month includes the surrender at Appomattox and Lincoln's assassination.

Personal Memoirs of U.S. Grant by Ulysses S. Grant (1885–1886): Written while Grant was dying of throat cancer, this candid memoir went on to become a hit with readers and critics alike. It is still considered a military classic.

Confederates in the Attic by Tony Horwitz (1998): This amusing work of nonfiction chronicles America's lasting obsession with the war, the Confederate flag and, most notably, the bizarre rituals of war reenactors.

Don't Know Much About the Civil War by Kenneth C. Davis (1996): Wonderful overview of the war's major moments and oddities delivered in elegant, bite-sized prose. Perfect primer.

Team of Rivals by Doris Kearns Goodwin (2005): Fascinating study of Lincoln's political mastery as he maneuvered his cabinet to reach consensus.

Fiction

Cold Mountain by Charles Frazier (1997): The story of a Civil War soldier trudging home from the battlefield to his native North Carolina in search of his true love became a best-seller and instant classic for Frazier.

Gone with the Wind by Margaret Mitchell (1936): An epic debut novel that swept readers away and won the Pulitzer Prize while introducing the indelible Scarlett O'Hara and Rhett Butler. The movie's not bad, either.

The Killer Angels by Michael Shaara (1974): Yet another Pulitzer winner, this kaleidoscopic account of the battle of Gettysburg offers deft portraits of participants such as Robert E. Lee and Joshua Lawrence Chamberlain as breathing, living people.

Oldest Living Confederate Widow Tells All by Allan Gurganus (1989): This raucous novel tells the story of the war-torn Reconstruction South through the eyes of a ninety-five-year old widow who is, yes, the oldest survivor of a Confederate veteran.

The Red Badge of Courage by Stephen Crane (1895): One of the finest novels written about any war, Crane's classic tells the story of a frazzled Union soldier preparing for battle.

THE WILDERNESS: COLD HARBOR AND CONCLUSION

The Wilderness Campaign launched by Ulysses S. Grant against Robert E. Lee's determined, but dragging, Army of Northern Virginia had already stretched nearly a month by the time the Spotsylvania battles petered out. In the wake of the Bloody Angle Union breakthrough in mid-May, the armies went back to mixed-bag battles and skirmishes that ended without surety of victory—or defeat—for either side.

In each case, Grant moved closer to Richmond, while Lee moved closer to running out of fighting men. Manpower had become a dwindling asset. The deadly spring offensive culminated with ruinous bloodshed at the Battle of Cold Harbor (May 31–June 12). By late June, Grant and the Union would lay siege to Petersburg, in the tactic used to take Vicksburg the previous year.

Before the siege, though, thousands died at Cold Harbor. In his excellent account of the bloody battles, Civil War historian Ernest B. Furgurson described it as "Not War but Murder." This sums up a Union soldier at Cold Harbor who described the disorienting vulnerability of a failed offensive in memorable fashion: "We felt it was murder, not war." The phrase "not war but murder" is often attributed to William Sherman, who used it to describe fighting in the western theater, though Sherman was not at Cold Harbor.

During a single hour of fighting on June 3, the Confederates inflicted seven thousand casualties on the Union. "I have always regretted that the last assault at Cold Harbor was ever made," Grant wrote years later. "At Cold Harbor no advantage whatever was gained to compensate for the heavy loss we sustained."

On June 7, the armies called a truce to tend to the dead. The toll alarmed Washington and the rest of the Union. "Butcher" Grant had gone from hero to goat in less than a year's time, only three months after being named head of all federal troops by President Lincoln.

The president, regardless, stood behind Grant. Union casualties were higher, with fifty thousand to fifty-five thousand during the Wilderness Campaign in most of May and June, as compared to thirty-two thousand Confederates. Casualties in terms of percentage were more even. For Lee and the Confederates, the population pool for reinforcements was already threadbare, a stark contrast to the North's situation.

Colorfully Named Units

- Pennsylvania Bucktails — 13th Pennsylvania Reserves. To be allowed to serve, a man had to produce a buck tail to prove his spot-on marksmanship. The men fastened the tails to their hats.
- Kentucky Orphan Brigade — 1st Kentucky Brigade. Confederate troops from the border state of Kentucky who, after the Confederacy abandoned occupation of the state in 1862, could not return home.
- Iron Brigade — I Corps, 1st Division, 1st Brigade. Named by Union Major Joe Hooker because of heroic actions at South Mountain.
- Garibaldi Guards — 39th New York. Including men of fifteen different nationalities, orders were often given in seven languages: German, Hungarian, Italian, French, Spanish, Portuguese, and English.

JOHN ROWLANDS, AKA HENRY MORTON STANLEY (1841-1904)

We're a little befuddled on whether or not to list John Rowlands as a "Confederate Soldier," or as a "Union Soldier." You see, Rowlands served on both sides. It's understandable how this came about, and if we were faced with the choice he was offered, we're not sure, but we might do the same thing, too.

Here's what we mean: Rowlands fought for the Confederate Army and was captured at the Battle of Shiloh. He was sent to Camp Douglas in Chicago as a prisoner of war. While he was there, languishing, he was offered an interesting proposal to get himself out of captivity. He could be released from prison into the service of the U.S. Army. He made his choice and never looked back.

We're getting ahead of ourselves, because the story of John Rowlands began long before Shiloh. He was born in Wales into a poor family and began his miserable life in a workhouse at the age of six. By his late teens, he had managed to get onto a ship sailing for America. Landing in New Orleans, Rowlands found work for a gentleman named Henry Hope Stanley and decided to assume a version of this name for himself.

From New Orleans, Rowlands/Stanley got caught up in secession fever, and he enlisted in the "Dixie Grays" with the 6th Arkansas Infantry. It's said that he really didn't care one way or the other about the Southern cause, but he enlisted to impress a lady. Men have done crazier things to impress women, after all. Anyhow, he first saw action at Shiloh, using an outdated musket, and we already covered how well that worked out.

Taking an oath of allegiance to the United States at Camp Douglas, Rowlands/Stanley became what was called a "galvanized Yankee." He was assigned to the 1st Illinois Light Artillery, but before seeing any action found himself in an Army hospital suffering from dysentery.

Still weak from his prison confinement, Rowlands/Stanley

decided he wasn't ready to go back into battle and set off to Cuba to look for Henry Hope Stanley. But his former benefactor had died, so the new "Stanley" returned to America and joined the U.S. Navy.

Again, Stanley soon saw that war was not for him. Assigned to the naval vessel Minnesota as the ship's writer, Stanley forged a pass from the commodore while in port in New Hampshire. He deserted to Canada, where he stayed until the end of the war.

By this time, our man was going by "Henry Morton Stanley." He returned to the United States and established himself as a newspaper reporter, first in Kentucky, and then in New York City. Working for editor James Gordon Bennett and *The New York Herald,* Stanley was assigned to cover the opening of the Suez Canal in Africa and to find Scottish missionary/explorer David Livingstone, who had gone missing while exploring the Nile River.

Stanley did locate Livingstone at Lake Tanganyika, and in the process, began a series of explorations that he would continue throughout his lifetime: Ghana, Lake Victoria, the Congo River, Sudan, Lake Albert, and Lake Edward. Stanley earned a name among African tribes as the "Rock Breaker," both for his blazing of trails as well as his sometimes ruthless treatment of the indigenous people.

Petersburg

On the heels of the Wilderness Campaign's carnage at Cold Harbor, Grant launched another attack. This time he surprised Robert E. Lee and the Confederates, opting to mount an offensive at Petersburg, the primary rail supply center for Richmond.

Union troops beat the Confederates to Petersburg with a significant advantage in men as ten thousand federals stood ready to assault three thousand Rebels led by P. G. T. Beauregard. The Union wasted their advantage under the ineffective leadership of Union commander "Baldy" Smith, and failed to make any substantive progress. Grant arrived on the scene shortly after and attempted subsequent attacks, but after being repulsed, he decided on a siege similar to the one he had overseen a year earlier at Vicksburg.

THE LOUISIANA TIGERS

First, a short bio of Chatham Roberdeau "Rob" Wheat (1826–1862). Wheat was a Virginia native, son of an Episcopalian minister. An 1845 graduate of the University of Nashville, Wheat volunteered in the Mexican War and rose to the rank of captain. Then he practiced law in New Orleans and served in the state legislature. Next he became a soldier of fortune, joining actions in Cuba, Mexico, Nicaragua, and Italy.

That gives you some background on Wheat's qualifications to raise an infantry battalion at the outbreak of the Civil War. He was joined by Alex White, who gathered a company from the dregs of local prisons and convinced a wealthy benefactor, Alexander Keene Richards, to outfit the group as Zouaves. They were hard not to notice:

- Scarlet wool fezzes with blue tassels
- Loose-fitting red wool battle shirts
- Red wool sashes
- Dark blue wool waist-length jackets with red trim
- Blue-and-white striped sailor's socks
- Baggy blue-and-white striped cotton trousers
- White canvas leggings
- Black leather grieves
- Bowie knives on their belts

Wheat himself wore a dark blue, double-breasted coat and trousers with a buff general's sash and a red kepi hat with gold trim.

The White/Wheat (sounds like some kind of healthy bread loaf, doesn't it?) "Tiger Zouaves" or "Wheat's Tigers" were accepted into the Confederate Army as the 1st Louisiana Special Battalion. Wheat was the major, and White was one of the captains.

In addition to former prisoners, the battalion was primarily made up of dockworkers, former soldiers of fortune, Irish immigrants, French-speaking Creoles, and other known "rough-and-ready" populations.

The Tigers soon developed a reputation as one of the toughest, most fearless forces in the Civil War, not afraid of pulling out their Bowie knives and moving to hand-to-hand combat on the battlefield. They were equally known for their thievery, drunkenness, and fighting in camp.

The "Louisiana Tigers" were first sent to northern Virginia just in time for First Bull Run. Wheat was wounded—a minie ball passed through both of his lungs—but he recovered.

Soon, the Louisiana Tigers were brigaded with four other Louisiana outfits, the 6th, 7th, 8th, and 9th Louisiana Volunteer Infantry Regiments, to form the Louisiana Brigade under General Richard Taylor.

The Louisiana Tigers fought at Front Royal, Winchester, Port Republic, and Antietam, as well as in the Valley, Peninsula, Northern Virginia, and Maryland campaigns.

At Gaines' Mill, Wheat was mortally wounded. With his death, the 1st Louisiana Special Battalion fell apart, and the soldiers were distributed among the four other regiments of the Louisiana Brigade. The battalion's men retained their spirit and ferocity, and soon the whole brigade became known as the Louisiana Tigers.

Of course, you can still watch the Louisiana Tigers in action today, especially on a fall Saturday afternoon, when you tune into a Louisiana State University athletic game.

UNION COMMANDERS: IRWIN MCDOWELL (1818-1885)

Character Description: "powerfully built," "frank," "agreeable," "oddly prim," indulging in no bad habits: no coffee, tea, or tobacco
Early Life: Born in Columbus, Ohio; educated in France
Military Training: West Point class of 1838 graduate; Artillery officer on the Canadian border; West Point tactics instructor, 1841
Military Experience: Mexican War (served as aide-de-camp to General John E. Wool); Performed staff work in the Office of the Adjutant General (1848–1861); Importantly, McDowell never gained any experience leading troops into battle.
Political Connections: As a career soldier, McDowell got to know General Winfield Scott and Secretary of Treasury Salmon P. Chase, among other high-ranking Washington officials.
Civil War Appointment: At the beginning of the war, Scott and Chase championed McDowell to President Lincoln as their choice for commander of the Union Army. They expected the war to end within ninety days with a Union victory, and so weren't worried about having a seasoned officer leading the Army.
The First Battle of Bull Run, July 18, 1861: To begin with, McDowell faced political pressures to get the war underway. He knew his forces were "green" and almost wholly unprepared to march into battle. McDowell led about thirty-five thousand Union soldiers to meet about twenty-nine thousand Confederate soldiers at Manassas.

To give McDowell credit, he had devised a good plan of attack. But, it turned out to be too complicated for his inexperienced men. Lack of coordination and communication between units, coupled with inadequate officer leadership and slow decisions, gave the Confederates ample opportunity to counterattack. Many Union soldiers simply turned and ran away.

Lessons from Bull Run: President Lincoln quickly figured out the Union Army needed a real military leader, not a friend of Winfield Scott's, in charge. Lincoln brought in George McClellan to replace McDowell.

McDowell was given command of a division in charge of defending Washington. He then led a corps at Cedar Mountain and Second Bull Run.

Second Bull Run: The battles that took place in Manassas turned out to be the undoing of Irwin McDowell. He was blamed for the Confederate victory due to his being slow to move, and was again relieved of his command. McDowell even took the matter to a court of inquiry, where plenty of evidence was brought against him.

The records show McDowell's name was cleared, but don't show why. Perhaps it was because of his friendships with Winfield Scott and Salmon P. Chase. Perhaps it was because he threw Fitz-John Porter into the ring as a scapegoat, testifying against Porter, who was court-martialed for failing to obey orders during the Second Bull Run.

McDowell's Civil War Combat Was Over: For the next two years, he served on boards and commissions in Washington and in July 1864 was given command of the Union forces in the Department of the Pacific in California.

McDowell in California: After participating in Reconstruction in the South, McDowell returned to California in 1876 to head the Department of the Pacific until he retired in 1882. As parks commissioner, he accomplished improvements to San Francisco's Presidio, a former Spanish garrison that is today a part of the National Park Service system. After his death in 1885, McDowell was buried in a cemetery on the Presidio grounds.

Union Commanders: Henry Wager Halleck (1815-1872)

Character Description: "brilliant," "ambitious," "pop-eyed," "flabby," "surly"

Early Life: New York native, raised by his grandfather, elected Phi Beta Kappa at Union College

Civil War Battles: Fort Donelson, Pea Ridge, Island #10, Shiloh

Military Education: 1839 West Point graduate, third in his class

Literati Achievements: An assistant professor of engineering at West Point before he even graduated; wrote for the U.S. Senate, Report on the Means of National Defense and Elements of Military Art and Science (widely used as a reference during the Civil War); translated Henri Jomini's *Political and Military Life of Napoleon* from French

West Point Nickname: "Old Brains," for his great intellect

Civil War U.S. Army Nickname: "Old Wooden Head," for his bumbling leadership

Military Experience: Served in administration in California during the Mexican War; Worked as a lighthouse and fort inspector and engineer on the Pacific Coast

Civilian Experience: Opened a successful law practice in San Francisco and helped write the State of California Constitution. For someone who ran away from home at a young age to avoid working the family farm, interestingly, he grew quite wealthy in California managing a thirty thousand-acre ranch in Marin County.

Personal Life: Halleck married Elizabeth Hamilton, granddaughter of Alexander Hamilton, in 1855.

Civil War Appointment: At the beginning of the Civil War, Halleck appeared to be "a soldier of great promise." He was appointed a major general, the fourth highest ranking officer in the U.S. Army.

Civil War Highlights: Halleck was first assigned to the Department of Missouri, where his great organizational skills were useful in following up the previous command of John C. Frémont. Promoted to general-in-chief of the U.S. Army in 1862, Halleck put to use his intellect in administrative duties. He acted more as a clerk, though, organizing army operations and supply chain.

Civil War Lowlights: Although he won victories at Pea Ridge, Island Number 10, and Shiloh, Halleck is known for his blunder in Mississippi. His incredibly slow advance to Corinth allowed the Confederates plenty of time to withdraw and thus earned Halleck a reputation as an inept field commander.

Halleck knew the theory of war inside and out, but he couldn't apply it to reality. His subordinates complained that he didn't share plans with them, or really, communicate at all about anything. He also had problems accepting responsibility, instead pointing fingers when things went wrong.

Halleck soon became known as "the most hated man in Washington," drawing criticism from the president, the cabinet, and fellow officers. Halleck clearly did live up to the expectations inspired by the incredible intellect he demonstrated at West Point.

Grant demoted Halleck to chief-of-staff early in 1864. This turned out to be right up his alley. He worked as an effective communication liaison between Grant and Lincoln.

After the Civil War: Halleck served as a pallbearer at Abraham Lincoln's funeral. A career soldier, Halleck remained in uniform and held various administrative posts. He died while in command of the Division of the South in Louisville, Kentucky.

Halleck at Berkeley

While in California, Halleck began gathering documents about the state's history, from mission reports to exploration notes and official government papers. (You could wonder if he came across some of these papers by less-than-legal means.)

Halleck eventually amassed one of the best collections of "Californiana" anywhere. As it turns out, it's now the only collection, because the official government archives were destroyed in San Francisco's Great Fire of 1906.

Halleck's collection is now housed in the Bancroft Library at The University of California, Berkeley.

UNION COMMANDERS: GEORGE ARMSTRONG CUSTER (1839-1876)

Early Life: Born in Ohio, raised in Michigan, briefly taught high school

Military Education: 1861 West Point graduate

Immediate Civil War Appointment: Commissioned Second Lieutenant of cavalry

First Assignment: Messenger between Lieutenant General Winfield Scott and Brigadier General Irvin McDowell during Bull Run preparations

Next Assignment: Aide-de-camp to Major Generals George McClellan then Alfred Pleasanton

Custer's Cavalry Brigade: 1st, 5th, 6th, and 7th Michigan Cavalry regiments. Following their leader's characteristic courage and aggressiveness, Custer's brigade suffered the highest losses of any Union cavalry brigade in the war: 525 men were killed or mortally wounded.

Civil War Battles: Custer was on almost every major eastern battlefield, including Brandy Station, Rappahannock, Gettysburg, Culpepper Court House, Yellow Tavern, Winchester, Fisher's Hill, Woodstock, Cedar Creek, Five Forks, Waynesboro, Dinwiddie Court House, and Shenandoah Valley.

Rank Achieved: Major General of Volunteers

Lee's Surrender: Custer received the first truce flag Lee's army offered. Then, after Lee and Grant signed the surrender documents in Wilmer McLean's farmhouse, Philip Sheridan bought the very table they worked from for Custer to give to his wife, Elizabeth Bacon Custer.

After the War: Custer remained in the Regular Army. Following a brief assignment with Reconstruction in Texas, he was named lieutenant colonel of the 7th Cavalry. He commanded them for many years on the western front, during which time he led a massacre on a Cheyenne village at the Washita River in 1868.

George Custer Trivia

- Custer was not a star student. His four West Point years were marked by excessive demerits, bad grades, and worse discipline. His only high point was excellent horsemanship. He was so close to being expelled, that he was actually on detention when he graduated last in his class.

- Some say that Custer received his appointment to West Point due to the influence of a local Monroe, Michigan, father who was motivated to separate Custer from his young daughter.

- Custer was tall and buff, and he had long, curly blond hair.

- George's nicknames: "Curly" (his troops); "Fanny" (his West Point buddies); "Armstrong" or "Audie" (his friends).

- Custer's basic battle strategy was, "Charge!" Beyond that, he let the chips fall where they may.

- Eleven horses were shot out from under Custer; he himself was only wounded once.

- At the war's end, the Armies of the Republic participated in a grand review in Washington, D.C. As the Army of the Potomac precisely marched down Pennsylvania Avenue, with pomp and circumstance, Custer lost control of his horse and galloped ahead of his column, his long hair flailing behind him.

- Custer was court-martialed in 1867 for leaving his post on the western front to make an unauthorized visit to his wife. His old comrade Philip Sheridan came to his rescue.

- Before his untimely death in Montana, whispers were circulating that Custer might be considered as the next presidential candidate.

Custer's Last Stand

No biography, short or long, about George Custer would be complete without mention of his famous "Last Stand" at the Battle of Little Big Horn. In May of 1876, Custer encountered Lakota Indians encamped on the Little Big Horn River in Montana. With 1,100 men, Custer underestimated the Lakota, both in their numbers (around nine thousand) and their capabilities. On June 25, 1876, Custer charged the Indians, expecting them to run. He found out too late that, supplied with repeating rifles, they had no intention of retreating. Custer and a third of his regiment were killed and buried where they fell.

UNION COMMANDERS: HENRY WARNER SLOCUM (1827-1894)

Background: Born in upstate New York, settled in Syracuse
Military Education: 1852 West Point graduate (Philip Sheridan's roommate)
Military Experience: Seminole Wars
Civil War Appointment: Colonel, 27th New York
Rank Achieved: Major General
Civil War Battles: First Bull Run (severely wounded), Peninsula Campaign, Second Bull Run, Antietam, Chancellorsville, Gettysburg, Chattanooga, Vicksburg, Atlanta Campaign, March to the Sea, Carolinas Campaign

Slocum was one of the officers who urged Lincoln to relieve Hooker of command of the Army of the Potomac after Chancellorsville. He came under considerable criticism himself for actions at Gettysburg—or more accurately, for his inaction. For whatever reason, Slocum didn't bring his troops to the battlefield until the very end of the day, earning himself the nickname, "Slow Come."

After the War: Settled in Brooklyn, practiced law, served in the House of Representatives, participated in building the Brooklyn Bridge.

CONFEDERATE COMMANDERS: STERLING PRICE (1809-1867)

Physical Description: handsome, tall, "stout"
Nickname: "Pap" Price
Early Life: Virginia native, relocated to Missouri at age twenty-one
Civilian Career: Tobacco Farmer (slave owner) and Lawyer
Military Career: Mexican War—Military Governor as a Brigadier General of Volunteers in New Mexico (1846–1848); Missouri State Militia head (1860)
Political Aspirations: Missouri state legislator (1840-1844); Missouri Congressman in the House of Representatives (1845–1846); Missouri Governor (1853–1857)
Political Opinions: Opposed secession, but agreed to fight against the Union anyway
Importance to the Confederacy: Not necessarily a successful commander, Price's value to the South lay in his great popularity with the people of Missouri
Civil War Service: Leading five thousand men from the Missouri state militia, Price experienced the victory of battle at Wilson's Creek and Lexington. Then he served with his forces under Earl Van Dorn in the defeat at Pea Ridge. After that loss, Price brought his militia with him when he joined the regular Confederate Army as a major general.
Other Civil War Battles: Iuka; Corinth; Helena, Arkansas; Second Lexington; Carthage; Prairie D'Ane, Arkansas; Pilot Knob, Missouri; Westport, Missouri; Mine Creek, Kansas.
Price's Civil War Objective: Throughout the Civil War, Price's general aim was to liberate Missouri. To that end, he began a major raid through Missouri in the fall of 1864 to recapture the state for the Confederates. It ended disastrously, with his surviving men forced to retreat all the way to Texas.
After the War: Headed to Mexico with his troops to offer their services to Emperor Maximilian. Returned to Missouri in 1866, could not to rebuild his tobacco fortune and died the next year.

THE CRATER

Welcome to Coal Miners' Slaughter.

As the siege of Petersburg got under way, a Pennsylvania regiment led by Colonel Henry Pleasants, a coal mine engineer, hatched a novel attack plan to carve out a large underground tunnel extending to Confederate defense lines and then blow it up. Amid the confusion, the federals would launch subsequent offensives. The regiment was made up of men who worked in mines, an affinity that made their unorthodox military strategy resonate with former Army of the Potomac commander Ambrose Burnside.

Pleasants presented the idea to Burnside, now a subordinate serving as a field officer to Grant. Burnside approved the plan and the Pennsylvanians dug in—and out.

The idea offered a potential breakthrough. The armies faced off with more than twenty miles of trenches and fortifications around Petersburg, extending all the way to the Cold Harbor battlefield. For Burnside, victim of a humiliating defeat at Fredericksburg, it offered a chance at redemption.

Grant remained skeptical. For him, it represented little more than busy work for some of the men while the frustrating siege dragged on. The miners, though, made surprising progress despite little enthusiasm or support from higher-ups. They disguised the tunneling even as they crafted clever systems to keep the growing subterranean work space ventilated with clean air.

By July 30, the 511-foot tunnel, lined with explosives, was detonated. The impact killed 250 Confederates.

Despite that initial success, "The Crater" soon swallowed up hopes for a Union victory as Burnside presided over a disastrous follow-up attack. The botched episode ended Burnside's career. If the black soldiers were slaughtered, George Meade reasoned, the criticism would be scathing. The message would be that black lives mattered less than whites'. Burnside bent to Meade's argument only after Grant sided with Meade—and despite the fact that the black troops in question were well-regarded and had been training for the follow-up attack.

That questionable decision was followed by a disastrous one. Burnside put the assault in the hands of James Ledlie, with the black troops under Edward Ferrero now in a secondary role. An ineffective and undistinguished general with a reputation for heavy drinking, Ledlie lived down to expectations at the Crater. He failed to prepare his men, and during the attack, was sequestered in a bunker quaffing rum while his men were dying.

Upon explosion, the Crater created a massive hole, estimated to be 170 feet long, sixty to eighty feet wide and thirty feet deep. The Union soldiers charged into the hole—not around it—and found themselves hopelessly trapped, perfect for Confederate target practice. A rebel commander described it as a "turkey shoot." Ledlie, too, would be bounced from the army in the wake of four thousand Union casualties compared with the one thousand Confederates.

"It was the saddest affair I have witnessed in the war," Grant wrote of the Crater.

In the Trenches

The siege of Petersburg offered a telling example of what modern warfare would become. With troops building fortifications and digging trenches that stretched twenty miles, the Civil War in general, and Petersburg in particular, portended much of what was to follow during World War I. Men dug ditches, lived in them in squalor, and in occasional bursts of fury, massacred one another before starting the same thing all over again.

DEATH, MEET TAXES

Next time you find yourself grumbling over tax season, thank Salmon P. Chase. President Lincoln's treasury secretary was responsible for paying for the Civil War (expenses reached $2 million a day in its latter stages) and proved himself more than worthy of the task.

The early part of the war effort in the North depended on private funds, and soon after that, the sale of government-backed bonds. Chase turned to noted Philadelphia banker Jay Cooke for help, prompting Cooke to devise an ambitious bond campaign that targeted wealthy and average earners alike.

At the same time, Confederate monetary policy devolved into spiraling inflation, useless, and oft-counterfeited currency. In addition, the Confederate government failed to assemble anything close to a cohesive tax structure and left its chief assets—land and slaves—untapped until the latter stages of conflict. By then, it was too late.

By 1862, Chase had secured approval for the first federal issuance of paper money. Congress granted authority for the first greenbacks at the same time it backed a wide-ranging tax law aimed at bolstering the Union's financial prospects.

Taxes were imposed on all matter of goods (alcohol, tobacco, jewelry, even playing cards) as well as assets (inheritance and income chief among them). Congressional legislation established a Bureau of Internal Revenue—the IRS—and introduced staggering personal income tax rates of 3 to 5 percent (yes, really).

Though the Civil War taxes were halted in 1872, they returned, soon after, for good. With the sixteenth amendment to the Constitution in 1913, federal taxation made Benjamin Franklin's assurance of life's certainties ring true in every American home. So next April 15, feel free to salute Chase and Lincoln in whatever fashion you consider appropriate for the gift that is the IRS.

PAPER MONEY

To discuss money circulated during the 1860s, we have to back up and talk briefly about silver and gold standards. During the American Revolution, patriots printed paper money that wasn't backed by silver or gold.

In essence, they were printing currency that actually was only worth the paper it was printed on. In today's terms, if you buy a ream of five hundred sheets of paper for $7.00, meaning each sheet of paper is worth $0.014. Simply writing or printing "$100" on the piece of paper does not increase its value from less than a penny to one hundred dollars.

Back to our founding fathers: When they drafted the U.S. Constitution, they included a provision for sound money in Article I, Section 10, which says, "No state shall [. . .] make anything but gold and silver coin a tender in payment of debts." In the following years, the American dollar was based on the value of gold if the coins were not made entirely from that metal. In fact, all the way until 1862, American money was all in coin form, although some states had already printed their own paper money.

Printed paper money simply meant that a $1 paper note was worth $1 in gold. In simplistic terms, you could take your $1 paper note to the bank and exchange it for $1 in gold.

Now that we've been through the most basic of discussions of money, let's apply it to the Civil War.

Federal Paper Money

In 1862, U.S. Secretary of the Treasury Salmon P. Chase introduced the Legal Tender Act to print paper money to help pay for war costs. This money featured pictures of Chase himself, and was soon called "greenbacks." More importantly, the paper money was actually backed by the value of gold.

Confederate Paper Money

The Confederacy printed up money to pay for war costs, too. The big difference was that Confederate money was not backed by any kind of precious metal, be it silver, gold, platinum, or even aluminum (which, incidentally, at the time was still a hard-to-obtain, semiprecious metal). They expected to win the war, and then the notes would be backed by cotton.

The Confederate government, as well as individual state governments, printed treasury notes in ever-increasing volume. Before they were finished, Confederate currency was not even worth the paper it was printed on. Confederate Treasury Secretary Christopher G. Memminger warned that with the printing of such valueless notes, "the large quantity of money in circulation must produce depreciation and disaster." He was right.

In fact, by the end of the war, even Southerners coveted the federal greenbacks for their purchasing power.

Inflation

Inflation affected both the North and South. Northern currency did decrease in value; at its lowest point, $2.59 in federal paper money equaled $1 in gold. But, at the same time, $1 in federal paper money was worth about twenty times that in Confederate money.

The worthless Confederate currency led to a state of hyperinflation in the South. Confederate money declined so much in value that eventually it took seventy Confederate dollars to equal one gold dollar.

Ironically, as a collector item, Confederate money today is worth far more than it ever was in circulation. A well-preserved $100 note goes for anywhere from $700 to $7,000.

ARTWORK ON CONFEDERATE MONEY

Confederate and state currency featured government officials and revered army officers, as well as depicted scenes of Southern belles and antebellum life.

Confederate Treasury Notes
One dollar: Lucy Holcombe Pickens, wife of the governor of South Carolina
One dollar: Confederate senator Clement C. Clay
Two dollars: Confederate cabinet member Judah P. Benjamin
Five dollars: Capitol of the Confederacy in Richmond, Virginia
Five dollars: State capitol of Columbia, South Carolina
Ten dollars: Women as Confederate warriors and patriots
Ten dollars: Confederate cabinet member R. M. T. Hunter and Treasury Secretary C. G. Memminger
Ten dollars: Horses pulling cannons
Ten dollars: Eating a sweet potato pie dinner
Twenty dollars: Tennessee state capitol at Nashville
Twenty dollars: Confederate Vice President Alexander H. Stephens
Fifty dollars: Confederate President Jefferson Davis
One hundred dollars: Railroad train with steam
One hundred dollars: Lucy Pickens and Confederate cabinet member George W. Randolph
Five hundred dollars: Stonewall Jackson and the Confederate Calvary

Other State-Issued Notes
Five cent Alabama fractional note: Cotton boll
Fifty cent Alabama fractional note: Juliet Hopkins, who established hospitals for wounded Alabama soldiers
Ten dollar Arkansas treasury note: Arkansas State Treasurer Samuel Adams

One dollar Georgia treasury note: steam locomotive

One hundred dollar Georgia treasury note: Georgia Governor Joseph E. Brown

One dollar North Carolina treasury note: Ceres, the Roman goddess of agriculture

One dollar Bank of Tennessee note: Women as patrons of home and agriculture

One dollar Virginia treasury note: A woman representing agriculture and prosperity

Five dollar Virginia treasury note: A woman destroying tyranny

One dollar and fifty cents, Bank of Rockbridge, Virginia: A woman destroying tyranny

Twenty dollar Missouri bond: Goddess of prosperity

Mangled Magnolia State

Mississippi sent over eighty thousand soldiers into battle and lost about one-third of those men who went off to war. An oft-cited statistic by historians demonstrates the breathtaking carnage for those who returned from the war: State spending on artificial limbs for Civil War veterans accounted for 20 percent of Mississippi's budget in 1866.

DAMN THE TORPEDOES!

These immortal words were spoken by Union naval commander David Farragut, who shouted them amid a cacophony of roaring guns and other weapons in Mobile Bay.

Farragut was an old hand, a veteran of the War of 1812 and the man behind the Union's successful taking of New Orleans in 1862. In August 1864, Farragut targeted the Confederates' primary port in the Gulf of Mexico—Mobile, Alabama.

His opponent was Franklin Buchanan, a former navy colleague whose Confederate military service included the captaincy of the ironclad at Hampton Roads.

Now Farragut faced Buchanan in a battle for Mobile Bay. The Confederates controlled the thirty-mile coastline with several fortifications as well as an ironclad (the *Tennessee*) and several gunboats. Torpedoes lined the channel leading into the harbor, presenting another deadly hurdle.

On August 5, Farragut decided to move. His Union fleet consisted of four ironclads and fourteen wooden ships. To better withstand the expected beating from enemy fire, the wooden ships were tied together in pairs. Farragut, aboard the lead ship *Hartford*, lashed himself to the rigging and stayed in place amid heavy gunfire.

After an ironclad sank, the Union ships listed into a logjam. Farragut urged his sailors on, "Damn the torpedoes! Full speed ahead!" It was a pivotal moment, spurring the Union to take two Confederate forts over the course of the next two days. Two weeks later, the Union seized control of the last remaining Confederate fort. The South had lost Mobile Bay, a crushing blow.

ELECTION BLUES

Matters looked hopeless for President Lincoln in the summer of 1864. Facing an election in November, the president noted that "it seems exceedingly probable that this Administration will not be re-elected."

Northerners were distraught. The war dragged on, with citizens frustrated by mounting casualties and a stalemate on the battlefield.

Lincoln selected a new running mate—Tennessee Governor Andrew Johnson—and dumped incumbent Hannibal Hamlin. The president's opponent was George McClellan, the Democratic nominee and the general Lincoln fired over his reluctance to attack the Confederates in Virginia. McClellan ran on a platform that promised to end the war, a move that some historians believe would have allowed slavery to continue in the South for years to come.

The president needed a significant military triumph to rally the Union and secure his reelection. Lincoln got just that in September 1864 when William Sherman captured Atlanta. "War is cruelty, and you cannot refine it," wrote Sherman, who blazed an indelible, punishing trail across the South. He made the civilians suffer the consequences of war as much as the rebel army.

Atlanta marked the turning point in the 1864 presidential campaign. Lincoln won 55 percent of the popular vote and enjoyed an even wider victory margin in electoral votes, defeating McClellan 212-21.

"Seeing the Elephant"

Soldiers described their first battle experience as "Seeing the Elephant." At that time, not many people had seen a real elephant. So a person's first battle experience was as unfamiliar and exotic as seeing an elephant.

BRITISH STEAL

Naval fleets and equipment represented yet another example of Northern superiority. To offset its disadvantage, the Confederacy turned to "privateers"—government-sanctioned piracy preying on commercial ships that flew the Union's banner.

The most famous ship was the thousand-ton sloop, C.S.S. *Alabama*. Originally commissioned and built by Great Britain (prone to ignoring its Civil War neutrality as a matter of convenience) in 1862, the ship had to be smuggled out of England. Union ambassadors narrowly missed seizing the boat. Instead, the Confederate navy secretary, Stephen Mallory, concocted a plan to have the British-made ship dart into the Irish Sea, where command was shifted to Captain Raphael Semmes, who boarded from another waiting vessel.

Semmes and the C.S.S. *Alabama* became legends during the next two years. The *Alabama* prowled major shipping lanes with Semmes at the helm, seizing sixty ships bearing cargo valued at more than $6 million.

In June 1864, Semmes landed at Cherbourg, France, to dock and have maintenance and repairs done. Under Captain John Winslow, the 162-man U.S.S. *Kearsarge* crew had been unsuccessfully trying to catch the *Alabama* for months. The *Kearsarge* captain had gotten wind of the *Alabama*'s Cherbourg stop and raced over from the Dutch coast in hot pursuit. Now Winslow had Semmes, and the *Alabama*, in his sights. Once in place, the *Kearsarge* waited at sea—three miles from shore in observance of international territorial water laws. Just a week after docking at Cherbourg, the Confederate raider left dock.

Semmes embraced the looming challenge. He steered the *Alabama* straight for the *Kearsarge*—and battle. After the ninety-minute engagement, the *Alabama* was history. The *Kearsarge* sank it with a barrage of targeted shots. Semmes was among those saved by a British vessel, allowing him to later return to the Confederate navy.

As for the *Alabama*, the ship's remains were discovered off the French coast in 1984. Twenty years later, combined efforts by French and American scientists remained in progress to research and excavate the Confederate ship's remains.

Check, Please

The havoc wreaked by the C.S.S. *Alabama* and other Confederate privateers lingered beyond the Civil War. American officials were furious over the losses incurred by commercial Union ships during the war due to the Confederates' piracy. A joint high commission arbitrated the dispute in 1872, awarding the United States $15.5 million.

THE HUNLEY

Although submarines had been conceived and built in crude form during previous wars, none demonstrated any military usefulness. Notice we said in "previous wars."

Three men—Horace L. Hunley, Baxter Watson, and James McClintock—joined forces soon after the war began. They aimed to conceive and build a submarine for the Confederate navy capable of disrupting the Union's military plan of strangling Confederate ports and waterways. Their first two attempts bore little fruit (one built in New Orleans and another in Mobile, Alabama), but the third, the aptly named *H.L. Hunley*, fared better.

The *Hunley*, also built in Alabama, was sent by rail to Charleston, South Carolina, for testing in Charleston Harbor. In the summer and fall of 1863, the 39-foot sub—with a wrought-iron hull and a glorified snorkel providing air for the submerged crew—began testing along the South Carolina coast. With capacity for nine crewmembers, the *Hunley* relied on a single propeller powered by crewmembers who manually turned the shaft from their seated positions.

Forget Tom Clancy-style nuclear subs. The *Hunley* had a single weapon, a 90-pound torpedo attached to the submarine by a spar extending from the bow. To stage an attack, the *Hunley* needed its crew to turn the propeller fast enough so that it could ram into an enemy vessel with enough momentum to plant the spar. Then the crew had to turn around and put 150 feet between the *Hunley* and the attacked ship before triggering the torpedo.

Tests in Charleston Harbor with the *Hunley* produced mixed results, at best. The *Hunley* struggled with buoyancy after test dives. Five crew members died during a test run in August 1863, followed two months later by the death of eight more sailors in another accident. The latter included Horace Hunley, the man the sub was named for.

Confederate commander P. G. T. Beauregard wanted no part of

additional *Hunley* tests or potential missions, but war conditions and persistent lobbying by Lieutenant George Dixon persuaded Beauregard to sign off on a mission using a partially submerged *Hunley*.

On February 17, 1864, the *Hunley*, boasting an eight-man crew helmed by Dixon, attacked a Union ship, the *Housatonic*, off the Charleston coast. Five *Housatonic* crew members were killed, but since the sinking Union ship was in shallow waters, no additional losses were incurred.

The *Hunley* retreated from the sinking *Housatonic* and disappeared. It sank with all eight of its crew aboard. Though its initial success influenced the future of naval battle, the *Hunley*'s lone foray made no difference in the Civil War.

Lost and Found

Nautical searchers, led by best-selling author and adventurer Clive Cussler, discovered the *Hunley* in 1995 while exploring waters in Charleston Harbor near Sullivan's Island. It was raised from the water five years later. Since then, an intense recovery campaign has been under way at the nearby Warren Lasch Conservation Center. Backed by a nonprofit organization, Friends of the Hunley, the research is driven by state politicians, prominent scientists, naval experts, backers such as Cussler, and media mogul Ted Turner.

The Last Farewell

The discovery of the sunken, long-lost Confederate submarine *Hunley* in 1995 led to much-belated funerals for the eight crew members who died in 1864. On April 17, 2004, horse-drawn caissons and a procession of nineteenth century-attired mourners marched four and a half miles through the streets of downtown Charleston. There, the *Hunley*'s crew—led by Lieutenant George Dixon—was buried next to other *Hunley* crewmen who died in earlier test missions. Three descendants of crew members attended, as did tens of thousands of people fascinated by what many billed as the last Confederate funeral.

WHERE EAGLES SOAR

The rare appearance of eagles was noted with awe. Watching the majestic birds soar in flight and having them land near the regiment—or vessel, if at port—was taken as a good omen for victory in upcoming battles. The most famous Civil War eagle was Old Abe.

- Often strolled around camp like he owned the place.
- Liked to perch on his specially-made red, white, and blue shield.
- Did soar above the battlefields, just out of firing range, watching the action.
- Attended at least thirty-six battle engagements.
- Captured and later sold by Chippewa Indian Chief Sky.
- Eau Claire Volunteers, Wisconsin 8th Regiment.

The young eaglet belonged to several different keepers before he came to the Eau Claire Volunteers. Private James McGinnis was assigned to his care, and Captain John Perkins dubbed him "Old Abe."

Old Abe was the pride of the regiment; the soldiers even saluted the bird in camp. The fowl actually participated in reviews, sharing the stand with high-ranking officers and civilian guests.

Often observed circling over battlefields, Old Abe became a familiar sight to all. Confederate troops referred to him as "that Yankee eagle" or "that Yankee buzzard."

Old Abe was given to the Wisconsin governor in 1864 and spent the rest of his days in a place of special recognition in the Wisconsin state capitol building. For the next twenty years, his honored falconers included many former Eau Claire infantrymen.

If you visit the Atlanta Cyclorama, look for Old Abe in the centerpiece painting. If you look on the shoulder of any soldier in the Army's 101st Airborne Screaming Eagles, you'll see Old Abe represented on the patch.

Some Horsey Facts

By the end of the war, the Union had purchased approximately 840,000 horses and 430,000 mules. To put this into perspective, the most Union cavalry soldiers ever fighting at one time was sixty thousand.

The price of horses rose throughout the war, from about $120 each in 1861 to about $170 each by 1865.

A trained cavalry mount's average speeds:

* walking = 100 yards per minute
* trotting = 200 yards per minute
* galloping = 400 yards per minute (equal to 15 mph)

Veteran cavalrymen learned that when their horses began nervously twitching their ears, enemy forces or raiders were probably nearby.

The last living horse of the Civil War was Old Jim, who survived a bullet in the neck to live until 1894.

Horses were included in Lee's surrender terms at Appomattox. He asked, and Grant allowed, that his men would be able to keep their horses, so they would have a means of plowing and making a living once they got back home.

Notable Numbers of Horses Shot Out From Under Commanding Officers
* Confederate Commander Nathan Bedford Forrest = 30
* Confederate Commander Joseph Wheeler = 16
* Union Commander George Custer = 11
* Union Commander William T. Sherman = 3 (all of them at Shiloh)

Favorite Horses of Union Commanders
- Benjamin Butler: Almond Eye
- Ulysses S. Grant: Cincinnati
- Joseph Hooker: Lookout
- Philip Kearny: Moscow
- George McClellan: Kentucky
- George Meade: Old Baldy
- William Sherman: Lexington

Favorite Horses of Confederate Commanders
- Patrick Cleburne: Dixie
- Richard S. Ewell: Rifle
- Nathan Bedford Forrest: King Philip
- Thomas Jackson: Old Sorrel
- Albert S. Johnston: Fire-Eater
- Robert E. Lee: Traveler
- J. E. B. Stuart: Virginia

Wirz of the Worst

The lone Confederate executed for war crimes was an obscure if notoriously cruel figure. Henry Wirz, who presided over the brutal Confederate prisoner of war camp at Andersonville, Georgia, was convicted of war crimes and sentenced to death after the Civil War. Nearly one-third of the forty-five thousand prisoners held at Andersonville died there, victims of disease, starvation, and other inhumane conditions. Wirz reveled in his reputation and touted his spiraling death count as more effective than that of the Confederate troops fighting the Union on the battlefield.

OTHER ANIMALS AT WAR, BESIDES HORSES

Although officially against the rules, many regiments included pets. The soldiers enjoyed them as a reminder of home. They also provided some entertainment and genuine affection during the long hours spent around camp between battles.

Camp pets were commonly dogs, cats, squirrels, raccoons, goats, and birds (roosters, pigeons, hens, and crows) and unusually badgers, bear cubs, and eagles. General George Custer kept several dogs with him, and included one puppy in a much-circulated photograph.

Some animals who made it into official records are:

- Sallie, a Staffordshire Bull Terrier of the 11th Pennsylvania, would not leave the dead and wounded on the battlefield; memorialized on a monument at Gettysburg National Park.
- Jeff Davis, Mongrel of the 6th Iowa
- Jack, a black and white dog of the 102nd Pennsylvania, was captured at Salem Heights.
- York, a large dog of the 3rd Illinois Cavalry, was memorialized in an engraving published in *Leslie's Illustrated Weekly.*
- Sawbuck, a black and white bird dog with the 4th Louisiana
- Douglas, a camel of the 43rd Mississippi, Company B, often spooked the horses and was killed at Vicksburg.
- Old Harvey was a white bulldog with the 104th Ohio. Other mascots of the regiment included a cat and raccoons.
- Major, a mutt with the 10th Maine/29th Maine, caught a Confederate minie ball in flight.
- Calamity, a mutt of the 28th Wisconsin Volunteer infantry helped the troops search for local food.
- Grace, a mutt with the 1st Maryland Artillery
- Jason, a donkey with the 3rd Louisiana, liked to sleep in the colonel's tent.

- Dick, a sheep of the 2nd Rhode Island, learned tricks for the soldiers, but had to be butchered to feed the men
- Stonewall, a mutt with the Richmond Howitzers, attended roll call and stood in line with the soldiers.

Lincoln's Lost Recruit

Before the Civil War began, President Lincoln made Robert E. Lee an offer he could refuse, though it pained him. Lincoln wanted Lee to lead the Union Army. Despite his belief that the Union should be preserved, as well as his personal disdain for slavery, Lee opted for the Confederacy. He declined Lincoln's offer, driven in large part by an unswerving loyalty to his home state of Virginia. A year after the war began, in 1862, Lee assumed command of the Army of Northern Virginia. He became the Confederacy's overall military commander in 1865, two months before the war ended with Lee's surrender to Grant at Appomattox.

TAKING ATLANTA

"War is cruelty, and you cannot refine it," William Sherman said in September 1864. He was responding to a plea from Atlanta politicians that the city not be forced to evacuate its citizens. Sherman captured Atlanta after a summer-long campaign of maneuvers and battles that began on the Tennessee-Georgia border three months earlier. In doing so, he delivered the 1864 election to President Lincoln.

He also introduced the concept of total war to the Confederacy. Sherman embraced a strategy that brought pain and suffering to the civilian population as well as the military enemy. Union troops seized property, food, and anything else they needed (or wanted), exacerbating Southerners' already miserable living conditions. In doing so, Sherman exacted a steep psychological toll on the popular will, sapping the South of its willingness to fight much longer.

Sherman controlled three armies encompassing close to 100,000 soldiers: the Army of the Cumberland (sixty thousand men led by George Thomas, the hero at the Battle of Chickamauga), the Army of the Tennessee (twenty-five thousand men under James B. McPherson) and the Army of the Ohio (fifteen thousand men commanded by John M. Schofield). He had been given the top role in the western theater soon after Lincoln tapped Ulysses S. Grant to lead the Army of the Potomac in March 1864.

Grant ordered Sherman to break Confederate commander Joseph E. Johnston's army, march toward the interior of the Confederacy, and damage their war resources. On May 7, Sherman and Johnston began a series of moves and countermoves—interrupted by occasional battle and skirmish—ruining the rail lines running between Chattanooga and Atlanta. Sherman made Atlanta his target because of its role as a primary transportation center (borne out in the city's original name, Terminus).

The back-and-forth maneuvers found Johnston backing up but maintaining strong defensive positions with his sixty-two thousand men. Sherman and the Union grew frustrated at their failed attempts to turn the Confederate flank. Both armies stayed in step, following one another to tiny Georgia towns such as Dalton, Resaca, and Cassville.

At Kennesaw Mountain, located just outside Atlanta, the armies engaged each other. Johnston and the Confederates enjoyed a fortified position high above the approach to the city. The Union troops under Sherman again attempted to flank the rebels. Johnston, though, expected Sherman's move, and on June 22, cut him off with forces led by John Bell Hood. But Hood grew overambitious and shifted from defensive mode to attack, incurring unnecessary casualties and sparking criticism from Johnston. On the Union side, Sherman and one of his subordinate commanders, Joseph Hooker, also began grousing at one another. Meanwhile, critics chided Sherman for not attacking the Confederates head-on. Goaded into action, Sherman mounted a disastrous assault that was turned back. The results gave the Confederates their lone victory during the Atlanta Campaign.

Undeterred, Sherman kept moving on Atlanta. Johnston again moved back while establishing a defensive position, this time along the Chattahoochee River, located on the outer edge of Atlanta. The Confederate commander wanted to drag out Sherman's inevitable victory long enough to cost Lincoln the election. He hoped that it would, perhaps, earn the South a peace negotiation with the Democratic candidate, George McClellan. That scenario would give the Confederates a resolution to the war, while possibly establishing the Confederacy as more than a temporary rebellion. It would also keep slavery alive.

Jefferson Davis and the Confederacy made a colossal blunder in mid-July, dashing any hopes inherent in Johnston's strategy by dumping him in favor of the hyper-aggressive but less-skilled Hood. In late-July, Sherman began cutting rail lines, battling Confederate troops and laying siege. Sherman remained frustrated at his lack of progress. By late-August, he feared that the standstill would allow Nathan Bedford Forrest and the rebel cavalry to sweep in and aid Hood.

On August 26, a day after Sherman ordered his men to stop firing on the Confederates in their fortifications, the Union army was gone. Hood assumed Sherman had abandoned his campaign. Instead, Sherman had taken the Union army south and cut the city's last surviving rail link, forcing Hood to flee with his troops. On September 2, Sherman claimed Atlanta.

A combination of Southern prevention and Northern aggression led to Atlanta's devastation in 1864. There were two sets of fires, with the combined effect leaving almost nothing intact. Just before the majority of Confederate troops abandoned Atlanta, Southern commander John Bell Hood ordered some of his men to destroy a Confederate train filled with ammunition, a measure designed to keep the invading Union army from making use of it. Sparks from that blaze caused extensive damage. Then in November, as Sherman prepared to make his exit and embark on the March to the Sea, he ordered Union troops to burn anything left in Atlanta that could be used for military advantage. Union troops applied a broad definition to Sherman's order. When they left several days later, little remained beyond ashes and cinders.

Southern Fried

Before William Sherman and his men began their path of destruction across Georgia and the Carolinas, the general's famed March to the Sea, the Union troops left Atlanta in tatters.

In an 1864 letter to Georgia Governor Joseph Brown, an Atlanta observer offered vivid details of the city's struggles in the wake of Sherman's claim on it three months earlier. W. P. Howard, ordered to inspect state property in Atlanta at the governor's behest, described a bleak landscape. Of usable materials, he wrote: "The [railroad] car wheels that were uninjured by fire were rendered useless by breaking the flanges. In short, every species of machinery that was not destroyed by fire was most ingeniously broken and made worthless in its original form—the large steam boilers, the switches, the frogs, etc. Nothing has escaped. "

Soon, much of the rest of the South would feel Atlanta's pain as Sherman marched onward, wreaking havoc and taking the war to the people.

MARCH TO THE SEA

With Atlanta handled, William Sherman decided to shift tactics by no longer chasing the Southern army. He had detached George Thomas to head back to Tennessee and attempt to finish off remaining Confederate forces there. Sherman set his sights on Savannah.

This was the basis for what became known as Sherman's famous—or infamous, depending upon perspective—March to the Sea in the fall of 1864. By mid-November, Sherman and his troops had left Atlanta in ruins. Having seen the psychological effect of waging a war of hardship on civilians as well as the enemy army, Sherman leaned on Ulysses Grant for permission to follow a similar strategy across Georgia.

Grant approved Sherman's plan, so Sherman set off with sixty thousand men in a march that lasted just over a month and encompassed three hundred miles. It left a staggering toll on Georgia and the Confederacy. Sherman estimated the damages at $100 million, with the Union troops destroying everything from railroad tracks to cotton mills. In fact, the twisted rails fashioned by soldiers over fires and left tied to trees became known as "Sherman neckties."

The troops lived off the land, with the men employing foraging units to seize crops, livestock, and supplies as they made their way from Atlanta to Savannah. Decimated Confederate troops put up some fight, but not much. Stragglers abounded, from slaves hoping to be emancipated by tagging along (they weren't) to poor residents hoping to get rations by helping the Union army.

The Northern troops left virtually nothing of use in their wake. They killed thousands of horses, mule, and cattle, seized nearly 10 million pounds of corn, wrecked any manufacturing sites they encountered, and disabled bridges and telegraphs along the way.

On December 22, Sherman sent Lincoln a telegraph, "I beg to present you as a Christmas gift the City of Savannah."

TENNESSEE TUSSLE

The Rock of Chickamauga, Major General George Thomas, detached from William Sherman's wrecking crew in the fall, just a few weeks removed from the dramatic taking of Atlanta. Thomas headed north, toward Tennessee.

His task was to finish off the Confederates in Tennessee. The Southern forces under John Bell Hood aimed to hit and disrupt rail supply and communication lines in Tennessee, hoping to draw Sherman's attention and score a dramatic victory over the Union forces. Instead, Sherman set out for Savannah and left Thomas to deal with Hood.

Thomas, as always, was up to the job. After taking on reinforcements in November, Thomas' Nashville-based Union forces numbered sixty thousand men. They were expecting battle with the overaggressive Hood and his forces, as well as Nathan Bedford Forrest's cavalry.

Before Hood reached Thomas in Nashville, he pursued Union troops under John Schofield, who retreated to Franklin, south of Nashville. On November 30, Hood once again committed a strategic blunder. Remember, his eagerness during the Atlanta campaign had been costly and led to a rift with erstwhile Confederate commander Joseph E. Johnston. This time, Hood pressed an ill-conceived frontal assault on Union troops tucked in with strong fortifications. Hood lost six thousand men to death and injury—three times as many casualties as the Union absorbed. The federals scored this decisive triumph in spite of being backed against the river.

Schofield continued on to Nashville, where he combined forces with Thomas, giving the Union a decisive advantage in troops. Thomas, always a deliberative commander, fell under intense pressure to pursue battle with the Confederates. Minor skirmishes at Murfreesboro and elsewhere took place while military leaders in Washington urged Thomas to take action.

Still, Thomas waited. As he readied a Union attack in early December, a winter storm forced further delays. Finally, on December 15, the Union moved against the rebel army. Over the next two days, the Union struck both Confederate flanks with varying success, and sent Hood's army scrambling out of town, heading south toward Franklin.

Thomas and his men pursued the Confederates, but the arrival of Forrest and his cavalry allowed Hood to escape. The Confederates retreated to Tupelo, Mississippi. In January 1865, Hood resigned as commander; what remained of the Army of Tennessee would have no impact on the remainder of the war.

Cluck Cluck

Robert E. Lee had an unusual traveling companion during his days leading the Army of Northern Virginia. In addition to his famous horse, Traveler, Lee nurtured a pet hen who accompanied the general on many of his military travels. The hen, according to some accounts, would often lay an egg beneath the sleeping general's cot. During Lee's lone foray into the North, culminating in the Battle of Gettysburg in the summer of 1863, Lee had his pet hen in tow.

REVENGE ON THE SECESH

William Sherman delivered Savannah as a Christmas present to President Lincoln at the end of 1864, the culmination of his March to the Sea. Next he planned to turn north and head for a reunion with Ulysses S. Grant and the Army of the Potomac in Virginia— which would certainly deliver a lethal blow to the Confederacy.

To reach Virginia, Sherman would first have to take his men through the Carolinas, starting with South Carolina, the first state to secede and home of the first battle of the war in 1861, at Fort Sumter. Aides in Washington encouraged Sherman to leave enough of a destructive impression in South Carolina to prevent future thoughts of secession and nullification. Sherman, already bent on making the civilian population feel the pain of war, needed little prodding.

"The whole army is burning with an insatiable desire to wreak vengeance upon South Carolina," Sherman said. "I almost tremble at her fate."

Sherman and his sixty thousand men arrived in Columbia, the state capital, on February 16. A day later the city surrendered. Soon after, Columbia was engulfed in flames, awash in the same destruction as Atlanta five months earlier. Resentment over Sherman's actions linger to this day in certain Southern circles, but historians dispute whether the destruction of Columbia began with Sherman's men or with cotton bales set afire by Confederates eager to keep anything of value from the Union army. Whatever the cause, it is beyond dispute that Sherman and his men left a large swath of devastation throughout Georgia and the Carolinas, looting and burning their way across the heart of the Confederacy.

Columbia's fall preceded Charleston's by a day. For the first time since April 1861, the American flag once again flew over Charleston.

THE SECOND INAUGURAL

Abraham Lincoln's most famous speech remains the Gettysburg Address, delivered at the dedication of a soldiers' cemetery at the battlefield in the fall of 1863. But many historians consider his greatest speech was delivered at the sixteenth president's second inaugural on March 4, 1865. Speaking from the East Portico of the Capitol, Lincoln faced an audience mired in mud, a result of weeks of wet weather in Washington. In his remarks, Lincoln began the long, painful process of reconciliation even as the Union and Confederacy remained at war.

The text of his remarks follows:

"Fellow Countrymen: At this second appearing to take the oath of the Presidential office there is less occasion for an extended address than there was at the first. Then a statement somewhat in detail of a course to be pursued seemed fitting and proper. Now, at the expiration of four years, during which public declarations have been constantly called forth on every point and phase of the great contest which still absorbs the attention and engrosses the energies of the nation, little that is new could be presented. The progress of our arms, upon which all else chiefly depends, is as well known to the public as to myself, and it is, I trust, reasonably satisfactory and encouraging to all. With high hope for the future, no prediction in regard to it is ventured.

"On the occasion corresponding to this four years ago all thoughts were anxiously directed to an impending civil war. All dreaded it, all sought to avert it. While the inaugural address was being delivered from this place, devoted altogether to saving the Union without war, insurgent agents were in the city seeking to destroy it without war—seeking to dissolve the Union and divide effects by negotiation. Both parties deprecated war, but one of them would make war rather than let the nation survive, and the other would accept war rather than let it perish, and the war came.

"One-eighth of the population was colored slaves, not distributed generally over the Union, but localized in the southern part of it.

These slaves constituted a peculiar and powerful interest. All knew that this interest was somehow the cause of the war. To strengthen, perpetuate, and extend this interest was the object for which the insurgents would rend the Union even by war, while the Government claimed no right to do more than to restrict the territorial enlargement of it. Neither party expected for the war the magnitude or the duration for which it has already attained. Neither anticipated that the cause of the conflict might cease with or even before the conflict itself should cease. Each looked for an easier triumph, and a result less fundamental and astounding. Both read the same Bible and pray to the same God, and each invokes His aid against the other. It may seem strange that any men should ask a just God's assistance in wringing their bread from the sweat of other men's faces, but let us judge not, that we be not judged. The prayers of both could not be answered. That of neither has been answered fully. The Almighty has His own purposes. 'Woe unto the world because of offenses; for it must needs be that offenses come, but woe to that man by whom the offense cometh.' If we shall suppose that American slavery is one of those offenses which, in the providence of God, must needs come, but which, having continued through His appointed time, He now wills to remove, and that he gives to both North and South this terrible war as the woe due to those by whom the offense came, shall we discern therein any departure from those divine attributes which the believers in a living God always ascribe to Him? Fondly do we hope, fervently do we pray, that this mighty scourge of war may speedily pass away. Yet, if God wills that it continue until all the wealth piled by the bondsman's two hundred and fifty years of unrequited toil shall be sunk, and until every drop of blood drawn with the lash shall be paid by another drawn with the sword, as was said three thousand years ago, so still it must be said, 'The judgments of the Lord are true and righteous altogether.'

"With malice toward none, with charity for all, with firmness in the right as God gives us to see the right, let us strive on to finish the work we are in, to bind up the nation's wounds, to care for him who shall have borne the battle and for his widow and his orphan, to do all which may achieve and cherish a just and a lasting peace among ourselves and with all nations."

SIEGE AND SUFFERING

As Abraham Lincoln began his second term in March 1865, Robert E. Lee's Confederate army was reeling. Lee had half as many men as Ulysses S. Grant, whose 125,000-strong force extended from Petersburg to Richmond.

Grant's siege—begun in June 1864—surrounding Petersburg had already exacted a steep toll. The Confederate soldiers lacked food, made do with shoddy uniforms and supplies, and in short, lived in horrid conditions.

Lee wanted to break the stalemate and attempted a push on Union lines to create a gap. He intended to create enough room to allow a portion of his men to break through and move out to unite with the tattered remains of Joseph E. Johnston's thirty thousand-man Army of the Tennessee.

On March 25, twelve thousand Confederates under Major General John Brown Gordon attempted just that, attacking a Union position known as Fort Stedman. After an initial, successful surge by the Confederates, the tables quickly turned. Gordon grew disoriented and could not determine where to attack, since Union troops occupied almost all of the surrounding area he had just penetrated. Those same federals soon regained momentum and meted out harsh retribution on the Confederates. Gordon lost one-third of his men to casualties, and the rebel army remained stuck in Petersburg with little prospect for breaking out. The Civil War was all but over.

CIVIL WAR BATTLE TIMELINE: 1865

January 13–15: Attack and capture of Fort Fisher, North Carolina

February 5–7: Battle of Hatcher's Run (Siege of Petersburg)

February 22: Capture of Wilmington, North Carolina

March 8–10: Battle of Kinston, North Carolina (Sherman's Carolinas Campaign)

March 16: Battle of Averasboro, North Carolina (Sherman's Carolinas Campaign)

March 19–21: Battle of Bentonville, North Carolina (Sherman's Carolinas Campaign)

March 22–April 22: Wilson's Alabama and Georgia Raid

March 23–April 23: Stoneman's North Carolina and Virginia Raid

March 25: Battle of Fort Stedman (Siege of Petersburg)

March 27–April 8: Siege of Spanish Fort (Mobile Campaign, Alabama)

April 1: Battle of Five Forks (Siege of Petersburg)

April 2: Petersburg lines breached (Siege of Petersburg)

April 2: Confederates evacuate Richmond and Petersburg

April 2: Battle of Selma, Alabama

April 2–9: Siege and Capture of Fort Blakely (Mobile Campaign, Alabama)

April 3: U.S. forces occupy Richmond

April 6: Battle of Sayler's Creek, Virginia

April 9: Lee surrenders at Appomattox Court House

April 12: Surrender of Mobile

April 13: Raleigh, North Carolina, occupied (Sherman's Carolinas Campaign)

April 14: Lincoln shot by John Wilkes Booth

April 18: Confederate General Joseph E. Johnston surrenders in North Carolina

May 4: Confederate Lieutenant General Richard Taylor surrenders in Alabama

May 12–13: Battle of Palmito Ranch, Texas

May 26: Confederate Lieutenant General E. Kirby Smith surrenders in New Orleans

June 23: Confederate Brigadier General Stand Watie surrenders at Doaksville, Indian Territory

Thank You Very Much

Elvis Presley hailed from the heart of the Confederacy—Tupelo, Mississippi—and yet one of his biggest hits borrowed the melody from a Civil War ballad beloved by the Union president. "Aura Lee," written by W. W. Fosdick and George Poulton, was used as part of "Love Me Tender," one of the King of Rock and Roll's many hit singles. President Lincoln counted "Aura Lee" among his favorite songs, along with, yes, "Dixie." Look away, Southerners: "Dixie" was not only a Lincoln favorite, it was written by a Yankee and featured during Lincoln's inauguration.

FIVE FORKS

Union commander Ulysses S. Grant kept increased pressure on Robert E. Lee and his weary, worn-out troops during the lengthy siege of Petersburg. As Grant stretched his seemingly inexhaustible supply of men into positions that created longer and longer lines, Lee found his army all but decimated.

Competing with the Union's deep resources was all but impossible, and Lee's pain was exacerbated by the shrewd general he now faced. Grant, unlike his predecessors, avoided rash, suicidal assaults, removing a key intangible—cautious and inept strategy—that had long worked in Lee's favor.

Those dynamics created a crucial confrontation for the two armies at Five Forks, a rail center valued for its critical supply-line connections. Lee also planned to use the Five Forks rail junction as a link with Joseph E. Johnston's Army of the Tennessee, now located in North Carolina.

George Pickett, the man whose resentment toward Lee would linger for years in the wake of his disastrous charge at Gettysburg, led ten thousand men to defend Five Forks for the Confederates. His opponent was Phil Sheridan, backed by twelve thousand federals.

The fight was hardly a fight at all. Sheridan's men had little trouble blasting Pickett's forces to bits. It marked yet another devastating defeat—and provided the latest evidence of the Confederacy's ever-dwindling prospects.

CONFEDERATE COMMANDERS: STATES RIGHTS GIST (1831-1864)

That is His Real Name

Yes, this Confederate General's given name was really "States Rights." Father Gist chose a name for his child that made it very clear on which side Papa fell in the debate between states' rights and national unity. It's a good thing Little Gist agreed with Daddy Gist, because that would be tough to explain otherwise.

Gist's Antebellum Activities

- Education — Graduated from South Carolina College (the University of South Carolina) and Harvard Law School
- Occupation — Practiced law in South Carolina
- Military Experience — Brigadier General in the South Carolina militia, training his countrymen for inevitable war; after South Carolina seceded, served as the state's Inspector General, responsible for gathering arms to attack Fort Sumter.
- Civil War Rank — Promoted to Brigadier General of the Confederate Army in 1862.

Gist's Civil War Service

- Fort Sumter — Although he did not take the first shot, Gist was in charge of the Confederate batteries.
- First Battle of Bull Run — A volunteer aide to Brigadier General Barnard Bee, Gist temporarily took over command when Bee was killed.
- Wounded in action — Chickamauga, Atlanta campaign, Franklin
- Other battles — Wilmington, Chattanooga, Vicksburg, Missionary Ridge

Just in case you didn't know, the word antebellum literally means "before the war."

Gist's Last Battle

Gist commanded a brigade under Major General John Brown during General Hood's Franklin campaign. Leading his brigade into battle, Gist was killed. He was one of six Confederate generals killed in action that day.

Gist's Family Connections

- His brother Joseph was a brigadier in the militia and a major in the 15th South Carolina.
- His cousin William Henry Gist was South Carolina's Governor, 1858–1860.
- Second cousin William Murena (William Henry's son), a major of the 15th, was killed in action at Knoxville.

Moving the Focus Northward

Where do you think the northernmost action of the Civil War took place? If you thought Gettysburg or Chambersburg in Pennsylvania, then you were thinking in terms of battles. Think raids. A group of Confederate agents raided the small quiet town of St. Albans, Vermont, on Lake Champlain, only fifteen miles south of the Canadian border.

It was an example of desperate measures called upon by desperate times. In 1863, the Confederate secretary of the Navy sent more than sixty officers to Canada to organize raids along the Canadian border. These men included C. C. Clay, Jr., George Saunders, Bennett Young, and John Wilkes Boothe.

The idea was to create such a disturbance on the Northern frontier that troops would be called away from the lines in the South to defend the Northern states. They planned to raid accessible Vermont towns, beginning with St. Albans. They also wanted to get some satisfaction after the burning of Atlanta.

CONFEDERATE COMMANDERS: EARL VAN DORN (1820-1863)

Earl Van Dorn is better known for how he died than for his achievements in battle. Unfortunately, he did not die a hero's death. But since that's what he's most famous for, we'll start his story at the end.

In 1863, while sitting at his desk in his Spring Hill, Tennessee, office, Van Dorn was shot in the back of the head. The gunman: Dr. George Peters. The motive: Peters said that Van Dorn was having an affair with his wife, Jessie Peters, while the good doctor was out of town. To be fair, Van Dorn did have a reputation as a womanizer. Some reports say that Van Dorn was even writing a pass for Dr. Peters when he was shot.

Dr. Peters was arrested for murder, but when the circumstances were revealed, was released. Dr. Peters was never tried for shooting Earl Van Dorn.

Here's where it gets sticky, though. Some say that Dr. Peters was a Northern sympathizer, and that's why he killed Van Dorn. Later, Dr. Peters divorced Jessie, but then they both turned up in Arkansas at the same time and reunited. Dr. Peters had received a federal land grant in that state, under circumstances that were never satisfactorily explained. So draw your own conclusions about the real motive.

Nevertheless, Van Dorn was the only Civil War officer killed in uniform by a jealous husband.

Other Not-Quite-As-Interesting Facts About Earl Van Dorn

- His great-uncle, Andrew Jackson, secured him an appointment to West Point, where he graduated fifty-second in his class of fifty-six in 1842. The West Point Class of '42 included seventeen future Civil War generals, Confederate and Union.
- At school, Van Dorn spent more time in mischief than studying, and his grades showed it. But he was a good horseman and soldier. He even displayed talent in drawing and watercolor

painting, although he spent time enjoying horse racing and excessive drinking.

- During the Mexican War, Van Dorn was badly wounded in the arm, stomach, and lung. He was highly decorated for his bravery.
- Confederate President Jefferson Davis offered both Generals Henry Heth and Braxton Bragg command of the western Mississippi River area. After they each turned it down, Van Dorn was tapped and accepted.
- Van Dorn, along with two other cavalry officers—none of them sailors—captured the *Star of the West* after it ran aground off the coast of Texas. *Star of the West* was the ship sent to resupply Fort Sumter, but was forced to turn back under fire from Citadel cadets, before the war officially started.
- Van Dorn's friends called him "Buck." However, his men called him General "Damn Born," and more than once accused him of negligence, disregarding their welfare, and failing to adequately plan a campaign. After Confederate disasters at Pea Ridge and Corinth, Van Dorn was tried in a court of inquiry. The court ruled negligence on his part, and he was never again trusted to command an army.
- Van Dorn was had a thing for the ladies, even though he was married himself. In Vicksburg, a newspaper article described him as "the terror of ugly husbands."
- Van Dorn was described as a handsome, blue-eyed blond. Although he was only five feet, five inches tall, he looked the part of the dashing Southern soldier romanticized in Civil War literature today.
- Van Dorn married Caroline Godbold, the daughter of a prominent Alabama plantation owner. They had a son and a daughter.

ACTION IN ST. ALBANS, OCTOBER 1864

Prelude: The Union army had just left town after purchasing seven hundred horses. The horse traders, shopkeepers, and banks were full of money.

Poor Security: Almost forty local politicians were away at the state legislature session. The town's lawyers were also away, as the Supreme Court was meeting.

The Uprising: Bennett Young and two other young men checked into Tremont House Hotel. Their cover story was that they were hunters on vacation from Canada. More men arrived in twos and threes over the next few days, some staying at the Tremont House, others at the American Hotel.

All were young, ages twenty to twenty-eight. They were friendly, showing an interest in firearms and horses—in keeping with their hunting story. No one in the little Vermont village suspected a thing.

Then with a flourish, the men threw off their overcoats. In his Confederate uniform, Young declared the city a possession of the Confederate States of America. Raiders stormed the three banks (St. Albans Bank, Franklin County Bank, and First National Bank), threatening tellers with their pistols. Young even forced the tellers to take an oath of allegiance to the Confederacy and Jefferson Davis.

In the meantime, other Confederates gathered the townspeople on the village green and stole their horses. They took saddle and bridle gear from the local leather shop. In all, they gathered about $200,000 in gold, and left about twice that much behind, all without firing a shot.

The Getaway: To keep the townspeople from fighting his men, Young ordered the town set on fire. They were armed with a new chemical hand grenade called "Greek fire." But there was no spectacular explosion (one raider even lit one in the American Hotel's water closet—aka restroom—but it didn't work, either).

The raiders rode their stolen horses all the way back to Canada.

The Vermont militia, led by Captain George P. Conger, eventually caught up with them, and the bank robbers were arrested. But Canada, known for its Southern sympathies, refused to extradite the men. They were tried in a Montreal court.

The Brilliant Defense: Canadian officials declared Young's men were soldiers under military orders. This defense was helped out by some hastily written orders supplied by Confederate Secretary of State Judah Benjamin. Therefore the raiders were accused of only violating Canada's neutrality. They were then acquitted and freed.

The Canadian government returned about $88,000 to the St. Albans banks. Young claimed that the entire $200,000 was turned over to Confederate Commissioners near Niagara Falls, Canada. Do you think he was implying that something else happened to the rest of it while in Canadian hands?

Bennett Henderson Young

A Kentucky native, Young participated in General John Hunt Morgan's 1863 raids through Indiana and Ohio. He was captured and imprisoned at Camp Douglas near Chicago. After escaping from Camp Douglas, he fled to Canada.

At the war's end, Young was excluded from President Johnson's amnesty proclamation. He spent several years abroad before returning to Kentucky to a successful law practice. Reports say he led an exemplary post-war life, never drinking, smoking, or swearing.

TARGETING THE NORTH, BUT NOT!

Confederate Secretary of State Judah Benjamin decided it was time to stir some conflict up North by targeting strategic cities such as New York City.

Eight Confederate agents, ticked off over the devastation in Atlanta and the Shenandoah Valley, were eager to retaliate by burning New York City hotels and other locations frequented by wealthy citizens.

Let's look at the plot described here in a November 27, 1864, *New York Times* article for its complete ineptness: "The plan was excellently well conceived, and evidently prepared with great care, and had it been executed with one-half the ability with which it was drawn up, no human power could have saved this city from utter destruction."

Like the boys in Vermont, the New York raiders began by checking into various hotels under alias names. They were armed with 140 "Greek fire" bombs, expected to explode when exposed to air.

The raiders did not know how to work the "Greek fire" grenades, and the chemical did not ignite properly. All they managed to do was set some pesky trash fires in about ten different hotels throughout the city.

They also caused a nuisance at the American Museum, Niblo's Theater, the Winter Garden Theater, and Barnum's Museum. At Barnum's, the damage consisted mainly of scaring a few animals and the seven-foot-tall woman. The fires were quickly put out, and the raiders fled to Canada.

One raider was later caught. Robert Cobb Kennedy, who had been expelled from West Point, was hung as a spy on March 25, 1865, in Fort Lafayette in New York Harbor. Heading the military commission that tried Kennedy, General John A. Dix wrote, "The attempt to set fire to the city of New York is one of the greatest atrocities of the age."

JOSIAH GORGAS: UNSUNG HERO, GENIUS (1818-1883)

General Josiah Gorgas has been called an "unsung hero," a "genius," an "extraordinary administrator," and many other complimentary superlatives applicable to a man who all but worked miracles in his service to the Confederacy. Gorgas's devotion to the South is all the more touching when considering he was one of the few Northerners who chose to side with the South after secession. Born in tiny Running Pumps, Pennsylvania, to a life of poverty, he managed to get an appointment to West Point and graduate sixth in the Class of '41.

After West Point, Gorgas joined the U.S. Army, specializing in ordnance, an efficient word for "getting and distributing military supplies, including weapons, ammunition, and combat vehicles." Gorgas spent about twenty years learning almost everything there is to know about acquiring arms, and he eventually rose to the rank of captain. Along the way, he met and married the lovely daughter of a wealthy plantation owner and moved to the South himself.

So when the South seceded, Gorgas was well-equipped (no pun intended) to take on the position of the Confederate Army's chief of ordnance. It was a challenge—considering the limited resources in that part of the country—but Gorgas rose to the occasion brilliantly.

At the beginning of the Civil War, the South only had one foundry that could handle manufacturing heavy artillery and only a couple of factories making rifles. Gorgas applied admirable ingenuity to acquire raw materials and produce weapons and powder.

- He supervised construction of arsenals, foundries, rolling mills, and factories throughout the South (for instance, the Tredegar Iron Works in Richmond produced 2,200 cannon).
- He found supplies of pig iron, sulfur, saltpeter, and other materials needed for manufacturing railroad track and weapons.

- He encouraged private entrepreneurs to manufacture rifles and pistols.
- He purchased arms from dealers in Europe and even from those in the North willing to make money on the war effort (the Ordnance Bureau under Gorgas was prepared to pay well for weapons and didn't care where the money went).
- He used his own fleet of blockade runners to smuggle foreign weapons into Southern ports.
- He instructed soldiers to seize from the enemy all of the usable small arms and artillery that they could (one year, Confederate soldiers collected more than 100,000 Union rifles).
- He appealed to Southern civilians for raw materials, such as iron, to make weapons from.
- He even explained to farmers how they could save animal manure and human waste to transform into niter.

The Ordnance Bureau was known for efficiency in delivering weapons and materials to the field, where they were needed. The Confederate Army suffered from lack of food, clothes, and other items. But under Josiah Gorgas's direction, Confederate forces never lost a major battle for lack of munitions.

Because of his outstanding performance in the face of daunting odds, Gorgas was promoted from major to lieutenant colonel, then to colonel, and finally to brigadier general.

After the war, Gorgas managed an Alabama ironworks from 1865 to 1869. Some credit Birmingham, Alabama's post-war emergence as a leading steel center to the genius of Josiah Gorgas.

Then Gorgas turned his attention to education, first teaching at the University of the South, in Tennessee, and becoming vice-chancellor there in 1872. In 1878, he returned to Alabama to serve as president of the University of Alabama. In bad health, he resigned a year later, and died in 1883 in Tuscaloosa, Alabama.

UNION COMMANDERS: OLIVER OTIS HOWARD (1830-1909)

O. O. Howard was an abolitionist, 1855 West Point graduate, and a math professor when he enlisted. He fought in the Peninsula Campaign, First and Second Bull Runs, Antietam, Fredericksburg, Chancellorsville, and Gettysburg.

Howard lost his right arm at Fair Oaks during the Peninsula campaign. After that, he preferred head-and-shoulders portraits so his empty sleeve was unapparent. The wound did not keep him out of battle. His leadership at Gettysburg earned him the Thanks of Congress. Accepting the document, Howard simply offered his left hand.

During the Atlanta Campaign, Sherman ordered by-then Major General Howard around the western side of Atlanta to sever Hood's communication lines. Hood fought back, protecting the railroad, but Hood was overwhelmingly outnumbered and so fell back. Howard later marched with Sherman to the sea.

General Oliver Otis Howard headed the Bureau of Refugees, Freedmen, and Abandoned Lands, an agency charged with transitioning freed slaves into a world of freedom. The agency was accused of corruption, and after a congressional inquiry, Howard was cleared of any wrongdoing.

Howard University

While with the Freedmen's Bureau, Howard used agency financial support to found several schools, including an all-black college in Washington, D.C. Originally conceived as a theological seminary for educating African-American clergymen, the college opened with the specific goal of training black lawyers, doctors, dentists, and teachers.

Howard served as president of the school named in his honor from 1869 to 1874. Today it is a premier university.

FATHER RYAN AND "THE CONQUERED BANNER"

A Southerner of Irish background, Catholic priest Abram Joseph Ryan enlisted in the Confederate Army and served as chaplain throughout the war. From his experiences on the battlefield, tending to the wounded and performing last rites, Ryan began to express his thoughts in verse. He wrote his first poem upon learning his brother had been killed in action.

Father Ryan soon became known as the "poet-priest" of the Confederacy; his best-remembered poem "The Conquered Banner" won national recognition. An excerpt:

Furl that Banner, for 'tis weary;
Round its staff 'tis drooping dreary;
 Furl it, fold it, it is best;
For there's not a man to wave it,
And there's not a sword to save it,
And there's no one left to lave it
In the blood that heroes gave it;
And its foes now scorn and brave it;
 Furl it, hide it—let it rest! [. . .]

Furl that banner! furl it sadly!
Once ten thousands hailed it gladly.
And ten thousands wildly, madly,
 Swore it should forever wave;
Swore that foeman's sword should never
Hearts like theirs entwined dissever,
Till that flag should float forever
 O'er their freedom or their grave!

Furl it! for the hands that grasped it,
And the hearts that fondly clasped it,
Cold and dead are lying low;
And that Banner—it is trailing!
While around it sounds the wailing
 Of its people in their woe. [. . .]

Furl that banner, softly, slowly!
Treat it gently—it is holy—
For it droops above the dead.
Touch it not—unfold it never,
Let it droop there, furled forever,
For its people's hopes are dead!

Thanks of Congress

These were resolutions passed by the Senate during the Civil War to recognize impressive action by military commanders. In receiving the Thanks of Congress after Gettysburg, Howard joined the ranks of such well-known generals as Ulysses Grant, Ambrose Burnside, Joseph Hooker, William T. Sherman, Philip Sheridan, and David Porter.

CONFEDERATE COMMANDERS: JOSEPH EGGLESTON JOHNSTON (1807-1891)

Background: Virginia native, 1829 West Point graduate

Military Experience: Seminole War, Mexican War, Kansas unrest

Civil War Ranking: Entered May 1860 as Brigadier General; switched to C.S.A. Army in 1861 as a Major General before being promoted to full General

Battles Participated In: First Bull Run, Yorktown, Williamsburg, Seven Days, Seven Pines, Stones River, Vicksburg, Chickamauga, Chattanooga, and Atlanta

Civil War First: To Johnston goes the distinction of being the first commander in history to strategically use the railroad for moving troops to position his men at Bull Run.

Johnston and Jefferson Davis: Johnston started out as Davis's commander in the East. At first everything was fine, but it seems that Davis was a micromanager. Johnston was put off by the president's detailed orders. In turn, Davis thought Johnston was spending too much money to accomplish his detailed orders.

In fact, when Johnston wrote his memoirs in 1874, he made sure to criticize how Davis (and other Southern generals) handled the Confederate military. When Davis published his own memoirs in 1881, he laid much of the blame for the Confederacy's losses on Johnston and P. G. T. Beauregard.

Davis so disliked Johnston, that when reviewing other incompetent generals, he would let their command stand if Johnston was the logical replacement. When Johnston was wounded in the Battle of Seven Pines outside Richmond, Davis quickly took the opportunity to replace him with General Robert E. Lee.

While Davis wasn't a fan, Johnston's men worshiped him for his fair treatment of his soldiers.

Wounded at Seven Pines: While riding on the front lines at twilight, Johnston was hit twice by Union fire, taking a bullet in the shoulder and shrapnel in the chest. The wounds were serious but not fatal.

The Army of Tennessee: General Bragg finally resigned after the Chattanooga disaster. Davis reluctantly charged Johnston with the Army of Tennessee, facing a much larger army under Union General Sherman.

With the 1864 U.S. presidential election coming up, and Abe Lincoln sinking in the polls, Johnston figured his best bet would be to avoid a major defeat, which was certain based on the numbers. To avoid defeat, his strategy was to avoid a battle. He figured that, without any momentum to spur on war fever, perhaps Northerners tired of the war might not reelect Lincoln. In Johnston's scenario, whoever beat Lincoln would end the war.

This in mind, Johnston decided to frustrate Sherman with little skirmishes here and there, advancing, dropping back, and advancing again. Unfortunately, he also ticked off Davis, who was quick to label Johnston a coward.

Davis fired Johnston, replacing him with John Bell Hood. Hood turned around and let Sherman capture and burn Atlanta.

Defending Richmond: Lee reappointed Johnston to lead Confederate forces in the Carolinas. Johnston gamely tried to halt Sherman's relentless advance but was grossly outnumbered. Lee tried to get his troops there to help out, but Grant blocked Lee's movements at every turn.

Johnston surrendered to Sherman almost a month after Lee met Grant at Appomattox. That same day, presidential assassin John Wilkes Booth was captured and killed.

The End: Johnston and Sherman developed a fast friendship after the war. When Sherman died in 1891, Johnston served as a pallbearer at the service, saying Sherman would have done the same for him. It was a bitterly cold day, and Johnston refused to wear a hat out of respect for Sherman. The old Confederate General caught pneumonia. Six weeks later, he died himself.

SPRING CLEANING

The Union finally began making progress after nine months of laying siege to Petersburg. On April 2, an attack by federal troops produced a decisive push, and Robert E. Lee had to evacuate his Confederate army. Beyond that, the Southern cause lost another general as A. P. Hill was killed in the fighting.

Those events led to the abandonment of Richmond. At last, the Confederate capital was ripe for the Union's picking. Jefferson Davis received word of Petersburg's collapse during a church service in Richmond. It convinced Davis to take his cabinet and government officials on an impromptu road trip. They retreated to Danville, Virginia, near the North Carolina border.

While Confederate officials sought safe havens and refuge, their capital devolved into chaos. Stores were looted, citizens scrambled to make hasty escapes, and everything from public drunkenness to open robbery roared before the looming horror of certain defeat. Richmond, much like cities in Georgia and across the Carolinas, became engulfed in flames. Confederate efforts to blow up docked ironclads led to inadvertent blazes in other parts of the city. Tobacco warehouses along the James River—near the ironclads—caught fire and the flames spread quickly. Sizable chunks of Richmond became heaps of cinders and ashes.

On April 3, President Lincoln joined Grant in the now-abandoned city of Petersburg. A day later, Lincoln walked the streets of Richmond, where he took time to visit the Confederate White House. The president was greeted with quiet indifference from white residents and rapturous praise from the soon-to-be freed slaves.

LAST GASP

Honor and duty demanded Robert E. Lee not give up the fight, despite the inevitability of surrender to the Union. Lee hoped to buy some time and better negotiating terms for the Confederates. He aimed to unite his troops with the Army of the Tennessee—located in North Carolina. At this point, Lee's Army of Northern Virginia consisted of fifty thousand bone-weary men. To make matters worse, they set on yet another arduous march without any rations, the result of bungled orders. Lee divided his army, heading west from Petersburg.

The Union troops in pursuit included a brigade led by George Custer, destined for an infamous, fatal attack on Native Americans at Little Bighorn in 1876. A series of small, ineffective Confederate skirmishes followed, with Union cavalry leader Phil Sheridan hitting the rebel army hard as often as possible. At Amelia Springs, Sayler's Creek, and other outposts, the Confederate army suffered additional casualties and endured the loss of supplies and wagons to Sheridan and federal troops.

Lee was being hemmed in, left to scramble away from the inescapable Union victory. By April 9, the Confederate army had dwindled to thirty thousand men.

They were located between Appomattox Court House and Appomattox Station, not far from Lynchburg, Virginia. Lee and his army had choice. The Confederate commander had no desire for additional casualties. Lee decided to surrender: "There is nothing left me but to go and see General Grant, and I had rather die a thousand deaths."

FAREWELL

Text from Robert E. Lee's final order to the Army of Northern Virginia upon completion of his surrender to Ulysses S. Grant and the Army of the Potomac:

Hd Qrs Army Northern Virginia
10th April 1865
General Order
No 9

After four years of arduous service, marked by unsurpassed courage and fortitude, the Army of Northern Virginia has been compelled to yield to overwhelming numbers and resources.

I need not tell the brave survivors of so many hard fought battles who have remained steadfast to the last, that I have consented to this result from no distrust of them, but feeling that valor and devotion could accomplish nothing that would compensate for the loss that would have attended the continuance of the contest, I determined to avoid the useless sacrifice of those whose past services have endeared them to their Countrymen.

By the terms of the Agreement, officers and men can return to their homes and remain there until exchanged. You will take with you the satisfaction that proceeds from the consciousness of duty faithfully performed, and I earnestly pray that a Merciful God will extend to you His blessing and protection.

With an unceasing admiration of your constancy and devotion to your country, and a grateful remembrance of your kind and generous consideration of myself, I bid you all an affectionate farewell.

R E Lee
Genl.

THEY'RE BACK

Remember Wilmer McLean? He was the man whose Virginia farm had the misfortune of being located on what became the Bull Run battlefield in Manassas in 1861. During that battle, the first significant action of the war, a shell exploded in McLean's farmhouse. Frustrated by that series of unfortunate events, McLean moved soon after to what he considered a distant place unlikely to be sullied by war: Appomattox Court House.

As Robert E. Lee readied for a personal negotiation with Ulysses S. Grant on April 9, 1865, to end the war, he sent an aide, Colonel Charles Marshall, to find a suitable meeting place. Marshall went to Appomattox Court House and addressed the first person he saw. It was Wilmer McLean. Soon enough, the men decided that McLean's house would be used for the meeting.

With that, as Civil War documentarian Ken Burns and others have noted, McLean claimed the mantle of having the Civil War begin in his front yard and end in his parlor.

At the McLean house, Lee and Grant met in the early afternoon. Lee arrived first, followed a half-hour later by Grant. Both men had staffers in the room during their conversation, which began with a handshake greeting.

Surprised by the earlier-than-expected Confederate surrender, Grant had only a rough field uniform to wear. By contrast, Lee, who told an aide that he expected to become Grant's prisoner, brandished a regal sword and wore a new, formal military uniform just for the somber occasion.

The two men discoursed on their shared past in the Mexican War, when Lee had held a higher ranking. Grant was uncertain whether Lee would remember him at all. Soon enough, they fell into a brief reverie.

"Our conversation grew so pleasant that I almost forgot the object of our meeting," Grant wrote in his memoirs twenty years later. "After the conversation had run on in this style for some time,

General Lee called my attention to the object of our meeting, and said that he had asked for this interview for the purpose of getting from me the terms I proposed to give his army."

Grant proved magnanimous in triumph. The federals allowed the Confederate soldiers to keep their horses (Grant said they would need them to plant crops in order to replace the ravaged agricultural landscape left in the war's wake), personal possessions, and sidearms. No treason charges were made against the rebel army, either. Lee was not to become a prisoner, remaining free just as his soldiers did. They were allowed to return home.

Grant, at Lee's request, also provided rations for the starving Confederate army. Although some troops remained in the field elsewhere, Lee's surrender effectively ended the Civil War after four bloody years and more than 600,000 soldiers' deaths.

Man on the Run: Davis' Southern Swing

A week before Ulysses S. Grant and Robert E. Lee met at Appomattox to end the Civil War on April 9, 1865, Confederate President Jefferson Davis went on the lam.

Davis fled Richmond—he had relocated the capital to Virginia in May 1861 after an abbreviated tenure in Montgomery, Alabama—by train and headed for Danville, Virginia. From there, employing subterfuge and hoping to unite enough troops to mount another battle, Davis went on the run for a month before being captured by Union forces in Georgia. He was apprehended only five days after a meeting between Davis and his cabinet that had dissolved the Confederate government. Davis served two years in a Virginia prison before benefactors raised enough money to have him freed.

Authorities indicted Davis on treason charges, but he never went to trial. In 1869, the charges were dropped, though Davis was stripped of his citizenship. A 1978 Congressional Act posthumously restored those rights to Davis, who died at eighty-one in 1889.

DARKEST DAY

Less than a week after the meeting at Appomattox Court House ended the Civil War, Abraham Lincoln decided to take in a popular play as part of a rare night of leisure.

The play was *Our American Cousin*, performed at Ford's Theatre in Washington. The Lincolns invited General Ulysses S. Grant and his wife, Julia, but the Grants declined the invitation. The president and his wife decided to attend the play anyway.

Several days before the Lincolns headed for Ford's Theatre, the president told his wife and a few other close friends of a strange recent nightmare in which the president, Lincoln, had been assassinated.

John Wilkes Booth, a popular young actor with a well-known hatred of Lincoln, had a similar dream, with one major exception—the notion of a dead Lincoln was anything but a nightmare for him. Booth had long agitated for the Confederacy. During 1864 and 1865, Booth and a motley crew of conspirators had attempted to kidnap Lincoln and envisioned other methods of aiding the doomed Confederacy.

With the war over, Booth no longer wanted to kidnap the president; Booth wanted to kill him.

He cooked up a plot that called for co-conspirators to kill Vice President Andrew Johnson and Secretary of State William Seward. In the case of Johnson, the man assigned to kill him had second thoughts and never made an attempt. As for Seward, he and several family members were attacked by Lewis Powell, a former Confederate soldier who had signed on with Booth's band of Southern sympathizers. The secretary of state, and everyone else injured in the attack, recovered.

Booth fared better than his comrades. At 10:15 p.m., Booth entered the president's box and shot him in the back of the head, firing on the president at the time of the play's signature joke, a guarantee that the distracted audience would not hear the shot. He then stabbed Major Henry Rathbone in the arm while scuffling with Rathbone, who was also seated in the presidential box.

What happened next is familiar to most Americans, but remains startling nonetheless. Booth leaped from the box to the stage, breaking his left leg in the process, and yelled out the Virginia state motto: Sic semper tyrannis ("Thus ever to tyrants"). Onlookers were so shocked at what had happened that they failed to give chase to Booth as he dashed out of the theater. He was on the lam for nearly two weeks before troops caught and shot him at a Virginia tobacco farm. Booth died on April 26.

The fallen president was taken across the street to the home of William Petersen. Doctors on hand had already confirmed they could do nothing to save Lincoln. At 7:22 a.m. on April 15, Lincoln died. Secretary of War Edwin M. Stanton, upon Lincoln's death, declared, "Now he belongs to the ages." Some historians argue that Stanton actually said, "Now he belongs to the angels."

Either way, he was right.

Hang 'Em High

Federal forces shot and killed John Wilkes Booth on a Virginia farm, but what of his co-conspirators? Seven of the eight were caught soon after the president's assassination. Of the seven arrested, four were sentenced to hang, including Mary Surratt, whose boardinghouse served as a de facto headquarters for Booth and his fellow plotters. Mary Surratt became the first woman in American history sentenced to hang. Three other conspirators were sent to prison, with one dying inside and the one paroled. As for the escaped conspirator, John Surratt (son of Mary), he was acquitted after spending two years on the run evading U.S. authorities.

IMPOSSIBLE TO REPLACE

President Lincoln's death vaulted Andrew Johnson into the White House, a stunning turn of events. Johnson, after all, had been part of the Lincoln reelection ticket in 1864 as an afterthought, included mainly to win over moderate voters as a Democrat. A Tennessean, Johnson's political resume included stints as a congressman, governor, and U.S. senator. When Tennessee seceded, Johnson remained loyal to the Union, a position that earned him the position of military governor when Union troops seized control of Tennessee during the Civil War.

Johnson lacked his predecessor's political acumen as well as his personal bonhomie. The result was predictable. Radical Republicans in Congress trampled on Johnson, who attempted to retain some of Lincoln's plans for Reconstruction. Congress overrode Johnson's vetoes to push reconstruction forward. Those battles led to the eventual impeachment showdown.

Too Young to Enlist

Although statistics from the Confederate Army are not available, researchers say about ten thousand underage boys enlisted on the Union side, where 127 soldiers were thirteen when they enlisted; 320 were fourteen, almost eight hundred were fifteen, more than 2,750 were sixteen, and about 6,500 were seventeen.

Recruiters were more concerned about filling their quotas than about an authentic birth certificate. They were more willing to take a tall, healthy farm boy (or a puny one, for that matter) at his word than to require proof of age. Because of this, young boys figured out how to avoid outright lying when saying they were "over eighteen:" they would write "18" on a piece of paper and put it in their shoe. That way, they would be standing "over 18."

JOHN LINCOLN "JOHNNY" CLEM TOP TEN LIST

1. When he was nine years old, Johnny Clem tried to join an Ohio army regiment. Because of his age, Johnny was sent home.
2. Later Johnny "joined" the 22nd Michigan unit, tagging along as they marched through town. They allowed him to remain as their drummer boy and camp "go-fer." Before long, the soldiers developed a genuine fondness for the boy and each chipped in to pay him $13 a month, the going rate for a soldier's wage.
3. During the Battle of Shiloh in April 1862, shellfire destroyed Johnny's drum. Newspaper reporters called him "Johnny Shiloh," and a battlefield song was written about him.
4. By September 1863, Clem was officially enrolled in the army. His comrades supplied him a downsized musket. During the Battle of Chickamauga, ten-year-old Clem shot a Confederate soldier who tried to capture him and shot another Confederate trying to take the caisson he rode on. Newspapers called him "The Drummer Boy of Chickamauga." General George H. Thomas promoted him to lance corporal.
5. In October 1863, while guarding a train, Clem was captured by Confederates and exchanged soon thereafter. He was promoted to sergeant.
6. Clem also participated in the battles of Perryville, Murfreesboro, and Atlanta.
7. After the war, Clem tried to enroll in West Point but, lacking a formal education, was unable to pass the admission exam.
8. In 1871, President Grant personally commissioned Clem as second lieutenant commanding a unit of black soldiers.
9. Clem spent his life in a military career, retiring as a major general just before World War I.
10. Clem died in 1937, and was buried with full military honors at Arlington National Cemetery in Washington, D.C.

Memorials to Johnny Clem

- A Newark, Ohio, public school is named John Clem Elementary School.
- In 1963, The Wonderful World of Disney released *Johnny Shiloh*, starring Brian Keith and Kevin Corcoran.

The Drummer Boy of Shiloh

On Shiloh's dark and bloody ground
The dead and wounded lay,
Amongst them was a drummer boy
Who beat the drums that day.
A wounded soldier held him up
His drum was by his side;
He clasped his hands, then raised his eyes
And prayed before he died.
He clasped his hands, then raised his eyes
And prayed before he died. [. . .]

Ye angels round the Throne of Grace,
Look down upon the braves
Who fought and died on Shiloh's plain,
Now slumb'ring in their graves!
How many homes made desolate?
How many hearts have sighed?
How many, like that drummer boy,
Who prayed before they died;
How many, like that drummer boy,
Who prayed before they died!

BROTHER VERSUS BROTHER

Much has been said about the Civil War pitting brother against brother. But it was also about father versus son and uncle against nephew, even mother versus son and friend against friend. Close relationships were destroyed during this war.

Border states were already conflicted in their beliefs, both pro- and anti-slavery. Families living there were ripped apart as their members took different sides. Even as they marched off to war, the men knew there was a good probability the next time they saw each other, it would be on opposite sides of a battlefield.

Most of the trained military boys were West Point graduates. When the war started, more than three hundred U.S. Army officers resigned to support the cause of the Confederacy. This meant that on any given battlefield, the possibility was high that the commanding officers had once been classmates.

Examples of "Brother versus Brother" run from the highest-ranking officials to the everyday man:

- President Abraham Lincoln: Lincoln's wife, Mary Todd Lincoln, was from the border state of Kentucky and rumored to have Southern sympathies. Her youngest brother, three half-brothers, and three brothers-in-law all fought in the Confederate Army. In fact, her West Point graduate brother-in-law, Ben Hardin Helm, turned down Lincoln's personal offer of a Union Army commission to become a general in the Confederate Army. He was killed at Chickamauga.
- Confederate Lieutenant General Stonewall Jackson: Thomas Jackson's sister, Laura Jackson Arnold, was a unionist who became estranged from her family for her view. Federal troops occupied her West Virginia hometown during the war, and she nursed the federal wounded in her home.

- Senator and former U.S. Attorney General John J. Crittenden: (author of the 1860 Crittenden plan to avoid war) One of his sons, Major General Thomas L. Crittenden, served in the Union, and two sons, Major General George B. Crittenden and Colonel Eugene W. Crittenden, fought for the Confederacy.
- Representative and Senator Henry Clay: (the "Great Compromiser") Clay's grandsons served both the Union and Confederate armies.
- McIntosh Brothers: Confederate Brigadier General James McQueen McIntosh (killed in 1862) and younger brother, Union Brigadier General John B. McIntosh
- Lea Family: Confederate Major A. M. Lea captured the U.S.S. *Harriet Lane* off the coast of Galveston, Texas. Upon boarding the Union ship, Lea found his son, Lieutenant Edward Lea, dying on the deck.
- Buchanan Brothers: During the battle of the ironclads C.S.S. *Virginia* and U.S.S. *Monitor*, another Union ship, the *Congress*, was sunk. The Virginia's commander: Franklin Buchanan. The *Congress*'s Paymaster: McKean Buchanan.
- Hubbard Brothers: At the First Bull Run, Frederick Hubbard fought with the New Orleans artillery unit. His brother Henry was with the 1st Minnesota infantry. Both wounded, lying side by side on cots in the field hospital, the brothers were reunited for the first time in six years.
- Culp Brothers: Confederate soldier Wesley Culp died during the Battle of Gettysburg, near Culp's Hill, on his uncle Henry Culp's land; William Culp fought with the Union and survived the war.
- The Cooke Family: Union Brigadier General Philip St. George Cooke saw his son, son-in-law, and nephew all join the Confederate forces.
  - Son: Confederate Brigadier General John Rogers Cooke
  - Son-in-law Confederate Cavalry General J. E. B. Stuart (who Cooke was at one time assigned to hunt down)
  - Nephew: John Esten Cooke, who rode with Stuart in the Confederate Cavalry

THE CURIOUS CASE OF JOHN C. BRECKINRIDGE

In the Service of the United States Government

John C. Breckinridge was vice president of the United States under James Buchanan. In the presidential election of 1860, he ran against Lincoln on the southern Democrat ticket. His platform was that the U.S. government should protect the rights of personal property (meaning "slavery").

Breckinridge, oddly, campaigned that his election would keep the Union together. Follow his logic: He made it clear that if Lincoln was elected for opposing slavery, then the South would secede. But if he was elected for advocating slavery, then the Southern states would not pull out.

President Buchanan and former Presidents John Tyler and Franklin Pierce all supported Breckinridge. He carried eleven of the fifteen slave states.

In the Service of the Confederacy

When the Civil War started, Breckinridge joined the Confederate Army as brigadier general and soon was promoted to major general. Thus he became the only former U.S. vice president, to date, who has ever taken up arms against the United States.

In battle, Major General Breckinridge was a snappy dresser, easily recognizable from a distance by his broad-brimmed felt hat.

During the course of the Civil War, Breckinridge participated in these battles: Shiloh, Baton Rouge, Newmarket, Cold Harbor, Hoover's Gap, Atlanta, Stones River, Chickamauga, Chattanooga, Jonesboro, and Monocacy.

In January 1865, Jefferson Davis appointed Breckinridge as the Confederate secretary of war, a position he held until the Confederacy fell to the Union. In April 1865, upon threat of being executed for treason, Breckinridge left Richmond to cool his heels in Europe by way of Cuba.

After three years in England and Canada, Breckinridge learned he had been pardoned. Returning to America in 1868, he resumed his law practice in Lexington, Kentucky, where he lived until his death in 1875.

Breckinridge Curiosity #1

During the Battle of Atlanta, Confederate General John C. Breckinridge was supposedly taken prisoner by his cousin, W. C. P. Breckinridge of the Union army.

Breckinridge Curiosity #2

John C. Breckinridge's daughter Margaret Breckinridge kept her loyalties with the Union, even though her father had joined the Confederacy. She served as an agent with the U.S. Sanitary Commission during the war.

Breckinridge Curiosity #3

During the Civil War, Mrs. Breckinridge was devoted to doing her part, which she regarded as accompanying her husband at headquarters. She determined that the regiment needed a new flag, and she thought she knew exactly how to get one.

John C. Breckinridge's wife remembered quite well the time she spent in Washington society as the country's "second lady." She particularly remembered a lovely silk dress she had worn at state dinners, and she imagined that its fabric would be well put to use as a regiment flag.

After much cutting and stitching, the cloth that had once shared a table with President Lincoln now would fly over the 20th Tennessee Regiment.

From its first debut at Hoover's Gap, Tennessee, in June 1863, "the Mrs. Breckinridge flag" proved quite unlucky to those who carried it:

- Hoover's Gap: The first color bearer was killed, and two more were wounded by gunfire.
- Chickamauga: Three color bearers were killed.
- Jonesboro: Every one of the color guard who carried the flag was killed or wounded.

CIVILIAN CLOTHING OF THE 1860s

Women

Most women wanted to imitate the close-fitting styles popular with European women. This required custom tailoring, at home, or from a dressmaker for those who could afford it. Cloaks, corsets, and hoops were purchased from a general store or catalog.

First we'll discuss fashionable dress in the cosmopolitan areas:

- Hooped Skirt: Women loved the new hooped skirt, which freed them from a bustle and all its petticoats (as many as fourteen). The hooped skirt draped over a crinoline. In the 1860s, the shape of the skirt changed from a dome to a triangle.
- Crinoline: A crinoline was a set of hoops connected to each other by tapes. It resembled a cage, but really let the dress to fall away from the body without having to wear so many petticoats. A crinoline made even thick-waisted girls have pinched waists in the wide skirts. It was flat in front, and the skirt was gored so that most of the cloth hung in the back.
- Petticoats: A modest girl would sometimes wear one petticoat under the crinoline. She might wear another petticoat over the crinoline to smooth away the hoops' lines.
- Waist: Women wanted a narrow waist—or at least look like it—so they laced their bodices as tightly as they could stand.
- Hems: The skirt's bottom edge came right to the ground, and it often brushed the floor as women bent over or walked on uneven ground. Dresses had special bands around the hems to protect and preserve the fabric; they were removable for washing or replacing.
- Shirts: Cuffs and collars on shirts were detachable so they could be washed.
- Headgear: Bonnets were in fashion until about 1865 with styles ranging from low brim to high spoon. Ladies of the South wore straw hats to protect their skin from the sun, as having a suntan did not come into fashion until many years later.

- Aprons: Women wore aprons of all sorts to protect their clothes from stains. A fashion statement in themselves, aprons were made of materials and colors that complemented the dresses, and they ranged from the quite simple to the fairly complicated.
- Gloves: Few women went out in public without gloves, whether wearing white kid for a formal affair, or cotton or linen, for everyday.

  Rural women needed practical dresses for their farm work, and often only had one or two. These dresses had no hoops or bustles and ended just above the ankle on grown women. They were most often one piece, but sometimes were in two pieces for easier dressing, mending, and cleaning.

Men

Men's looser-fitting styles could be sewn on an assembly line in Northern factories.★

- Coat, vest, and trousers: Usually black, dark blue, brown, or green.
- Shirt: White cotton or linen.
- Neckwear: Tight collars and ties.
- Headgear: Usually a cap or hat, especially for protection from the elements outside. Professionals wore top hats; farmers wore broad-brimmed hats.
- Trousers: Held up by suspenders, button-flied, fitted around the waist, loose around the legs and seat, with pegged ankles.
- Aprons: Laborers wore aprons to protect clothes or carry tools.

★This leads to a quick discussion of industrialization. The ready-to-wear industry began with sizing standards and simple designs evolving in men's clothing. With the Civil War, garment factories saw their production orders increase to meet the demand for uniforms.

While this was good for factory owners who found themselves building new plants, it also led to a new class of female workers in sweatshops: seamstresses.

JOURNALIST HORACE GREELEY (1811-1872)

New Hampshire native Horace Greeley started his career as a newspaper apprentice in Vermont. In 1841, he founded his own newspaper, *The New York Tribune*, in the face of the sensational tabloids prevalent at that time.

In *The New York Tribune*, Greeley voiced his opinions on social fairness, abolition, monopolies, and land speculation. The newspaper was successful and regarded as one of the most influential in the country. Greeley remained the editor for thirty-one years, for a time even employing Karl Marx as a European correspondent.

Greeley did not like Abraham Lincoln, and it sometimes seemed Greeley opposed Lincoln even when Lincoln's policies matched his own beliefs.

- When Southern states first began floating the idea of secession, Greeley urged to let the Southern states leave peacefully.
- When the Southern states seceded, Greeley urged to get the war started.
- When war broke out, Greeley urged Lincoln to free the slaves.

After the Civil War, when former Confederate President Jefferson Davis had been captured and held at Fort Monroe Prison, Greeley heard of the deplorable dungeon-like conditions in Davis' cell. Greeley took Davis' side in his newspaper. He even joined other abolitionists who signed Davis' $100,000 post-war bail bond, although he knew it would affect his newspaper's circulation.

In 1872, Greeley was nominated for president, receiving support from liberal Republicans as well as Democrats. Some say he might have won if his opponent had not been Ulysses S. Grant.

CIVIL WAR-ERA NEWSPAPERS

Born in England in 1821, Henry Carter came to America at age twenty-seven and changed his name to Frank Leslie. In 1854, he founded *Frank Leslie's Ladies' Gazette of Paris, London, and New York Fashions.*

The next year, Leslie began an illustrated weekly newspaper, called *Frank Leslie's Illustrated Weekly*. It was one of the earliest papers to use woodcuts and engravings for illustrating a weekly publication.

Once the Civil War started, the paper's popularity grew. Frank Leslie's Illustrated Weekly provided a look into the Civil War battles for the families back home. He published more than two hundred issues during the conflict, which are collector's items today. Historians now look to Leslie's weekly for realistic Civil War art.

Buoyed by his illustrated weekly's success, Leslie soon launched more magazines: *Boys' and Girls' Weekly Sunday Magazine, Jolly Joker, Comic Almanac, Chatterbox, Ladies' Magazine,* and *Ladies' Journal.*

A remarkably cross-eyed editor, James Gordon Bennett founded *The New York Herald* with $500 in a New York basement. From its humble origins in 1835, the paper grew into one of the most popular and widely-read in the country. As one of the first true newspaper reporters, Bennett focused on reporting events rather than just writing his editorial opinion. He reported on sports, business, stocks, and crime.

At the outbreak of the Civil War, Bennett sent his *New York Herald* reporters out to the field to cover and report what they saw. The other major New York papers scrambled to do the same. Thus was born the first war correspondents, the forerunners to those we rely on today to provide information from their "embedded" assignments.

In 1857, the Harper brothers (James, John, Fletcher, and Wesley) of publishing fame (think HarperCollins and *Harper's Bazaar*), founded *Harper's Weekly* on the heels of his successful seven-year-old venture, *Harper's Monthly*. Widely read in both the North and South, the weekly took a moderate stance on slavery but fully supported Abraham Lincoln and the Union.

Harper's Weekly, the "Journal of Civilization" according to its masthead, featured lithographs and articles documenting the Civil War. It was published until 1916 and revived in 2000 as a brief weekly e-mail dispatch.

By the start of the Civil War, the ten-year-old *New York Daily Times* newspaper had already changed its name to *The New York Times*, and it was making a reputation for itself as the paper containing "all the news that's fit to print." The public was so eager to have news from the battlefield, that during the Civil War, her editors began printing a Sunday edition along with daily issues.

Founded in 1860, *The New York World* was a longtime Lincoln enemy, sure to publish unflattering views of the president and his policies. Although not particularly successful during the Civil War years, *The New York World* is known for publishing a forged document in 1864 from Abraham Lincoln calling for 400,000 more troops. As a result, the press was shut down for three days.

The New York World was bought in 1883 by journalist Joseph Pulitzer, who focused on human-interest instead of hard news stories. *The New York World* ceased publication in 1931.

Horace Greeley's *New York Tribune* was one of the most influential newspapers in the country of its time. In 1924, the paper merged with *The New York Herald* to become *The New York Herald Tribune* and was published until 1967. A new *New York Tribune* was published for about ten years, beginning in 1983; it was not associated with Horace Greeley's newspaper.

Nellie Bly made her famous race around the world as a reporter for *The New York World*.

URBAN LEGEND NUMBER 1:
THE ORIGIN OF "TAPS"

First, we'll share a condensed version of the e-mail that we received not too long ago:

In 1862 Union Captain Robert Ellicombe was near Harrison's Landing in Virginia during the Seven Days' Battles. During the night, he heard moaning on the field. Without knowing if the soldier was Union or Confederate, Ellicombe crawled on his stomach to rescue the man and bring him to the medics in camp. The soldier died during the rescue, and Ellicombe discovered he was actually a Confederate—and his own son.

The boy had been studying music in the South and enlisted in the Confederate Army. Ellicombe was denied permission to bury his son with military honors, but allowed to have one bugler play a funeral dirge. Ellicombe asked the bugler to play a series of notes he found on a paper in his son's uniform pocket.

How much of that widely circulated e-mail is the true origin of "Taps?" The date (July 1862) and the place (Harrison's Landing).

Here's the truth, as much as anyone can be sure:

There's no record of a Robert Ellicombe in the Union Army. There was no dead Confederate son, or dead Union son. So of course, there was no bugler playing at the nonexistent boy's funeral, and of course the phantom boy did not write the tune.

Union General Daniel Butterfield decided that he wanted his brigade to have a different bugle call for lights out. Before this particular day in July 1862, the camps played a French bugle call, "Tattoo," to signal to the men in the garrison to wrap it up and go to bed.

When asked about the particulars, years after the war, the by-then elderly Butterfield and his equally-senior bugler Oliver W. Norton were both a little hazy on the details. They did agree that Butterfield decided to change the call, and asked Norton to help him work out the tune. Since Butterfield didn't read music, everyone is pretty sure he didn't write the new tune; he most probably arranged "by ear" a variation on "Tattoo."

Once Butterfield and Norton got the piece to sound the way they liked it, Norton played it that same night. It didn't take long for neighboring camps to pick up the tune, and it spread throughout both the Northern and Southern armies. There are no official words to "Taps," but some verses people sing are:

Day is done, gone the sun,
From the hills, from the lake,
From the sky.
All is well, safely rest,
God is nigh.

Go to sleep, peaceful sleep,
May the soldier or sailor,
God keep.
On the land or the deep,
Safe in sleep.

Love, good night, Must thou go,
When the day, And the night
Need thee so?
All is well. Speedeth all
To their rest.

Fades the light; And afar
Goeth day, And the stars
Shineth bright,
Fare thee well; Day has gone,
Night is on.

Thanks and praise, For our days,
'Neath the sun, 'Neath the stars,
'Neath the sky,
As we go, This we know,
God is nigh.

URBAN LEGEND NUMBER 2: SON OF A GUN

As long as we're telling urban legends of the Civil War, we have to include this one. It's far too outrageous to actually believe. And yet it managed to get published in the *New York Journal of Medicine* as fact. That's what makes it so incredibly unbelievable!

The Legend:

During the Battle of Raymond, Mississippi, in May 1863, a soldier was shot clean through a particularly personal private area. In the meantime, a young Southern belle was standing on the porch of her family home that bordered the battlefield, about one hundred or so yards away. The minie ball that injured the soldier kept flying, and inflicted a second wound, lodging in the girl's abdomen.

The same surgeon who attended the soldier on the field also was called to the farm house to administer to the young lady. Nine months later a baby was born, although the belle claimed she had never "known" a man. This same surgeon removed a minie ball from under the newborn baby's skin.

Eventually the soldier, being a gentleman, married the young mother and made her an honest woman. This is where the term "son of a gun" supposedly came from.

Perpetuating the Story:

The American Medical Weekly published an article by Dr. LeGrand G. Capers (note the name) on November 7, 1871. The article, a gag, claimed this really happened during the Vicksburg Campaign. Some clueless doctors didn't get the joke, and the incident was cited in the *New York Journal of Medicine* in 1959.

As if we didn't already know, the "Son of a Gun" legend was ruled impossible—it's a one in a million shot—in the Discovery Channel program *Mythbusters* (Episode 30).

URBAN LEGEND NUMBER 3: THE VISITING LINCOLN

Former slaves often claimed Abraham Lincoln visited them individually. The basic story:

- Slaves working in the fields near the road were approached by a tall man walking down the dusty lane. He asked for a drink of water, which they gave to him. He drank the water, thanked the slaves, and walked away.
- The slaves never asked the man his name. Many of them had never even seen a picture of Abraham Lincoln. But all the same, they knew it was him.

It had to be true, because it happened to the daughter of a friend at the next plantation. Or the preacher's son. Or ...you get the idea.

The story was probably based in fact, though. Lincoln did visit Richmond, Virginia, after the Union soldiers captured the town in April 1865. He walked through the city's streets and addressed the negroes who gathered around him, telling them, "You are free—free as air."

Slaves also shared stories of their version of Lincoln's meeting with Jefferson Davis, which ultimately led to war. They had heard that Lincoln told Davis to free the slaves. Davis refused. So the war started. In truth, Lincoln did not travel to South Carolina to meet with Davis, and certainly no discussion of this sort ever happened.

Other oft-repeated sightings surround Lincoln's tomb in Springfield, Illinois—the usual footsteps, voices, bumps in the night. From 1865 to 1871, Lincoln's body was placed in a temporary grave in Springfield's Oak Ridge Cemetery while a permanent tomb befitting a best-loved president was built.

During the time until the new crypt was constructed, many people reported seeing an Abe-Lincoln-shaped ghost pacing from the current grave to the new site, as if he was checking on the progress of his final resting place.

ABRAHAM LINCOLN, MARFAN SYNDROME, AND MULTIPLE ENDOCRINE NEOPLASIA

We all can describe "Honest Abe" as taller than average with long, thin limbs and a solemn face featuring sunken eyes. Some researchers have considered those features as possibly characteristics of a particular disorder.

Beginning in the 1960s, scientists put forth a theory diagnosing Lincoln with Marfan Syndrome. This is a hereditary condition of the connective tissue holding the body together. With Marfan Syndrome, the defective tissue affects many body systems, including the skeleton, eyes, heart and blood vessels, nervous system, skin, and lungs.

French pediatrician Antoine Marfan described the condition in 1896. Since the Marfan Syndrome diagnosis wasn't around in Lincoln's day, the only way to determine if he had it is to review his written medical records and old photographs.

When Marfan Syndrome affects the skeleton, people are very tall (or taller than other family members), slender, and loose jointed. In Marfan Syndrome, arms, legs, fingers, and toes are much longer than other bones. Some people with Marfan Syndrome have a long, narrow face and flat feet.

This description fits Lincoln perfectly. However, while historians were looking at evidence to apply Marfan Syndrome to Lincoln, other scientists were discovering another hereditary disorder, multiple neoplasia type 2B. Called MEN2B, it is characterized by overactive endocrine glands causing skeletal features almost identical to Marfan Syndrome.

MEN2B physical characteristics include a slender body build, long and thin limbs, loose joints, and enlarged thick lips. MEN2B also results in cancerous tumors. So, if this is what Lincoln did have, he might have already been dying from cancer when John Wilkes Boothe took his shot.

THE AFFAIR OF THE
DAHLGREN PAPERS

In January 1864, Lincoln approved a two-part plan by Brigadier General Judson Kilpatrick. First, free prisoners of Belle Isle and Libby Prison, and secondly, destroy Confederate communications.

Fact: Kilpatrick met separately with Secretary of War Edwin Stanton.

Assumption: During this meeting Stanton added a third objective, to enlist the help of the released prisoners to kidnap or kill Jefferson Davis and his cabinet.

Kilpatrick did not share his specific plans with his superior, General George Meade. Kilpatrick enlisted the young Colonel Ulrich Dahlgren, who had no command experience, to help with the operation.

The raid failed. Kilpatrick's group abandoned their plans, and Dahlgren's group was ambushed by Confederate cavalry under Lieutenant James Pollard. Dahlgren was killed.

After the attack, thirteen-year-old William Littlepage searched the colonel's pockets. Instead of money, he found papers and a pocket notebook. Littlepage's booty came to be known as "The Dahlgren Papers."

It's hard to question the authenticity of the first document because it was:

1. Written in ink
2. On Union Army stationery
3. The header said, "Headquarters Third Division, Cavalry Corps"
4. It was signed, "U. Dahlgren, Col. Comd." and written to address a regiment.

The most incriminating section said:

"We hope to release the prisoners from Belle Island first & having seen them fairly started we will cross the James River into Richmond, destroying the bridges after us & exhorting the released prisoners to destroy & burn the hateful City & do not allow the Rebel Leader Davis and his traitorous crew to escape."

Although the second paper was not signed, it takes a stretch of the imagination to think it a forgery. In the same handwriting on the same Cavalry Corps stationery, it looked like instructions for another party (Kilpatrick's group). It also said:

"The men must keep together & well in hand & once in the City it must be destroyed & Jeff. Davis and Cabinet killed."

There's no doubt as to whom the notebook belonged, as it had Dahlgren's signature and rank on the first page. Along with plans about the raid, it said, "Jeff Davis and Cabinet must be killed on the spot."

Smart boy that he was, Littlepage gave the documents to authorities. Within two days, the Confederate government released their contents to the media.

Dahlgren earned the posthumous nickname of "Ulrich the Hun."

When General Meade read the Richmond newspapers, he realized that things were much worse than a failed raid and a dead colonel. The big problem was that in warfare, it's accepted to capture leaders and military figures, but targeting civilians and civilian leaders goes against the codes of war.

Meade asked Kilpatrick if Dahlgren really had any such papers on him. Kilpatrick admitted he had seen the papers and signed off on them, but said the papers he saw did not include anything about killing Davis and his cabinet. His brilliant move: claiming the papers must have been forged by the Confederacy.

With that, Union officials claimed that no one had ordered or authorized Dahlgren's plan to kill civilians. They said the colonel acted alone. They held onto that claim forever. When Richmond fell and Union soldiers reclaimed the town, Stanton regained possession of the papers and burned them before they could be reviewed further.

Most historians agree that the papers were not a forgery. If the plan had been carried out, the war would have been escalated to a new height altogether. As it was, Confederate leaders viewed the orders as the North's "gloves off" message, and were now, as a matter of self-defense, free to take the same "all's fair" approach to warfare.

When Could the Dahlgren Papers Have Been Forged?

The Dahlgren Papers certainly made the rounds between the time young Willie Littlepage discovered them, and history has places and names for those rounds. They were handed over to newspaper reporters less than forty-eight hours after being discovered. This is one reason experts are sure they couldn't have been forged—possession of the papers was carefully documented, leaving no time for such an operation to have been accomplished:

1. Littlepage gave the papers to his home guard commander, Captain Edward W. Halbach.
2. Halbach shared the papers with his superior Captain Richard Hugh Bagby.
3. Bagby and Halbach turned the papers over to Lieutenant James Pollard.
4. Pollard gave the papers to Colonel Richard L. T. Beale, who ordered Pollard to take them straight to Richmond the first thing the next morning.
5. In Richmond, Pollard delivered Dahlgren's papers—and his wooden leg—to cavalry Major General Fitzhugh Lee (Robert E. Lee's nephew).
6. Lee immediately took the papers to Jefferson Davis, who read them with Secretary of State Judah Benjamin. When he read "once in the City it must be destroyed & Jeff. Davis and Cabinet killed," Davis laughed. "That means you, Mr. Benjamin," he said.
7. Davis told Lee to deliver the papers to the War Department.
8. Secretary of War James A. Seddon decided, with Davis's approval, to release the contents to the newspapers.
9. The newspaper editors rushed back to their presses to print the contents in the next morning's editions.

HUGH JUDSON "KILL CAVALRY" KILPATRICK (1836-1881)

Judson Kilpatrick was nicknamed "Kill Cavalry" because of the unusually high body count among his men as well as the enemy's. He was known to push his men and horses to the absolute end of their endurance. Some examples of his losses of Union soldiers:

- Bull Run: As the sun set at the end of the first day, Kilpatrick ordered a cavalry charge that ended in losing most of the men in his command. The twilight firefight was spectacular in itself, if not for the heavy casualties. It did earn Kilpatrick his hell-bent-for-leather reputation, though.
- Gettysburg: Kilpatrick missed out on the first full day because he didn't follow orders (not as punishment, mind you, but because he was traipsing around the countryside looking for Confederate troops who weren't there). On the third day, Kilpatrick ordered Brigadier General Elon Farnsworth's cavalry to charge, even though Farnsworth's brigade was grossly outnumbered. Farnsworth and most of his men were killed as a result of Kilpatrick's poor judgment.

Some of the more colorful words used to describe Judson Kilpatrick include ruthless, reckless, ambitious, popular, confident, inspiring, daring, brilliant, and aggressive. It's also been said that his men liked him, probably because of his lack of discipline and order in camp. Kilpatrick was a professed temperance man—and heavy drinker—who made a great effort to support the working girls, even though he had a wife and daughter at home.

A farmer's son from Deckertown, New Jersey, Kilpatrick spent his life wheeling and dealing to better his social and professional position. When he registered at the U.S. military academy, Kilpatrick omitted his first name, "Hugh," which he had always thought was effeminate. And from then on, he went by "Judson Kilpatrick."

Kilpatrick graduated from West Point in May 1861 and three days later was promoted to captain in the 5th New York Infantry, also known as "Duryea's Zouaves." Kilpatrick gained some fame in the Northern press as the first officer from the regular army to be wounded in action when he took some grapeshot in the backside at Big Bethel.

By the fall of 1861, Kilpatrick was promoted to brigadier general and transferred to the 2nd New York Cavalry. From then on he led mounted men in every important engagement in the war's eastern theater.

Kilpatrick had a busy year in 1864. In February, commanding the 3rd Division of the Army of the Potomac's Cavalry Corps, he led the ill-fated plot to capture and kill Jefferson Davis and the Confederate Cabinet. Then in May, he was wounded at the Battle of Resaca. Finally Sherman requested Kilpatrick to lead the cavalry in his March to the Sea.

Sherman reportedly said of General Kill Cavalry, "I know Kilpatrick is a hell of a damned fool, but I want just that sort of man to command my cavalry."

Kilpatrick managed to attain the rank of major general by the war's end.

After the war, Kilpatrick served as minister to Chile from 1865 to 1868. He returned home, ran unsuccessfully for Congress from New Jersey, and accepted President Garfield's appointment back to Chile in 1881.

Kilpatrick died in Santiago nine months later. He is buried at West Point. His daughter burned all his papers after his death.

The United States Naval Surface Warfare Center, Dahlgren Division in Dahlgren, Virginia, is named for Admiral John A. Dahlgren.

THE DAHLGREN MEN: PAPA DAHLGREN

The name "Dahlgren" was well-known during the Civil War, especially in naval operations. That's because Dahlgren smoothbore guns, named after inventor John Adolphus Bernard Dahlgren (1809–1870), were widely used during the war. Dahlgren's bottle-shaped smoothbore cannon were standard arms found on all U.S. Navy ships.

A Philadelphia native, Dahlgren was a lifetime sailor, joining the U.S. Navy at age sixteen as a midshipman. He eventually rose to the Navy's ordnance bureau, and by 1861 was over the Washington Navy Yard. There he often hosted President Lincoln, who shared Dahlgren's fascination with new technology in warfare. They became friends.

Although he had a good position over Naval Ordnance, Dahlgren wanted to see real action. He petitioned his close friend Lincoln, who overruled any misgivings expressed by Secretary of the Navy Gideon Welles. In July 1863, Lincoln promoted Dahlgren to rear admiral.

Dahlgren was given command of the South Atlantic Blockading Squadron. In that capacity, he helped in the captures of Charleston Harbor and Savannah.

After the war, Dahlgren served time commanding the South Pacific Squadron. He returned to the Washington Navy Yard in 1869, serving as commander until he died the following year.

Admiral Dahlgren was deeply disturbed by the way his son Ulrich was portrayed in the press after the failed raid on Richmond and plot to kill Jefferson Davis. The elder Dahlgren went to his grave convinced that incriminating papers found on his son's body were undoubtedly forgeries.

THE DAHLGREN MEN: DAHLGREN THE YOUNGER

The son of Admiral John Dahlgren, Ulrich Dahlgren (1842-1864) profited from his father's close relationship with President Lincoln. Lincoln secured Ulrich a commission when he quit college to go to war in 1862.

Dahlgren has been described as tall, fair-haired, dashing, adventurous, low on common sense, reckless, immature, and careless.

- Fredericksburg: Captain Dahlgren was known for helping sixty Union soldiers hold the city for three hours against almost six hundred Confederates. Dahlgren's regiment even managed to take a few prisoners during the heavy Union loss.
- Gettysburg: With only one hundred Union men, Captain Dahlgren attacked a Confederate cavalry brigade, capturing two hundred prisoners. Afterwards, during a cavalry skirmish, he was wounded in the right leg, which had to be amputated. He was promoted to Colonel and fitted with wooden leg—one that apparently was of better-than-average quality, if you consider all that has been written about Ulrich's "fancy" cork leg.
- Richmond Raid: The still-recuperating Dahlgren had no true experience commanding soldiers when he offered his help to Judson Kilpatrick in a raid to Richmond to liberate prisoners of war. Fatally shot during the mission, twenty-one-year-old Dahlgren was found to be carrying papers suggesting a plot to capture and kill Jefferson Davis and the Confederate Cabinet.

In 1836, John A. Dahlgren was almost blinded from directly viewing a solar eclipse.

BLOODIEST BATTLES OF THE CIVIL WAR

Gettysburg (July 1–3, 1863): The most famous and important battle of the war also represents an unprecedented three-day torrent of blood. The two armies suffered a combined fifty-one thousand casualties as the Union repulsed Robert E. Lee's Northern invasion.

Chickamauga (September 18–20, 1863): Loosely translated as an Indian word meaning "river of death," Chickamauga lives up to its morbid billing. The temporary setback for the Union cost the two sides nearly thirty-five thousand casualties.

The Wilderness (May 5-6, 1864): With twenty-six thousand casualties, this Virginia clash is just as it sounds—a battle in thick, dense woods rife with confusion and carnage. Though inconclusive, it marked Grant's first step in a vicious war of attrition aimed at making Lee and the Confederates surrender their will—and the war.

Spotsylvania (May 8–21, 1864): Step two in the Grant-Lee death grip with twenty-eight thousand casualties, including eighteen thousand Union men. The Confederates had barely half as many men (fifty-two thousand) entering the battle and suffered twelve thousand casualties.

Chancellorsville (April 30–May 6, 1863): A signature victory for Robert E. Lee as a series of bold maneuvers paid off handsomely. The armies combined suffered thirty thousand casualties.

Shiloh (April 6–7, 1862): At the time it was fought, Shiloh was the bloodiest battle in American history, though future Civil War battles would surpass the butcher's bill in this engagement. More than twenty-three thousand men were killed, wounded, captured, or missing.

Stones River (December 31, 1862–January 2, 1863): An inconclusive battle, it carried the highest casualty rate for both sides, as nearly one-third of the eighty-one thousand men in the battle—twenty-four thousand soldiers—wound up as casualties.

Antietam (September 17, 1862): The bloodiest single-day battle, according to the National Park Service, noting that nine times as many Americans (twenty-three thousand) were killed or wounded as on D-Day during World War II. The Union victory delivered a strong rebuke of the Confederate army's invasion of the North, with twenty-three thousand casualties.

Fort Donelson (February 12–16, 1862): The battle that earned Ulysses S. Grant the nickname "Unconditional Surrender" included more than sixteen thousand casualties, with Confederates accounting for nearly fourteen thousand of those.

Did You Know?

The death of Albert Sidney Johnston in action at the Battle of Shiloh still represents the highest-ranking Union or Confederate military commander's death in battle in the Civil War.

ONE OF THESE THINGS IS NOT LIKE THE OTHERS

Look at the list of Confederate officers below, and see if you know how Benjamin Cheatham is not like the others.

- John Adams
- John C. Carter
- Benjamin Cheatham
- Patrick Cleburne
- States Rights Gist
- Hiram B. Granbury
- Otho F. Strahl

Give up? Of these men, Cheatham is the only Confederate general who was not killed at the Battle of Franklin, Tennessee, on November 30, 1864. Under John Bell Hood's Army of Tennessee, the Confederates executed an ill-planned attack on the Union army.

The Battle of Franklin was one of the few engagements that took place at night. Hood's first assault did not get started until 4:00 in the afternoon, when dusk was falling on the late-November day. Hood's final major assault was at 9:00 p.m. By midnight, Union commander John Schofield began withdrawing his troops. Counted as a Confederate victory—one of the last—it was also one of the bloodiest battles fought in the western theater. One Union general was wounded; six Confederate generals were killed.

Mexican War veteran John Adams (1825–1864) graduated West Point in 1846. He participated in the battles of Vicksburg, Jackson, and Sherman's Atlanta campaign. At Franklin, although wounded early in the day, he continued to fight with his men. Eventually taking nine shots, Adams' final words were, reportedly, "It is the fate of a soldier to die for his country." Adams achieved the rank of brigadier general.

A Georgia native and Tennessee resident, John C. Carter was

known for his gentle nature and courage in battle. He is said to have rescued his regiment's flag to lead the charge at Shiloh. Carter was mortally wounded during the fighting at Franklin and carried to the nearby Harrison House residence. He died ten days later. He also fought at Stones River and Chickamauga. Carter achieved the rank of brigadier general.

Tennessee farmer and Mexican War veteran Benjamin Franklin Cheatham (1820–1886) was said to have a band of spies working for him while in the Confederacy's service. In addition to Franklin, Cheatham also participated in Belmont, Shiloh, Corinth, Perryville, the Tullahoma Campaign, the Atlanta Campaign, Chickamauga, Nashville, and the Carolinas Campaign. Cheatham achieved the rank of Major General. After the war, Cheatham returned to farming and served as Nashville's postmaster.

Ireland native Patrick Ronayne Cleburne (1828–1864) told his troops before heading into battle at Franklin, "If we are going to die, let us die like men."

Harvard Law School graduate States Rights Gist's (1831–1864) Civil War participation included Fort Sumter, First Bull Run, Chickamauga, the Atlanta Campaign, Wilmington, Chattanooga, Vicksburg, and Missionary Ridge.

Mississippi native and Texas resident Hiram B. Granbury (1831–1864) served in the battles of Fort Donelson, Port Hudson, Raymond, Chickamauga, and Chattanooga. Captured during Fort Donelson's surrender in early 1862, Granbury spent five months as a prisoner of war in Boston's Fort Warren Prison. His young wife of five years died of ovarian cancer in March 1863. Granbury achieved the rank of brigadier general.

Ohio native and longtime Tennessee resident Otho French Strahl (1831–1864) was an Ohio Wesleyan University graduate. He participated in the battles of Shiloh, Chickamauga, and Chattanooga. When he arrived at Franklin, Strahl was still recovering from a serious wound incurred during the recent Battle of Atlanta. Strahl achieved the rank of brigadier general.

WEALTH MEETS WARFARE: JOHN JACOB ASTOR III (1822-1890)

John Jacob Astor III, unquestionably the wealthiest man in America and grandson of the über-rich fur trader of the same name, wanted to do more than hire a substitute to enlist in his place. He became a volunteer aide-de-camp to Major General George McClellan.

Astor showed up at the Army of the Potomac in November 1861 with his own chef, steward, and valet in tow. He remained with McClellan for eight months. Though he never actually ventured out onto a battlefield, in 1865 Astor was awarded a brevet of brigadier general for his services during the Peninsula Campaign.

You'll recognize John Jacob Astor's name from the Waldorf-Astoria hotel in New York City. His son, William Waldorf, built a hotel, the Waldorf, on the site of the family house at the corner of 5th Avenue and 33rd Street. Then John Jacob Astor IV built an adjoining inn, the Astoria Hotel. The combined building was called the Waldorf-Astoria Hotel. Today, the elite establishment is located between the 47th and 50th Street on Park Avenue. The Empire State Building now stands at the original site on 5th and 33rd.

Several men in the Astor family were given the name "John Jacob," though it wasn't necessarily handed down from father to son. If you're confused, and we'd not blame you, we've mapped out the John Jacobs by generation:

1. John Jacob Astor (1763-1848)
2a. John Jacob Astor II (1791-1879) (no children)
2b. William Backhouse Astor (1792-1875)
3a. John Jacob Astor III (1822-1890)
4a. William Waldorf Astor, 1st Viscount Astor (1848-1919)
5a. William Waldorf Astor, 2nd Viscount Astor (1879-1952)
5b. John Jacob Astor V, 1st Baron Astor of Hever (1886-1971)

3b. William Backhouse Astor, Jr (1830-1892)

4a. John Jacob Astor IV (1864-1912) died when the RMS *Titanic* sank

4b. Vincent Astor (born in 1892)

4c. Ava Astor (born in 1902)

5. John Jacob Astor VI (1912-1992)

Presidential Timber

The Civil War featured many notable future leaders on the battlefield. Among the most memorable was Oliver Wendell Holmes, who went on to become one of the most distinguished Supreme Court justices in American history. Holmes, who endured several serious wounds including one at Antietam, served in the Union ranks and once yelled at President Lincoln during an ill-timed visit to the battlefront. Spying a civilian in peril as shots rang out, Holmes barked, "Get down, you fool!"

Though few could match Holmes for moxie, seven future presidents also served in the war (all on the Union side, obviously). The roster: William McKinley, Benjamin Harrison, James Garfield, Chester A. Arthur, Rutherford B. Hayes, Ulysses S. Grant, and Andrew Johnson, who served as military governor of Tennessee.

Another future president, Grover Cleveland, avoided serving in the war. Instead, he paid to have a substitute enlist in his spot, a practice permitted under the Conscription Act of 1863.

CONFEDERATE COMMANDERS: SIMON BOLIVAR BUCKNER (1823-1914)

West Point graduate Simon Buckner fought in the Mexican War, then taught infantry tactics at his old school. By the beginning of the Civil War, he was commander of the Kentucky Militia.

The Surrender of Fort Donelson

Under siege from Union General Grant's troops, the Confederates inside Fort Donelson tried to break through Union lines. Confederate General Gideon Pillow, who was commanding Fort Donelson with former Secretary of War John Floyd, led the advance, but chickened out and withdrew his men.

Both Pillow and Floyd were too proud to surrender to Grant. They didn't want to be the first Confederate officers to admit defeat. Buckner volunteered to do it, to spare any more needless killing.

Pillow and Floyd went so far as to sneak away under cover of darkness. *The New York Times* reported that some Confederate soldiers were so mad about this that they fired on Floyd as he slunk off.

Buckner sent a note to Grant asking for surrender terms. Grant responded, "Unconditional and immediate surrender," which earned him the nickname, "Unconditional Surrender" Grant. Buckner gave up the fort and fifteen thousand men.

The Union win meant control of the Cumberland and Tennessee Rivers and access to Tennessee, Mississippi, and Georgia.

Buckner eventually attained the rank of brigadier general. After the war, he served as Governor of Kentucky from 1887 to 1891 and ran as the Democratic candidate for vice president during the 1896 election.

Family Traditions

Abraham Lincoln's Brother-in-Law

Confederate Brigadier General Benjamin Hardin Helm (1831–1863) joined Lincoln's family tree when he married Emilie Todd, Mary Todd Lincoln's half-sister, in 1856.

A West Point graduate, Helm turned down Lincoln's personal offer of a commission as paymaster in the Union army to command the 1st Kentucky Cavalry for the Confederate army. In March 1862, Helm was given command of the 1st Kentucky Orphan Brigade, named so because Kentucky never actually seceded from the United States, although natives of the state supported the Confederacy as much as they did the Union. Helm achieved the rank of brigadier general after fighting at Shiloh, Baton Rouge, and Tullahoma.

In September 1863, Helm was killed at Chickamauga. His death deeply saddened his in-laws in the White House, although publicly Mary Lincoln professed that she hoped all her Confederate relatives were killed. She verbally reasoned they themselves would be happy to kill her own husband and destroy the federal government if they could.

Robert E. Lee's Distinguished (?) Family Tree

- Ancestors: Richard Henry Lee issued the motion calling for independence at the Continental Congress in 1776; Francis Lightfoot Lee signed the Declaration of Independence; Arthur Lee, chief minister to France during the Revolution, served in the Continental Congress.
- Father: Major General Henry "Light-Horse Henry" Lee III, served in George Washington's cavalry, served as Virginia's governor, and was a U.S. Congressman.
- Half-Brother: Henry "Black-Horse Harry" Lee IV fathered a child with his wife's teenage sister and embezzled his in-laws' money.
- Half-Brother: Charles Carter Lee squandered what was left of the family fortune.
- Wife: Mary Anna Randolph Custis was the granddaughter of George Washington's wife, Martha Custis Washington.

CONFEDERATE COMMANDERS: JOHN C. PEMBERTON (1814-1881)

A Pennsylvania native and 1837 West Point graduate, John Clifford Pemberton fought in the Seminole and Mexican Wars as a career U.S. Army officer. At the outbreak of the Civil War, he sided with his Virginia-born wife to join the Confederacy.

John C. Pemberton is best known for his role in the surrender of Vicksburg, Mississippi. In the autumn of 1862, Pemberton's troops were able to check Union General William T. Sherman's advance toward Vicksburg at Chickasaw Bluffs.

Then the Union decided to try a siege approach, completely surrounding the town by mid-May of 1863. Following Jefferson Davis's urgently wired instructions to hold the city at all costs, General Pemberton and thirty-one thousand Confederates were trapped with no means of getting new supplies. Union gunboats blocked the Mississippi River from any Confederate ships, and Union troops blocked any land shipments as well.

General Grant heated the pot by ordering artillery to continually bombard the city. By July, the Confederates were starving. On the fourth, while another battle raged in Gettysburg, Pennsylvania, Pemberton surrendered. The Mississippi River was now completely open to the Union.

The Northern-born Pemberton was accused of lacking dedication to the Confederacy and of disobeying orders at Vicksburg. After surrendering Vicksburg, Pemberton showed his loyalty by resigning his lieutenant General's commission and serving as a lieutenant colonel of artillery, defending Richmond.

Union Commanders: Philip Kearny (1815-1862)

When Phil Kearny's parents died, his wealthy grandfather John Watts, founder of the New York Stock Exchange, took in the young New York City lad to raise himself. Grandpa Watts did not want young Phil to follow his dream of a military career, so Kearny earned a law degree from Columbia University and settled into business as a lawyer.

Then in 1836, John Watts died, leaving his grandson to inherit a windfall upwards of $1 million. That's when Phil Kearny decided to do things his own way, and he headed off to France to study at the Saumur cavalry school.

Kearny's military training served him well as he began a new career. In Algiers, in Africa, as a cavalry leader, he excelled and earned the French Legion of Honor as well as the nickname "Kearny the Magnificent." He was noted for charging into battle with a sword in one hand, a pistol in the other, and his reins held between his teeth.

During the Mexican War, Kearny lost his left arm in Mexico City. Back in Europe, he furthered his battle experience in the Crimean War, where he was known as the "One-Armed Devil."

So by the time the Civil War started in the United States, Kearny was more than qualified to lead first a New Jersey brigade and then the 3rd Corps through the Peninsula Campaign, Williamsburg, Seven Pines, Fair Oaks, Malvern Hill, Seven Days, and Second Bull Run.

A Better Death for Major General Phil Kearny

On September 1, 1862, the day after Second Bull Run, Kearny rode out to check a gap in Union lines near Chantilly. He accidentally rode into the Confederate lines and refused to surrender. While riding away, he was shot in the back and killed instantly.

Kearny's old friend, Confederate General A. P. Hill, was deeply affected, and publicly stated that Kearny deserved a better death than that. Confederate General Robert E. Lee himself proposed a "gesture of courtesy" which his officers all agreed to. A truce was called to escort Kearny's body back to the Union lines and return Kearny's riderless horse.

Back in New York City, Kearny's funeral was closed to newspaper reporters, although some managed to attend, dressed as clergy, to cover the event.

Phil Kearny Trivia

- Kearny made good use of his millions of dollars, taking care to always ride into battle in top form. He had twenty custom-made uniforms on hand so that he could look "fresh" at all times. He was known for his spotless dress and gold-braided kepi, riding into battle in the manner of the elite he was. His regiments could also always count on dining in fine style courtesy of Kearny's deep pockets.
- At Williamsburg, Kearny led the charge to take back the Federal battery that had been captured by the Confederacy. Guns waving, he galloped forward, shouting to his troops, "Don't flinch, boys! They're shooting at me, not at you!"
- Kearny served under General George McClellan, to whom he gave the nickname "the Virginia Creeper," for the commander's hesitance at taking action anytime, ever.
- Kearny's favorite horse, Moscow, was a beautiful solid white, making a highly visible target in battle. Therefore, he sometimes rode the less-conspicuous mounts Decatur and Bayard.
- Kearny attained the rank of major general.
- Kearny was the first to have his division wear red diamond patches on their caps, so he could identify his own men. The idea soon spread and was the basis for shoulder patches still sported by different regiments today.

SENATOR JAMES HENRY LANE (1814-1866)

A quick reminder about the Kansas-Nebraska Act of 1854: it allowed each territory to decide by vote whether or not to be admitted into the Union as free or slave. This act, therefore, ended the practice from the Missouri Compromise of alternating free and slave state admittances.

Indiana native James Henry "Jim" Lane's early political career included representing his home state in the U.S. Congress from 1853 to 1855. During that time, he voted in favor of the Kansas-Nebraska Act.

Then Lane had a change of heart and decided that he was for all free states, all the time. He moved to the Kansas Territory and ramped up his support of abolition. If you'll remember, in Kansas, those who wanted it to be a free state and those who supported slavery were in great conflict, and the territory was fraught with violence. Those supporting Kansas as a free state were known as "Jayhawkers."

There was so much guerrilla warfare and other "means of persuasion" used to influence the vote, that the area became known as "Bleeding Kansas." This was the state from which Lane was elected to the U.S. Senate, serving from 1861 to 1866.

While in Washington, as the Civil War began, Lane pulled together a voluntary guard to protect the White House grounds. But that only lasted a few months.

Lane returned to Kansas and decided to take things into his own hands. He gathered and trained the completely unauthorized 1st Kansas Colored Volunteers. The regiment was included in the Union Army in 1863, although they had already unofficially participated in action before that time.

Jim Lane Runs Afoul of William Quantrill: You've read that Quantrill was a Confederate "Bushwhacker" (a Kansas pro-slave guerrilla) whose purpose was to forcefully convince residents of border states that they should be loyal to the South. Keep that in mind.

Jim Lane and his Jayhawkers decided to punish anyone in Kansas supporting Confederate soldiers. Translated, that means women and children who offered food or shelter. The Jayhawkers burned down entire towns.

In retaliation, the Bushwhackers also leveled homes where Union sympathizers were known to live. In addition, Quantrill swore he would burn Jim Lane at the stake. Lane barely escaped Quantrill's midnight raid of his house, slipping out the back door and disappearing into an adjoining cornfield, dressed only in his nightshirt.

Some Jim Lane Trivia:

- Words used to describe Jim Line include "ambitious," "unscrupulous," "rash and impulsive," and "an unsafe leader."
- While stationed at the White House, Lane was often seen walking the halls of the First Residence wearing denim overalls and a leather vest.
- Lane was more than a little attached to his bearskin overcoat, which he always wore outdoors, no matter the season.
- Lane committed suicide, shooting himself in the head after fellow senators accused him of fraud and improper handling of Indian contracts.

CONFEDERATE COMMANDERS: JOHN BANKHEAD MAGRUDER (1807-1871)

The Skinny on John Magruder

- Virginia native
- Attended the University of Virginia; graduated West Point, 1830
- Veteran of Seminole and Mexican Wars
- Civil War battles—Big Bethel, Peninsula Campaign, Yorktown, Malvern Hill, Galveston
- Achieved the rank of major general in the Confederate Army
- Various descriptive words: "dashing," "energetic," "loud," "overzealous," "cautious," "bumbling"

"Prince John" Magruder earned his nickname by indulging his expensive tastes. He also loved hogging the spotlight and enjoyed bringing out the drama in situations. His fellow soldiers also soon quickly became accustomed to his quirky way of whiling away camp time by staging amateur performances.

There's even a story about his production of Shakespeare's *Othello* during the Mexican War, in which none other than Ulysses S. Grant tried out for the part of Desdemona. (By the way, if you're not familiar with all the works of the Bard, Desdemona is the female lead. In Shakespeare's day, men played all the roles, both male and female. You can imagine that in a military setting, men would be required to play the female roles, too.)

The Battle of Big Bethel, June 1861: Magruder was assigned to protect Richmond from the Union. Although only a small number of soldiers were involved (1,200 South versus 2,500 North), Big Bethel is often considered the first battle of the Civil War. When it was over, Magruder claimed victory, estimating the number of Union to Confederate casualties at more than nine to one.

Yorktown, the Highlight of Magruder's Career: Magruder's best achievement of the war resulted from employing his great flair for theatrics. At Yorktown, Magruder's, eleven thousand Southern troops were vastly outnumbered by Union General McClellan's forces. But Magruder devised a ruse that scared McClellan into believing that the numbers were the other way around.

- He scattered artillery around the grounds and initiated sporadic bombardment that seemed to be coming from all sides.
- He had the musicians play loudly and continuously after dark.
- He paraded one battalion in an endless circle through a clearing and back into the woods.
- He strategically placed Quaker guns (wooden cannon made out of trees to look like the real thing) around the encampment.

Although the hours of marching were tiring, the plan worked beautifully. The ever-hesitant McClellan thought he counted at least 100,000 Southern soldiers. He waited. Lincoln urged him to attack. McClellan waited some more. This gave Confederate General Joe Johnston time to bring in reinforcements for the battle.

Malvern Hill, Magruder's Exact Opposite of Yorktown: Magruder destroyed any expectations of his potential during the Seven Days' Battles, at Malvern Hill. He marched his units away from the battlefield. The stories range from claims that Lee's orders were delivered hours later than they should have been, to the idea that Magruder marched down the wrong road and got lost, to blaming a guide who led Magruder's units the wrong way. In any event, Magruder was roundly blamed for the Confederate loss at Malvern Hill.

A New Assignment: After the debacle at Malvern Hill, in October 1862, Magruder was transferred to command the District of Texas, New Mexico, and Arkansas. There, he saw action in minor battles and was instrumental in recapturing Galveston for the Confederacy.

A Career Soldier: At the end of the Civil War, Magruder moved to Mexico. He took a position as a general in the Imperial Mexican Army and served under Emperor Maximilian until the ruler's death. He returned to Texas and retired in Galveston.

GRANT'S SALUTE

Ulysses S. Grant paid tribute to Union efforts as the war came to an official close. This is the text of Grant's message to his soldiers:

War Department, Adjutant General's Office
Washington, D.C., June 2, 1865
Soldiers of the Armies of the United States:

By your patriotic devotion to your country in the hour of danger and alarm, your magnificent fighting, bravery, and endurance, you have maintained the supremacy of the Union and the Constitution, overthrown all armed opposition to the enforcement of the laws and of the proclamation forever abolishing Slavery—the cause and pretext of the Rebellion—and opened the way to the rightful authorities to restore order and inaugurate peace on a permanent and enduring basis on every foot of American soil.

Your marches, sieges, and battles, in distance, duration, and resolution, and brilliancy of results, dim the luster of the world's past military achievements, and will be the patriot's precedent in defense of liberty and right in all time to come.

In obedience to your country's call, you left your homes and families, and volunteered in her defense. Victory has crowned your patriotic hearts; and, with the gratitude of your countrymen and the highest honor a great and free nation can accord, you will soon be permitted to return to your homes and families, conscious of having discharged the highest duty of American citizens.

To achieve these glorious triumphs and secure to yourselves, your fellow countrymen, and posterity, the blessings of free institutions, tens of thousands of your gallant comrades have fallen and sealed the priceless legacy with their blood. The graves of these a grateful nation bedews with tears, honors their memories, and will ever cherish and support their stricken families.

U.S. Grant, Lieutenant-General.

Coming Home From War: A Soldier's Experience

For soldiers, their homecoming experiences were the difference between night and day, depending on their Army.

Northern Soldiers

Northern troops participated in a review of the Grand Armies of the Republic in Washington, D.C. on May 23, 1865. Soldiers proudly marched in parade down Pennsylvania Avenue from the capitol before President Johnson and Generals Grant and Sherman, to the reception of singing schoolchildren and cheering adults.

Then they went home to their houses, families, and livelihoods.

Southern Soldiers

In the South, especially for those who lived near the trail Sherman blazed to the sea, there was nothing to come home to. There was no unscorched land to raise crops on, and nowhere to support a family. Houses, if they were still standing, had been raided until they were empty. Farm animals had either been taken by Union troops or killed. In fact, without field animals, many men, women, and even children soon found themselves hitched to a plow.

Sherman defended his actions as the punishment for treason. His severe punishment included destroying anything that could be used in farming or manufacturing, including all the railroads. This meant, when the war was over, many Southern soldiers had to walk home, some all the way from Virginia.

Understandably, many former Southern soldiers returned home suffering from depression. They chased away demons with liquor, and alcoholism was common. Opium addiction was also common, for both Northern and Southern soldiers. It had been used as a painkiller by army medics on both sides without regard for its dependence.

Always Look on the Bright Side

- The railroads to Atlanta were restored even before Reconstruction started.
- Memphis, Chattanooga, and Birmingham moved toward heavy manufacturing.
- The cotton industry, which had been completely shut down, had a whole world waiting for more of its product.

Quotes of Union Generals

"Stand up, you cowards. They couldn't hit an elephant at this distance."
John Sedgwick, in challenge to his artillery corps at Spotsylvania, just minutes before he was fatally shot in the head by a Confederate sharpshooter

"No terms, except unconditional and immediate surrender, can be accepted."
Ulysses S. Grant, in response to Confederate General Buckner's call for truce during the Battle of Fort Donelson, earning the Union General his nickname, "Unconditional Surrender" Grant

"War is cruelty, and you cannot refine it. But when peace does come, you may call on me for anything. Then I will share with you the last cracker."
William T. Sherman, to Atlanta's mayor, just before burning the city

CONFEDERATE MEMORIAL DAY

Confederate Memorial Day predates the Memorial Day federal holiday that we celebrate each year on the last Monday in May.

Several cities claim to be the first to celebrate Confederate Memorial Day. They all began honoring those who died while serving the Confederate forces almost as soon as the Civil War was over. Women's groups throughout the South took on the loving tribute of decorating the graves of their fallen soldiers with flowers.

Different Southern states chose different dates to observe their Memorial Day, based on significant dates:

- April 26: Anniversary of General Joseph E. Johnston's surrender in North Carolina
- May 10: General "Stonewall" Jackson's death, and Jefferson Davis's capture.
- June 3: Jefferson Davis's birthday

It is said that the sight of the Confederate graves decorated in Arlington National Cemetery was so moving, that Congressman and former Union General John A. Logan worked to found Memorial Day as a national holiday to honor soldiers from both the North and the South. At the time, it was called Decoration Day, celebrated on May 30 each year.

After World War I, observance of the holiday also included those soldiers who bravely gave their lives in any American conflict. The name officially changed to Memorial Day after World War II, and in the 1970s, the date was changed to the last Monday in May.

Some Southern states still honor the Confederate dead:

- Florida: April 26
- Georgia: April 26
- Alabama: The last Monday in April
- Mississippi: The fourth Monday in April

- South Carolina: May 10
- North Carolina: May 10
- Virginia: Last Monday in May
- Kentucky: June 3
- Louisiana: June 3
- Tennessee: June 3

Arkansas and Texas hold joint celebrations of the birthdays of Robert E. Lee and Dr. Martin Luther King, Jr. on the third Monday in January.

A Few Confederate Quotes For Good Measure

"It is well that war is so terrible; else we should grow too fond of it."
Robert E. Lee

"I always thought the Yankees had something to do with it."
George Pickett, in response to being asked why the Confederates lost at Gettysburg

"Always mystify, mislead, and surprise the enemy."
Stonewall Jackson, battle strategy

SONS AND DAUGHTERS OF THE CONFEDERACY

Out of the Civil War grew many local groups who intended to honor the memory of those who served and died in service to the Confederacy. These organizations eventually joined forces and are still in existence today, with a double purpose of preserving their ancestors' memory by educating the public and providing charity services to worthy causes.

United Daughters of the Confederacy

The United Daughters of the Confederacy was organized in 1890, and today has chapters in thirty-three states and the District of Columbia. With the motto "Love, Live, Pray, Think, Dare," the national organization's membership requirements are quite specific:

- Members are women.
- Members are blood descendants of Civil War veterans (men or women).
- Members' ancestors must have honorably served the Confederate cause.
- Members' ancestors either fought in the Army, Navy, or Civil Service, or gave material aid to the cause.

The United Daughters of the Confederacy's stated objectives include preserving the history of the Civil War, honoring the memory of those who served in the war, educating descendants of its veterans, lending aid to any descendants, and sustaining the information available on women's roles in the war.

Sons of Confederate Veterans

The Sons of Confederate Veterans organized in 1896 in Virginia to ensure the history of the Civil War is carried on. It is a historical, patriotic, and nonpolitical organization. Devoted to preservation, their services to the community and memory include marking soldier's graves, exhibiting historical reenactments, distributing scholarly publications, and discussing the war's military and political history.

Sons of Confederate Veterans' membership requirements:

- Members are men.
- Members are descendants of Civil War veterans who served honorably in the Confederate armed forces.
- Members' ancestors must have honorably served the Confederacy.
- Members' ancestors must have fought in the Army, Navy, or Civil Service.

What is Impeachment?

When most Americans hear then word "impeachment," they think of a president being driven from office. The term describes the first part of a two-step process—the bringing of charges before a legislative body—for involuntarily forcing a public official to leave office. After the charges are brought, a vote by a predetermined governing group or committee must decide whether the official is guilty or innocent of the charges.

Andrew Johnson became the first president to be impeached, in 1868. He was subsequently acquitted. The only other president to be impeached is Bill Clinton, who faced charges of perjury and obstruction of justice. He, too, was cleared of impeachment charges and remained in office.

Another president, Richard Nixon, faced certain impeachment in the wake of the Watergate scandal during the 1970s. Instead, Nixon resigned in 1974 before Congress brought charges against him. Gerald Ford replaced Nixon and later pardoned the disgraced president—preventing a post-presidential indictment—for his role in the cover-up of various administration scandals involving spying, sabotage, and payoffs.

IMPEACHED

Andrew Johnson's ascension to the presidency radically altered the landscape for Reconstruction—and the common ground between the executive and legislative branches of the federal government.

Johnson and Congress engaged in a vicious tug-of-war over Reconstruction policy and governmental power. In most cases, Congress proved the victor. With the passage of the Tenure of Office Act in 1867—aimed at keeping Radical Republican ally and Secretary of War Edwin M. Stanton in Johnson's cabinet—a showdown became inevitable.

Johnson sought Stanton's resignation, with approval by the Senate required to make the move official. The Senate instead overrode Johnson's decision in January 1868. When Johnson moved to appoint a replacement for Stanton, he was impeached by Congress.

Charges were heard by the Senate during a trial that lasted throughout the spring. It was obvious that political rancor, not illegal actions, drove the case against the president. Johnson's job was saved by a one-vote margin. Conviction would have required a two-thirds majority vote.

Stanton stepped down in May 1868.

FORTY ACRES AND A MULE

This is the compensation that was supposed to go to every freedman, or former slave, at the end of the war. The idea was that all the land that had been abandoned or captured and claimed for the Union by Northern troops, especially Sherman, would be divided up into forty-acre tracts and redistributed. With each tract of land would be supplied a military animal—a horse or mule—that was no longer needed.

The plan never quite panned out. Only a small percentage of the 4 million former slaves actually realized the dream of land ownership, with estimates on how many range from five thousand to forty thousand. Instead, a couple of things happened to the 800,000 acres under federal control:

- Speculators, lumber companies, and railroads snapped up large portions of land.
- Former large plantation owners petitioned President Johnson to get their land back, and he approved their requests.

This left most free blacks with few options except to secure sharecropping arrangements. As sharecroppers, they—alongside poor whites who had lost everything during the war years—worked as tenant farmers who paid for their seed and supplies with a portion of their crops that left little in the form of profit. In fact, the landowners made sure that the cost of seed and supplies would almost equal the expected profit. This form of debt slavery became known as the "new slavery."

Government did recognize that former slaves were not one bit prepared for emancipation and a life of freedom. So, in March 1865, Congress established the Bureau of Refugees, Freedmen, and Abandoned Lands, known simply as the Freedmen's Bureau. It was a temporary federal agency under the War Department to oversee everything relating to freedmen's conditions and treatment in the South.

With nine hundred agents, the Freedmen's Bureau spent the next year distributing trainloads of food and clothing, fuel, and medical supplies and other provisions from the federal government. The supplies went to both impoverished freed slaves and southern white refugees.

The Bureau regulated wages and working conditions and handled legal affairs for freedmen. During its relatively brief one-year existence, the agency spent $17 million* in direct aid.

- More than four thousand schools were built for former slave children.
- Many major African-American colleges were founded with the bureau's assistance.
- Hospitals were updated and rural health clinics established. The bureau helped almost 500,000 freed slaves receive medical attention.

*As a reference point, after the December 2004 tsunami in the Indian Ocean, the American Red Cross reported having spent $283 million in emergency response and recovery over the subsequent thirty months.

Forerunner to Bureau of Refugees, Freedmen, and Abandoned Lands

New Hampshire native John Eaton, Jr., was a former teacher who enlisted in the Union Army as chaplain with the Ohio Twenty-Seventh Regiment. In that role, he worked with runaway slaves in the Union lines, insisting they deserved an education and a job. For doing his level best to provide both, Eaton was awarded the honorary title of brevet brigadier general.

The Freedman's Bureau was in part modeled on Eaton's Civil War successes. Eaton later served as the U.S. Commissioner of Education from 1870 to 1886.

CARPETBAGGERS AND SCALAWAGS

To be fair, many well-meaning Northerners headed south to help freedmen adjust to emancipation. Teachers, doctors, and clergymen accomplished good things. They established the leading African-American colleges in the South, helped former slaves get the franchise to vote (and even serve in Congress), and provided much-needed economic stimulation. These good people were not what many in the South remember of the immediate post-war years.

Carpetbagger (kär-pet-ba-ger) n.:
Unscrupulous Northerner who rushed South with the intent of stimulating his own economic situation. Called "carpetbagger" for the "carpet bag" luggage hastily packed on the way out the door to travel South.

Political cartoons showed men pouring into the South with their carpet bags, and these scoundrels soon became the universal symbol for everything that Southerners hated about the North and Reconstruction.

Carpetbaggers were seen as political opportunists who manipulated issues and situations for personal financial gain. They managed to get themselves appointed to political positions, then, instead of attending to the concerns of their constituents, would find a way to arrange for public money to be used to their own benefit.

Scalawag (ska-li-wag) n.
A former Confederate who took the position of the North, joined the Republican Party, and agreed with the Reconstruction policies.

While the Southerners hated Northern carpetbaggers, they at least could understand their motivation. Much worse were their friends and neighbors who they saw treasonously deserting the Southern cause. Scalawags were viewed with disgust, and they were despised.

The most hated scalawag was General James Longstreet, who Robert E. Lee once called his "warhorse." Also hated were ranger John S. Mosby and Colonel Franklin J. Moses, Jr.

(Many so-called scalawags simply believed that accepting the Reconstruction Acts was the quickest route back to normal life.)

Tenure of Office Act

This obscure act formed the basis for President Andrew Johnson's impeachment. Passed in 1867 despite Johnson's veto, it required the president to win Senate consent whenever he sought to remove office holders who had been Senate-approved, such as Cabinet secretaries. When Johnson attempted to dump Edwin M. Stanton, the secretary of war, in August 1867, the matter quickly spilled over into a political bloodbath. Congress had been out of session during Johnson's attempt, so when the Senate returned to work in January 1868, it promptly overrode Johnson's dismissal of Stanton.

Undeterred, Johnson sought to name a replacement as secretary of war. Congress responded with a forceful answer of its own—impeachment. Johnson survived and held on to the presidency, though he was greatly weakened.

The Tenure of Office Act was repealed in 1887. In 1926, in a case involving similar questions of presidential power, the U.S. Supreme Court ruled the act was unconstitutional.

NO APPETITE FOR RECONSTRUCTION

Historians note the miraculous nature of the Civil War in America. Unlike most other countries, the United States healed and became a unified nation after the war ended in 1865. Guerrilla warfare and endless smoldering feuds did not follow in the wake of the bitter, divisive struggle.

All of this is true, and should be commended. But the Civil War also left deep, lingering scars. The pain of healing from such a bloody, deadly war was exacerbated by the radical Republican agenda in Congress. The combination of Abraham Lincoln's assassination and Andrew Johnson's impeachment left the group unchecked.

Some of the steps taken by those radicals were necessary, such as greater equality in schools, jobs, and other facets of daily life for freed blacks. In many cases, these changes were forced upon Southerners. Other steps, however, were aimed with vengeance and the intent to humiliate Southerners, such as repeated episodes of putting ill-prepared freed slaves in political office. Radical Republicans revenge on the former Confederate states on a regular, protracted basis. For the South, already mired in stifling poverty, failing educational systems, and a torpid economy, the radical Republican agenda served to sow greater resentment while leaving the region even more depleted.

Those pains were punctuated by the arrival of Northern "carpetbaggers"—opportunists who came to the South seeking political patronage, payoffs, and other schemes aimed at hurting the old Confederacy while filling their pockets. Southerners who helped the carpetbaggers came under even greater scorn, denounced as "scalawags." As prominent historians, including Eric Foner, have demonstrated, the stereotyping of carpetbaggers and scalawags overlooks a number of people (Northerners and Southerners alike) who were dedicated to reviving the South. However, corruption and mismanagement were rampant in many rebuilding efforts, whether intended or not. And, to make all of these circumstances worse, the people with the most to gain from the arduous war—freed blacks— bore brunt of the punishment. Humiliated and downtrodden, Southerners opted to carry out their resentments and frustrations over Northern injustices by subjugating basic rights and dignity owed to the freed slaves.

"Forty acres and a mule" and other attempts at redistribution of land to the former slaves ultimately proved to be failures. As whites reclaimed lands divided after the war, blacks found themselves in the midst of a newly oppressive agrarian economic system, sharecropping. Instead of slavery, blacks now faced an only slightly less humiliating and limiting system of life, one that required much of the harvest and profit from designated land plots to be given to the white property owners.

Jim Crow laws, segregation, and senseless violence fell upon Southern blacks for a century after the war ended, leaving a permanent stain on the region.

CIVIL WAR BY THE NUMBERS

4,000,000: Slaves in America in 1860

3,000,000: Soldiers and sailors who fought in the war (2,100,000 North; 900,000 South)

2,500,000: U.S. dollars per day spent on the war effort

600,000: Soldiers who died serving their country (360,000 North; 258,000 South)

200,000: Soldiers were killed in battle or died of battle wounds

500,000: Dollar ransom demanded by Confederate General Jubal Early to not burn the Chambersburg, Pennsylvania, business district to the ground

400,000: Men who died from disease

185,000: Black soldiers in the Union army

150,000: Soldiers engaged at Gettysburg

51,112: Dead or wounded at Gettysburg (23,049 North; 28,063 South)

35,825: Dead or wounded at Vicksburg (4,550 North: 31,275 South)

35,000: Dollars Jeb Stuart netted from raiding Union General John Pope's headquarters

34,633: Dead or wounded at Chickamauga (16,179 North: 18,454 South)

30,500: Dead or wounded at Chancellorsville (16,792 North; 12,764 South)

25,000: Bales of cotton captured with the city of Savannah

22,719: Dead or wounded at Sharpsburg/Antietam (12,401 North; 10,318 South)

17,900: Dead or wounded at Fredericksburg (12,600 North; 5,300 South)

16,500: Doctors in the medical corps in 1865 (13,000 North; 3,500 South)

13,000: Union soldiers who died at Andersonville Prison Camp

11,386: Dead or wounded at Petersburg (8,150 North; 2,970 South)

10,455: Military engagements

8,000: Beds in Richmond's Chimorazo army hospital (the biggest and best, North or South)

7,000: Union soldiers who fell in the first 20 minutes at Cold Harbor

6,500: Confederates lost in Pickett's Gettysburg Charge (of 13,000 total)

3,500: Miles of Confederate coastline guarded by the U.S. Navy

23,741: Dead or wounded at Shiloh (13,047 North; 10,694 South)

3,000: Dollars bid for original copy of Lincoln's Emancipation Proclamation in a Sanitation Commission fundraiser

2,400: Population of Gettysburg, Pennsylvania during the Civil War

200: Miles of Southern railroad track destroyed by Union soldiers

1,500: Blockade runners seized, sunk, or burned by Federal troops

1,000: Number of deaths Confederate General Lee proclaimed he'd rather die, before going to meet Union General Grant at Appomattox Court House

500: Foot length of tunnel dug by Pennsylvania coal miners under Confederate lines near Petersburg

450: Brothels in Washington, D.C.

300: Dollars' commutation fee to avoid the Federal draft

180: Miles Grant's army marched in three weeks during the Vicksburg campaign

166: All-black Union regiments

150: Residents of Lawrence, Kansas, murdered by Confederate guerrilla William Quantrill

115: Doctors in the medical corps in 1861 (88 North; 27 South)

119: Estimated number of citizens killed in New York City draft riots

101: Days to build the ironclad U.S.S. *Monitor*

90: Days in original militia enlistment tours

82: Percent of the 1st Minnesota regiment lost in one charge at Gettysburg

70: Mills destroyed by Union General Philip Sheridan in the Shenandoah Valley

68: Union men inside Fort Sumter on April 12, 1861

63: Age of Union Admiral David Farragut when he ordered, "Damn the torpedoes, full speed ahead!" in Mobile Bay

55: Percent of the popular vote carried by Lincoln in the 1864 Presidential election

48: Days Vicksburg remained under Union siege before surrendering

39: Regiments from Missouri (22 North; 17 South)

30: Horses shot from under Confederate General Nathan Bedford Forrest in battle

25: Average age in years of any soldier

27: Total number of Confederate sailors who died aboard the submarine *Hunley*

18: Generals killed or wounded at Sharpsburg (9 North; 9 South)

13: Charges ordered by Confederate General Hood during the Battle of Franklin

11: States in the Confederacy

8: Hours for Union engineers to build a 2,100-foot pontoon bridge across the James River

6: Years in Jefferson Davis's term as president of the Confederacy if the Civil War hadn't ended

Grant's Second Act

In 1868, Ulysses S. Grant ran for president and won, assuming the top political job in the land without ever having held public office. His two-term presidency reflected his political inexperience. Grant's tenure as commander-in-chief has become infamous for its constant scandals within the administration.

Fraud and financial schemes within the public sector marred Grant's presidency—and left him with an enduring reputation as one of the worst presidents in history. Among the worst examples of the pervasive skimming was the transcontinental railroad that was built and bungled during Grant's time in the White House.

The former Union general's integrity rarely came into question. Instead, Grant's lassitude and laissez faire attitude toward lower-ranking officials came under attack. The president, critics contended, allowed government fraud to reign supreme during his terms in office.

During Grant's presidency, white supremacy ran rampant despite the Civil War hero's opposition.

ONE OF THE WORST SCALAWAGS

Franklin J. Moses, Jr., (1838–1906) didn't accomplish much during the Civil War, but he is known today as one of the worst of the scalawags of Reconstruction. A strong secessionist-turned-Republican, Moses was known as the Robber Governor, and critics even called him Franklin Judas Moses.

Antebellum Sentiments: By all indications, Moses had the makings of a classic Southern supporter. He was a South Carolina native, son of a state Supreme Court justice, local lawyer, and editor, secretary to South Carolina Governor Francis Wilkinson Pickens in 1860. He personally raised the Confederate flag over Fort Sumter in 1861. He even joined the Confederate Army ranked as a colonel in charge of the Confederate Conscription Acts (not much has been written about his wartime service).

Reconstruction Activities: After the war, Moses changed his allegiance and joined the Northern Republicans. He was elected in 1868 as South Carolina's adjutant and inspector general and as Charleston's delegate in the South Carolina House of Representatives, where he was speaker.

The state legislature made him a trustee for the University of South Carolina in 1869. Moses so greatly lowered admission standards to that institution, that the state General Assembly closed the school in 1877. This is the same school from which, in 1855, Moses himself had been dismissed during his freshman year.

In 1870, Moses was reelected to the House, but it wasn't long before he began accepting bribes and participating in other forms of corruption. By 1872, only four years, the state's debt had tripled.

The Republican candidate for governor in the 1871 race, Moses was elected for the 1872–1874 term. He immediately began dipping into the state treasury, using $40,000 to buy the Preston Mansion (now a historic museum) for his official residence and spending $50,000 on living expenses.

By 1874, it was clear he was using state funds for his own use, and Moses was indicted. To keep from being arrested, he employed three companies of state militia to protect him. Fortunately for Moses, the South Carolina Supreme Court ruled he couldn't be prosecuted while governor.

Things Get Worse: In 1874, Republicans of the South Carolina General Assembly selected Moses for a seat on the circuit court, but temporary Governor Daniel Henry Chamberlain did not approve the appointment. In 1878, Moses' wife filed for divorce. Moses relocated to Massachusetts.

In Winthrop, Massachusetts, Moses settled into a job editing the local newspaper. But he didn't settle down, and instead continued his thievery and fraud, including forging the name of author Thomas Wentworth Higginson. He was tried for his crimes and sentenced to three years in the Massachusetts State Prison in 1885.

Moses must have been a smooth talker. In 1887 he managed to convince Massachusetts Governor Oliver Ames that he was a sick man and did not have long to live. In 1887 Ames pardoned Moses, who lived another nineteen years. By the time he died in 1906, Moses had been completely disowned by his family in South Carolina. He was buried in Massachusetts.

Who Was Thomas Wentworth Higginson?

The author Thomas Wentworth Higginson is best known for being a mentor to recluse poet Emily Dickinson. In April 1862, Higginson published an article in the *Atlantic Monthly* that attracted the attention of the young Dickinson. They began a lifelong letter-writing correspondence in which Higginson offered critique and advice to Dickinson.

After Dickinson's death, Higginson worked with Mabel Loomis Todd to edit and publish volumes of Dickinson's poetry. It is to Higginson's credit that we have most of Dickinson's classic poems to read and study today.

COST OF THE CIVIL WAR

When talking about money, we like to see these numbers with all the zeroes. But, we'll help out by showing you what they mean, too.

- $2,500,000 — By 1863, the Civil War cost the federal government $2.5 million. That's per day.
- $6,190,000,000 — Final official estimate of total money spent by the federal government on the Civil War. That's $6 billion.
- $2,100,000,000 — Final educated guess of total money spent by the Confederacy on the Civil War. $2 billion this time.
- $8,300,000,000 — Total combined cost of the Civil War across the North and South. $6 + $2 = $8 billion.

Compare these numbers to:

- The United States' Cost of World War II — $288,000,000,000 ($288 billion).
- The National Debt — Hovers around $9,000,000,000,000 ($9 trillion).

How They Paid for the War in the North

In the beginning, when everyone thought this little war between the states would only last about ninety days, the federal government relied on private donations to fund the war. In a matter of months it became clear that things were going to get more complicated.

Secretary of Treasury Salmon P. Chase put his thinking cap on and came up with creative ways to get money for the war effort:

- He issued war bonds, which brought in more than $1 billion.
- According to the Legal Tender Act, Chase began printing paper money (known as "greenbacks") backed by real gold.
- Congress passed the Internal Revenue Act, the beginning of income tax as we know it.

How They Paid for the War in the South

Secretary of the Treasury Christopher Memminger didn't have nearly the resources at his disposal that Chase had. So while Chase was creative, Memminger was often downright desperate. His solutions at times mirrored those in the North, and at other times were unique to the South:

- He issued war bonds that could be redeemed when the war was over. Right after Fort Sumter, war bonds were a hot ticket, both with Southern citizens and foreign countries. In 1861, the Confederacy raised $15 million from bond sales. But, as you can guess, when the war's outcome became inevitable, bond sales came to a screeching halt. Obviously, these bonds were worthless by the war's end.
- The South really expected to get European loans and other foreign money by selling cotton overseas. This only worked until the U.S. Navy successfully blockaded all the Confederate ports.
- The Confederate Treasury printed more than $1.5 billion in paper money. But since it was not backed by gold, once again, these were worthless.
- The Confederate Congress passed a tariff in 1861 that only brought in $3.5 million throughout the war.
- The Confederate Congress passed income taxes and an "in kind" tax requiring farmers to turn over 10 percent of all their crops to the government. This was especially hard on the poor farmers.

Christopher Memminger's Great Gold Caper

The Confederate secretary of the treasury devised a scheme to deplete the Union's gold supply and to hopefully create a financial panic in the North. He asked Southern sympathizers in Northern states to convert paper money to gold and horde it. He also had Northern Confederate agents buy up huge quantities of U.S. gold to export.

The plan did manage to get about $2 million in gold out of the country before the plot was discovered.

CIVIL WAR REENACTMENTS

Civil War reenactment has been going on almost since the conflict ended. But as a hobby, it really heated up around the time of hundred-year anniversaries of battles. Reenactment, in particular, has risen in popularity during the nation's bicentennial celebration in 1976.

The goal of reenactment is to interpret history. Reenactors select a regiment, a rank, and then portray that soldier as authentically as they can. They study historical documents for specifics about their soldier, such as uniforms, flags, supplies, and weapons. When specifics are not available, they apply generalities from Civil War times, such as general period dress and society.

Reenactors try to provide accurate information to spectators, and spend much time and money making sure they portray the right uniform and know how to wear it correctly. They also learn how to use equipment as if they were 1860s soldiers, such as learning to load and clean weapons from that age. They even create back stories for the soldiers they portray to explain how their civilian home and family life provides their motivation. It's a lot like acting.

Reenactments are staged not just for the participants' enjoyment, but also for spectators to learn about the Civil War from a living history display. So, if you visit a reenactment, you are encouraged to take a walk through the camp and observe the soldiers. Both through scripted interactions and informal talks, they try hard to explain the how and why of what you see. Reenactors want you to leave with a better understanding of a soldier's life both on and off the battlefield.

- Reenactors have been used as extras in epic Hollywood movies and miniseries, as well as in historical documentaries.
- Not all reenactors choose to portray soldiers. From surgeons and sutlers to engineers and blacksmiths, and just about any other civilian role in history, men have many other choices. Women, too, can participate, as camp followers, nurses, vivandières, even

local townswomen selling their wares or tending to the soldiers.

- Reenactors become very attached to their personae. Many choose to wear their uniforms during their own wedding ceremonies, and just as many request to be buried in their uniforms.

- Reenactors have a word for materials not authentic to the Civil War period: "farb." For example: "I know your Merrell shoes and Under Armour are more comfortable, but they are so farb!"

- Participants are allowed to use modern-day concessions, as long as they are not visible. For instance, adhesive bandages can be worn under socks to help prevent getting blisters on the feet. It's allowed to wear any modern perspiration-prevention products or performance garments under a hot wool uniform, as long as the "farb" items don't show through any authentic holes.

Historian Versus Reenactor

A common argument between professional historians and amateur reenactors goes something like this (both views have their merit):

Historian: "Those weekend reenactors don't get the big picture. They're more interested in the events than in the significance of the events."

Reenactor: "Those professors can read history books, but books don't show you how battle really felt, and smelled, and sounded, and even tasted."

HAIR-RAISING CIVIL WAR GHOST STORIES

Whether or not you believe in ghosts, plenty of ghost stories are still told about the Civil War. Keep in mind, these are stories. They've likely been changed many times over from the first telling.

- Former slaves in the Shenandoah Valley have told of hearing gunfire and horse hooves, bugles and drums.

- Civil War reenactors tell of unknown participants who join them around the campfires at night, but who are not around the next morning. They hear shooting at night, smell gunpowder fumes, and see hazy visions. Get this—reenactors have even come home with pictures showing extra soldiers who no one knows or remembers marching next to.

- Chickamauga, Georgia: After the battle ended late in the day, local women searched the battlefield for injured or dead loved ones. Today still, you can see lantern lights in the darkness punctuated by anguished cries.

- Fredericksburg, Virginia: As the Union troops stormed Marye's Heights during the Battle of Fredericksburg, Mrs. Charles Stevenson worked in her garden in Henrietta, New York. She sensed someone behind her, feeling a warm breath on her cheek.

- Her husband, Sergeant Charles Stevenson of the 108th New York Infantry, was standing right there. The vision quickly evaporated. Later she learned that he had been killed at Fredericksburg that same day.

- Cedar Creek, Virginia: Neighbors tell of a Yankee soldier wearing cavalry boots whose ghost took up residence in a local barn. He was often seen standing on the steps, but never threatening.

- Gettysburg, Pennsylvania: Gettysburg College's Pennsylvania Hall was used as a hospital after the battle. Students report seeing soldiers in the building's halls. Some staff members riding the elevator have been carried to the basement instead of their floor.

The doors open onto a horrible Civil War hospital full of wounded soldiers, complete with a pile of amputated limbs. Then the doors close.

- Montevallo, Alabama: Reynolds Hall on the University of Montevallo campus was used as a Confederate convalescent hospital building under the protection of Captain Henry Clay Reynolds. When Union soldiers swept through town on their way to destroy the nearby Brierfield Ironworks, they brutally massacred all the Confederate soldiers in the hospital.

- Captain Reynolds roams the halls of the building in sorrow over the loss of his men to Sherman's troops.

- Hopewell, Virginia: A sympathizing nurse hid a Union soldier inside her home's basement wall when Confederate troops came searching for Yankees. She was arrested, but the soldier was not discovered. However, he could not get out of the hiding place without her help, and he died. His body was found almost one hundred years later when the house was renovated. Even today, you can hear scratching inside the wall as he tries to get out.

- Francisville, Louisiana: We had to include the Myrtles Plantation, known as one of America's most haunted houses. Visitors to the house today report seeing many different ghosts, including a slave, Chloe.

According to story, Chloe was a house servant who the plantation owner took as a mistress. She was caught eavesdropping, and one of her ears was cut off as punishment.

Chloe got her revenge by crumbling up oleander leaves (a known poison) in a birthday cake she baked for one of the daughters. The mother and two daughters, including birthday girl Sara, ate the cake and died—the father was not home at the time.

Other slaves feared they would be implicated in the plot, and hanged Chloe before the master returned home. Today, Chloe and Sara are two of the figures seen floating around the home and grounds.

Two Shots for Ruffin

Edmund Ruffin, a farmer and slaveholder from Virginia, became known as the man who fired the first shot of the Civil War at Fort Sumter in 1861. A zealous proponent of Southern secession, he gained further notoriety when he killed himself in June 1865, two months after the war ended. Historians invariably point to Ruffin's rabid final diary entry as a barometer of Southern resentment toward the Union in the era of Reconstruction, which lasted from 1865 to 1877.

An excerpt from Ruffin's diary:

I here declare my unmitigated hatred to Yankee rule—to all political, social & business connection with the Yankees and to the Yankee race. Would that I could impress these sentiments, in their full force, on every living Southerner & bequeath them to everyone yet to be born! May such sentiments be held universally in the outraged & downtrodden South, although in silence & stillness, until the now far-distant day shall arrive for just retribution for Yankee usurpation, oppression & atrocious outrages, & for deliverance & vengeance for the now ruined, subjugated & enslaved Southern States!

… And now with my latest writing and utterance, and what will be near my latest breath, I here repeat and would willingly proclaim my unmitigated hatred to [. . .] the perfidious, malignant, & vile Yankee race.

THE KLAN

Confederate cavalry hero Nathan Bedford Forrest gained notoriety on the battlefield for his daring tactics and strategic brilliance. After the war, he became even more notorious as the founder of the Ku Klux Klan—a group best described as an efficient sponsor of racist-inspired intimidation and terrorism.

The name of the organization came from the Greek word kuklos, which means "circle." The KKK formed in December 1865.

A year later, Forrest was named the group's first "Grand Wizard," the equivalent of Racism Inc.'s CEO. Though the familiar image of men adorned in white robes and sheets is accurate, the KKK, in short order, emphasized violence above all else. Beatings and raids were familiar tactics in the long-running campaign to stamp out all vestiges of racial equality.

Violence escalated to the point that Forrest—hardly a shrinking violet in light of his leadership at the Fort Pillow Massacre during the war—renounced KKK tactics. Federal legislation sought to limit the Klan's violence, as well.

Despite those moves against it, smaller branches and offshoots continued to pop up intermittently well into the twentieth century. The first major revival came in 1915, when religious groups and immigrants were targeted as well as blacks. KKK activity roared back to life during the tumultuous Civil Rights era in the South during the 1960s. Lynching, murder, and rape occurred all too frequently as white resistance to the federally imposed basic equalities for blacks finally came to pass.

Hanging Chads?

The contested 2000 election between Al Gore and George W. Bush was hardly America's first controversial national vote, as the 1876 race for the White House demonstrates. Southern activists (known as redeemers) and strong support for Democrats in the now "Solid South"—Republicans were vilified as Lincoln's party and were the authors of radical-fueled Reconstruction policies—pushed Samuel J. Tilden to the presidency.

There was one small problem, though. Tilden, a Democrat, never made it to the White House, despite winning the popular vote over Republican Rutherford B. Hayes. Radical Republicans subverted the results, citing tenets of Reconstruction and arguing that Tilden's election was invalid. That sent the contested election to Congress. Still, no consensus emerged. Newfound threats of Southern secession emerged. A little more than a decade after the wrenching agonies of the Civil War, the American experiment again seemed to be on the brink.

At last, they found compromise. Republicans and Southern Democrats agreed to name Hayes president in exchange for assurances from Republicans to allow Southern states to carry out their race agendas.

The ascension of Hayes, known derisively as "Your Fraudulency," signaled the death of Reconstruction. Until the 1960s, Southern blacks would suffer both from the cruelty of oppression of local politics and the indifference of national politics.